KILLING WOMEN

Cultural Studies Series

Cultural Studies is the multi- and interdisciplinary study of culture, defined anthropologically as a "way of life," performatively as symbolic practice, and ideologically as the collective product of media and cultural industries, i.e., pop culture. Although Cultural Studies is a relative newcomer to the humanities and social sciences, in less than half a century it has taken interdisciplinary scholarship to a new level of sophistication, reinvigorating the liberal arts curriculum with new theories, new topics, and new forms of intellectual partnership.

The Cultural Studies series includes topics such as construction of identities; regionalism/nationalism; cultural citizenship; migration; popular culture; consumer cultures; media and film; the body; postcolonial criticism; cultural policy; sexualities; cultural theory; youth culture; class relations; and gender.

The Cultural Studies series from Wilfrid Laurier University Press invites submission of manuscripts concerned with critical discussions on power relations concerning gender, class, sexual preference, ethnicity, and other macro and micro sites of political struggle.

For further information, please contact the Series Editor:

Jodey Castricano
Department of Critical Studies
University of British Columbia Okanagan
3333 University Way
Kelowna, BC V1V 1V7

KILLING WOMEN

The Visual Culture of
Gender and Violence

Annette Burfoot and
Susan Lord, editors

Wilfrid Laurier University Press
[WLU]

This book has been published with the help of a grant from the Canadian Federation for the Humanities and Social Sciences, through the Aid to Scholarly Publications Programme, using funds provided by the Social Sciences and Humanities Research Council of Canada. We acknowledge the financial support of the Government of Canada through the Book Publishing Industry Development Program for our publishing activities.

Library and Archives Canada Cataloguing in Publication

Killing women : the visual culture of gender and violence / Annette Burfoot and Susan Lord, editors.

(Cultural Studies Series ; 6)
Includes bibliographical references and index.
ISBN-13: 978-0-88920-497-3
ISBN-10: 0-88920-497-7

1. Women murderers in motion pictures. 2. Women murderers in mass media. 3. Women murderers in popular culture. 4. Murder victims in motion pictures. 5. Murder victims in mass media. 6. Murder victims in popular culture. 7. Women—Crimes against—Social aspects. 8. Motion pictures—Social aspects. 9. Mass media—Social aspects. I. Burfoot, Annette, 1958– II. Lord, Susan, 1959– III. Series: Cultural studies series (Waterloo, Ont.) ; 6.

HQ1206.K53 2006   305.4'896949   C2006-904585-2

Cover design by P.J. Woodland with a contribution from Tyler Clark Burke. Cover photograph by Keri Knapp. Text design by Catharine Bonas-Taylor.

© 2006 Wilfrid Laurier University Press
Waterloo, Ontario, Canada
www.wlupress.wlu.ca

∞

This book is printed on Ancient Forest Friendly paper (100% post-consumer recycled).

Printed in Canada

[contents]

[illustrations]

[acknowledgements]

Killing Women started with Annette's recognition that popular representations of women who killed related to representations of women's violent deaths. While it is a hard truth that there is never an untimely moment to think and write about gender and violence, this collection comes at a moment in history when women suicide bombers appear on the front pages of newspapers, when Amnesty International publishes its report on the violence involving, and the murders of, First Nations women in Canada, when Robert "Willy" Pickton is on trial for the murder of women from the Downtown Eastside of Vancouver, when Karla Homolka is released from prison, and when rising tides of protest address the murders of four hundred women in Juarez and Chihuahua, Mexico.

This collection brings together a group of engaged writers with whom it has been both a pleasure and an education to work. We thank them for their patience, diligence, and thoughtful contributions.

Thanks to Dave St. Onge from the Prison Museum for helping us gather images from the Archives, and for permission to these images. We acknowledge *Screen* for permission to reprint Jyotika Virdi's essay, Routledge (UK) for permission to publish a substantially revised version of a chapter from

Belinda Morrissey's book *When Women Kill: Questions of Agency and Subjectivity*, and Sage Publications Ltd. for permission to reprint Sharon Rosenberg's essay, previously published in the journal *Feminist Theory*.

We are grateful to the skilled students who helped with the preparation of this anthology. Thanks to Carla Henderson, Ryan Higget, Kristy Holmes, Marlene Little, Erik Martinson, Jocelyn Purdie, Stephen Rifkin, and Aimee Skelton. Special thanks to Tyler Clark Burke for her contribution to the cover design and to Vidisha Kapil for her thorough work on the index. We are grateful to the Queen's University's Office of Research Services for funds to complete the index.

It was always a pleasure working with members of the Wilfrid Laurier University Press, including Heather Blain-Yanke, Brian Henderson, Carroll Klein, Rob Kohlmeier, and Jacqueline Larson.

Thanks also to the rich and varied forms of support and encouragement from our family and friends: Mary Louise Adams, Frank Burke, Karen Dubinsky, Myra Hird, Paul Kelley, Catherine Krull, Frances Leeming, Janine Marchessault, and Dorit Naaman.

[introduction]

ANNETTE BURFOOT

SUSAN LORD

On 4 October 2004 Amnesty International released *Stolen Sisters: Discrimination and Violence against Indigenous Women in Canada: A Summary of Amnesty International's Concerns*. The summary states:

> A shocking 1996 Canadian government statistic reveals that Indigenous women between the ages of 25 and 44, with status under the Indian Act, were five times more likely than all other women of the same age to die as the result of violence. Understanding the true scale and nature of violence against Indigenous women, however, is greatly hampered by a persistent lack of comprehensive reporting and statistical analysis...the role of discrimination in fuelling this violence, in denying Indigenous women the protection they deserve or in allowing the perpetrators to escape justice is a critical part of the threat faced by Indigenous women. (http://web.amnesty.org/library/Index/ENGAMR200012004)

On Tuesday, 5 October, the CBC presented the following headline for its Web story: "Canada Accused of Ignoring Violence against Aboriginal Women." The opening line of the story reads: "Canadian officials and police are failing to protect aboriginal women from violent attacks and ignoring the acts when they occur, according to a report from Amnesty International" (http://www.cbc.ca/story/canada/national/2004/10/04/ai_aborigina1041004.html). If you click on the "In Depth" button to the left of the story, the link takes you to a sublime image of Mount Saint Helens—the soon-to-erupt volcanic mountain in Washington State. The other possible in-depth stories available to the reader anxious to know more about the Aboriginal women are listed with the following keywords and in the following order: Montreal Expos, Deadly Dust, Assisted Suicide, Afghanistan, Face-Off, Sudan, and so forth. There is no in-depth story available. The Aboriginal women are missing.

There is, however, an "in-depth" story about rape in Darfur, written by Martin O'Malley: "Consider the use of government-sanctioned rape to humiliate, terrorize and control black Africans in the Darfur region at the western edge of Sudan. Amnesty International released a report this week that says government-backed Arab militiamen—*janjaweed*—are raping and killing pregnant women and girls as young as eight. Pregnant women are a favourite target, with rapes followed by mutilation and killing done in public, in daylight, in front of their husbands and families with Arab women watching and singing songs of praise" (http://www.cbc.ca/news/viewpoint/vp_omalley/20040722.html). The Darfur rapes were part of the Canadian international news for the better part of a week—*after* the United Nations raised the Genocide Convention to address the violence in the region.

Both of these stories were found on the same day in Canada's national news broadcaster's website; in both cases Amnesty International is cited; in both cases the cause and the potential solution to the problems is referred elsewhere—that is, the media do not reflect on their role in the production, reproduction, and dissemination of the relationship between gender, violence, and representation. More than coincidence brings these two stories to our attention for there is something horribly familiar about the hide-and-seek the major news organizations play with the representation of women and violence. Amnesty International's report on the issue of violence and Aboriginal women makes a clear case for the role the media have played in the perpetuation of the racism and sexism that lie at the heart of these women's deaths. In O'Malley's story the role of misogyny in the long history of rape during wartime is deflected onto the spectacle of *Arab* women "watching and singing songs of praise." And, of course, when a woman murders, the media is saturated with details of her private life and her manner of killing. What is it that one wants of representation in such situations? What would a just representation be? Is the representation of violence drawn so heavily from genre and gender codes that even the most horrific realities are destined to become "stories"—normalized and folded into the everyday racist and sexist ideologies that form our senses of belonging to a nation, a gender, a race, an ethnicity, a class?

The chapters in *Killing Women* address these questions by focusing on the conceptual space that connects two powerful images in the contemporary social imagination: women who are killed and women who kill. The theme of women and violence is hardly new; however, traditionally it has been restricted to only one-half of the spectacle—women who are killed or who are the victims of violence. When women murderers (fictional and actual) make a rare appearance, their representation tends to be restricted to reactive roles, such as the vengeful wronged woman and the maternal protector. Recently, there have been significant shifts in the characterization of women who can kill, which may be seen in both popular culture (e.g., the character Ripley from the film series *Aliens* has been joined by the female kung fu fighter, Lara Croft, Buffy, and *Kill Bill*) and in the current global political landscape (e.g., the so-called angels of death of Palestine).

The purpose of this collection is to explore the territory of gender and violence anew by focusing on visual culture—both historical and contemporary—in fiction and non-fiction film, museums, art, archives, and the news media. This focus is presented within a broad cultural context and engages with contemporary theories, the practice of identity politics, and the debates over the ethics and politics of representation itself. The contributions intentionally weave between fact and fiction in order to illuminate engendered violence as a form of cultural materialization and, thus, to recognize the powerful role culture plays in the production and reproduction of social meaning.

Killing Women offers fresh analyses of well-established sources for the study of women and violence: the horror film genre and the court trials of women who have killed their abusive husbands. It also adds significant new dimensions to the characterization of gender and violence by looking at nationalism and war, feminist media, and the way in which violence is circulated through non-obvious sources, such as medical cultural practice and the information society. The collection thus moves beyond what Jyotika Virdi describes as "the static two-dimensional portrayals of women as victims or vamps, madonnas or whores, suffering mothers or pleasing wives." Nor is this simply a celebration of vibrant new roles for women involving kick-boxing, butt-kicking, and killing—even though these images may be welcome as apparent antidotes to the conventional controls prevalent in the cultural materialization of femininity. The chapters gathered here explore how violence is culturally produced in complex and sometimes contradictory forms; how feminist resistance appears in unexpected places and in unusual ways; and how traditional forms of the patriarchal imaginary re-emerge in postmodern style. They also critically investigate women's varied resistances to and engagements with violence in light of contemporary problematic social and political contexts: "postfeminism," the discourses and technologies of dematerialized identity, and globalization.

In gathering the chapters for this collection, we wanted to give priority to visual culture within a global context and to make space for new methods of historiography, media analysis, and critical writing alongside the well-established illuminations of textual and genre analyses. Our decision to focus on women and the representation of femininity and violence is a political one, as we state above and as is evident in all of the chapters compiled here. It is also meant to point to and to provide an alternative to the problematic erasure of feminism and women from the new discourses on screen violence (Prince 2004; Karl French 1996). Notably, many of the contributors refer to foundational theoretical works about gender and screen violence, such as those by Carol Clover (1992) and Barbara Creed (1993), and they rework them by filtering them through more recent cultural studies approaches. Sociological literature is vital to many of the chapters compiled here as well as to the overall approach of the collection, which is adopted from cultural studies. However, our focus on representation meant that we could not include social science approaches (such as those undertaken in sociological and political studies) to the question of gender and violence. New literature on violence against women, analyzed from social science perspectives on gender, race, and class, has been recently compiled by Katherine M.J. McKenna and June Larkin in their anthology *Violence against Women: New Canadian Perspectives* (2002). Other recent avenues of social and political inquiry include analyses of girlhood violence and bullying (Artz 1998); stalking (Davis, Frieze, and Maiuro 2002); violence against women of colour (Bannerji 2002) and immigrant and refugee women (Moussa 2002; Agger 1993); women and terrorism (Randall 2003); women and development (Kapadia 2002); and the politics of culturally specific violence, such as Veena Talwar Oldenberg's study of dowry murder (2002).

Helen Birch's ground-breaking *Moving Targets: Women, Murder and Representation* (1993) remains the only collection on the portrayal of women who kill and women who are killed. *Killing Women* is both an update and an expansion of the largely Anglo-American views provided in *Moving Targets*. Readers will note that we did not include analyses of already well-covered territory, such as Ripley in the *Alien* films (Bundtzen 1987; Creed 1990; Tasker 1993, 1998; Taubin 1993; Davies 2000) or Buffy, Xena, and so on (Early and Kennedy 2003; Inness 1999; Wilcox and Lavery 2002). Also, we found that books such as *When Women Kill: Questions of Agency and Subjectivity* by Belinda Morrissey (2003),

Discerning Eyes: Viewers on Violence by Julie Firmstone (2002), *The New Avengers: Feminism, Femininity and the Rape-Revenge Cycle* by Jacinda Read (2000), *Lustmord: Sexual Murder in Weimar Germany* by Maria Tatar (1997), and *Over Her Dead Body: Death, Femininity and the Aesthetic* by Elisabeth Bronfen (1992), as well as articles such as Elayne Rapping's fascinating discussion of US television dramas, "The Politics of Representation Genre, Gender Violence and Justice" (2000), covered their specific areas so thoroughly that we were permitted to attend to many as yet unwritten histories and analysis of gendered violence.

The chapters collected here are framed by questions and debates that have been part of the feminist public sphere for at least three decades. Does representation produce or reproduce the conditions of violence? Is representation itself a form of violence? If we consider the discursive constructions of violence—the "rhetoric of violence"—are we abandoning the material body and the conditions of its suffering? If we look only at the empirical, can we comprehend psychic and symbolic forces and their role in oppression, power, and, ultimately, the struggle over the meaning and value of a person?

In the mid-1970s through the 1980s violence-against-women debates, as set out by the American cultural feminists (Andrea Dworkin, Susan Brownmiller, Mary Daly, Susan Griffin, Robin Morgan, and Catherine MacKinnon), were linked to pornography. Robin Morgan and Susan Brownmiller's (in)famous equation "Pornography is the theory, rape the practice" was situated within a heteronormative, white framework of essentialism (one of the dicta of the day was "All men are potential rapists") and found its legal argument in the Dworkin-MacKinnon anti-pornography bill of 1983—the Minneapolis Ordinance—which defined pornography as: "the graphic sexually explicit subordination of women through pictures or words" (MacKinnon 1987, 176). The critical responses within feminism to this position were both politically and philosophically motivated: the conflation of sexually explicit material with sexual violence, as anti-censorship authors argued, fed into patriarchal forms of control over images without confronting social and economic inequities, and it also fed into a moral majority agenda. While the anti-censorship position opened the pornography debate to a more complex set of social and sexual contexts, it is important to remember that the body politics of feminism that drove the anti-pornography movement in the 1970s and 1980s was, like other social projects related to the violence and exploitation of women's bodies (e.g., rape relief centres, women's shelters, abortion clinics, women's medical centres, etc.), tied directly to feminist legal struggles around rape and sexual violence, domestic violence, and abortion rights.

The feminist poststructuralist theories that were being articulated in the 1980s and early 1990s presented a nuanced critique of the cause–effect thinking at the heart of cultural feminism's critique of violence and its link to pornography, looking instead to the complexity of representation itself (see Hanssen 2000). Central to the poststructuralist project is a twofold analysis: the institutional production and circulation of discourses and techniques of power and knowledge, on the one hand, and the psychic complexity of the female subject in relation to symbolic meaning, on the other. In 1989 Teresa de Lauretis wrote a critique of French theorist Michel Foucault's blind spot with regard to gender, in which she argues that Foucault's discourse analysis of the technologies of sexuality needs to be balanced with an analysis of the technologies of gender. She spots a danger in the foundation of the theory (what is known as the "linguistic turn") and calls for a more instrumental turn in the theory, which would allow for the analysis of "the techniques and discursive strategies by which gender is constructed and hence…violence is en-gendered" (de Lauretis 1987, 38). The 1990s saw the debates about identity politics, cultural relativism, and media politics address the problematics of violence and representation within three constellations of inquiry: (1) the history and memory debates (the interrelation between trauma, fantasy, archives, and historiographies); (2) technologies and techniques of violence (the discourses and institutions that construct identity—and the body—through scientific or legal methods); and (3) nationalism (neo- and postcolonial subjects, war and representation, and ethnicity and violence). The chapters in *Killing Women* are situated within these arenas and the book is organized to reflect this. The book as a whole considers how representation functions as a materialization of violence: that is, how violence is "engendered in representation" (de Lauretis 1987, 33); how "epistemic violence" (Spivak 1988) is a political and juridical tool used to maintain a phallogocentric and racist system of knowledge and power; and how "feminist counter-violence" is a strategic response to the saturation of violence in the linguistic, legal, and media worlds that comprise the everyday. However, our focus on representations, strategies, and institutions does not eclipse either the murdered or the murdering women. In several of the chapters the very problem of the techniques and technologies of representation are analyzed in the shadow of the ongoing murders of women in Juarez (Zoey Michele) or in the ongoing searches for the missing women of downtown Vancouver (Margot Butler). Likewise, Dorit Naaman's analysis of the images of the female suicide bomber works to show how specificity is eclipsed by media spectacles of the Middle East and by discourses of nationalism. Sharon Rosenberg's analysis of the monuments erected in memory of the women murdered in the Montréal massacre is set beside the analyses of archived lives and murderers' testimonies in Sylvie Frigon's and Kathleen O'Shea's chapters, respectively.

Killing Women is organized so as to highlight the constellations of inquiry mentioned above: history and memory, techniques and technologies, and national cultures. Clearly, there is overlap between the three parts, with the matter, for example, of the abject body being of concern for several authors, and with the issues of specific representational modes, media, or genres being found across several chapters. Part 1 presents chapters that consider the way we live with, and construct histories and memories of, gendered violence. The complex relationship between history and memory has been a focus of much feminist research, connecting it to other studies of trauma and violence, such as those concerning the Holocaust, colonialism, and war. The chapters in Part 1 consider issues of how an archive is made to tell a certain truth about gendered violence, how the record is mediated by the subjective work of memory and repression, and how contemporary writing about or representations of the victims or murderers of the past must reflect upon the processes of history making and memory work.

The collection opens with Sylvie Frigon's historiographical analysis of how women accused of, and often imprisoned and executed for, killing their husbands were depicted between 1866 and 1954. Unable to appreciate domestic violence, Canadian society throughout this period mediated women who had murdered in public representations as either the sexualized family traitor (e.g., Evelyn Dick in the so-called Torso Murder Case) or the protective mother (e.g., Angelina Napolitano, seven months pregnant and with four children at home). With revealing excerpts from contemporary press releases, court transcripts, and popular culture (plays, songs, novels, and films based on some of the cases), Frigon brings to light the historical depth of the problem of representing women who kill in modern society. She points to more recently contested ground in her comparison of historical characterizations with contemporary, Western popular film portrayals of murderous women, where the traditional stereotypes persist but are accompanied by more complex and feminist renderings.

Sharon Rosenberg's chapter on the politics of memorials and memory relating to the Montreal Massacre traces the ways in which the murders at the Ecole Polytechnique have been publicly remembered through tenth anniversary commemoration. She argues that, far from settled (and hence a matter of "the past"), "what remains is an ambivalence in memory that cannot be addressed without an opening of present-day frames and commitments." The profound emotional experience of loss and grief have been recorded in particular ways, thus constructing not just the past of this terrible day but also the present. She works with the monuments and other public memorials by analyzing "public memory as those selective and contested social formations that circumscribe a set of terms and bounded symbolizations, through which past events are remembered and living attachments to that past are formed."

Zoey Michele's chapter on the contemporary case of over three hundred murdered women in the Mexican border town of Ciudad Juarez examines how documentary and media representations of the victims further violate the women by affording them meaning only through the frameworks of "truth" that are reproduced by racist and sexist institutions. She engages with feminist and poststructural theories of representation, particularly Jacques Derrida's metaphysics of presence, Laura Marks's metaphors of fetish and fossil, and bell hooks's insistence on including personal and political contexts when considering domination and oppression. In pointing out the oversimplification, mystification, and exoticization of the murdered Other found in the depictions of what happened in and around Ciudad Juarez, Michele attempts to stifle any further violation of these women.

Kathleen O'Shea's personal reflection on her work with women on Death Row in the United States plays between the intensely personal and the public with regard to state-sanctioned killing and its ideological rationalization in the American media. O'Shea focuses on one highly visible character condemned to death, Karla Faye Tucker, and demonstrates how she is played by the media to fit social norms of femininity (much as are the Canadian women analyzed by Frigon). Through the use of diary-like prose, O'Shea also draws a quiet comparison between Tucker and another Death Row inmate, the much less-known Cherokee woman Nadian Smith. The connections between trauma, testimony, and memory are shown to mediate each other and to condition the way in which the official histories are written.

Part 1 ends with an examination of the media and legal frameworks that represent convicted murderer Karla Homolka. Australian legal theorist Belinda Morrissey offers some critical distance on a very sensitive case that is extremely well known within Canada. For Canadian analyses see Davey 1994; Dorland and Walton 1996; Crosbie 1997. Morrissey considers the framework and the gendered discourses within which the public has come to know Homolka and offers a way of thinking about a figure that even feminism has had difficulty approaching. By offering an analysis not only of media representation but also of representation within legal theory, Morrissey asks us to struggle with our sense of horror and our designation of Homolka as evil and to instead consider her within the psycho-sexual framework of sadism—a framework usually reserved for men.

Throughout Part 1 there is a significant movement between (1) actual women's lives and their experiences of violence and (2) the characterization of those lives when the women turn to murder or when they are memorialized or forgotten as victims of violence. Part 2 focuses on that process of mediation as a political and aesthetic force with the power to make bodies and their social contexts appear or disappear, on the one hand, or to make them perform and signify strategic or critical alternatives, on the other. The chapters in Part 2 focus on the strategies, discourses, and technologies of the representation of violence.

Annette Burfoot opens Part 2 with an unusual but revealing study of eighteenth-century anatomical models. The models are an important example of the early modern treatment of the female body and femininity both as pacified by male desire (carefully disguised as scientific objectivity) and as posing an active threat (in the form of the abject). In terms of this collection, these models represent the feminine as both murdered and murderous. The analysis of these models, the comparisons between the female and male models, and an appreciation of their historical context demonstrates how medical visual culture renders sexual difference in terms of violence as well as how the female form figures as a prime arbiter of life and death. Also significant here is the reassignment—from the Church to modern medical science—of the authority to publicly characterize femininity as something inherently dangerous.

Lisa Coulthard also engages with the terrain of medical science, in this case through the "the forensic aesthetic" in feminist artworks. In her close and critical reading of two feminist exhibits centring on women and violence, *Bloody Wallpaper* and *Lustmord*, Coulthard demonstrates the operation and significance of absence: "the hidden and quotidian aspects of violence against women." She expands on oversimplified conceptions of violence and the violated subject, and criticizes the exploitative nature of normative renderings of murdered women in terms of forensic "debris."

Like other contributors to *Killing Women*, Jack Boozer examines the realm of representation and its connection to material conditions; however, he turns to the images of violent women in American film and considers them in terms of "televisuality," or the materialization of subjectivity within the context of the "contemporary simulational environment." His close reading of the films *To Die For* and *Nurse Betty* pays crucial attention to an obsession for violence within virtual representations or simulations themselves. In this virtual space of highly figurative subjectivity, gender and violence become part of a much more complex arrangement that includes the techniques and technologies of representation itself.

The disappearance and murder of women in San Diego and Vancouver compels Margot Butler to engage the reader in the act of probing the telling of the tales of these murdered women. Butler's chapter recreates parts and processes involved in the No Humans Involved exhibition, which focused on forty-five unsolved murders of women in the San Diego area, and she uses this as a foundation for addressing the techniques, ethics, and politics of representing the immediate and ongoing horrors of the BC Pickton farm investigation and excavation. She works through visions and voices: hers and those of other women associated with the constellation of events in both cities. "Implicatedness" is central to this piece—who is in the picture from the gallery of murdered women's faces? Why? When? How? Configuration and subjectivity are not secure in that the treatment of the stories further violates the murdered women and extends the violence to others.

Susan Lord concludes Part 2 with an analysis of feminist films that feature female murderers, arguing that a strain in feminist media performs a "strategic counter-violence." She demonstrates the significance of time for feminism and how the violent sites in feminist cinema can be analyzed as a response to the lack of futurity to which images of women are subjected in Western culture. As a project of creating and reflecting upon representation as a collective formation of a social imaginary, feminist cinema and its discourse of violence permits the complexity of gendered subjectivity to enter and to disrupt the image bank of media culture.

Which leads us to Part 3, where collectivity, in the form of national cultures, figures prominently in the discussion of women and violence. Whether they consider the relationship between gendered violence and nationalism or between the representation of gender within specific national cultural traditions, the chapters in this part have something interesting in common: all of the central characters/subjects are women who kill. This tells us less about specific women than it does about the imaginary for female agency within a national context in which the female character is either a surrogate for the nation or, due to cultural tradition, is imagined to have autonomy. However, curiously, in the case of the horror genre, whether in Italy or in the United States, the image of female agency is tied directly to the character's body as a site of desire, abjection, or rage.

Frank Burke's chapter on Italy and its specific variant of the horror film turns to the representation of a female violence and its conditioning by national culture and traditions. In the reading of one film in particular, *The Bird with the Crystal Plumage,* Burke demonstrates how it is possible to reinterpret female protagonists within the problematic genre of horror "beyond a misogynist projection of male anxiety." Especially when considered in terms of its national socio-political context, the film can be seen as a representation of women's rage based in a collective experience of violence against, and the suppression of, women in Italy by a dominant masculine culture.

Suzie Young's chapter examines the connection between the gendered identity of its subjects, cultural tradition, and recent popular representations of femininity. She addresses this connection through an analysis of flight in two recent films featuring violently active yet lighter-than-air Asian martial artists: the well-known *Crouching Tiger, Hidden Dragon* and the much less well known but ultimately more progressive (argues Young) *Wing Chun*. These almost hyperactive female fighting bodies obviously control the scene and narrative as embodiments of justice, courage, and honour. But Young asks, "how far do they push the limits of cinematic femininity in neoconservative culture?" At the crux of this question lies a much older ambiguity regarding the popular and public mediation of female figures that defy, as well as take flight from, social norms.

Steven Schneider explores representations of women and violence within the American horror film, focusing on the female psycho-killer. Schneider finds some common ground between the female psycho-killer and her male counter-part: early childhood abuse. In an extensive overview of the Hollywood slasher horror film, Schneider comes to a novel conclusion regarding the significance of the female crazed killer: he sees this figure as representing a form of animated femininity—one that provides political resistance to patriarchal gender stereotyping within the framework and history of American popular genre cycles.

Within the context of popular Hindu cinema (particularly its "woman's film") and the national women's movement, Jyotika Virdi investigates women who kill. She challenges feminist charges that recent reinscriptions of women as avenging dare devils continues to panders to male desires. As with Young, Frigon, and Schneider, Virdi is interested in whether these new representations of the avenging female body inspire a political transformation by providing women with an active and possibly feminist role. She explores three films, *Teesri Manzil/Third Floor, Aradhana/Prayer,* and *Insaaf Ka Taraazu/Scales of Justice,* each of which depicts rape as the motive for the female avenger. Virdi examines feminist criticisms of the popular depiction of rape-revenge and offers a crucial contextualization of the woman's film in terms of the Indian women's movement, which was founded on issues of sexual violence.

To conclude Part 3 and the collection, Dorit Naaman enters the highly contested ground of Palestinian and Israeli women fighters, suicide bombers, and "angels of death." If, historically and recently, Western ideology has struggled with the spectacle of women-who-kill and has tended to force them into constraining gender stereotypes, then the same can be said for how contemporary media and film treat Middle Eastern women warriors. Significantly different however, and presaged by Virdi and Burke's attention to national political contexts of violence against women, is the interaction between the brutal struggle for nationhood and the public materialization of gender. Naaman examines a selection of films devoted to the struggle for national liberation in Algeria, Palestine, and Israel, all of which feature women combatants and guerrillas. She interweaves this analysis with crucial information on Middle Eastern politics as well as with excerpts from interpretations found in both the Western press and the Middle Eastern press. She discovers crucial differences between the ideological manifestation of freedom fighters of Israel and Palestinian angels of death—differences that co-implicate engendered violence and international hostilities.

The process of developing *Killing Women* was facilitated by an e-mail listserv and two focus panels at the 2002 Congress of the Humanities and Social Sciences. The authors were encouraged to recognize points of contact and to share resources, thus enabling us to build a bibliography and a list of visual resources for the volume. This process also permitted us to highlight the politics of representation as a particularly powerful and complex process of social meaning production. Whether in the pages of *Adbusters* or in a news report from Ciudad Juarez, the globalization of media culture and the geo-politics of gendered violence find in the image of the female body a familiar and horrible home. The chapters collected here are meant to provide critical distance on the visual culture that we—broadly and globally—share.

[section one]

History, Memory, and Mediations of Murder

FIGURE 1 Women prisoners at cells (possibly Kingston Penitentiary), c 1900 (with permission from Canada's Penitentiary Museum Collection, Kingston, Ontario).

Mapping Scripts and Narratives of Women Who Kill Their Husbands in Canada, 1866–1954: Inscribing the Everyday

SYLVIE FRIGON

[1]

Fallen women. Unruly women. Deviant women. Women who kill. They are dark creatures, dark characters who disturb and fascinate. Although many contemporary films and prime-time television shows have been devoted to crime, this interest in the representation of crime for public edification is not a new phenomenon. The fascination for crime and violence has been inscribed in mythology, ballads, plays, and early journalism. Shakespeare's crime stories are a case in point, and Lady Macbeth is an examplar[1] of the depiction of the violent, murderous woman. And throughout modern history representations of women who kill oscillate between fascination, eroticization, pity, disgust, and repulsion. Straddled between these characterizations, the actual women who kill in this visual culture, in fact, disappear; they are effectively erased. The very construction of their evilness rests on this. Moreover, there is a simultaneous construction of her *body in danger* as a *dangerous body* (Frigon 1996, 1999, 2000, 2001, 2002). In this chapter I aim to demystify fallacies by exploring how these images are framed and constructed, how they gain currency, and how they are contested. In mapping out the historical foundation for a particular set of these images, I begin to sketch some possible points of counter-inscription.

Theorizing Female Conjugal Homicide as Narratives in a Historical Context

A historical basis for modern fascination with women-who-kill may be found in the trial narratives of women condemned of murder, in which the representations of actual women killers are strongly coded and mingle with a public fascination. Prominent cases include those of Ruth Ellis in 1954 (the last woman to be hanged in England), Myra Hindley[2] (also of England), and, more recently in Canada, Karla Homolka. The mythologies of Ruth Ellis, Myra Hindley, and Karla Homolka and the related public outcry and condemnation of them reveal, above all, "that we do not have a language to represent female killing, and that a case like [these] disrupts the very terms which hold gender in place" Carlen 1993, 61). The acts of these women rightly invoke moral condemnation, but we lack feminist explanations of women murderers who have not killed in self-defence because their deeds fall between the cracks of the normative representation of women.

Typically, violence done to women, but not violence committed by women, is representable. Woman-as-murderer is unspeakable and does not fit social norms and codes of femininity. Despite the fact that they have been portrayed as evil, deceitful, and cunning, female murderers throughout history are usually common people, and female-perpetrated murders occur in disturbingly ordinary circumstances. Often, their stories function to illuminate women's daily lives and common experiences of violence. In what ways can these counter-images of murderous women negotiate with public spectacle?

Traditional portrayals of women killers are saturated with images of particularly sexual and evil creatures randomly killing. However, the scientific literature, accounts from actual murderers, and court evidence suggest that women who kill do not usually kill strangers but, rather, loved ones (e.g., partners, children). Nor do they kill randomly—often, they kill their violent partners.

Life with Billy (1994) is a fictional film based on the life of Jane Stafford, a woman condemned for killing her abusive partner in Nova Scotia. Documentary filmmakers deliver striking and sensitive portraits of women, their lives, their stories, and the abuse they have had to endure before they finally defended themselves. As these women typically claim: "It was my life or his," and "There was no other way out."[3] Other such counter-inscriptions of women killing their partners are offered in *The Provoked Wife* (1991), *Why Women Kill* (1992), *Women Who Kill* (1994), *Defending Our Lives* (1993), *Stories from the Riverside* (1994), and *When Women Kill* (1994), and all provide a key understanding of real life stories and "survival killers" (i.e., spouses who kill in order to survive) who commit conjugal homicide.

Iconographies of Women Who Kill and Theorizing Female Conjugal Homicide within a Historical Context

Historically, the criminal justice system's treatment of women who have killed violent husbands has been harsh. The violence endured by these women and by women in general was, in fact, condoned by society, as is suggested by the so-called "rule of thumb." This alluded to the fact that it was legal for a man to beat his wife with a stick so long as it was not thicker than his thumb. This violence was also epitomized in femicide or uxoricide (the killing of a wife by a husband). Interestingly, there is no term for the killing of a husband by a wife.

Between 1351 and 1828, under English law, women who killed their husbands could be charged with "Petit Treason" and could be executed. Until 1790, if found guilty of this crime, women could be burned at the stake (Gavigan 1989). The 1763 case of Marie-Josephte Corriveau in Lower Canada (Quebec) illustrates this situation. "La Corriveau" admitted to killing her husband, Louis-Hélène Dodier; however, she held that his death was the result of his

FIGURE 2
"La Corriveau," cartoon depicting the public exhibition of Madame Corriveau by Henri Julien in *La Cage*, Beauchemin Press, 1916.

violent treatment of her. The sentence was justified by Lieutenant Colonel Morris as follows: "The sentence must be strong enough to prevent other crimes in the years coming [note the political instability]. If all wives, unhappy with their lives, killed their husbands there would be no more men left in the colony" (Lebel 1981, 180; translation mine). As was the practice at the time, Marie-Josephte Corriveau was executed and publicly exposed for a month in an iron cage at a crossroad in Lauzon, Quebec. After more than 200 years, the public fascination with the story of "La Corriveau" (as she will be referred to hereafter) has become a part of Quebec mythology. Her story has been re-enacted repeatedly in ballads, books, poetry, songs, visual art, and plays.

Depictions of Women Condemned for Killing Their Husbands in Canada, 1866–1954

In this section[4] I explore the historical context of the years between 1866 and 1954 by studying the relevant trials and providing an analysis of gender construction in the public narratives of these trials. More than one hundred years after the execution of "La Corriveau," between 1866 and 1954, twenty-eight Canadian women were found guilty of killing their husbands and were condemned to death. In the end, seven of these women were executed. The archival record, *Persons sentenced to death in Canada, 1867–1976* (Gadoury and Lechasseur 1994), provides a list of convicted women as well as their case reference numbers. These cases were retrieved and analyzed at Archives Canada in Ottawa. The content of the accumulated records included: court transcripts; police reports; correspondence (i.e., letters, telegrams, memorandums); reports made by judges, lawyers, and justice ministers; witness statements; confessions; Tickets of Leave; coroners' reports; doctors' evaluations; notices and judgments of appeal; petitions; newspaper clippings; photographs; and fingerprints. A variety of documents from the types mentioned above were found for each case. A search provided a complementary source of information for those cases that did not include sufficient archival newspaper clippings.[5]

The purpose of the research was to determine how the incident of murder and the women involved were constructed throughout the trial and afterwards. This was primarily achieved by eliciting the different accounts of the major actors who participated in the courtroom proceedings and the subsequent post-trial procedures as well as from recorded comments made by concerned members of the respective communities. Throughout our research we discovered several interesting phenomena that contributed to our analysis of these women's lives. Of course, these "lives" were constructed within a courtroom; that is, they were constructed within legal discourse, through adversarial means, and within a male dominated arena. The readings of the contents of the trial transcripts, confessions, newspaper clippings, and testimonies evoked a feeling similar to that aroused upon reading a trial drama (see also the Ruth Ellis trial in 1954–55). Dramatic effect was achieved by the use of different rhetorical devices, and some of these "stories" (because they did become stories) are even presented in a detective-story format. This is exemplified in the popular representation of the 1946 trial of Evelyn Dick in Ontario, referred to as the "Torso Murder Case":[6]

> On March 16, 1946, the headless, limbless body of John Dick was discovered by a group of schoolchildren in the lonely outskirts of Hamilton, Ontario. So began the most shocking murder investigation ever undertaken in Canadian history. This is a true-life crime story with all the ingredients of the best detective stories: lurid sex, seething passion, spine-tingling suspense and gruesome murder. And it stars a genuine *femme fatale*, Mrs Evelyn Dick—a strikingly beautiful woman whose extraordinary sexual proclivities and bizarre testimony shocked the nation. (Campbell 1974, back cover)

The outcome of the trials studied here (acquittal, sentence, execution, commutation of sentence, and sentence reduction), as well as the trials themselves, unfold, in part, according to the dramatic construction of the moral character and history of the women involved. Often, it seems that the actual evidence becomes secondary, being deemed inferior to the prevalent narratives that repeatedly emerged throughout the trial.

In order to explore the construction of these narratives, I consider a number of questions: How is the crime represented in the courtroom? What are the social and legal representations of femininity, sexuality, marriage, fidelity, and motherhood? What is the legal relevance of violence against women? Which factors will affect the trial outcomes? With the support of this empirical material, I attempt to examine some dominant representations of women who kill their partners. These images are gathered through the eyes of different social actors especially "norm definers" (Lévesque 1989) such as: legal representatives (police, lawyers, judges); medical professionals (doctors, psychiatrists, coroners); religious leaders and the Church; the press; family members; neighbours; and petitioners. Drawing on the work of Pat Carlen (1983) and others' work in related areas, I suggest that, as with fictional representations of women-who-kill, the trial narratives indicate that women are punished for having stepped out of their social norms as women, wives, and mothers. As the Poulin case (in 1874)[7] and the Smith case (in 1946)[8] put it, murder by women is a "transgression to the Law of God and the law of man."

Trials of Women in Canada, 1866–1954

The archival documents from Confederation to the abolition of the death penalty in 1976 include the files of some 1,300 men and fifty-eight women. Twenty-eight women were initially condemned to death for killing their husbands. The distribution of these homicides is as follows: seven in Ontario, seven in Quebec, four in Alberta, three in New Brunswick, three in Saskatchewan, two in Manitoba, one in British Columbia, and one in Nova Scotia. The periods during which these twenty-eight cases of homicide occurred are as follows: seven cases occurred between 1866 and 1899; nine occurred between 1900 and 1929; and twelve occurred between 1930 and 1954. In terms of final trial outcome, we know that seven women were executed, that fifteen had their death sentences commuted, and that six were acquitted.

The women ranged in age from twenty-five to fifty. Most of them were mothers, and almost half of them had been victims of domestic violence. Three sentences were commuted because the women were pregnant. Firearms were used in ten out of the twenty-eight cases and poison was used in eight (five in Quebec). In the other cases, the weapons used were the axe (four) and the knife (six). It is interesting to note that all seven executions were performed either in Ontario (three) or in Quebec (four), and that five out of the seven women executed (70 per cent) allegedly had lovers.

"The most atrocious crime of the century"

In many cases, these stories were described in headlines as being the most disgusting crimes in Canadian history. For example, in the case of Phoebe Campbell (1871, Ontario),[9] the *London Free Press* wrote that proof "renders this woman the most atrocious criminal of our century" (8 August 1871). But more important, judges also participated in this construction even though, in the name of justice, they were meant to be fair, impartial, and objective. The judge's address to the jury in Marie Beaulne's case[10] in 1929 (Quebec) illustrates the subjective, value-laden, and unfair treatment of women: "We have to study together the story of a crime, maybe the most atrocious one in our judicial records." Comments made by the trial judge in the case of Tommasina Teolis in 1934 (Quebec)[11] also stand as an example of the inappropriate conduct of judges and of the lack of objectivity afforded to women on trial: "We are in the presence of a hateful crime, perhaps the most brutal one registered in our annals of justice."[12]

Gendered Trial Dramas and Narratives of Gender

As I proceeded with the archival work, I found that a series of factors on the characterization of the woman played a role in the final outcome of the trial and were dominant in the petitioners' request for mercy, commutation of the death penalty, and sentence reduction. Three narratives of appropriate gender roles emerged around the triangle of femininity/wifehood/motherhood.

Femininity on Trial

During the trials the femininity of the accused was put into sharp focus and questioned by emphasizing appearance, behaviour, feminine attitude, and mental instability. The physical appearance of the accused women was also central to press coverage. The most striking example of this is found in the media attention given to Evelyn Dick in Ontario (1946). The *Hamilton Spectator* (8 October 1946) describes Dick as follows: "Shiny black curls beneath her sequin-studded skull cap; a beauty spot on her right cheek; finely-shaped nose, large dark eyes. Her dress: black, sleeveless, perhaps revealing her gain in weight; toeless, heel-less shoes; matching lipstick and nail polish." More descriptions of Dick follow. The magazine *New World* (December 1946) sold, at ten cents an issue, a six-page story with photographs that consecrate Dick as the most murderous and sordid femme fatale in Canada. In the documentary *The Notorious Mrs. Dick* (2001), one comment linked her beauty to her evilness: "Of course, she was as evil as she was beautiful."

Other women condemned for killing their husbands also see their appearance take a prominent position in the courtroom and in the media. As early as 1871 Phoebe Campbell's appearance was scrutinized, as these newspapers clippings indicate:

> She appears to be somewhat thinner than she was when arraigned; her hair is dressed in the same ringlet fashion as it was at the trial. (*Globe and Mail*, 20 June 1872)

> Her face still has the ruddy and healthful glow which it bore at the time of her trial. (*Adviser*, 19 June 1872)

> She was dressed in a black gown, without ornament, and her hair was done up in a plain manner after the fashion she has followed since her incarceration. (*Adviser*, 20 June 1872)

Women's behaviour was also an object of fascination, especially if it deviated from the expected, naturalized gender roles of the period. In 1897 Cordélia Viau, who lived in a small village in Quebec, was deemed to be an inappro-

FIGURE 3
Charlotte Corday by Louis
Muller, c 1880 (with permission
from Canada's Penitentiary
Museum Collection, Kingston,
Ontario).

priate woman because she was independent and did not adopt a conventional lifestyle.[13] She was also seen as the man in her marriage, as this question from the Crown illustrates:

> Q. Who appears to have been in charge among these two, the husband or the wife?
>
> A. It was Mrs. Poirer.[14]

In certain trials the judges urged members of the jury (which were always all-male) to examine the facts in light of what a "reasonable man" would do and think, and not to take into account that they were judging a woman. For example, in the 1935 trial of Mary Cowan (Ontario) Judge Keiller asserted that: "In this case a woman is on trial. She must receive exactly the same treatment as if a man were on trial. The law applies equally to women and men."[15] In the 1922 trial of Irene May Christensen in Alberta, Judge MacCarthy addressed the jury in a similar way: "We have got to face this situation boldly…there should be no sympathy for her by reason of the fact that she is a woman and broken down in health…we must face the issue boldly."[16]

In the 1923 trial of Catherine Tratch in Saskatchewan, Judge Embury asserted that her crime was "dastardly" because she had poisoned her husband at the family table in front of his children:

This woman administered to him strychnine, he not knowing it, taking it from her hand, at his own table, with his own children, in his own home…it is one of the most dastardly crimes that have ever been known in this country. And so, gentlemen of the jury, while this is a woman, you and I are faced with an undoubted responsibility.…We are faced with a moral responsibility of not being afraid to do our duty.[17]

Another instance in which men (read: the law) construct a woman's character is in their consideration of the appropriateness, legitimacy, and authenticity of her reaction to the crime. Certain ideals regarding women's sensitivity and emotional nature are reaffirmed in the courtroom drama: if she did not cry (or did not cry sufficiently), then she was seen as guilty. The 1946 trial of Elizabeth McLean in Manitoba provides an example of this. Two police officers testified as witnesses for the Crown. Officer Nicholson described her weeping: "She wept some.…She wept a little on occasions.…She didn't weep, it wasn't hysterical weeping.…She would burst out and cry, and then compose herself almost immediately.…In my experience a person who is hysterical carries on for some considerable time. They don't break down for a short period and then compose themselves."[18] However, if the woman cried too much, this was not necessarily considered to be a sign of her innocence. In the 1917 trial of Carmello Marablito in Nova Scotia, the trial judge commented:

> The evidence is that the woman was crying, no doubt she would easily cry, whether she was guilty or not guilty: I would not wonder at her being found in tears, for it is only women of the firmness of Lady Macbeth that could carry out a project like that without some time or other giving way and showing signs of a woman's weakness. She was not Lady Macbeth, but only an ordinary, commonplace human being, and it is not at all unnatural that she would be found in tears after she realized the enormity of the crime that had been committed.[19]

The moral character of the women on trial is constructed around dichotomous notions of good and evil. For example, in Ontario Olive Sternaman (1896) and Elizabeth Tilford (1935) were tried differently from one another, even though the circumstances surrounding the murders were very similar: both women were accused of single-handedly poisoning their husbands with arsenic; neither had a lover; rumours circulated to the effect they had both killed their first husbands; their alleged motive was insurance money; there was no issue of domestic violence; and both claimed their innocence. Sternaman was portrayed as being very pious and religious. According to the *Globe* (1 January 1898): "The explanation is that she is a simple, emotional, deeply spiritual and religious unworldly woman."[20] Another newspaper article stated: "She has not a high nervous organization, and she has the deepest religious trust that I have ever seen in a human being" (unknown source, 22 December 1897). The *Toronto World* (9 December 1897) described Sternaman's reaction after hearing the guilty verdict: "She threw herself to the floor as if her heart would break." After the public outcry around her conviction, she was finally acquitted.

In contrast, Tilford is portrayed as a bad woman, a witch. On 6 December 1935 Margret Sim wrote that the death penalty was inappropriate, even for such evil creatures: "That a woman so sick a mind as that woman has, should be kept under restraint so that she may work no more evil, we verily believe, but to perpetuate a lust for blood will work ourselves harm."[21] The chilling headline of the *Daily Mirror* (8 December 1935) indicates that Tilford was publicly perceived as cold and cruel: "Icy Wife Sees Rise of Gibbet." This woman was hanged.

In other cases, physical and emotional disturbances attributed to femininity were highlighted in order to shed light on the killing. In the cases of Napolitano (1911), Shulman (1918), and Pogmore (1936), their instability was believed to rest on their being pregnant. Shulman had a miscarriage two days before the crime, and this came to be seen as the precipitating factor. Menopause was seen as a contributing factor in the cases of Tilford (1935) and Harrop (1940). In the case of Tilford, a letter sent by Mr. Fraser on 6 December 1936 to the minister of justice recommends the commutation of the death penalty on those specific grounds:

> From her age given in the papers, [we] realize that she must have passed through the menopause quite recently, or that she is not yet passed that trying period....A woman may be absolutely sane, and yet, because of weakness and functional disturbances, may be unable to control certain tendencies—tendencies entirely foreign to her under normal conditions.[22]

The coroner in the Harrop case evoked mental weakness as the cause of the woman's emotional break:

> This is a very unusual and a very sad case of a prolonged quarrel between husband and wife; when you have a case like that you have a domestic volcano which may erupt at any moment, and the result depends on which one of the parties has the most intense mental obsession, and there was probably in her mind that she was going to be killed by her husband. People like that have what the French called "the fixed idea."[23]

Hysteria was seen as a form of mental instability and was believed to have contributed to the commission of the crime in the trials of Jackson (1920) and Dranchuk (1934).

The Sacrosanctity of Marriage

In the late eighteenth and early nineteenth centuries, women were not legal persons in the eyes of the law. A woman had to be submissive and to obey her husband, and those who deviated from the norm paid dearly. Of course, women who were thought to have lovers and who were also condemned for having killed their husbands were condemned for their infidelity as well. Eighteen of the twenty-eight women convicted of murder were presumed to have had lovers. The trial judge of Angèle Poulin in 1874 in New Brunswick emphasized her "sexual appetite." Women in Quebec (Cordélia Viau, Marie Beaulne, Emily Sprague, Marie-Louise Cloutier, and Tommasina Teolis) were the most harshly punished—presumably for their alleged infidelity as they lived in a society where religious beliefs about sexual propriety were paramount and any deviation was inexcusable (Bernier and Cellard 1996, 38). We have already seen how the infidelity of Poulin (1874) and Smith (1946) was described as a transgression against the laws of God and man. The trial of Angelina Napolitano is instructive because, even though her husband was known to have had many mistresses, her infidelity removed any credibility she might have had in the eyes of the judge.

The execution of Cordélia Viau in the film *Cordélia* (1976) features a double hanging: Cordélia and Samuel Parslow, hired help and presumed lover and accomplice. The sexually active, immoral woman, the seductress, is punished before our eyes. The supposed lover is presented as being not particularly bright, and the ensuing public reaction to him is not on the same register as is that for Cordélia. He is presented as having fallen for the woman's charms. We, as movie-goers, look at the crowd looking at the double hanging and share in the spectacle, especially during the very long take of Cordélia ascending the gallows.[24]

Women who were presumed to have had lovers were seen as temptresses and manipulative seductresses. Their lovers were often seen as puppets in the hands of these crafty, sexual women. Examples of the murderous woman as temptress are found in the cases of Carmello Marablito, who was forty-three years old, and Mary Cowan, who was twenty-seven years old. Both of these women allegedly had younger lovers. According to the judge, Neri, who was twenty-two years old and was Marablito's lover, "was a victim, in a sense, of the woman, and…she got possessing the young fellow's mind and soul [sic], and brought it about that he was hardly a free agent."[25] A letter from the Crown's counsel to the minister of justice concerning eighteen-year-old Allan Cowan, who was Mary Cowan's lover, suggests the same: "This boy has appeared to me all through as a submissive easily led type and it is not surprising to me that Mary Cowan, 27 years old, a moron, but much more aggressive, a woman who has been gratifying his sexual appetite, has had such control over him."[26]

The 1954 infidelity of Lina Thibodeau (New Brunswick) is perceived differently from that of Cowan and Marablito, but to the same effect. Although she is perceived as being excessively sexual, this is represented and excused by the trial judge as a freak of feminine nature and as something of which her male lover took advantage: "Furthermore, she was gratified by Nature with nice features, and I am inclined to believe, with a sexual urge which her husband could not possibly fully satisfy. She met a wolf who took advantage of her weakness."[27] The murder trial as representation of gender extremes, but not of gender deviation, effectively reifies the norm.

The Holy Nature of Motherhood

During the period between 1866 and 1954 the primary social role of women was to bear and rear children. Women who did not conform to this standard were made into outcasts. Childless women were, in fact, perceived to be potentially bad women. In the trials of Emily Sprague, Marie-Louise Cloutier, and Cordélia Viau in Quebec, their childlessness was seen as central to their crime. In the trial of Cloutier, the trial judge asked: "What could a woman with no children and no tenure in a home do?…When there are no children, a woman alone in a house may be victim to many errors."[28]

However, when the accused women were mothers, the holy mother figure became central in the petitioners' appeals for reprieve, commutation of the death sentence, or early release. The respective communities' opinions on the appeals were forwarded to the minister of justice and typically referred to two major problems associated with punishing women who are mothers: First, it was seen as socially dishonourable to kill and/or imprison a woman who was perceived as a creator and nurturer of humanity; second, citizens were concerned with the welfare of the children should their mother be executed or incarcerated. In Elizabeth Coward's case the Coral Council of Women wrote to the minister of justice, pleading that "Mrs. Coward has proved to be an affectionate and worthy mother as shown by the love and solicitude for their mother's release and their engaging to provide a home."[29] The accused herself appealed her sentence to the minister of justice for the sake of her children: "This wretched life of mine is wanted by my children, they need me, especially my youngest daughter of 15 years old."[30]

Sarah Jackson also benefited from having had children: a petition asked for leniency "in mercy of her five children who have to face life with so great a handicap."[31] Letters submitted by the children themselves were also important in the construction of the social significance of a mother's role. For example, Jackson's daughter, Beatrice, undertook a crusade to have her mother released: "I have spent many a sad and lonesome heart broken day waiting for my dear mother. It would make life worth living if she was only free to come home to me."[32] Even though very few petitions were sent on behalf of Dina Dranchuk, a letter signed by L.M. Clark to the minister of justice emphasized her role as a mother: "I beg of you to do all in your power to get this woman reprieved for her dear children's sake. I feel as other mothers do that it is a terrible thing for a woman to be hung in this country especially in these distressing times after all we should show a little forgiveness."[33]

Angelina Napolitano, seven months pregnant and already having four children, was undoubtedly the one to receive the most support simply for being a mother.[34] In a letter signed by Frederick Scroggie and sent to Lord Earl Grey, a member of the public states: "I appeal to your Excellency to take into consideration the fact that this woman is to give birth a month before she is hanged to a child. I think it was Coleridge who said 'A mother is a mother still, the Holiest thing alive.'"[35] Another letter, submitted by Anna Hurtubis, called her crime honourable: "Thank God the little woman had the courage (that of the tigress protecting her young) to slay the villain who should have been the first to protect her honour, her children and her home."[36] Another letter, sent from Alexandra Allma to the minister of justice, called for clemency "in the name of motherhood, the base of all civilization and in the name of the home, the bulwark of civilization."[37] Tilford (nine children), Jackson (five children), Tratch (eight children), and Harrop (four children) all received support on this basis.

However, the appeal to their role as a mother was not always sufficient to win clemency for the accused women. For example, Tilford provoked sympathy and a critique of the criminal justice system but was, in the end, executed. On her behalf, Countess F. Fontaine wrote on 15 December 1935:

> A mother is the holiest entity on Earth. Remember that a mother of nine children had a great reason, perhaps even a sacred duty in killing a bestial vile creature....Perhaps he abused the children, as well as her, or even attempted to rape his own daughters. There are many vile creatures in human form, not fit to live. Nature gave women a very rotten deal, for they have to suffer the agony of motherhood, sacrifice their life each time they give birth to a child, while most men, are just selfish bestial creatures only seeking to inflict cruelty upon women.[38]

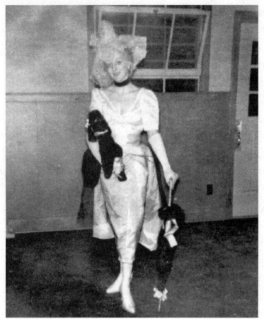

FIGURE 4
Prisoner dressed up with poodle
at Kingston Prison for Women,
c 1950 (with permission from
Canada's Penitentiary Museum
Collection, Kingston, Ontario).

As I have suggested, the outcome of the trials (acquittal, sentencing, execution, commutation of sentence, and sentence reduction) and the dramatic quality of those trials are due in large part to the construction of the moral character and the history of the women concerned. The evidence, as I have said, becomes secondary. The trial-as-drama rests upon the construction of the moral characters and histories of the persons involved. The narratives of appropriate gender roles pivot around the role of the woman as wife and mother and are central to the (re)production of these homicidal wives thus influencing the legitimacy of the narratives of domestic violence.

Suffice it to say that, in nearly half of the cases (thirteen out of twenty-eight), the accused had been a victim of domestic violence; however, if we exclude Quebec, the percentage rises to more than 70 per cent. This factor is not significant in terms of the acquittals related to a self-defence plea but it might play a role in the length of the sentence or even the sentence itself. In fact, in almost all the cases the death sentence was to be commuted to long terms of incarceration. Even if the violence endured by the "accused" from the "victim" was well documented by doctors, police, children, family members, and neighbours, its relevance was modulated by narratives of appropriate gender roles and the context of the time (Frigon 1995, 2002).

Conclusion

As I have suggested, the trial narratives construct appropriate gender roles around the triangle of femininity/wifehood/motherhood. These narratives also reflect the shift in the representation of women killers in contemporary popular culture from the femme fatale to the battered woman and beyond. Through assessing the foregoing analyses of historical trial documents, we are able to see how court discourse and media reporting relies upon and reproduces the cultural myths and figures of femininity.

By exploring the so-called offending women involved in actual crime we can see how representation becomes cultural artefact and social norm. In fact, films, plays, documentaries, and TV shows can be charted through the blurred boundaries of fact and fiction as participating in the evolution of the characterization of women as fallen. The historical analysis of women and conjugal homicide is interesting in light of the women-who-kill genre, from the "femme fatale" to the "super-bitch killer beauties"[39] to the "survival killers" subgenres in cinematographic and other artistic representations.

In order to offer a space for theorizing gender, I conclude this chapter by providing a brief exploration of the fictitious scripts and characterizations of women who kill. The 1940s film noir's construction of the femme fatale paved the way for a "decade of deadly dolls" (Birch 1994) and for Hollywood's productions of super-bitch killer beauties. In the late 1980s and early 1990s movies in this category included: *Fatal Attraction* (1987), *The Hand That Rocks the Cradle* (1991), *Single White Female* (1992), and *Basic Instinct* (1992). These productions introduce pathologically manipulative and violent females who threaten or take the lives of men and other women but whose beauty and charms mask their evil natures. Over the past four decades portrayals of women's violence have consistently relied upon the same formulaic stereotypes. As a case in point, *Swimfan* (2002) is a *Fatal Attraction* for teenagers and relies on the same plot: a young, blond, unstable, sexual, and manipulative teenage girl sleeps with a young popular guy from the swimming team. She reassures him that she does not want to tie him down but eventually stalks him, tries to kill his girlfriend, and so on.

In contrast, *Crimes of the Heart* (1986), *Fried Green Tomatoes* (1991), *Life with Billy* (1993), *The Burning Bed* (1984), and *Dolores Claiborne* (1993) all offer weak resistance to the typical characterization of women-who-kill. Here, femmes fatales or beautiful killers do not occupy centre stage. In *Life with Billy*, for example, the daily experience of terror and a pervasive climate of fear are well established and replace stereotypical characterizations of the

woman-who-kills. This representation of the severely abused woman resort-
ing to murder epitomizes, and introduces, the survival killer subgenre.
Although it differs from the earlier characterization of women-who-kill, this
subgenre is still designed to entertain. In Steven King's *Dolores Claiborne*
(1993), for example, the ordinary circumstances of a conjugal murder committed by an ordinary, middle-aged, plump mother provide a thrilling account
of domestic homicide. A notable and exceptional case is the film *Thelma and
Louise* (1993), which offers a significant shift in the women-killer movie genre
by providing a feminist space, shifting from a "genre that shows women turning *at* each other for empowerment to turning *to* each other for empowerment" (Travers 1992, 72).

Women who kill, in fiction and in real life, fascinate because murder itself
is so final, so irrevocable. Also, these people are triply deviant—they are women,
they are criminals, they are murderers—and they have stepped out of the
stereotypical bounds of femininity, family, and society (Carlen 1983). Commit-
ting murder contradicts their socialized roles, which depict them as being naturally loving and nurturing. More important, their expected passivity is
replaced by a violent agency.

Although these feminine characterizations remain species and spaces of
fascination and fantasy, there is some political hope. In contemporary, popular representations there seems to be a shift from reading killing women as
turning *on* each other for empowerment (*Fatal Attraction* and *The Unfaithful Wife*) to representations of women killing as turning *to* each other for
empowerment (*Thelma and Louise* and the rescued historical accounts of
women killing to protect their children and themselves from violent spouses).
They represent a more politically realistic and emancipatory image: a shift
from the *femme fatale syndrome* to the *super-bitch killer beauties* to the *survival
killer* protecting herself and her children from their abusers is also in the making.[40] Historical cultural work such as this also counters the erasure of women's
identity, factual and fictional, now and then.

Notes

1 I discuss the trial of Carmello Marablito in Nova Scotia in 1917, in which the accused
   woman is compared to Lady Macbeth.
2 In 1965, Myra Hindley was accused and sentenced, with her lover Ian Brady, for taking part in the murders of five children. For an excellent thought-provoking essay
   on the case, see Birch (1993).
3 These recurring themes emerged from interviews conducted within the context of our
   research in Canada, France, and Belgium (Frigon 1999, 2002, 2003).

4 Special thanks goes to Peggy Chrisovergis and Gabriela Pedicelli, research assistants, who actively participated in the archival work.

5 This search was conducted manually through the use of microfiches in the University of Ottawa and Concordia University. Since the *Canadian Periodical Index* does not include such early dates as the nineteenth century, the clippings were retrieved from major newspapers, which were available in these libraries. We found these clippings by searching significant dates surrounding the incidents in question. Since local community newspapers were inaccessible and many of the microfiches of the major Canadian newspapers were not available during these times, our search was often frustrated.

6 See *Torso* (2002) and *The Notorious Mrs. Dick* (2001), a documentary based on the Evelyn Dick story.

7 Reported in the trial of Angèle Poulin, Archives Canada (hereafter AC), Ministry of Justice Archives (hereafter MJA), RG 13, vol. 1411, file 83A.

8 Reported in the trial of Mary Charlotte Smith, AC, MJA, RG 13, vol. 1599 (1,2,3), file CC439.

9 Phoebe Campbell, AC, MJA, RG 13, vol. 1409, file 47A.

10 Marie Beaulne, AC, MJA, RG 13 C-1, vol. 280–281 (pt 1), vol. 1555, 1.

11 Tommasina Teolis, AC, MJA, RE 13 C-1, vol. 1593, no. 348–349 (pt. 1), 437–38.

12 Translation; trial of Tommasina Teolis, AC, MJA, RG 13 C-1, vol. 1593, no. 348–349 (pt. 1), 437–38.

13 *La lampe dans la fenêtre* (Cadieux 1979), a novel, is the basis for the film *Cordélia* (1976) in French with English subtitles.

14 Crown's interrogation in the trial of Cordélia Viau, AC, MJA, RG 13 C1, vol. 1436, no. 6; vol. 1, 299.

15 Judge's address to the jury in the trial of Mary Cowan, AC, MJA, RG 13, vol. 1600 (1.1,1.2,2), file CC443.

16 Judge's address to the jury in the trial of Irene May Christensen, AC, MJA, RG 13, vol. 1524 (1,2), file 704 A/CC197, 249–50.

17 Judge's address to the jury in the trial of Catherine Tratch, AC, MJA, RG 13, vol. 1528 (1,2,3,4), file 722A/CC216, 191.

18 Testimonies in the trial of Elizabeth Maud McLean, AC, MJA, RG 13, vol. 1661 (1.1,1.2), vol. 1662 (2), file CC619, 174, 181, 239–40.

19 Judge's address to the jury in the trial of Carmello Sofie Marablito, AC, MJA, RG 13, vol. 1487 (1,2), file 595 A/CC61.

20 Trial of Olive Adèle Sternaman, AC, MJA, RG 13, vol. 1431, file 286A.

21 Trial of Elizabeth Ann Tilford, AC, MJA, RG 13, vol. 1598 (1.1,1.2), vol. 1599 (2, 3.1,3.2), file CC437.

22 Letter sent during the trial of Elizabeth Ann Tilford, AC, MJA, RG 13, vol. 1598 (1.1,1.2), vol. 1599 (2, 3.1,3.2), file CC437.

23 Testimony in the case of Frances Harrop, AC, MJA, RG 13, vol. 1625 (1,2,3), file CC514, 19.

24 In the film *Cordélia* it is said that only men could attend public hangings, which were performed as entertainment.

25 In the trial of Mary Cowan, AC, MJA, RG 13, vol. 1600 (1.1,1.2,2), file CC443.

26 Ibid.

27 Judge's address to the jury in the trial of Lina Thibodeau, AC, MJA, RG 13, vol. 1741, (1.1,1.2,2.1,2.2), file CC803, 14.

28 Translation; judge's address to the jury in the trial of Marie-Louise Cloutier, AC, MJA, RG 13 C1, vol. 1617 VI, no. 387–388; vol. 4, 1261, 1266.

29 In the trial of Elizabeth Coward, AC, MJA, RG 13, vol. 1485 (1.1,1.2), vol. 1486 (2.1,2.2), file 555A/CC56.

30 Letter from Elizabeth Coward, AC, MJA, RG 13, vol. 1485 (1.1,1.2), vol. 1486 (2.1,2.2), file 555A/CC56.

31 Petition on behalf of Sarah Jane (Sadie) Jackson, AC, MJA, RG 13, vol. 1509 (1,2), file 654A/CC147.

32 Letter sent for the release of Sarah Jane (Sadie) Jackson, AC, MJA, RG 13, vol. 1509 (1,2), file 654A/CC147.

33 Petition on behalf of Dina Dranchuk, AC, MJA, RG 13, vol. 1592 (1,2), file CC418.

34 See the play *The Angelina Project* (Canino 2000), which focuses on the Napolitano trial and is based on a historical article by Karen Dubinsky and Franca Iacovetta (1991).

35 Petition on behalf of Angelina Napolitano, AC, MJA, RG 13, vol. 2698 (1,2,3,4,5), file 446A/CC22.

36 Ibid.

37 Ibid.

38 Petition on behalf of Elizabeth Ann Tilford, AC, MJA, RG 13, vol. 1598 (1.1,1.2), vol. 1599 (2, 3.1,3.2), file CC437.

39 The term is from Karlene Faith (1993).

40 These shifting images are portrayed in various artistic manifestations. For example, the two-act monologue by Newfoundland playwright Berni Stapleton, *Offensive to Some* (1996), takes place in a prison cell where a woman is serving a sentence for the murder of her abusive husband. It explores not only the murderous climax of her character's married life but also the climate of terror that cumulated in the murder.

Neither Forgotten nor Fully Remembered: Tracing an Ambivalent Public Memory on the Tenth Anniversary of the Montreal Massacre[1]

SHARON ROSENBERG

[2]

> Although social power regulates what losses can be grieved, it is not always as effective as it aims to be. The loss cannot be fully denied, but neither does it appear in a way that can be directly affirmed.
>
> —Judith Butler, *The Psychic Life of Power*

In the early evening of 6 December 1989 a twenty-five-year-old white man by the name of Marc Lépine entered l'Ecole polytechnique (the School of Engineering) at the University of Montreal in Quebec, Canada. Armed with a semi-automatic rifle, he walked into a fourth-year mechanical engineering class of sixty (Rathjen and Monpetit 1999b, 10), ordered the male students, and two professors, to leave—which they all did—and shot six women to death, screaming the accusation that they were a "bunch of feminists." He then walked through hallways and entered other classrooms, murdering eight more women. In addition to these dead, Lépine injured nine women and four men—the latter having been shot at, it is generally presumed, because they attempted to impede his rampage. At the end of this massacre he killed himself. In the three-page suicide note found on his body, but not released into public circulation for a year, Lépine described the murders as a political act and blamed feminism for ruining his life.[2] Key sentiments in this letter (in translation) read:

Would you note that if I commit suicide today 89–12–06 it is not for economic reasons…but for political reasons. Because I have decided to send the feminists, who have ruined my life, to their Maker.…Even if the Mad Killer epithet will be attributed to me by the media, I consider myself a rational erudite that only the arrival of the Grim Reaper has forced me to take extreme acts.…Being rather backward-looking by nature (except for science), the feminists have always enraged me. (in Malette and Chalouh 1991, 180–81)

The text of the letter is followed by a "hit list" of nineteen prominent Quebec women and a note, "the lack of time (because I started too late) has allowed these radical feminists to live" (in Malette and Challouh, 1991, 181).

Like many others, my life was pierced by these killings. Studying at another university at the time, not 200 miles away from Montreal, having made Canada my home for a decade and for close to as many years named myself a feminist, my identificatory proximity to the women murdered was high, even though in life they were unknown to me. More than twelve years later I recall with visceral texture the moment I received a call from a friend, telling me to turn on the television, sitting vigil in front of that small screen deep into the night, rigid with shock. While that rigidity gradually eased, I continued to live with the murders, which are a haunting presence in my intellectual and political life.

This is a haunting that turns me not to the past, as though it were suspended from the present, but to keeping a past–present relation animated and open. As Wendy Brown (2001, 171) elucidates, drawing from the work of Benjamin, at stake here is "making a historical event or formation contemporary, making it an 'outrage to the present' [Bloz and van Reijen] and thus exploding or reworking both the way in which it has been remembered and the way in which it is positioned in historical consciousness as 'past.'" This chapter endeavours to make the massacre at the Poly such an "outrage to the present." Tracing the ways in which it has been publicly remembered through tenth anniversary commemoration, I argue that, far from being settled (and hence a matter of "the past"), the Montreal massacre remains an ambivalent memory that cannot be addressed without an opening of present-day frames and commitments. I begin by recalling the texture of the loss, grief, and shock that was expressed in the aftermath of the murders and how these have been named in the historical record. I then outline the conceptual terms of reference upon which the chapter draws—terms that are then put into play through an analysis of how the massacre is being remembered and how the strategies of that remembrance position the living. I end the chapter with a call to take up the fraught ambivalence of memory as a resource for opening the present so as to more fully encounter the loss(es) of the massacre.

FIGURE 5   Bench, Marker of Change—Nathalie Croteau, Vancouver (with permission of Sharon Rosenberg).

Shock, Grief, and Early Expressions of a Legacy of Loss

Named as the "deadliest single-day mass shooting in Canadian history" (Charles Grandmont, *National Post,* 5 December 1999), the massacre in Montreal registered widely in the social domain in a manner unprecedented in Canada. These comments, fashioned in the immediate aftermath of the killings, characterize the shock and horror that many expressed:

> This week, the unimaginable happened. A 25 year-old man...strode into the University of Montréal and opened fire on innocent students....The shock, horror and grief reverberating throughout the country are all prefaced with the question, "Why?" Why Lépine? Why female victims? Why now? Why Canada? (Lois Sweet, *Toronto Star,* 9 December 1989)

> Now our daughters have been shocked to the core, as we all have, by the violence in Montréal. They hear the women were separated from the men and meticulously slaughtered by a man who blamed feminists for his troubles.... Fourteen of our bright and shining daughters won places in engineering schools, doing things we, their mothers, only dreamed of. That we lost them has broken our hearts; what is worse is that we are not surprised. (Stevie Cameron, *Globe and Mail,* 6 December 1990)

> You're 30, you're 43, you're 50, you're reading the newspaper or someone calls you, you can't believe it, you're numb or you feel angry. You're a feminist. You've spent five, or 10 or 15 years going to meetings, organizing demos, publishing/ writing/fundraising/speaking/marching. Suddenly, you're tired, or you're burnt out, or demoralized, and you cry for the deaths of 14 young women you've never met. You grieve also for the literal expression of a hatred for feminism that you

know to be embedded in your culture. You feel targeted. Your heart feels cold.
(Marusia Bociurkiw 1990, 7)

In Canada such expressions of grief, shock, and anger provided the impetus
and form for a diverse number of what I have come to think of as activist-
memorial responses. From anniversary vigils, to the design and production of
monuments, to days of education, to the naming of December sixth as the
National Day of Remembrance and Action on Violence Against Women, the
Montreal murders were widely marked, narrated, and commemorated in
the years following their occurrence. Named in the list of the top twenty-five
Canadian news events of the twentieth century (J.L. Granatstein and
N. Hillmer, *Maclean's*, 1 July 1999), the massacre in Montreal has not been forgotten in the Canadian historical record, nor does this appear to be an immediate risk. This stands in notable contrast to the United States, where an initial attention to the massacre (in its immediate aftermath) has long been
replaced by other, more local "school shootings"—most notably, perhaps,
those at Columbine, which occurred almost a decade later.[3]

Indeed, over these ten years in Canada the massacre has continued to be
felt as a profound loss for many. In particular, for those close to the women
murdered, the deaths linger as a constant reminder of what was and of who
no longer is. As Elena Cherney (*National Post*, 4 December 1999) comments
in the introduction to her piece on "the ones…left behind," "in the decade
since the massacre, each family has tried to find its own way of understanding what happened that day. Many of the parents have stopped asking questions, because they know there are no answers. The families have all been
marked by the shooting, although each in a different way. Some try to keep their
daughter alive by talking about her, while others can hardly bear to speak their
child's name." While it is not surprising that the family members, friends, and
lovers of the women murdered, along with fellow students, continue to grapple with their deaths, what is less known and publicly discussed is how the
lives of other people have been profoundly shaken by this mass murder. Among
these people are those who, through their professions, came into contact with
the slaughter and its wake. For example, Jacques Duchesneau, who was chief
inspector of the organized crime division in Montreal at the time of the murders, recalls: "I was 21 years at homicide as a detective. I was used to seeing dead
bodies.…But 15? No.…That was a Wednesday. It was only Saturday that I
could sleep" (quoted in Linda Slobodian, *London Free Press*, 5 December 1999).
Others, like the mortician at the morgue where the dead women's bodies were
laid out, never returned to work ("Legacy of Pain," *The Fifth Estate*, 1999).
Montreal journalists too remember the killings as a deep resonance; Lynne

Moore, the only reporter who managed to enter the Polytechnique on the night of the shootings, notes simply, "the chill still lingers" (Lynn Moore, *Montreal Gazette*, 6 December 1999). For some, this chill led to the taking of their own lives. At least five people have killed themselves as a result of their connection to the massacre and its devastating effects ("Legacy of Pain," *The Fifth Estate*, 1999).

How are we to understand the relationship between such anguish, lived individually and personally, and the memorial legacy of the massacre as a social and public domain? Certainly, there are vague references to these murders as a trauma that extends beyond individuals and that affects a city, a community, and, to some extent, a nation. The following phrases are illustrative: "even now [a decade later], Montréalers recall where they were, what they were doing, when they heard the news" (Peggy Curran, *Montreal Gazette*, 4 December 1999). "On December 6th, 1989, Montréal trembled, Montréal was wounded. *Nef pour quatorze reines* [Nave for 14 Queens, a memorial square and monument to the women murdered, unveiled for the tenth anniversary] allows us to overcome another phase in our mourning. We are offering this place to Montréal's collective memory: a place to contemplate, a place for reflection" (the mayor of Montreal, quoted in Isabelle Hachey, *La Presse*, 6 December 1999, translation). Beyond Montreal, the massacre is remembered as a national tragedy that "shattered the innocence of Canadians" ("Legacy of Pain," *The Fifth Estate*, 1999) as "a whole nation was plunged into mourning" (*Hamilton Spectator* [no author], 3 December 1999). While such comments are evocative in that they allude to a traumatic legacy with a wide memorial reach, this is a legacy that, I contend, has been only partially faced. Francine Pelletier has argued that the killings were "so loathsome, so unimaginable, [that] it has taken 10 years to come to terms with [their] sheer brutality" ("Legacy of Pain," *The Fifth Estate*, 1999). On a personal level, as individuals who experienced the massacre as a compelling legacy work through its meaning in their/our lives, I expect Pelletier is correct: the tenth anniversary marked a watershed for coming to terms with these murders. However, I argue that such a coming to terms has been, and can only be, partially and insufficiently supported by the formation of a public memory that, over the past decade or more, has sedimented in Canada. While this public memory is considerable, particularly when compared to the sparsity of memorial attention that is sustained for many other acts of violence (raising the ongoing question of what events are produced as "(un)worthy" of remembrance, and with what implications for people's lives and deaths),[4] I argue that it has been fraught with ambivalences that circumscribe sustained encounters with the loss(es) of the massacre.

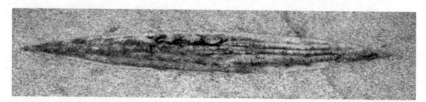

FIGURE 6 Bench, Marker of Change—indentation from top, Vancouver (with permission of Sharon Rosenberg).

Public Memory, Pedagogy, and Ambivalence

To explore the argument outlined above, I turn to the tenth anniversary representation and circulation of the memory of the Montreal massacre in the Canadian media. As Chun (1999, 114) remarks, in the absence of any juridical forum, "the mediatization of the event" has become particularly important to "the task of comprehending the massacre and placing it within [a] historical or societal context." In contrast to the previous years (and, indeed, since), during which mainstream media attention to the murders had waned significantly, the tenth anniversary was marked and commented upon in daily newspapers, in broadcast news and documentaries, and in a full day of memorial representation and discussion on *Newsworld*—an all-day, all-news television station owned by the Canadian Broadcasting Corporation (CBC), Canada's national public broadcaster. In this anniversary reporting, a series of issues was repeatedly identified as marking the legacy of the massacre. This series included: the efforts and relative successes of gun control; the creation of monuments to mark and remember the deaths; the traumatic impacts on family members and those close to the women who were murdered; the correspondence between the massacre and the more usual, daily violence against women in North America; and the relation between Lépine and "men" as a social group. I do not provide a detailed reading of the coverage of these issues; rather, I look at what they suggest about the public memory of the massacre, beginning with the following questions: From the perspective of the present, some distance from the immediate and fraught aftermath of the murders, what are the substance and character of their public memory? Given the decisively gendered constitution of the massacre, how are questions of gender, violence, and public memory now being grappled with?

The conceptualization of memory that I am putting into play here is informed by an interdisciplinary theorization of public memory as those selective and contested social formations that circumscribe a set of terms and bounded symbolizations through which past events are remembered and living attachments to that past are formed. Iwona Irwin Zarecka (1994, 56) artic- ulates what is at issue: "how people attend to the past, if at all, and how they make sense of it is very much grounded in their experience. At the same time, and allowing for this, the public framing of remembrance does matter. Beyond providing resources to work with, public discourse may validate (or discour- age) particular ways of seeing the past." She further notes that such public discourse is shaped by "established structures of thinking and feeling" (121), an important reminder that public memories are not simply generated by information but must engage the living at the level of affect and attachment as well—an idea I explore a little later on. As David Gross (2000, 83, empha- sis mine) explains, recalling the 1930s work of Frederic Bartlett, such structures (or what he calls "schemata") do not simply tell of the past but actually con- stitute its memory: "when we remember, we grasp patterns in or impose pat- terns upon the material remembered; what we ultimately recall is what the patterns bring out, *while what we forget is what the patterns prevent us from grasping or even discerning.*" I also draw upon the work of contemporary trauma theorists who point to the particularities of remembering–forgetting events of violence, loss, and suffering, events that demand paying attention to how social frames of memory engage and/or displace psychical effects. As Cathy Caruth (1995, 256) notes, "trauma can be experienced in at least two ways: as a memory that one cannot integrate into one's own experience, and as a catastrophic knowledge that one cannot communicate to others." From a concern with the formation and contestation of public memories of trau- matic events, then, what becomes central is a concern with the limits of intel- ligibility, representation, and communication.

Some theorists, myself included, have begun to argue for conceptualizing what is at stake here—that is, not only how public memories are produced but also how they are and are not attached to—as a question of pedagogy.[5] Much more than a method or strategy of classroom exercises, pedagogy in this sense is tied broadly to cultural practices and to any public, cultural endeavour to shape political visions of the past, present, and/or future. Thus, in regard to questions of public remembrance, memorial practices (from monument designs to news documentaries) can be read as carrying (explicitly and/or implicitly) particular conceptions of what is to be remembered of the massacre, by whom, for whom, how, and with what potential effects for "securing" memorial significance in the present. Public remembrance practices can be understood, therefore, as practices of teaching and learning, attempts to prompt and engage people in the development of a historical consciousness that might affect their perceptions of, feelings about, identifications with, and the meanings they attribute to the massacre. Moreover, these are communicative practices that intend, however obliquely, to bequeath a memorial legacy to those whom they address. As a memorial address, a public remembrance practice can be understood as something that attempts to bind the living in a particular relation not only to the dead but also to each other. Such bindings might be produced on any number of terms. For example, in regard to the massacre, practices of public memory have variously undertaken to bind the dead and the living as women, as feminists, as Montrealers, as citizens, and/or as Canadians.[6]

Drawing on the forgoing frame to read tenth anniversary coverage, I argue that we are faced with an ambivalent and uneasy public memory of the murders in Montreal. This ambivalence is an effect, I propose, of the dominant pedagogy of remembrance as a "strategic practice" (Simon, Rosenberg, and Eppert 2000, 3–4). In this memorial pedagogy public responses to an act of atrocity are designed to stabilize and to transmit particular versions of the past from the perspective of current socio-political struggles, mobilizing attachments and knowledges that serve specified present-day interests. Such practices are often aligned with the anticipation of a reconciled future, hope for a new and better tomorrow. With regard to the massacre, from one political perspective such strategic pedagogies take shape in the form of calls for stricter gun control; from another, they take shape in the form of the insistence that what happened be recognized as a crime not against humanity in general but, rather, against women in particular. I argue that, while not to be disregarded, such strategic memorial practices cannot fully console people for the loss of the women murdered in Montreal—nor for the rupture of taken-for-granted frames that assumed women were safe and welcome in universities in the late twentieth century, that feminism was passé, and that mass shootings were an American rather than a Canadian phenomenon. These "difficult returns" (Simon, Rosenberg and Eppert 2000, 4–5) demand practices of remembrance that can attend to the absent presence of who and what has been lost—not as a matter of history but as a matter of what it might mean to live in relation with the past, endeavouring to face its claim on the present of one's life. Such disquieting remembrances are not readily aligned with efforts to remember for a reconciled future; rather, they trouble such consolations in their efforts to face rather than to soothe the social and psychic "wounds" caused by the murders. The ruptures, instabilities, losses, and displacements that are initiated as an effect of such memorial attention rub against the grain of more strategic efforts to stabilize memory, with their accent on the socio-political significance of the murders to contemporary endeavours. Where strategic remembrance practices invest in moral lessons—addressed to others—for the future, memory as a difficult return disrupts the certitude of the dichotomies of self/other, present/future, grieving/activism, and teaching/learning.

In this chapter I consider in some detail the uneasiness and ambivalence that is an effect of the incommensurability of these memorial practices, tracing their presence in public memorial formations that constituted the massacre first as an "event" and, second, as an event that has increasingly been read as "emblematic" of men's violence against women. I argue that this emblematic practice has produced ambivalent memorial relations to the massacre in both women and men. I argue for reading these ambivalences as *both* a limit and a resource for those of us committed to extending and elaborating understandings of the legacy of the massacre in Canada. Rather than argue for one memorial formation over another in absolute terms, I am particularly interested in what can be made from this ambivalence. What does an ambivalent public memory suggest about the difficulty of coming to terms with and working through the legacy of the massacre? If it suggests, as I propose, that contemporary social and political conditions constrain memorial politics, then how might engagement with ambivalent memory act on those conditions?

FIGURE 7 Nave for Fourteen Queens—"G" in Steel, Montreal (with permission of Sharon Rosenberg).

The Ma(r)king of an Event

Gun control legislation, efforts to increase the number of women in engineering programs, and the design of monuments[7] can be readily understood as strategic remembrance practices—practices that tie the legacy of the Montreal massacre into contemporary political efforts to achieve a redeemed future. Indeed, such practices are easy to identify as having helped "us" move on. As Peggy Curran (*Montreal Gazette*, 4 December 1999, emphasis mine) puts it, commenting on the national campaign for stricter gun control that was initiated as a result of the massacre, "[this campaign is] without question, still *the most significant memorial* to the Montréal killings." However, I propose that strategic remembrance is not limited to specific political strategies per se but, rather, is widely constitutive of the prevailing public memory of the massacre. This is a memory that can be read as containing the motivation for the killings and, concomitantly, a way to remember both the women murdered and Lépine.

I propose that one of the formative strategic remembrance practices has been the ma(r)king of the murders as *an event* in and for public memory. This is a practice that results in a deeply ambivalent memorial relation to the killings and their legacy. On the one hand, such demarcation renders the murders distinct and out-of-the-ordinary; on the other hand, the very character of this distinctness functions as a limit on interpreting what has occurred. In de Certeau's (1988, 96) terms, delimiting the murders as an event "is the means thanks to which disorder is turned into order. The event does not explain, but permits an intelligibility. It is the postulate and the point of departure...of comprehension." Such demarcation has been centrally fashioned through constituting the murders under a proper name: outside of Montreal the murders are known by the sign "Montreal massacre," within the locale they are known by the sign "Polytechnique" or, more starkly, "Poly." What is it that is made intelligible by these orderings? First, the term "massacre" means "to kill indiscriminately or in large numbers." While this is a naming practice that brings to the fore the impersonal relation between the women killed and their killer, it makes inconspicuous the gendered nature of his act; for he did not kill indiscriminately, he targeted women whom he constituted as feminists and thus as his enemy. Moreover, "Montreal" inscribes a geographic reference but obscures the specificities of the site, the victims, the political motivation, the killer. Similarly, "Poly," while referencing the site, depends heavily for its interpretation on access to and knowledge of local discourses.

I suggest that these are not inconsequential memorial naming practices. The obliqueness with which they signify the killings can be understood as a distancing of "us" from "them" (both those murdered and their killer)[8] and a strategic containment of the losses resulting from the murders. For what neither naming calls attention to is the specific "ruptural character" (Johnson 1999, 23) of the murders,[9] which Collette Guillaumin describes as "a shock of the known." According to her:

> One cannot regard the slaughter in Montréal as an act devoid of meaning, a *senseless* act, just a break in the normal course of events, an unpredictable event that is limited to creating a "shock." Yes, it is a shock, but it is not a shock of the unknown, it is a shock of pain, of anger. In fact, it is a shock of the known, the "I can't believe it" of the known that is not acknowledged—of *unbearable* reality. (Guillaumin 1991, 12–13, emphasis in original)

The shock that Guillaumin directs us to is the shock of the known that cannot be borne, a shock forged through a decisive linkage between the traumatic impact of two distinct ruptures initiated by the murders in Montreal. The first of these was the rupture of what was expected and anticipated for women attending an institution of higher learning in late twentieth-century North America (i.e., that they [we] were [are] safe, welcome, and therefore could attend classes without the threat of death). The second was a rupture of the necessary and everyday systemic refusals to attend to the horrors of oppression that pass as normal—refusals that are, paradoxically, necessary to the very continuance of daily life. These are key markers of the massacre's

FIGURE 8
Nave for Fourteen Queens—Steel Pillars in Snow, Montreal (with permission of Sharon Rosenberg).

"difficult returns." While I am not suggesting that a different naming practice (e.g., "anti-feminist massacre" or "mass killing of women in an engineering school") would be all that is needed to address these rupturing effects, I do suggest that their explicit absence from memorial namings can be read as a trace of how the legacy of the massacre has been (and is being) constituted as a limited and limiting memorial event.

Emblematic Memory

In the immediate aftermath of the killings, and during the early anniversary years, there was enormous debate in the mainstream media regarding how to make sense of Lépine and his actions. The interpretation circulating widely in the media within hours of the killings constituted the murders as "incomprehensible" (in Lakeman 1992, 94), "one man's act of madness" (in Nelson-McDermott 1991, 125), in which "the victims just happened to be women" (in L. Schmidt, *Kinesis*, 7 February 1990). This is a reading that individualized and pathologized Lépine, and, if it worried about the women at all, refused them a gendered identification. A year later, on the first anniversary, this headline in the *Globe and Mail*, Canada's national English-language daily newspaper, illustrated the tenor of the moment: "Remembering: the act of a madman or a tragedy sparked by society's pervasive sexism? That is still the question being asked today" (6 December 1990). By the anniversary date the following year, the weight of that question had begun to ease, with the declaration by the Canadian federal government that it would mark December sixth as a national day of remembrance—a day to remember not only the women murdered in Montreal but also all women harmed by men's violence.[10] Thus, December 1991 marked the opening of a discursive shift in memorialization, such that it has now become quite common to hear the Montreal massacre referred to as a signifier for violence against women in Canada (although this is not without contestation—an issue to which I will return).

However, it needs to be remembered that this reading of the massacre was initiated by feminists during the urgency of contesting the individualizing of Lépine, noted above. In this reading, the massacre is produced not as an aberrant act but as "emblematic." The term "emblematic" refers to the practice of producing a specific act (in this case, Lépine's slaying of women) as standing for a range of other acts that are understood to be constituted in similar terms (e.g., battering, abuse, rape, and other such practices that are marked by beliefs in men's rights to women's bodies, spaces, conduct, invisibility, and so on). As a family of resemblances, these acts are assumed to share certain characteristics, hence the remembrance of one gestures towards the remembrance of all. The most dominant feature of the emblemization of the Montreal massacre, thus, has been to read it as standing for, or as symbolic of, mass systemic violence perpetrated by men against women.

In this framing, therefore, public remembrance of the massacre involves not only a call to remember the women murdered by Lépine on 6 December 1989 but also a call to remember all violence enacted in similarly gendered terms. One important dimension of emblemization is that it emphasizes an identity-based resemblance between the massacre and more daily violence against women—a memorial logic in which "men" are aligned with Lépine and "women" are aligned with his victims. This comment in *The Globe and Mail*, within days of the massacre, illustrates well the workings of this remembrance politic:

> It does not matter that the man who decided to kill fourteen women—and he clearly did decide to do that—killed himself afterward; it is not of him that I am afraid. I am afraid of what he represents, of all the unspoken hatred, the pent-up anger that he expressed. Hatred and anger that is shared by every husband who beats his wife, every man who rapes his date, every father who abuses his child, and by many more who would not dare. (D. Bronson, *Globe and Mail*, 8 December 1989)

While a response that emphasizes the socio-political character of the murders has been absolutely necessary, and continues to be so, emblemization is clearly not unproblematic. It is to these problems that I now turn.

Emblemization and "Difference"

While many feminists have put forward an emblematic reading of the massacre, other feminists have long argued that this is a reading that prioritizes identity politics and gendered power relations at the expense of recognizing complex identity formations and inseparable relations of power—such as "race," class, and sexuality—which shape the meanings of gender for women (in life and in death). I recall, for example, Marusia Bociurkiw, who was writing before the emblemization of the massacre had settled into a stable practice but who was anticipating, even then, the paradox of positioning these particular deaths as a "national tragedy." She observes:

> Without diminishing the horror and waste of these women's deaths, and the unimaginable grief inflicted upon their families, friends, and lovers, it is important to examine the dynamics of the response. The deaths of 14 white, relatively privileged young women was recognized as a national tragedy, while recent

police shootings of Black people have been dismissed either as an accident or
a necessary evil. Meanwhile, poverty, that insidious hired gunman of the state,
stalks women daily. (Bociurkiw 1990, 9)

Caffyn Kelley, writing some five years later and in reference to a Vancouver-
based monument project to memorialize the women murdered in Montreal,
further complicates the issues of remembrance and identity. She writes:

> The names inscribed on the monument will not be the First Nations women of
> the neighbourhood who have been murdered in back alleys and beer parlours,
> left to die in garbage dumpsters or thrown out of hotel windows. In this neigh-
> bourhood where women are six times more likely to be murdered than in the
> city overall—10 to 20 times more likely if they are between the ages of 20 and
> 45—the monument will be inscribed with the names of fourteen, white, mid-
> dle-class women from four thousand miles away. (Kelley 1995, 8)

Counter to a straightforward emblematic reading of the massacre, then,
Bociurkiw and Kelley, among others,[11] gesture to an understanding that recognizes resemblances *and* differences between women (and between acts of violence). While this reading is important for how it complicates an emblematic
reading that traces a single line between the massacre and "violences against
women," it nevertheless faces an unresolvable contradiction as a practice of
public memory. This is because the reading of resemblance and difference
must simultaneously *accept and refuse* the massacre as emblematic. In other
words, we are dealing with a position that argues for recognition of the massacre's partiality within a structure that depends, for its intelligibility, upon
seamless symbolic substitutability.

In the resulting ambivalence and difficulty of this position, it is perhaps
not surprising that critiques of emblemization, by feminists and with regard
to women's lives, are largely absent in tenth anniversary popular media coverage of the massacre. I would argue that, in the emblematic narrative binding of "fourteen women murdered by Lépine" to "women subject to men's
violence," a reading of differences between women risks destabilizing emblemization and its memorial-pedagogical force. When emblemization (which, to
recall, was initiated as a feminist response) has taken hold in public memory
as a counter-narrative to "Lépine as a madman," I suspect that to risk its reading in more complex terms may be regarded (at least by those invested in this
narrative) as risking its complete undermining. Nonetheless, this is an issue
that should, I propose, continue to draw feminist attention.

In contrast to this lack of attention in the mainstream media, questions
of emblemization, identity, and difference continue to be at the forefront in
tenth anniversary reporting with regard to the memorial positionings of Lépine

and, concomitantly, "men." While an emblematic narrative normalizes Lépine as enacting a prevailing practice of men's violence against women (albeit more drastically than is typical), such normalization is by no means secured in public memory. Upon studying the daily newspaper coverage of the tenth anniversary, I was surprised to come across repeated phrases that trouble, if they do not subvert, the apparent acceptance of the argument that Lépine did not act in a social vacuum. He is described, for example, as a "crazed young man" (*Globe and Mail* editorial, 6 December 1999), "wretchedly angry and broken" (Herman Goodden, *London Free Press*, 8 December 1999). In this coverage, Lépine was a "disgruntled loner…[who] roamed the school" (Thanh Ha Tu, *Globe and Mail*, 7 December 1999), "striking blindly at women he did not know" (Charlie Fidelman, *Montreal Gazette*, 6 December 1999), "fired by a pathological hatred" (*Hamilton Spectator*, 3 December 1999). Repeatedly, the killings are described as a "senseless horrific act" (Linda Williamson, *Toronto Sun*, 5 December 1999), "cruel and senseless" (Isabelle Hachey, *La Presse*, 6 December 1999).

In rereading these phrases, I am not interested in entering into a discussion of the usefulness of a psychological versus a sociological interpretation of Lépine and his actions; rather, what I want to underscore is the continued ambivalence within an emblematic public memory regarding Lépine. On the one hand, his *act* of murdering fourteen women in an engineering school is now predominantly remembered as being connected to the daily and more insidious violence committed against women; on the other hand, Lépine as a *person* continues to be distanced from "normal men" through the deployment of a psychologizing vocabulary ("deranged," "crazy," "disgruntled," "loner," "pathological"). When there are no actual diagnoses of Lépine available,[12] I am left to wonder at the adoption of such language and what it suggests about the difficulties, admittedly profound, of coming to terms with the legacy of the massacre as an act of violence supported by dominant relations of power that *privilege* the lives (desires, needs, rights, etc.) of men over those of women.

Such difficulties can be traced further by looking at how men respond to the pedagogical address to remember the massacre *as men*, who, in those emblematized terms, are aligned as guilty by association.[13] For some men, emblemization produces a corresponding position that "accepts" this guilty charge: this stance is most commonly represented by those who take up subject positions offered through the discourse of the White Ribbon Campaign. This campaign represents a coalition of men, formed as a response to the massacre, who organize and speak against men's violence against women. Jack Layton, then Toronto politician and now leader of the New Democratic Party and co-founder and president of the coalition, states: "We need to have men denouncing violence against women; men who are admired like athletes, heads of enterprise and union officials. These are the people that other men respect in daily life" (quoted in Isabelle Hachey, *La Presse*, 1 December 1999, translation). Counter to this memorial positioning are men who refuse the terms of emblematic identification for men, arguing that "[the massacre] was perpetrated by one man...Lépine doesn't represent all men. Many of us refuse to wear the white ribbon each year because the campaign is always posited in terms of male violence against women, ignoring the fact that twice as many men are murdered in this country each year as women" (Herman Goodden, *London Free Press*, 8 December 1999).

The following comments by a psychologist are more nuanced than are those that appear above, but they risk leading to similar refusals on the part of men to bear witness to a massacre that rests, in part, on the presumption of men's privilege and a concomitant right to enact violence:

> That tragedy [the massacre] psychologically injured hundreds of people....Students, male and female, thought their last hour had arrived. But the boys [*sic*] were not listened to, in terms of what they had lived through....We have to teach men and women that they can be victims of violence, injustice or a lack of understanding. If we want to sensitize the population to victims' experiences, we have to recognize the victims, regardless of their gender. (Odette Arsenault, quoted in Sophie-Hélène Lebeuf, *Le Devoir*, 6 December 1999, translation)

While Arsenault registers the traumatic resonances of the massacre (and this is important), her comments reflect an ambivalence in which gender is either fully explanatory of differential relations to the killing or a worthless limit. In this, she risks collapsing a myriad of experiences of harm, anxiety, and distress into a single narrative of victimization—a narrative that cannot maintain a distinction between the women murdered and those who witnessed their deaths (whether women or men).

While it is beyond the purposes of this chapter to explore the terms upon which men might develop and/or sustain complex memorial relations to the event of the massacre and its legacy, I argue that emblemization severely limits such terms. As the previous comments illustrate, in its binding of "men" to Lépine emblemization constitutes, unsurprisingly, a dichotomy of memorialization within which men are positioned—and must position themselves— as *either* recognizing (taking in, accepting) *or* refusing (disregarding, ignoring) a social alignment with Lépine. This creates a fraught ambivalence in memory as a public domain, leaving those men who do feel a relation to the massacre with little to rely on other than guilt and shame. Moreover, shrouded by

FIGURE 9
Plaque—Ecole Polytechnique,
Montreal (with permission of
Sharon Rosenberg).

this ambivalence, there is slight reckoning in public memory with the massacre as a difficult return, a loss that was motivated by gender hatreds but that cannot be faced within the binds of identity-based resemblances. I further consider the problems raised by these bindings in the following section.

Anti-Feminism as a Difficult Return

I want to look again at the pedagogy of emblematic public memory, but this time through a different lens. Specifically, what I think warrants our further consideration is how *anti-feminism* is displaced by an emblematic narrative. What repeatedly occurs is a not inconsequential slippage in the naming of the dead from "feminists" to "women"—a discursive shift that, however inadvertently, turns memorial attention *away* from Lépine's declaration that this was an anti-feminist slaying. Rather than being simply a matter of attention to detail, I suggest that emblematic memory partially constitutes this turn away from anti-feminism as a reading of the killings. These comments, from tenth anniversary reporting, are indicative of the discursive slippage that I am referencing:

> It was the last day of classes before exams. "Men on one side, women on the other!" yelled a gunman. "You are a bunch of feminists!" Fourteen young girls are dead without knowing why; without knowing either that after their deaths—by their deaths—they would become symbols of violence against women. (Louise Leduc, *Le Devoir*, 6 December 1999, translation)

In official statements out of Ottawa yesterday, Marc Lépine's violent act was cast as a symptom of widespread violence against women. "It is important that we honour these young women," said Hedy Fry, Secretary of State for Multiculturalism and the Status of Women. "The senseless loss of their young lives has become symbolic of the experiences of all women whose lives are shattered by deliberate acts of gender-based violence," she said. (Luiza Chwialkowska, *National Post*, 7 December 1999)

These 14 women died simply because they were women. (Claire Roberge quoted in Clark Campbell, *National Post*, 6 December 1999)

I am underscoring such comments neither to suggest that the murders were *not* an act of violence against women nor to unhinge the categories "feminist" and "women"; rather, what concerns me is the absent presence of anti-feminism in the constitution of this public memory of the Montreal massacre. A decade after its occurrence, I find myself asking: "What are the risks of basing the legacy of the massacre on this absence? Why is the massacre not remembered as an anti-feminist slaying? What difference would that make to the massacre's memory and what constitutes its legacy?"

As I contemplate these questions, I remember how feminists and feminism were positioned in the wake of the murders. As Heidi Rathjen, a student at the Poly and on campus at the time of the shootings, recalls: "Feminists got a really bad rap out of what happened at the Polytechnique. I mean, people were telling them to shut up before they had even begun to say anything. There was a mass denial of what had happened…and *part of that denial was to blame feminists*" (quoted in Chun 1999, 124, emphasis in original). In commenting on Rathjen's observation, Chun argues: "The logic ran something like this: if feminists had not talked of gender difference, none of this would have happened—look, even now they can't even shut up, no wonder Lépine was driven crazy!" (125). While such sentiments are not widely repeated in current memorial discourses, they are not entirely without representation. For example, in response to an eleventh anniversary faculty-wide email announcement of a memorial activity on campus, a University of Toronto professor wrote:

It is obvious that the point of this [memorial event] is not to remember anyone. The point is to use the deaths of these people as an excuse to promote the Feminist/Extreme-left-wing agenda. It is no different, and no more justifiable, than when organizations such as the Klu-Klux-Klan [*sic*] use the murder of a white person by a black person as an excuse to promote their agenda….Please do NOT respond to me complaining about this message….If you are offended by this message, this is nothing compared to how offended I am by this "memorial." (Charles Rackoff, email correspondence, 5 December 2000, emphasis in original)

Taken together, what these comments by Rathjen, Chun, and Rackoff underscore is a particularly troubling logic pertaining to the contemporary public memory of the massacre. On the one hand, feminists are to blame—both for the murders and for continuing to signify the murders as a site of remembrance-activism; on the other hand, anti-feminism is rendered largely invisible—either as a reason for the killings or as a force shaping counter-memory. What is striking is that anti-feminism does not disappear in this logic at all but, rather, functions as a structuring presence that cannot be readily discerned; for it is only through this circuitous route that *feminism can be blamed for the murders*, when Lépine himself testified to *anti*-feminist motivations and gunned down fourteen women whom he constituted as feminists.[14]

While a lack of memorial attention to anti-feminism cannot be fully accounted for by the (now) wide appeal of an emblematic interpretation of the massacre, I maintain that the force of the emblematic narrative, with its concomitant constitution of anti-feminism as an absent presence, signals a particular ambivalence with regard to the memory of the massacre and its legacy. Far from questions of memory being settled by a broader social "acceptance" of emblemization as *the* interpretation of the massacre, the repeated displacement of anti-feminism signals a set of deeper questions. What would it mean *to bear* these murders as anti-feminist, particularly for those of us for whom this naming—feminist—however fraught and complex, continues to compel our interest, commitment, energy, and identification? Are current socio-historical conditions insufficient to "our" bearing *this* loss? More specifically, if, following Butler (1997, 167), we understand "psychic and social domains [to be] produced in relation to each other," then might it be argued that feminist discourses of men's violence against women have constituted a late twentieth-century social domain in North America that allows for a grieving of the *women* lost but not of *feminists* lost?[15]

While it is largely beyond the scope of this chapter to meditate on such disturbing questions, tenth anniversary reporting offers some hints as to their pertinence. For example, references to the next generation of women engineering students suggest that they may experience the (anti)feminist legacy of the massacre as, at best, a disagreeable inheritance. As Andréane Meunier, an engineering student at the Poly in 1999, comments, "Sometimes we feel like saying, 'Stop talking to us about it,' we want to live normally" (in Isabelle Hachey, *La Presse*, 7 December 1999, translation). "Normal," in this instance, appears to rest on a distancing from the massacre—a distancing that, at its most pointed, refuses to address its public memory either as an identification with the victims and/or with feminist struggles against violence and/or with anti-feminism as a particular force, or at a minimum, as an understanding of oneself as coming after the dead, as having inherited their deaths. After ten years of public memory, what I hear in this student's comment is a sense of exasperation at this inheritance, at the continuing difficulties of constituting oneself as "just another engineering student" within the domain of the Poly. Rather than read this exasperation as an individual problem, I propose reading it as constituting a pressing question of cross-generational public memory.

How might this memory be sustained in the face of the ambivalences traced above? As Jane Davenport notes in her tenth anniversary report in the *Montreal Gazette*, "Ten years later, a new generation of female students at Ecole Polytechnique politely but firmly shrugs off the feminist label Lépine tried to impose on them" (5 December 1999). In addition to gesturing to issues of generational difference, this comment is noteworthy for its repetition of a logic that conflates feminism with anti-feminism, so that what is being "shrugged off" is not only Lépine's deployment of "feminist" as an accusation but also any possibility of taking on "feminist" as a relevant and productive subject position. This is a stance that is perhaps more broadly signalled by the following observation in *Le Devoir*: "Other than those who took an active part in the commemorative activities (such as student representatives, or others), youths in their early twenties were quite scarce at yesterday's ceremonies [in Montreal]" (7 December 1999, translation). While we cannot know to what extent such responses are connected to the ambivalence with which (anti)feminism is rendered in public memory of the massacre, it bears emphasizing that it is time to grapple with the recognition that anti-feminism is not outside of that memory but, rather, is an ambivalent marker of its very constitution.

In stark contrast, anti-feminism is a marked presence in tenth anniversary reporting, which generates from a *proximity* to the murders—a proximity that may be geographic (in that the news reports are in Montreal dailies), relational (in comments made by family members of those murdered), or the result of having been named by Lépine as a target (the key figure here is Francine Pelletier). The following comments are illustrative of this marking of anti-feminism as crucial to the memorial legacy of the killings:

> "A man appeared in a classroom. He separated the men from the women, and he screamed that they were feminists. How could it be any clearer?" asks Thérèse Davieau. (quoted in Leduc, 7 December 1999, translation)

> Some have accused feminists of trying to appropriate the event. Wrongly so, says Claire Roberge [stepmother of Geneviève Bergeron, one of the murdered

women]. "The massacre was addressed to them. The man who murdered our girls screamed 'I hate feminists' before he started firing. For me, feminism doesn't mean taking men's place, it's placing women by their sides. That's where our girls were!" (Sophie-Hélène Lebeuf, *Le Devoir*, 6 December 1999, translation)[16]

So in this case [the massacre], it was not just another [act of] male aggression... he was picking a whole new category of women, that was the scary, scary thing, that anyone now, even the strongest ones...the new women champions could also be vulnerable. (Francine Pelletier on *Newsworld Reports*, 6 December 1999)

In the city of the murders, for those related to the women murdered and/or named as intended victims, I propose that it is far more difficult to emblemize the massacre, to produce the women murdered as "symbols" or "tragic representatives" of a broader violence against women. Symbolization requires a distance or a difference (geographic, relational, emotional) that was not readily available for those who felt themselves "appointed" (Felman and Laub 1992, 2–4) to remember the massacre one woman at a time rather than as a collective representation of women. Françoise David, president of the Quebec Federation of Women, offers some support for this interpretation: "It was difficult for feminists to work on this [characterizing the event as an act of violence against women] and be respected in terms of public opinion....In other provinces in Canada, it was quickly interpreted [in this way], but we were so caught up emotionally here. Québec had a much more difficult time" (quoted in Jane Davenport, *Montreal Gazette*, 5 December 1999).[17]

Reopening the Question of Memory: Ambivalence and Difficult Returns

While Françoise David's comment cites emotional proximity as a hindrance to claiming a memorial narrative of emblemization, I suggest that this proximity may be read, instead, as indicative of how *difficult* (emotionally, politically, socially, publicly, etc.) *yet necessary* it is to face Lépine's accusatory hatred of feminists (feminism) as a reason for murder. Perhaps this is how the next decade of public remembrance practices might be oriented: not as a displacement of the memory of the victims but, rather, as a layering of what constitutes the massacre's legacy in Canada. This means beginning to come to terms with the massacre as the difficult return of a series of losses that include, but are not limited to, the lives of the women Lépine murdered. To publicly remember the massacre *as a loss* is to face the social wounds it has inflicted—to prevailing notions of Canadian civil humanity, to feminism as a tolerated set of discourses, to liberal claims of gender equality, to universities as "safe places"— to name only the most obvious.

A rare exception in tenth anniversary coverage—two columns by Nathalie Petrowksi, a reporter for *La Presse*—offers resonant gestures towards one aspect of what it might mean to face the memory of the massacre as a difficult return of multiple losses. These columns are remarkable not only for their distinct rumination on the men who left the classroom that Lépine first entered at the Poly but also for the particular questions they raise about this leaving. Petrowski writes: "Between the victims and the assassin, there was not nothing. There was a handful of young men [approximately fifty] who didn't react and whose passivity we never questioned, nor even analyzed, when it would have been in our every interest to do so" (*La Presse*, 7 December 1999, translation). Petrowski goes on to note that, although panicked and distressed, these students (and I would add the two professors) were not held hostage; once they left the room, they were out of Lépine's sight and immediate reach.

While Petrowski's analysis initially concerns itself with why these men did not attempt to protect the women in their class, her closing remarks are pointed and, I think, much more productive. She writes:

> We have never appealed to people's public-spiritedness, nor to their personal responsibility, nor to their instinct to protect human life. *Never have we said to people that indifference is also a form of violence.*...Ten years later, the story is still the same: that of a murderer and his fourteen victims. Between the two, we obstinately continue to believe that there was nothing and nobody. Ten years later, it is still the same terrible reality we are fleeing. (*La Presse*, 7 December 1999, translation, emphasis mine)

What Petrowski gestures to here is one of the central difficulties of remembering the massacre, a difficulty that continues to rupture emblematic memory as fully explanatory or consoling—namely, while Lépine was motivated by identity-based hatreds, public memory of the massacre and its legacy is horribly foreclosed when remembrance (through emblemization) is bound too tightly to already constituted identity categories in which "women" are readily aligned with "the fourteen victims" and "men" with their killer, "Lépine." As Wendy Brown (2001, 39) argues, "identitarian political projects are very real effects of late modern modalities of power...[but] they are symptoms of a certain fragmentation of suffering, and of suffering lived as identity rather than general injustice or domination...suffering that cannot be resolved at the identitarian level."

It is on these terms that I want to argue for ambivalence, as a resource, in the public memory of the Montreal massacre. In other words, I want to attend to what is displaced by an emblematic reading (differences, the complexities of identification, anti-feminism, what it means to be bound to others through a trauma). I want to call for a suspension of prevailing feminist investments in the pedagogy of memory as a strategic practice, with its socio-political accents and its emphasis on remembering to educate "others." This was an understandable reading during the late 1980s and early 1990s, constituted as it was by the urgency of contesting the "madman" interpretation and the broader socio-political climate within which feminist concerns about "violence against women" were barely registering. However, more than twelve years later, the stark and difficult reality is that an emblematic reading, and strategic memorial practices such as gun control legislation and a federally declared day of memory, have neither secured a decrease in violence nor opened to scrutiny the precepts of moving on, healing, progress, and so on that diminish what might be learned from—and what needs to be faced in the memory of—the 1989 murders at the Poly.

It is in this regard that I find the second of Petrowski's columns so pertinent to an endeavour to face the massacre as a difficult return. She writes: "I may not have written it on Tuesday, but that doesn't mean I think it any less. If I had been at Poly on December 6th, I would have fled as well. Would I have been right to do so? That is my question" (*La Presse*, 9 December 1999, translation). If Petrowski's question is broadened here to "would *we*, would *you*, have been right to do so" then it points us to a particularly productive re-opening of the question of the massacre and its legacy. While recognizing that we all stand in different and complex relations to the event of the massacre—and, thus, must anticipate multiple and nuanced responses—the question remains: How will I (you, we) live after the massacre? More than a decade later, when, as Charles Foran writes, the massacre has "seemed frozen in meaning" and "journalists [grant] that with each passing year the 'story' [grows] tougher to write" (*Saturday Night*, June 1999, 78), that question has a particular urgency. For it holds the promise of re-opening "us" to the inheritance of these killings and their public memory—and not so as to make an effort to staunch the wound of the loss through strategic memorial pedagogies and practical-political responses. These have been important and necessary; however, they are insufficient to another ten years of feminist memorial-activism. We cannot bring these women back: but we can and need to ask, when they died in "our" name, what are the memorial responsibilities of feminism to the dead? What do these imply for my, your, our living—now? What practices and formations of public memory might help ready "us" for these encounters—with the dead and with each other?

Notes

1 Reprinted by permission of Sage Publications Ltd. from *Feminist Theory*, vol. 4, no. 1 (2003). This chapter is informed by extended conversations I have had over the years with a number of people on questions pertaining to the massacre's public memory. For sharing their insights and support, I am indebted to Roger I. Simon, Cathy Caruth, Tanya Lewis, Susan Heald, and Lorie Rotenberg. I also appreciate the attention given to this chapter by anonymous reviewers, and I extend my gratitude to Amy Patterson for her research assistance and to Anna Isacsson for her wonderful translation work.

2 Almost a year after the killings, Lépine's letter was sent anonymously to Francine Pelletier, a Montreal journalist and one of the women Lépine had named as a potential target. Pelletier determined that it was important to release the letter publicly; it was first printed in the 24 November 1990 edition of *La Presse*, the Montreal French-language daily newspaper for which Pelletier worked. The letter is reprinted in English translation in Malette and Chalouh 1991.

3 This chapter was completed before the occurrence of the events known by the mnemonic "9/11." Living in relation to the first year of public memorial response to these events—the magnitude and intensity of which is unparalleled in living memory—tends to overwhelm and displace the memory of prior acts of mass violence on and beyond the landspace of the Americas. What implications this will have for how past and future acts of violence are remembered is yet to be seen.

4 I recognize that this chapter is necessarily entangled in the dynamics of remembrance. In whatever small way, each writing about the memory of the murders becomes part of that memorial discursive field, further sedimenting its significance. While I do think that this attention is warranted, the concern, always, is that this risks an undesired displacement of the question "why?" Not the why of the murders but the why of marking these murders—*but not others*—as particularly worthy of continued theoretical and political attention. This tension underlies this chapter, and it is one to which I endeavour to attend.

5 For a formative essay on this topic, see Felman in Felman and Laub (1992); for a more extended conceptualization of memorialization in regard to a diversity of events, see Simon, Rosenberg, and Eppert (2000).

6 I return to the problem of memorial bindings in following sections of the chapter.

7 It might be argued, appropriately I think, that completed monuments exceed the claims of strategic memory in that they become a site for recognizing the difficult return of the massacre as a loss or a wound. However, what I want to emphasize here is the work of putting a monument into place (i.e., holding design competitions, fundraising, and negotiating with city officials for property use), which I understand to be part of memorial-activist politics, which tend to be strategic in their impulse. For more on monuments and/in the formation of public memory with regard to the massacre, see Rosenberg (2000).

8 The "us" here refers to a public that is outside the domain of the Poly. It is noteworthy that there is no commonly circulated phrase for the killings *within* the Polytechnique community/ies—at least none that is referenced publicly.

9 I recognize that the use of the term "massacre" might be read as referencing a circumstance of significant rupture in "civil humanity," but I would argue that this is not a

guaranteed reading at the end of the twentieth century—a century in which massacres, genocides, and mass violence cannot be regarded as out of the ordinary.

10 This commemorative date was established as a result of intense lobbying by the National Action Committee on the Status of Women, a federally funded body that represents "women's groups" in Canada.

11 In addition to the texts by Bociurkiw (1990) and Kelley (1995), see Chun (1999), Kohli (1991), Rosenberg (2000), and Rosenberg and Simon (2000).

12 Chun (1999, 115) notes that "Lépine had no prior psychiatric history…his insanity could only be determined, after the fact, by his murderous act."

13 As I write this phrase I recall a rather different instantiation of these words, with startling effect. Lin Gibson, a Canadian visual artist, used similar phrasing in one of her early installation pieces on remembering Montreal. Following a list of fourteen feminists' names (each name aligned with the name of one of the women murdered by Lepine), she wrote "guilty as charged" (see Yeo 1991). When emblemization positions men as guilty by association it repeats the logic of Lépine's accusation, although in reverse: now it is not women who are guilty of being feminists but men who are guilty of being "Lépines." This is a telling reversal, highlighting precisely the concern with emblemization, and the problem of fixing identities in public memory, that concerns me here.

14 Chun (1999, 119) cautions against "privileging the perpetrator's [Lépine's] testimony" for it risks "unwittingly undercut[ting] the significance of the testimony of Lépine's actual victims." While I concur with her caution, in this instance I think it is important to underscore Lépine's own reasoning for the killings.

15 In posing psychoanalytically oriented questions, I am not intending to suggest that there might not also be other reasons for why there is a deep ambivalence towards antifeminism in public memory of the massacre. However, since I am particularly interested in emblemization, which originated as a feminist response, I wonder what else may be at issue "for us"?

16 We might note that Roberge's comments here, in contrast to those above, evidence the slippage between "feminists" and "women" that I previously highlighted. What this speaks to is the particular ambivalence of this aspect of the massacre's memory: in a sense, both identity hailings are true and neither alone is fully explanatory.

17 As I continue to ponder this question of proximity and emblemization, I wonder if there might be some explanatory value in the degree to which emblemization of the massacre has seemed to displace a pathologizing interpretation of Lépine and the murders. While on the one hand this might be read "positively" as an indicator of the mainstreaming of a feminist argument, on the other hand its distance from Feminism (read as "overtly political") means that there was little explicit feminist presence and debate in the tenth anniversary reporting. It is perhaps for this reason also that anti-feminism receives such little attention, except in cases where, for "personal reasons," a strategic emblematic memory is regarded as too limiting.

Missing: On the Politics of Re/Presentation[1]

ZOEY ÉLOUARD MICHELE

[3]

Since 1993 the people of Ciudad Juarez, Mexico, have lost more than 300 women to murder. The details of the case are appalling but, sadly, not unique: Canadians, for example, need only think of the as-yet unsolved case of sixty-three women who have gone missing from Vancouver's Downtown Eastside over the last twenty years[2] (see Margot Leigh Butler's chapter in this volume). Given the interest that this sensitive story has elicited from foreign—including US and European—journalists, the Juarez case raises serious theoretical and methodological questions about the politics of representation. These questions are further complicated by certain developments in poststructuralist social theory—developments that have gone a long way towards challenging conventional assumptions about representation and interpretation.

The topic of representation has been examined in depth by authors from disciplines like film theory, feminist theory, and philosophy. My interest lies somewhere in between, therefore this chapter marks an encounter between feminism, philosophy, and film.[3] Further, after bell hooks's (1989) challenge, in "Feminist Theory: A Radical Agenda," that feminists take responsibility for the promotion of critical thinking among the public at large, my intent is to provide an issues-based discussion that will be of practical use both to academics and to the average, non-academic reader.

47

My profile of the Juarez case serves to ground an exchange between three disparate thinkers on the theme of representation. I wish to employ the philosopher Jacques Derrida's (1996) influential work on the metaphysics of presence to introduce and extend film theorist Laura Marks's (1999) use of the metaphors of fetish and fossil with reference to documentary film. In my discussion of Derrida and Marks, my intention is to spark the reader's imagination on the topic of representation. Then, through the use of another selection by feminist theorist bell hooks (1990)—in which she insists that those who write about oppression and domination acknowledge the painful nature of these conditions—I mean to emphasize that theories of representation must also be guided by a deep-felt respect for the personal/political context within which the topic is situated. Specifically, I examine what it means to think critically about the political issues raised by documentary representation. I do so motivated by the firm belief that, with an open and reflective awareness of the issues and emotions involved in the telling of stories marked by violence, investigators and audiences can minimize the extent to which these complex human stories are oversimplified, mystified, and exoticized in academic and popular modes of representation.

Ciudad Juarez: Setting the Scene

Ciudad Juarez, the largest city in Mexico's largest state (Chihuahua), is also the fourth largest city in the country. Situated along Mexico's northern border, just across the Rio Grande from El Paso, Texas, Juarez is a hub of industrial activity. Its 400 *maquiladoras* (foreign-owned assembly plants) attract 50,000 new economic migrants each year (Wolff 2002). The prospect of cheap labour and financial incentives offered by the Mexican government make Juarez a haven for international corporations eager to keep production costs down and profits up. The savings enjoyed by these companies come at the loss of potential tax revenue—revenue badly needed to finance Juarez's crumbling infrastructure. Although official estimates put the population at 1.3 million people, hundreds of thousands more eke out a kind of a living at the city's margins—in shantytowns strung together by a tangle of wires that surreptitiously (and dangerously) tap into the city's electrical grid (Wolff 2002).

Many of the workers who labour in the *maquilas* live in these places. The industry employs more than a fifth of the city's workers (Nathan 1999, 24) as "operators" (Wright 1999a); about 60 percent of them are women (Wolff 2002). In a workforce that is typically young and where the legal minimum age of employment is sixteen, it is not uncommon for fourteen-year-old girls to use false birth certificates to find work here. Labour controls are among the incentives provided by the Mexican government to attract foreign investment, which has led to a business climate hostile to labour organizing. As a result, wages are low—five to seven dollars per day—annual turnover is 100 percent, and unions are rare (Wolff 2002; Nathan 1999, 25). Because it has traditionally been dominated by women, *maquila* assembly work has become feminized, a pink ghetto established and reinforced by plant managers who regard "nimble-fingered" women as well suited to the boring, repetitive routines (Wright 1999a). This view of women as desirable workers does not, however, include their reproductive capacity. From the point of view of managers, pregnancy is unproductive. Women must submit to a pregnancy test before they are hired, are sometimes made to demonstrate that they are still menstruating after being hired, and those workers who become pregnant are often harassed into quitting (Wright 1999a, 467). Male *maquila* labourers, stigmatized by the feminized association of the job, are sometimes moved from segregated areas to work alongside women as a form of punishment for bad behaviour or poor quality of work (Nathan 1999, 27).

Yet it would be unfair to simply regard *maquila* workers, male or female, as passive victims of this poor treatment. Debbie Nathan (1999) and Melissa Wright (1999a) have documented numerous instances in which workers have resisted and even derived some pleasure from these problematic working conditions. It has been observed that factory work provides some measure of financial independence for women and serves as a means by which both skilled and relatively unskilled labourers can contribute to a family income.

For whatever else the *maquilas* have brought to Juarez, the boost the industry received when the North American Free Trade Agreement went into effect in 1994 correlates in a very disturbing way with a rise in the number of recorded homicides (Nathan 1999, 25). Ciudad Juarez now has the unenviable reputation of being "the most dangerous city in the Americas" (*City of Dreams* 2001). The dead include victims of neighbourhood gang fights, the city's illicit drug trade, and, by last count, more than 300 women (Houston Chronicle News Services, 22 March 2002). Some sources attribute most of the latter category of deaths to what the Knight Ridder/Tribune News Service (1 December 1999) has described as "domestic disputes." Even if this is accurate, it represents a vicious trend that puts Juarez at the highest level of reported domestic violence in Mexico (Nathan 1999, 30).

Many others—some seventy to ninety women—are said to have been the victims of serial killers, and even according to official estimates most of these cases remain unsolved (MacCormack 2002). Certain patterns have been observed by investigators: the discovered bodies appear to match a consistent profile, both in the physical characteristics of the victims and in the condition of the remains. It appears that many of the murdered women worked in the *maquilas*, sometimes disappearing along dimly light pathways on their way to or from work, or from buses hired by the companies to transport workers to the job site. Wright (1999a) has documented the industry's attempts to avoid taking responsibility for the part it may have played in the deaths of its workers.

The record of police (in)activity in this story is almost as appalling as are the murders themselves. In addition to the growing pile of unsolved homicide cases, there have been allegations that the police have fabricated evidence and relied upon torture-induced confessions (Romo 2001). The lawyer for two bus drivers charged in connection with the case was shot by police during a car chase in February of 2002: executed, some say, to silence his criticism of alleged police mistreatment of his clients (MacCormack 2002). These recent actions stand in stark contrast to the lack of interest displayed by police in earlier years. Authorities have in the past attempted to shift blame to the victims themselves, arguing that the women courted danger by spending time in the city's nightclubs and in dressing "provocatively" (Romo 2001; Wright 1999a). Most disturbingly, accusations have been made of police involvement in some attacks (*Senorita Extraviada* 2001). Meanwhile, the killings have continued. Eight bodies were found in November 2001 (Romo 2001), and two more were discovered on 19 March 2002 (Houston Chronicle News Services 2002).

As this cursory review indicates, there are numerous complex issues that underlie the cases of murdered women in Juarez. I refer the interested reader to the literature on Ciudad Juarez for an extended discussion of these points.[4] While it is important to note the socio-economic and political context in which these deaths are situated, we must also be careful to question the nature of the facts themselves. The information that I have relayed in this section was gathered from a variety of news and journal articles. It is worth remembering, as we move on to the topic of documentaries, that printed sources *document* lived reality in many of the same (problematic) ways as do documentary films. On the other hand, different modes of representation (e.g., print, video, radio, etc.) evince challenges that are unique to their particular medium. For example, in contrast to radio listeners, television audiences must contend with both auditory and visual information. While some viewers may be led to accept that they are receiving "the complete picture," others may be provoked into questioning how sound and image reinforce or contradict each other in televised stories. I would therefore challenge the reader to consider all representations as problematic, though in different ways, as we continue our discussion.

Rough Cuts: Documentary Film

This complicated story has attracted considerable attention from journalists and documentary filmmakers over the years. There have been several films made on or relating to this subject, including *Juarez, The City of Dead Women* (1998); *Maquila: A Tale of Two Mexicos* (2000); *City of Dreams* (2001); and *Senorita Extraviada: Missing Young Woman* (2001).[5] In keeping with my discussion of re/presentation (see below) and my stated intention to straddle film, feminist, and philosophical theory, I concern myself less with an analysis of the *content* of these examples and more with an examination of their *functioning*—their operation as *documentary films*. In the examples used to illustrate the points that follow, I draw primarily from the film with which I am most familiar, Norelli's (2001) *City of Dreams.*[6]

If the growing number of venues for their viewing is any indication, documentaries are enjoying a new popularity. In Canada the publicly held Canadian Broadcasting Corporation (CBC) has traditionally scheduled a number of television programs showcasing Canadian and international documentaries (which are, however, increasingly compromised by dwindling financial support and air time). Among these programs are *The Passionate Eye, Rough Cuts,* and *Witness.* It was *Witness* that first broadcast *City of Dreams* to Canadians (and sparked my own interest in this topic) in the fall of 2001. Film festivals that screen documentaries are flourishing around the world, including here in Canada: Doxa, the Vancouver-based documentary film and video festival, is held biannually, while each May Toronto hosts Hot Docs, a major international documentary film festival. As well, Canada's National Film Board has contributed a great deal to the production of Canadian-made documentary films. On the small screen, television companies are now offering the Documentary Channel as part of their cable packages. Then there is the ever-increasing list of so-called reality TV programs (e.g., *Survivor, Extreme Makeover*). When, for many of us, life has taken on a routinized, mundane quality, perhaps documentaries serve as a non-threatening means with which to connect with people whose lives are different from our own, conveniently delivered via media that do not require that we depart from the security of our customs and communities. Given their value as an accessible form for the dissemination of information, it is all the more important to critically consider how documentary films operate.

Documentaries are a unique media form. They combine the visual quality of film, the accessibility of television, and the opportunity for research and reflection found in (magazine or newspaper) investigative and feature articles, all in a compact package that serves both to inform and to entertain. Documentaries are also subject to many of the same limitations faced by other media forms. Producers and directors may be pressured to alter their films' content and approach to satisfy outside investors. Concern with the saleability of a film means that some stories are picked up while others are not, and some details are emphasized while others are ignored.

Within the field of film theory there is a substantial literature on the relationship between cinematic representation and reality. In *Representing Reality: Issues and Concepts in Documentary*, Bill Nichols (1991) includes documentary among what he terms the *discourses of sobriety*. Although Nichols associates documentary with other "sober" discourses like science and education, he points out that documentary, because of its close relationship to fictional film, is viewed with suspicion from the perspective of the other discourses of sobriety. He explains that the "discourses of sobriety are sobering because they regard their relation to the real as direct, immediate, transparent. Through them power exerts itself" (4). This is an important point to which I return in the section on Marks. Nichols also advances the concept of *epistephilia* in this text, described as "a pleasure in knowing" (178). Epistephilia, which Nichols associates with documentary realism, further complicates those other pleasures—voyeurism (see below), identification, and fetishism (the subject of a later section)—also associated with fictional film. This pleasure in knowing can have positive consequences as the viewing audience may be moved to progressive action based on the information relayed in a documentary. This was certainly my own response to viewing Norelli's *City of Dreams* (2001). Still, as Nichols (1991, 179) points out, this orientation presupposes and perpetuates a certain distance between audience members (as Self) and the Other, whom documentary film represents. This distance is obscured in documentary by the claim to transparency that defines its realist style.

Film theory also alerts us to the operation of the *gaze* in documentary. Laura Mulvey (1989) is an important contributor to theorizing the *male gaze* as the masculinist voyeurism of female film characters. The *colonialist gaze* serves a similar function in documentary, where the Other is represented as an exotic object for voyeuristic consumption by privileged "First World" spectators. As a discourse of sobriety documentary may disguise the extent to which it is affected by the male, colonialist gaze in its emphasis on educational and scientific goals. In her critique of the documentary *Paris Is Burn-*

ing, bell hooks (1992) isolates and critiques the role of the director in the operation of the gaze. A lesson to be taken from this example is that a filmmaker who carries a certain (economic, social) privilege relative to his/her cinematic subjects must actively ensure that this privilege is not reflected in how power is negotiated between them, both on and off-screen.

Speaking generally about the risks involved in media production, artist Lani Maestro (*Globe and Mail,* 20 April 2002) has warned that

> "the media" is itself a kind of violence, as well as the fact that photographic representations are always violent in their mode of operation (framing: cutting and fixing)....If one wants to do something on a topic such as violence or war, then it requires simultaneously a subversion of basic media principles and representation in general—otherwise one is simply perpetuating the problem one wants to address.

While we may not want to privilege technology's role in representation to the extent Maestro does in this statement, I think she rightfully alerts us to the influence of the "how" in representation—that is, *how* we go about representing individuals and societies. We might ask, to what extent do documentaries sensationalize their subject matter by the manner in which these stories are presented (think, for example, of the title to *Juarez, The City of Dead Women* [1998])? Where is the line that separates education from exploitation, and observation from voyeurism? This point leads to another: the relation between the truth (presence) of a thing and its representation in (cinematic) production. This idea is especially marked in documentaries, which many writers, including Marks (1999, 228), define as "a cinema whose indexical relation to the real is of central importance." It is this relationship that I discuss next.

Jacques Derrida: The Play of Presence and Absence

Various scholars have written on this notion of presence. Michel Foucault wrote about *truth.* Jean Baudrillard (1999) talks about *the real.* Derrida (1996, 438) relates his use of the word "presence" to a string of synonyms—essence, existence, consciousness, the transcendental signified, God, Man—all standing for this fundamental principle, which, he argues, animates traditional Western thinking.[7]

Applying his interpretation to a linguistic model, Derrida demonstrates what is at stake. He argues that philosophy suffers from a phonocentric bias that privileges speech, as being closer to thought or consciousness (presence, again), over writing. According to this system, speech represents thought, and writing, in turn, represents speech. Writing, seen as further removed from speech than thought, is viewed as at a greater risk for distorting thought. Derrida counters this by insisting that all language functions as a kind of writing. As the linguist Ferdinand de Saussure (1983) observed, language is not ruled by some transcendental force; rather, meaning is created in the play of presence and absence implied in each sign as one signifier leads inevitably to another and another. Derrida (1996, 439) concludes that language is "a system in which the central signified, the original or transcendental signified, is never absolutely present outside a system of differences. The absence of the transcendental signified extends the domain and the play of signification infinitely." Language can never fully re/present meaning; rather, meaning is created, indeed is made possible, in the *play* that characterizes the process of signification itself (447). So, thought is as vulnerable to the "distortions" of speech as it is to writing; but, more to the point, thought is not properly regarded as the source of meaning. Meaning is instead *produced* through the medium of language.

Looking to cinematic and theatrical modes of production, this relation between presence and representation is made clearer. As Roger Copeland (1990, 35) outlines: "A representation cannot be fully 'represented' precisely because it signifies or alludes to something that isn't fully there, whose 'real' existence lies elsewhere, beyond the confines of the stage." What is perhaps less evident is the degree to which we have come to rely on second-hand representations. Although there are advantages and disadvantages to every medium, (e.g., while breaking news can be televised live, such pieces tend to lack the considered analysis of print articles [Benedict 1992]), we are almost completely dependent on (corporate) mass media to stay informed about world events.[8] However, as Copeland suggests, "ironically, there's no reason to believe that 'being there' is always preferable to the omniscient detachment provided by advanced technology" (1990, 40). This point is well demonstrated in Norelli's (2001) film, *City of Dreams*, which indicates that evidence of police misconduct in the investigations of the murdered Juarez women may be seen in how the authorities represented their actions in the media.[9]

Returning to Derrida: if we reckon with poststructuralists that there is no essential, universal truth out there (the logical extension of Derrida's semiology), what is left? Derrida (1996, 445) explains: "One could say—rigorously using that word whose scandalous significance is always obliterated in French— that this movement of play, permitted by the lack or absence of a center or origin, is the movement of *supplementarity*." Lacking access to a single source of meaning, which cannot be said to exist, we have only *mediations*; *intermediaries* that both defer to and differ from that which they signify (Derrida 1976,

157). This idea is encompassed by Derrida's use of *différance*. It also relates to the in/famous phrase from *Of Grammatology*: "*There is nothing outside of the text* [there is no outside-text; *il n'y a pas de hors-texte*]" (158). In addition to being a comment on the absence of the core idea (truth/presence/transcendental signified) that I have been describing, Walter Truett Anderson's (1995, 87) reading of this statement is useful: "I think he means that human experience is inseparably entangled with our descriptions of it." In a broad sense that which Jean-Jacques Rousseau invoked by his reference to the "dangerous supplement" is dangerous because it competes with, and ultimately displaces, the real, "natural presence" (Derrida 1976, 159). With these ideas of presence and supplementarity comes the understanding that our access to the real is always mediated by our representations, which is to say, of course, that we cannot gain access to the real *because it does not exist.*[10] Our very conception of what is *real*, what is *true*, is formed by language, by representations, by culture. I consider the implications of this reading with reference to Juarez, but first I examine important points on the fetishization of the documented.

Laura Marks: On Fetishes and Fossils

In "Fetishes and Fossils: Notes on Documentary and Materiality," Laura Marks (1999) offers two metaphors to illustrate how documentaries both fetishize and fossilize their subjects. In this article Marks focuses on the operation of documentary films as intercultural phenomena, where the documentary marks a relationship between cultures. Drawing on the scholarship of William Pietz, Marks describes fetishes and fossils as "two kinds of objects that condense cryptic histories within themselves. Both gather their peculiar power by virtue of a prior contact with some originary object. Both are like nodes, or knots, in which historical, cultural, and spiritual forces gather with a particular intensity" (224). Early on, she makes a point of recounting the history of "the fetish" as an idea first employed during the period of imperialist expansion (226). In relations between Portuguese colonists and traders and West African peoples, the fetish served a dual purpose: to the colonists it represented the spiritual practices of the peoples they encountered; to the West Africans, it served to satisfy the visitors' curiosity about their traditions while deflecting attention away from those practices they wished to keep private. This research supports the claim that the fetish has always been "an intercultural product" (226) rather than a "simple" artefact. It also highlights the active role played by subjects in how they represent themselves and the distance between people that much documentary representation strives to bridge.

The fossil metaphor is invoked by Marks in its Deleuzian sense: it refers "to the power of memory images to embody different pasts. When an image is all that remains of a memory, when the memory cannot be 'assigned a present' but simply stares up at one where it has been unearthed, then that image is like a fossil" (Marks 1999, 227). Marks notes that Gilles Deleuze regards fossils as dangerous; like Rousseau's "dangerous supplement," the uncovered fossil is a sign that is related to other signs along a chain of signification that cannot be delimited or suspended. While it is possible to trace the histories of fossilized images, such efforts also risk disturbing "other memories, causing inert presences on the most recent layer of history themselves to set off chains of associations that had been forgotten" (227).

Documentaries behave in this way because they carry images that hold particular meanings in one culture and relay them to audiences from different cultures, for whom the images may have no, or a very different, significance. The filmmaker may attempt to provide some historical context or the viewer may be inspired to pursue the subject further. In either case, there is no way to guarantee which meanings will be drawn. While Norelli (*City of Dreams* 2001) attributes the Juarez murders to the city's drug trade and to a pattern of male *macho* backlash against the growing social and economic independence of female *maquila* workers, Portillo (*Senorita Extraviada* 2001) emphasizes the role of the police in the carrying out and covering up of some of the killings. Without Portillo's perspective and without a more nuanced understanding of the history of gender relations in Mexican society, northern[11] viewers of *City of Dreams* may be tempted to simplistically and dismissively draw on stereotypical beliefs about Latino men and women in thinking about this story. This example illustrates Marks's reminder that history is necessarily unfinished and that we must resist the urge to come to any definitive conclusions. To suggest such conclusions would be to lapse into stereotype and unhelpful cultural generalizations that would foreclose on empathy and understanding across cultures.

In her analysis, Marks (1999, 224) emphasizes the material, tactile quality of film: "My use of the fetish and fossil metaphors relates to the materiality of film itself as witness to an originating object: to documentary's indexical quality. To think of film as fetish or fossil requires an archaeology of sense experience and draws on an epistemology based on the sense of touch." This effort to materialize human practices—phenomena that ultimately resist being captured or contained in any medium—may fail if this indexical quality to film becomes obscured. Indexicality is what gives film its representational power, particularly in the case of documentaries, which, as I observed earlier, are traditionally directed towards representation of the real. Marks explains that "by approaching the indexicality of film as a fetishlike or fossil-like quality, I mean to emphasize that this trace of the real on film is embalmed in layers of historical use and interpretation, which obscure and ultimately transform any original meaning it might have had" (228). So, we must bear in mind that such representations of other cultures may be in some sense fetishized and fossilized: decontextualized, oversimplified, or distorted images created for purposes that may not be immediately apparent to the documentary's subjects, the filmmaker/s, or the audience(s).

Given the above discussion of Derrida's treatment of presence, what meaning do words like "distorted" have here? If the presence of representation is elusive at best, then what is there to be distorted in documentaries? There are, I think, several modes of distortion possible in documentary and other forms of representation. First, the filmmaker or author may "misrepresent" the intended image projected by her subjects. Although Derrida (1976, 158) has endeavoured to complicate the relation between intention (consciousness), representation, and interpretation, even he has no wish to dismiss the significance of intention entirely. This distortion of subjects' self-representation occurs when the filmmaker is insufficiently knowledgable about the historical and cultural context within which particular practices are situated (i.e., Marks's documentary as fossil).[12] Without presuming to offer the definitive representation of what's *really* going on in Juarez, we could ask: (how) do the backgrounds of filmmakers affect their accounts and analyses? For instance, does Lourdes Portillo's Latina heritage and experience provide her with certain advantages in the making of her film, *Senorita Extraviada: Missing Young Woman* (2001)?

Second, misrepresentation can take place when the filmmaker intentionally or unintentionally imposes a theoretical framework of interpretation on a culture for which such a framework is unknown and/or inappropriate. Indeed, individual subjects may be more aware of the potential for this form of distortion than are the investigators. Thinking back to Marks's history of the fetish as intercultural product, we are reminded of its decoy function.

Returning to the example mentioned earlier, in *City of Dreams* (2001) the narrative turns from a description of Juarez's criminal underworld to a presentation of a backlash theory of male violence against women as the more compelling explanation for the murders. This analysis accords nicely with a (Northern) feminist political framework, making the problem more comprehensible to a Northern audience. While I do not wish to discount this theory, I am concerned that not enough historical and cultural specificity was provided in the analysis of gender relations in the Juarez context. Without this complexity, audiences may be unwilling to reconcile the large numbers of murdered women with a breakdown in gender relations, as represented in the film. The danger here is that audiences may choose to attribute this violent behaviour to some essential quality of Juarenses, Northern Mexicans, or Latinos generally.

Scholars in anthropology and sociology who are acquainted with the history of their fields also know the damage done by past investigators whose work was tainted by fetishizing practices. Although reports of researchers grossly distorting their subjects have become less common in these disciplines, what Marks describes as the fetishizing and fossilizing effects of documentary film speaks to the risk with which all authors who engage in cross-cultural research, and who wish to avoid contributing to mediated neocolonization, must still contend.

Most important, because of the risk of potentially hurtful distortions, the metaphors of fossil and fetish identify the inherently political nature of (not only) cross-cultural representation. Marks (1999, 228–29) writes:

> I want to stress that the intercultural space in which fetishes and fossils are produced are charged with power; it is not a neutral ground. Colonial power relations in particular, with their propensity for cross-breeding indigenous and imported meanings, are prime sites for the production of these objects. Where two or more material discourses crash together are formed any number of peculiar artifacts.

In thinking of the documentaries made about Juarez, we must consider the various economic, cultural, historical, linguistic, and other issues that inform this story. We must consider the significance of the story itself, how it is told, by whom, and why. With the exception of *Maquila* (2000), all of the other documentaries identified earlier focus their attention on the circumstances surrounding the deaths of so many women. To me, this is certainly the most wrenching aspect of the story. Yet, it also seems disturbingly consistent with the character of much of Western popular culture, in which sexually exploitative and violent depictions of women have become commonplace. With regard to the representation of women who murder, a similar point is discussed by Sylvie Frigon (chapter 1 in this collection). While the filmmakers' motives for drawing public attention to the murder of Juarez women may be laudable (as a strategy for pressuring federal authorities to take more of an interest in the case, for example), by their very existence these documentaries add new images of battered and violated (Latina) women to the public imagination.[13] Could the salacious details of this case explain, in part, why Juarez has received so much attention by the media over the years? Many of the murdered women were very young (teens and twenties), their corpses showing evidence of sexual assault. In one scene from *City of Dreams* (2001) the screen is filled by the image of a dead woman who has been dumped in the desert. Although her face is obscured, her naked abdomen and thighs are clearly visible. In considering Mexico's colonial history and, in particular, the stereotypical depiction of Latinas, especially in the US media (see e.g., Valdivia 2000), we are justified in critically considering the impact (positive and negative) these representations are likely to have.

Following Derrida, we can identify a third form of distortion that relates to Marks's reasoning: this occurs when the documentary itself supplants, as the source of meaning, that which it represents. We have established that documentary film mediates intercultural relations. Like fetishes and fossils, "they are those historical objects that contain the histories produced in intercultural traffic" (Marks 1999, 228). Documentaries, as with the Juarez example, *document* lived experiences and communicate something of those experiences to audiences who may be far removed—geographically, economically, culturally, and linguistically—from *maquila* life. To the extent that they serve to fix these experiences—this unfinished history—and are allowed to stand in place of the (absent) truth, documentaries distort their subject matter. As *intermediaries* these films act to displace, to supplement the presence of their subjects (e.g., what is happening in Ciudad Juarez and why)? If such a question is ultimately unanswerable, then how can a film, especially one made by a stranger, hope to answer it? Of what good are documentaries? Or, for that matter, representation in general?

Interstitial Spaces and Irreducible Difference

In her article Marks emphasizes the potential volatility of both the fetish and fossil (a quality of all forms of representation). Their initial appearances are deceiving as they "carry within them histories that, once unravelled, make the fixity of the present untenable" (Marks 1999, 229). On the surface, these objects may give some clue to the histories out of which they emerged. The danger comes when living history is reduced to an object that is itself a product of an intercultural encounter. There are many stories one could tell about Ciudad Juarez, as the literature demonstrates (see note 4). That so many of the city's cases of murdered women remain open only underscores the provisional nature of any attempt to tell a particular story. Documentaries, like fetishes and fossils, are usefully conceived, in Marks's words, as *interstitial spaces* (1999)—(intermediaries)—which designate the site of an exchange of meanings. Some mutual understanding is certainly one possible outcome of this exchange, but we must also accept that "untranslatability...is part of the intercultural experience" (236). Within the context of our earlier discussion on media politics, in which we considered the financial and institutional barriers to cinematic production, we can better appreciate that with the decline in the variety of views represented in film comes a decline in the likelihood that audiences will come away from a film with the kind of understanding that Marks's point on documentaries as interstitial spaces seeks to convey.

Inevitably, Marks (1999, 240) says, documentaries will function as fetishes and fossils so long as they are said to represent a real event. Given the medium's technological capacity—action, colour, sound—the audience may experience sensations that are almost like those they would experience upon being there. This experience may be productively deployed in the interests of cross-cultural understanding and political action only when the fetishizing/fossilizing aspect of documentaries is allowed to fade away with the last flickering images of the film.

It is possible to harness the representational power of documentary film for progressive social change. To do so requires that we engage the form with the express purpose of subverting its potential to do harm. Returning to philosophy for a moment, Derrida (1996) makes a similar argument in "Structure, Sign, and Play in the Discourse of the Human Sciences." In this article he uses the example of ethnology to demonstrate how it is possible to work critically from within a politically problematic tradition with the goal of producing different outcomes.[14] Derrida explains that, "here it is a question both of a critical relation to the language of the social sciences and a critical responsibility of the discourse itself. It is a question of explicitly and systematically posing the problem of the status of a discourse which borrows from a heritage the resources necessary for the deconstruction of that heritage itself" (440). We are all invested in discourses—dominant ways of thinking that regulate the production of knowledge. There is no viable alternative if we are to make ourselves understood and be taken seriously. What Derrida is saying is that to resist the oppressive qualities that foreground discourses like the one/s found in ethnology requires that we use discursive concepts and premises in unanticipated and subversive ways.

In thinking about presence and representation, we might look to Derrida's (1996, 448) assessment of interpretation for added direction:

> There are thus two interpretations of interpretation, of structure, of sign, of play. The one seeks to decipher, dreams of deciphering a truth or an origin which escapes play and the order of the sign, and which lives the necessity of

interpretation as an exile. The other, which is no longer turned toward the origin, affirms play and tries to pass beyond man and humanism, the name of man being the name of that being who, throughout the history of metaphysics or of ontotheology—in other words, throughout his entire history—has dreamed of full presence, the reassuring foundation, the origin and the end of play.

Rather than deciding between these two irreducibly different perspectives, we ought instead to find out what they have in common. For, in addition to serving as an intermediary or interstitial space between (absent) presence and representation, the idea of the supplement—like Derrida's other "hinge-words" (Young 1981, 18) (e.g., *trace, différence*)—suggests that divisions like the one between presence and representation may be more ambiguous than is traditionally thought.

bell hooks: Pain as Catalyst and Conduit

So far, we might tentatively conclude that Derrida and Marks are attempting to unsettle whatever established ideas we might have held about the nature of truth, the transparency of linguistic and documentary forms of communication, the political nature of discourses and other forms of representation, and advocate for ways in which we might "trouble" these conventionally held ideas and techniques in subversive and emancipatory ways. This effort, particularly as it touches on "truth," is characteristic of the movement of poststructuralism. It has also been the target of intense criticism.

If we confuse the definition of what is true, what is real, what are the consequences for people like the families of the murdered Juarez women, who are suffering under conditions that have very real and very violent effects? Who is to be believed (e.g., the police, representatives of women's organizations, the survivors) in a situation where there are competing truth claims? A reply from poststructuralist theory might be that conventional ideas about truth have all too frequently been used against marginalized populations. As Derrida and Marks have indicated, discourses are not neutral—they are politicized by the circulation of power relations that have historically privileged some groups of people at the expense of others. And as Derrida asserts, the point is not to exchange one notion of truth for another but, rather, to remain critically aware of the limitations of these notions, even as we depend on them to make sense of our world.

While criticizing the "nihilist extremism" of Baudrillard's poststructuralist view of the real, Bill Nichols (1991) appears to sympathize with Derrida and Marks, but only to a point. He insists that the human element absolutely compels a distinction between reality and representation: "The reality of pain and loss that is not part of any simulation, in fact, is what makes the difference between representation and historical reality of crucial importance" (7). Documentaries have the capacity to draw attention to this distinction, according to Nichols.

To address further what is the raison d'être of many documentaries—that is, the communication of urgent stories of human suffering to a wider audience—I turn, finally, to the work of bell hooks. hooks takes up the idea of emotional pain in a manner reminiscent of *ethics* in the work of Michel Foucault (1987): as a catalyst for social change. In "An Interview with bell hooks by Gloria Watkins: No, Not Talking Back, January 1989," hooks (1990, 215) writes:

GW: Why remember the pain, that's how you began?

bh: Because I am sometimes awed, as in finding something terrifying, when I see how many of the people who are writing about domination and oppression are distanced from the pain, the woundedness, the ugliness. That it's so much of the time just a subject—a "discourse." The person does not believe in a real way that "what I say here, this theory I come up with, may help change the pain in my life or in the lives of other people." I say remember the pain because I believe true resistance begins with people confronting pain, whether it's theirs or somebody else's, and wanting to do something to change it. And it's this pain that so much makes its mark in daily life. Pain as a catalyst for change, for working to change.

This passages raises several issues that I think authors (including film-makers) and audiences need to be made aware of and/or reminded about. First, hooks highlights the need for authors and audiences to remain mindful of the pain experienced by actors in stories marked by violence. To be open to the pain experienced by research subjects, and the pain we may feel in empathizing with these subjects, is to keep the stories that we tell as free from externally imposed distortions as possible and to resist the tendency towards objectification. In this way, pain may serve as a conduit across the interstitial space occupied by documentary film, between those who are being represented and those who would represent them. When we remember the suffering of the people whose stories we seek to tell, we gain a greater appreciation of the sensitive nature of our task, and, it is to be hoped, take greater responsibility for the potential repercussions generated by our actions.

Second, to be open to these painful feelings helps us to re/affirm our priorities. This is pain as catalyst. In working with people who have been touched by oppression and domination—in dealing with this topic—when we allow ourselves to feel the pain that this oppression creates, we become aware of our political choices. Of course, the relatively straightforward act of taking a political position is only the first step in the more difficult journey of implementing that position.

Third, we cannot enter into the study of oppression and domination and expect to emerge unscathed. Borrowing from hooks's (1989) terminology, *white supremacist capitalist patriarchy* is the source of much pain and suffering, and we are all implicated in this. If we wish to address these conditions we must be prepared to submit our work, and ourselves, to scrutiny. In our reading and in our creative production we must be wary of the operation of oppressive relations of power even if issues of domination are not our focus. This is because their influence upon diverse phenomena is still being charted. If we are not willing to be "honest" with ourselves and our audiences about our biases, positions, and motivations, then our audiences will do it for us, and by then it will be too late.

Fourth, we need to reconsider how we think about pain and suffering. Painful feelings, such as the ones that surface when we are confronting internalized racism and white supremacism, can be helpful in alerting us to areas that require our attention. Pain can also be a signal of growth. As Derrida and Marks caution, we must avoid at all costs becoming too comfortable, too certain in our understanding.

Marks also shares with hooks a desire to integrate a sense of the tangible into her writing. Their approach illustrates that creative production (whether textual or cinematic) can be an emotional—even a physical experience—as well as an intellectual one. Social scientists and journalists are often expected to maintain an "objective" stance in relation to their subjects. Within the social sciences at least, this orientation—which, at best, represents a dubious ideal and, at worst, obscures the subjective basis of so-called "objective" behaviour—has been roundly criticized. Again, while there is no reason to exchange one (problematic) interpretation for another, a greater appreciation of the human element to stories can only aid in representation.

Recalling Nichols's criticism of epistephilic pleasure, it may be that the most effective demonstration of the filmmaker/researcher's empathy with his/her cinematic/research subjects is to dissolve the line that traditionally separates one role from the other—that is, to blur the boundary between Self and Other—without shrinking from the new political challenges to be faced in such a move. In the end, this strategy may well have the most potential for the promotion of a progressive model of representation.

Conclusion

Marks's discussion of the fetish and fossil captures the distance between cultures that is mediated (more or less successfully) by documentary films. Emotional distance from the pain caused by oppression and domination that hooks describes further alienates the filmmaker/author from the people whom she is representing. As Derrida observed, (good) intentions are not enough. However, I do believe that a sincere commitment to remain open to the raw experience of human suffering—a feeling to which all people can relate—can help to minimize the fetishization and fossilization that threatens scholarly and popular modes of representation.

Notes

1 Grateful thanks to Annette Burfoot and Susan Lord for their support and help in the preparation of this chapter.
2 As of this writing, eleven murder charges have been laid against one suspect in connection with the case.
3 My thanks to Susan Lord for her suggestions on how to frame this thesis.
4 They include: the historical relationship between the United States and Mexico; the significance of the border between the two countries, its meaning economically, politically, and symbolically (e.g., Wright 1999b); colonial history and its impact on Mexican cultural history and imagination (Nathan 1999); gender roles and relations in northern Mexico (e.g., Salzinger 1997); economic and other forms of exploitation by foreign powers and companies (Wright 1999b); and rapid industrialization and its effects on urban development (e.g., Young and Fort 1994).
5 Another film that touches on this topic is Ursula Biemann's videoessay (1999) *Performing the Border.*
6 Thanks to Gianfranco Norelli for his assistance in providing materials from *City of Dreams.*
7 The history of Western metaphysics—that branch of philosophy that attends to the "big" questions about the nature of being and reality—Derrida asserts, is the determination of Being as presence. It is the drive to find and fix a stable, originary truth (sometimes called the *logos*) at the centre of (not only) philosophical thought, the purpose of which is to serve as an anchor for ontological insecurity. Simply put, typically we feel more in control when we have answers to such "big" philosophical questions as: who are we? why are we here? what is "here"? and what is our relation to it?

   Derrida (1996) traces this entire effort back to the classical Greek philosophers, to Plato and others. He says that this idea of a core belief serves as an unstable foundation for other beliefs—binary oppositions like nature/culture, masculine/feminine, presence/absence—which further structure Western thought. These polarized binaries, and the differing values signified by each pole, are all implicated in this troublesome idea of truth. Consider that most of what we think of as "knowledge" is based in some notion of truth.

8 My knowledge about the events that have taken place in Ciudad Juarez is wholly dependent on the "accuracy" of the sources I have cited above, just as the reader's knowledge, in turn, may depend on my interpretation of these sources.

9 For example, in spite of alleged weaknesses in the original case against one favoured murder suspect, Abdel Latif Sharif (spelled differently in different sources), police used the media to present their ever more elaborate and improbable (according to Sharif's lawyer, Irene Blanco) accounts of his involvement in the killings, which continued even after his arrest and imprisonment. This was done, from the point of view of Blanco and an investigative journalist interviewed for the documentary, Rosa Isela Perez, to provide a scapegoat and to restore the public's faith in the much criticized police force (*City of Dreams* 2001).

10 With Derrida, I do not claim that there is nothing "out there," no reality beyond our representations, but, rather, that our perceptions of reality are always already mediated. Whatever the "real" might be, we can never come to know it objectively. Therefore, it is not the real per se, but our conventional conceptions of the real—as fixed and transparently accessible—that cannot be said to exist.

11 I use the distinction "North/South" to draw attention to the hemispheric (economic, political, and socio-cultural) divide between Canada, the United States, and European countries on the one hand, and the South and Central American, African, Asian, and South Pacific countries, on the other. As with the more common "East/West" binary, this tool has its limitations and should not be regarded as either stable or monolithic. I regard the differentiation between North and South as especially useful in the case of Mexico, which does not neatly line up on either side of the Western divide.

12 From this point we might infer, following philosopher Olufemi Taiwo (2002), that the ability to combine lived experience (a Mexican or Latino background, for example) with a theoretical framework constitutes a distinct advantage for someone seeking to represent some aspect of Mexican culture. On the other hand, such "insiders" still must struggle with the intercultural divisions (e.g., class, gender) that separate them from their subjects, while foreigners may contribute a valuable "outsider" perspective to their own investigations. Yet I maintain that all filmmakers and researchers who engage in cross-cultural analysis assume a certain responsibility to critically reflect on the part they play in the process of fetishization that Marks describes.

13 To the extent that these images are balanced with more empowering representations of women in Juarez, their overall negative effects may be mitigated (e.g., interviews with Latina journalists and activists who supply a theoretical framework in which to interpret these events [*City of Dreams* 2001]).

14 For a critical discussion of ethnography from the perspective of film theory, see Hamid Naficy and Teshome H. Gabriel, *Otherness and the Media: The Ethnography of the Imagined and the Imaged* (1993); and John King, Ana M. Lopez, and Manuel Alvarado, *Mediating Two Worlds: Cinematic Encounters in the Americas* (1993).

FIGURE 10 Angels softball team, Kingston Prison for Women, 1950s (with permission from Canada's Penitentiary Museum Collection, Kingston, Ontario).

Killing the Killers: Women on Death Row in the United States

KATHLEEN O'SHEA

[4]

It's 8:00 PM and unseasonably warm for December. The night is calm. The stars are bright. The moon is almost full. Except for two groups of people and a wrought iron sign like one you might see over a cemetery gate, there is little to indicate we have just arrived at the Oklahoma State Penitentiary in McAlester. We left Oklahoma City three hours ago in such a rush that the camera and sound women ended up carrying equipment on their laps. We are here to film the events surrounding the execution of Nadean Smith, a native Oklahoman— a Cherokee woman. Lethal chemicals will start flowing through her veins at 9:00 PM. I pray she dies quickly. A five-woman crew, we have been together twenty-four hours a day for almost a week filming and interviewing events surrounding this moment. Yet, as Nadean's final moments draw near, we find less and less to say.

Introduction

Since the mid-1930s executions in the United States have been closed. This means there are few witnesses, and even though we appear to support legal murder we don't really want to see it. In truth, we are happy to let the media shape our imaginations in this regard. For the most part, the media is more than willing to oblige us on TV, radio, newspapers, and movies as well as through documentaries and docudramas. And in recent years there has emerged a whole subgenre of writing that might appropriately be termed "execution literature."

When asked to contribute to this volume I was both honoured and concerned. I have no credentials in communications nor am I a film critic. I have never ventured into film studies although I do understand something of feminism. What I know best are women on death row (O'Shea and Fletcher 1997, 1999; O'Shea 2000).

These women have been sentenced to death either for capital murder or for having been an accomplice to a capital murder. For the purposes of this chapter I focus on the media presentation of the case of Karla Faye Tucker, whose execution ushered in a new era of executing women in the United States. I pay particular attention to the construction of Karla through television. Interspersed with the presentation of her televised story is a personal story from a time I spent in the State of Oklahoma with an all-female film crew to record the events preceding the execution of another woman on death row, Nadean Smith. This was on 1 December 2001. These reflections appear in italics throughout the chapter.

The Setting

Historically, public executions, especially the executions of women, were always a draw (Gatrell 1994). During the late 1800s and early 1900s the day of an execution was considered a time for social gathering. Flyers were posted, invitations sent out, and discussions held about how to accommodate a multitude of dignitaries. It was considered fashionable to attend an execution, and often the time of an individual's ultimate demise was determined by what was convenient for the greatest number of people. On at least one occasion we know an execution was postponed until the next day because a train with invited guests was late (O'Shea 1999, 5). As time passed, due to changing laws and what those involved in the business call "more sophisticated methods" (O'Shea 1999, 218) of execution, these events were moved from the public arena. Individual states now set the time when executions will take place and decide how many people can be accommodated at each event. State officials also allow victims' families and the person being executed to invite a limited number of people.

Despite increased restrictions, members of the press have always been among execution witnesses and have sought creative ways to inform and, darkly, to entertain the absent public (Shipman 2002, 4–5). On 12 January 1928 a man named Judd Gray and a woman named Ruth Snyder were both executed in the electric chair at Sing-Sing prison in Ossining, New York. Cameras had been banned from the execution chamber but Thomas Howard, a reporter from the *New York Daily News*, had a small one strapped to his leg when he entered the witness room. As the switch was pulled and the first bolt of elec-tricity surged through Ruth's body, Howard took a picture (O'Shea 1998, 251). It remains the only photograph ever taken of a woman being executed. The picture, which has recently resurfaced on the Internet, shows bolts of elec-tricity forming an outline of Ruth's body against a dark background.

In 1998 audiotapes recorded by the Georgia Department of Corrections at twenty-two state executions were subpoenaed in a lawsuit by criminal defence lawyer Mike Mears. Mears was in the process of challenging the state's use of the electric chair. Later, these tapes were acquired by *Sound Portraits*[1] of National Public Radio (NPR) and produced on the radio as *The Execution Tapes*.[2] The broadcast, hosted by Ray Suarez, marked the first time an audience was able to hear what takes place during an execution. One particularly gruelling recording has the audio portion of an electrocution that had to be done twice.[3] The inmate in question was still alive after the first surge of electricity, which lasted two minutes. On the tapes the order to electrocute him again can be clearly heard. Today, prisons routinely videotape executions for their own files, and last year a judge in Florida ordered that pictures of a man executed in Florida's electric chair be posted on the Internet. He felt the public should see exactly what happens.[4]

The debate about whether executions should be open to the public or even broadcast on TV continues. This debate is fuelled partly by prisoners' requests to have their final moments witnessed by the world and partly by anti-death penalty activists who feel public opinion would surely change if people were forced to view the brutality of an execution.

Enter Karla Faye Tucker

The 1998 execution of Karla Faye Tucker provided us with the first "almost-televised" execution in history. There was so much media coverage (leading up to the actual execution day) that, by the time it arrived, most of us felt we knew Karla intimately.[5] The extent of this coverage was partly because she was the first woman to be executed in Texas since the Civil War and in the United States since 1984 (*Post Dispatch*, 4 February 1998), and partly because Karla was a made-for-TV woman. She was young, attractive, white, articulate, and a born-again Christian—basically a reporter's dream. The *Houston Chron-*

icle described Karla as "a Bible-reading angelic-looking woman with pink-tinged lips, lightly freckled face and cascading dark curls" (Shipman 2002, 287). Listening to and watching her on numerous TV talk shows it was easy to forget she had committed a brutal crime.

By the age of eight Karla was doing hard drugs and by eleven she was mainlining heroin (O'Shea 1998, 343-44). In *Crossed Over: A Murder, A Memoir* Beverly Lowry tells us Karla was a "doper at 8, a needle freak behind heroin by the time she was 11" (quoted in Sam Howe Verhovek, *New York Times*, 1 January 1998). According to Karla, she was never without drugs from ten years of age until four months before her twenty-fourth birthday, when she was incarcerated. Karla had dropped out of school before completing the seventh grade and had had her first sexual encounter at twelve or thirteen. According to Lowry, Karla first "turned tricks with her mother" around the same age.

Karla started shooting heroin while living with her father at the age of twelve. When she was thirteen her mother let her tour with the Allman Brothers Band, and on these trips she started using cocaine. In a *New York Times* interview Lowry admitted, "I had a lot of sympathy for Karla's mother despite the fact that she was a woman who encouraged her teen-age daughters in drug abuse and prostitution" (quoted in Francine Prose, *New York Times Book Review*, August 1992).

Karla worked as a prostitute to support her drug habit until a few months before the murders of Gerry Dean and Deborah Thornton, for which she was executed. As previously published accounts tell us, Karla knew Dean and Thornton, and the murders were said to be unplanned. Karla's narrative tells us of a plan initiated by a friend, Danny Garrett, to steal Dean's motorcycle. Karla, Danny Garrett, and Jimmy Leibrant (another friend) then went over to Dean's to "case the place out." They thought they would then return another night to break in.

When they got to Dean's apartment, Karla opened the door, saw Dean lying on a mattress on the floor, sat on him, and then started wrestling with him. Danny Garrett eventually intervened, hitting Dean repeatedly over the head with a hammer. When Karla turned on the lights Dean was lying face down on the mattress. Blood was pouring from his mouth and he was making gurgling sounds. Karla said at her trial that she didn't like that sound and wanted to make it stop (Court TV 1998). With this in mind she picked up Dean's pickax, which was leaning against the wall, and hit him several times. When he kept making the same gurgling sounds Karla told Garrett it bothered her. Garrett then took the pickax and hit Dean until the noise stopped. Shortly after Garrett killed Dean, Karla noticed someone else moving under the covers. She grabbed the pickax from Garrett and hit the other person in the shoulder. Garrett was in the other room when Deborah Thornton stood up and tried to take the pickax out of her shoulder. When he came back, Karla left the room. At her trial, she testified she returned to see Garrett kill Deborah Thornton. Garrett left the pickax embedded in Deborah's chest, which is where the police found it the next day (Mike Ward, *American Statesman*, 28 January 1998).

After the murders, neither Garrett nor Karla Faye attempted to leave town. In fact, they continued living at home and occasionally bragged about what they had done. Ultimately, eight months down the line, they were turned in by their respective siblings: Danny Garrett's brother, Doug, and Karla's sister, Kari. Doug Garrett recorded Karla on tape telling him how she had an orgasm every time she swung the axe that killed Jerry Dean. She later recanted that statement, saying she had only spoken that way to impress him (O'Shea 1999). Both Garrett and Karla were sentenced to death. Liebrant testified against them for a life sentence.

During the fourteen years of her incarceration Karla received a lot of support from Christian groups, especially a Texas group called "Family Life."[6] Family Life members said they believed that Karla had changed (Shipman 2002, 290) during her years of incarceration. Apparently her situation had changed others too. Ultra-conservative Pat Robertson did a complete turnaround after meeting Karla. Always known for his pro-death penalty stance, with regard to Karla he told his national TV audience "in every law there has to be an exception for mercy...she's not the same person as before...what you have now is an absolutely vulnerable, wonderful human being whose life has been transformed" (Bill Geroux, *Richmond-Times Dispatch*, 3 February 1998).

In 1995, while still on death row, Karla Faye Tucker married prison ministry worker Dana Brown. Since prison policy forbids weddings, Karla and Dana were married by proxy in separate ceremonies inside and outside of the prison, respectively. Before marrying, Brown and Tucker enjoyed the privacy afforded the chaplain-prisoner relationship. After the marriage he could no longer serve in that capacity. Of their relationship, Karla said, "Since we don't have a physical relationship to get in the way, we have a totally spiritual relationship that's so deep, a lot of people wouldn't understand."

Brown was present at Karla's execution and said, "Her gain today was our loss...she was someone who literally reached thousands of people for Jesus and probably will continue to do so through her testimony. Even though she cried out for forgiveness, God gave her just what she needed. That was love" (Ann Hodges, *Houston Chronicle*, 4 February 1998). After the execution Brown took her body to an undisclosed funeral home and said he had not decided where she would be buried.

Cut to...

In the months preceding her execution, Karla was seen by TV audiences coast to coast. Nationally syndicated columnists took up her cause and reporters dropped everything to interview her. Once her execution became imminent, the prison received more than 300 phone calls a week about her. During that time Karla spoke with a number of prominent talk show hosts.[7] Even the US Information Agency, an arm of the federal government that deals with foreign press, called the prison regularly with questions from around the world.

With the help of every available form of media, Karla managed to make allies of Pat Robertson, Bianca Jagger, Mike Farrell, Pope John Paul (William F. Buckley, *Houston Chronicle*, 3 January 1998), and the American Civil Liberties Union. For at least one moment, religious conservatives and civil libertarians were in agreement (Allan Turner and T.J. Milling, *Houston Chronicle*, 3 February 1998). Neither the best of times nor the worst of times, this was a time when closed minds opened if only for a moment. One Christian broadcasting network explained: "She didn't fit what we thought people on death row were like" (Ellen Goodman, *Boston Globe*, 6 February 1998). When speaking of Karla, watchwords shifted from vengeance to redemption, from justice to mercy (Jan Ferris, *Sacramento Bee*, 3 February 1998).

Some citizens felt uncomfortable at having to face Karla Faye Tucker every day. People didn't like seeing her on television smiling and looking beautiful just before being executed. Her whiteness, her femaleness, her photogenic Christian-ness made her the exception to almost every rule. Watching her on TV, it was easy to forget her fourteen-year-old crime. Those who "fit" the image of people on death row in the United States are disproportionately black and almost entirely male. As the Reverend Jim Wallis, editor of the Christian magazine *Sojourners* said, the test would be "to apply that same compassion to a young black man who's had a conversion to Islam...or to someone who's had no religious conversion at all (Carol Fennelly, July/August, 1998).

Huntsville, Texas, had witnessed many executions but none came close to the media circus of Karla Faye's last days. There were throes of media encamped there, and witnesses say conversations with Huntsville residents were mainly about the streets lined with satellite trucks downtown near the Death House and the stadium-sized lights pointed at the Walls Unit, where executions take place. According to locals, however, the day of her death was a typical one in the east Texas town. "This isn't as unusual an occurrence for us as it is for everyone else," explained one person. "This just happens to be the town where the executions take place" (Don McLeese, *American Statesman*, 4 February 1998).

Inside the Walls Unit Karla began her last day like everyone else, waiting to see whether the US Supreme Court might issue a stay of execution or whether Governor George W. Bush would grant a thirty-day reprieve (Jay Root and John Moritz, *Fort Worth Star Telegram*, 4 February 1998). Reporters and camera crews clearly outnumbered protesters that day (Bruce Tomaso and Lee Hancock, *Dallas Morning News*, 4 February 1998). Ken Shimomura, a New York-based Japanese correspondent in Huntsville for the execution, said people in Japan were intrigued that Karla's gender caused such a commotion. "Why is the fact that she is a female such a big issue?" he asked. "In Japan there are very few executions, and there is a big argument every time. But in that argument, gender is never a factor" (Don McLeese, *American Statesman*, 4 February 1998).

A music store in Huntsville advertised: "KARLY FAYE TUCKER SALE—KILLER PRICES—DEALS TO DIE FOR." A student from Sam Houston State University claimed to represent the victims and held a sign that read, "FORGET INJECTION—USE A PICKAX" (Don McLeese, *American Statesman*, 1998). Another sign seen that day read "DIE LIKE A MAN" and yet another, referring to both the crime and Karla's religious conversion, said "AXE AND YOU SHALL RECEIVE, TEXAS 2:98" (Peter Canellos, *Boston Globe*, 4 February 1998). As the afternoon wore on, the crowd grew larger and edgier. Chants of "mercy for Karla" were shouted down with "Kill her, kill her!" and "She sliced, she diced, and now she's got to pay the price!" (Allan Turner and T.J. Milling, *Houston Chronicle*, 3 February 1998). Police tried to calm things down several times, but the only time it got quiet, at least temporarily, was when a music video by Karla's Houston church showed her image on a giant screen across the street from the prison. In the video Karla was swaying and signing the words of a hymn a woman vocalist sang, "When Jesus, my precious Savior, comes to take my soul away." A preacher in front of the screen spoke about "the glory of forgiveness" (Bruce Tomaso and Lee Hancock, *Dallas Morning News*, 4 February 1998).

The *Dallas Morning News* reported that shortly after six in the evening, everyone learned that Karla's appeals had been denied. A loud cheer went up from the pro-death penalty crowd and Karla's supporters began singing "Amazing Grace." Those who supported capital punishment periodically shouted the singers down and several ministers led groups in prayer (Bruce Tomaso and Lee Hancock, 4 February 1998). "We're going to pray for Karla Faye Tucker, for the victims and their families, for everyone involved," said the Reverend James C. Morgan of St. Stephen's Episcopal Church. "Outside the prison, you have people for the death penalty and protesters opposed. I have a feeling that a lot of people are in the middle. We have to come together and acknowledge that we live in a very violent society and acknowledge our failure in dealing with that violence" (Allan Turner and T.J. Milling, *Houston Chronicle*, 3 February 1998).

> As the camerawoman makes broad sweeps of the area, I focus on two groups that have formed on either side of the gate in front of the prison. On the left, the pro-death penalty people arrive and begin to unpack. They have posters with victim pictures and greet each other as old friends. It seems more like a backyard party than like an execution. They are sitting on the tailgates of pickups and going in and out of camper vans. Some are lighting charcoal in barbecue grills. The aroma of fried bacon fills the night air.
>
> A symbolic gesture is performed at each Oklahoma execution: on the right, there is a circle-of-prayer. A Roman Catholic priest encourages new arrivals to take a book and a candle. The number of executions in Oklahoma has generated a book of prayers to be used at executions. This group is quiet, making every effort to ignore the assembly on the other side. Many are familiar with the routine.
>
> I look at the prison. It is situated on a massive hill in front of us on a blanket of soft sculptured grass. There is absolutely no movement, no sign whatsoever that there is any form of life inside. Except for the wire fence rising out of beds of overflowing flowers one might mistake this for a museum. A closed museum. It is eight thirty by my watch. This means the order has been given for "strap down." With Nadean on the table someone is probing her arms looking for a suitable vein to insert a needle. I wonder what Nadean is thinking and feeling. Who does she see as she looks around for the last time? I have a hard time grounding myself in the moment. Everything seems surreal. I have known Nadean for ten years. She is the first woman I met on death row. I do not know how to be at this moment. I am grieved beyond any words I know.

Karla's final TV appearance was on *The 700 Club*, a program hosted by the Christian Coalition founder Pat Robertson (Bill Geroux, *Richmond-Times Dispatch*, 3 February 1998). She said her supporters should not question God if she were to be executed. "If I go home February third, don't take that as God not answering our prayers," she said. Robertson, normally a death penalty supporter, used her appearance on his program to tout her religious conversion and urged his viewers to pray for her survival.

Asked what her thoughts would be when strapped to the gurney, Karla replied, "I'm going to be thinking about what it's like in heaven. I'm going to be thinking about my family, my friends and the pain. I'm going to be thank-

ful for all of the love, probably wishing there was a way to give everybody a hug"
(Michael Graczyk, Associated Press, 4 February 1998). An Associated Press
report published 4 February 1998, the day after Karla's execution, tells us she
went to her death "calm, composed and contrite." Michael Graczyk, the only
reporter among Karla's witnesses, gave the account. He says that she was already
strapped to the gurney, with leather belts across her chest, body, legs, and
arms, when they went in. The warden stood near her head and the prison
chaplain at her feet. When the warden asked if she had a final statement she
turned to the window where the victim witnesses were and said, "Yes sir. I
would like to say to all of you—the Thornton family and Jerry Dean's family—
that I am sorry. I hope God will give you peace with this." Karla then turned
to the window with the witnesses she had invited and spoke to her husband,
Dana Brown, saying, "Baby, I love you." To Ron Carlson, the brother of the
woman she killed, who befriended her and who opposes the death penalty, she
said, "Ron, give Peggy a hug for me. Everybody has been so good to me."
Finally, she said, "I love all of you very much. I am going to be face to face
with Jesus now. Warden Baggett, thank all of you so much. You have been so
good to me. I love all of you very much. I will see you all when you get there.
I will wait for you." She then closed her eyes, licked her lips, and began to pray
silently. When the order was given to let the drugs flow into her veins, she
gasped twice, she let out a five to ten second wheeze as the air escaped from
her lungs. She died with her eyes open. Her mouth was also slightly open. It
all took about four minutes.

After the people outside were notified that Karla had been executed her
friends and supporters held a spontaneous rally, singing gospel songs to the
accompaniment of an electric keyboard. There was clapping and dancing.
"We're celebrating that God has called her to heaven," one of the ministers
explained (Bruce Tomaso and Lee Hancock, *Dallas Morning News*, 4 February 1998). *A Question of Mercy: The Karla Faye Tucker Story*, a documentary,
was broadcast on Court TV later in February of that same year (1998). It featured interviews with Karla, her lawyer, family members of the victims, the
arresting officer, and the prosecutor. The show focused on both the victims'
side and Karla Faye Tucker's side, stressing the human, not just the legal, issues
involved in the case.

It's a Wrap

In the early 1980s there was a shift of focus in feminist thinking from concern
with the concept of "woman" to a concern with the concept of "gender"

(Brasher 1999). With this shift, feminist theorists began defining gender as a socially constructed category that encompassed sex rather than constructing sex as a biological condition that determines gender. According to Brenda Brasher (1999), by redefining these concepts many new and important areas of analysis opened up for feminists. Judith Butler(1990a, 7) tells us that it allowed feminists to critique "the very apparatus of production whereby the sexes themselves are established...[and] the discursive/cultural means by which *sexed nature* or *natural sex* is produced and established as *prediscursive* prior to culture, a politically neutral surface on which culture acts."

In her paper "The Portrayal of Women on Television" Helen Ingham (1995) tells us that "television is regarded by many viewers to be the most real form of media." This is one of the reasons that everyone in America felt they were at Karla's execution. I briefly look at how Karla was portrayed on television and try to determine what it was that made people across all walks of life identify with her. In an unprecedented manner, television cameras and crews, as well as talk show hosts and TV evangelists, were given free rein to interview and photograph her. Since men dominate the production side of television, a masculine and, at times, patriarchal representation is presented as the norm. Laura Mulvey (1975) examines this ideology in her well known work in film studies, "Visual Pleasure and Narrative Cinema." According to Mulvey, the classical sequence of narrative cinema is that the spectator looks, the camera looks, the male character looks, and the female character is looked at. This sequencing lends itself to sex-role stereotyping and contributes to the objectification of women. Although Mulvey specifically refers to films, it is also what happens in live television, as in the case of Karla Faye Tucker. In another study that specifically deals with how women are presented on television, Saveria Capecchi and Cristina Demaria (1997) delineate the ways in which television, as a medium, devalues women. I looked at two of these processes in considering the case of Karla Faye Tucker.

The first way television devalues women, as Capecchi and Demaria mention, occurs in/during personal interviews. According to their study men often interview women, especially when an issue is controversial and particularly when much has already been made of how a woman looks.

When Karla was interviewed by Larry King he began by referring to her looks: "You're a very attractive young woman. What happened?" Capecchi and Demaria argue that, in this type of situation, the man who does the interviewing often adopts a patriarchal attitude by bringing up gender stereotypes that emphasize a woman's expected roles. Again we see this in the King interview: "The argument for you gains a great deal of attention because you are a woman. We could dare say if you were a man we wouldn't be here and you wouldn't be getting a lot of attention."[8]

When Peter Jennings interviewed Karla with a panel of eight male "experts" he continually referred to her gender. In his introduction to the program (which was called "A Closer Look") Jennings said, "tonight we're going to take a 'closer look' at whether the death penalty is fairly applied. We have been struck by how much attention a woman on death row in Texas has been getting....Our aim is to understand whether women in the system get a better deal than men." By making this statement Jennings clearly notified the audience that the main issue would be gender. He kept this issue before the audience with various types of questions, such as:

Jennings: Does a woman have an edge?

Bill Lane (panel expert): No question she does, Peter. Prosecutors time and time again ferret out and weed out cases in which women are involved in potential death-qualified situations and they don't charge them.[9]

Capecchi and Demaria (1997) indicate that male interviewers often do not trust women experts or a woman's answer and seek confirmation from a male expert. Thus, in the Jennings interview with and about Karla, there is a panel of eight men. The only woman interviewed (besides Karla) was a female reporter who made one statement referring to the brutality of the crime.

A second way television devalues women, according to Capecchi and Demaria, occurs when women are framed by the camera so as to highlight their bodies: the whole body or parts of it might be framed via tracking shots that run all the way up a female figure, shots from overhead when the woman is wearing a low-cut dress, close-up shots of the face, or through full-figure shots that reveal a woman's legs and thighs. The freedom of the camera's gaze was restricted in the interviews with Karla because she was filmed in a small room in the prison, and we (the public) saw her projected onto a large monitor. Nevertheless, even with these limitations, the camera made it evident, over and over again, that it was Karla's woman-ness that we needed to consider. The *Dallas Morning News* described her as the "soft-spoken, curly-haired Mrs. Tucker" (Bruce Tomaso and Lee Hancock, 4 February 1998). Typically, the Associated Press recounted Karla's execution by beginning with what she was wearing "a prison-issue white shirt and pants and white running shoes" (Michael Graczyk, 4 February 1998). Baggaley, Ferguson, and Brooks (1988) have noted that "a full face shot suggests less expertise and power than a profile shot since in popular broadcasting those who address the camera directly are typically anchormen." Shots of Karla during the broadcast interviews were always full-face, filling the entire screen in close-up or extreme close-up.

In his book *The Hidden Dimension* (1966) Edward T. Hall writes that physical distances in face-to-face interaction (on camera) convey various degrees of formality. Hall finds four specific ranges and refers to anything up to eighteen inches as "intimate." After several weeks of this kind of interviewing prior to her execution, and in keeping with Hall's thinking, this may be the reason so many people felt they knew Karla so well.

Returning to Capecchi and Demaria's (1997) point about devaluing women on camera by focusing on body parts, it can be noted that, when Karla was seen on television, aside from the full-face shots, the camera frequently focused on her eyes, her lips, and her hands. In 1975 Trevor Millum did a study of advertisements in women's magazines and came up with ten categories of female expressions that can be recognized in the eyes. Of the ten, the two that seem to describe Karla's on-camera look are "carefree" and "kittenlike" (Millum 1975). Karla Faye Tucker most likely displayed some of these qualities before being on death row. After fourteen-years on death row, clean and drug-free, as she described herself, they only became more evident. One can imagine her at the age of twelve travelling with a rock band and turning tricks, appearing somewhat nymph-like. This may have worked in her favour in those days and thus, due to arrested development, may later on have been the only way she knew how to be in a public sphere. Her long, dark hair, which often appeared slightly wind-blown, made her attractive, seductive, and camera-ready. Everyone who came in contact with Karla found her to be friendly, almost "girlish," somewhat naive, and always smiling.

Ultimately, it seemed most significant that, when Karla was being interviewed, cameras frequently moved from her face to her hands. It was with those same hands that she took a pickax and brutally hacked two people to death. Yet it was her face, her looks, that people found so appealing—appealing enough to even forgive and forget. The *Houston Chronicle* reported Andy Kahan, the Houston mayor's crime victims advocate at the time of Karla's execution, as saying: "The only reason we're paying any attention is that she [Karla] looks like one of the Brady Bunch girls and not Granny Clampett... she's being presented as a fuzzy-wuzzy bunny and everybody goes boo-hoo because the bunny is going to get stepped on. Well, this fuzzy bunny stuck a pickax into two people...and left it embedded in a woman's chest" (Allan Turner and T.J. Milling, 3 February 1998).

Karla did not grow up with traditionally desirable family values (her mother led her into prostitution), and although she was married twice—once before her incarceration on death row and once after, she never had children or set up house in a conventional-style home. The fact that the murders were so brutal, the fact that Karla and her companion were smug enough not to run away afterwards, the fact that Karla bragged of the murders being pleasurable enough to cause an orgasm, all run against female gender stereotypes.

The one thing about Karla that fit morally acceptable gender norms was her religious conversion. By emphasizing her status as being "born again" the media saved her from her transgressions and simultaneously glorified her in the role of the repentant, passive, and sacrificial woman. As spectators, we were privy to her public redemption through a visit with Sister Helen Prejean. Sister Helen later described Karla as "a gentle, beautiful Christian woman" (*Houston Chronicle*, 1 February 1998). By this visit Karla was immortalized as the poster child of the anti-death penalty movement. The picture of her and Sister Helen together, smiling and hugging as though they were college roommates, is still seen wherever this is a rally today.

On 14 January 1998 Karla appeared on *Larry King Live*, and the presentation forced us all to identify with her conversion from a gender-role transgressor to a patriarchal icon of femininity.

King: Never were a churchgoer or anything?

Karla: I was never—no. And had never been in jail. I didn't know that they gave out Bibles free to those who needed them. So I took this Bible into my cell, and I hid way back in the corner so nobody could see me, because I was really proud. I didn't want anybody to think I being weak and reading this Bible. I realize now, you have to be stronger to walk with the Lord in here than you do to not walk with Him…It's a whole lot harder, let me tell you. But anyway, that night I started reading the Bible. I didn't know what I was reading and before I knew it, I was just—I was in the middle of my floor on my knees and I was just asking God to forgive me.

King: How do we know, as a lot of people would ask who don't know you, that this isn't a jailhouse conversion?

Karla: I don't try and convince people of that. For me, if you can't look at me and see it then nothing I can say to you is going to convince you. I just live it every day and I reach out to people and it's up to them to receive from the Lord the same way I did when somebody came to me. And then there are fruits in people's lives. There is evidence, consistent evidence, in a person's life. And I'll tell you what, I've been in here fourteen and a half years and it can be a pressure cooker. I mean, you have different personalities. You have people who are still violently acting out in here. If I was going to do anything, it would have happened by now, but it hasn't.[10]

Despite these serious transgressions against ideological representations of women, in her last days Karla fit another gender stereotype: that of the repentant woman. The media focus on the stereotypically beautiful repentant bad woman made the image of Karla at the end of her life undeniably appealing. In an attempt to emphasize that expected repentant role, Larry King probed further:

> King: Do you think that a part of the anger that the state may have, or people may have, is the method by which the victims died?
>
> Karla: Oh, yes.
>
> King: Because there were axes—axes were involved, a lot of blood. It was a horrible death, right? Do you think that plays into this?
>
> Karla: Yes, I do. And if—if you were to execute me, you could…using the…brutality of the crime itself.
>
> King: In other words, ax you to death?
>
> Karla: Yeah…it was horrible. It was. And there are people out there who are in pain because [of it].…They [re]live it every day with birthdays and holidays, and maybe a smell that triggers a memory, so…I realize that. I…think about them all the time and I know that they're going through pain.[11]

Later in the interview King returns to the same theme:

> King: They were axed and bludgeoned to death. And the victims' bodies had more than twenty stab or puncture wounds. A three-foot ax was left embedded in Deborah Thornton's chest, which you did.
>
> Karla: No, I didn't.
>
> King: He did that?
>
> Karla: Yes.
>
> King: When you hear this and you have come through so much since this, how do you—and you feel new, how do you separate the two for yourself?
>
> Karla: It's very hard, except to know that—that the—that the things that were in me when I did that fourteen years ago, I guess I would say it this way—that God reached down inside of me and just literally uprooted all of that stuff and took it out, and poured himself in.[12]

Karla Faye Tucker will be remembered as a woman whose seeming lack of morality directly affected her mortality, as the fallen woman who was born again, as a murderer who, in the moment of death, chooses life. Prison officials decided not to allow the public to see the hearse with Karla's body driving away, even though it is a custom carried out in every other execution to verify that the state has fulfilled its duty. Karla herself said her gender should not be an issue in the decision about whether she should live or die. And she was right. But everything we heard or saw before her death was presented in such a gendered way that no one could forget she was a woman. We came to know Karla only as she was presented to us over and over again by the male-directed gaze of the TV camera. Perhaps no one really knew Karla Faye Tucker, but many became enamored of her media constructed image: the repentant murderous woman.

> It is ten past nine. I have to assume the execution is over. That Nadean has succumbed and that the prison will begin preparing for its next date with death in two days. Nothing has happened to signal that it is over. One group is still praying, the other talking. Then one of the three guards that have been at the gate all evening goes over to the anti-death penalty group and says something. They begin kissing each other good-bye and pack up their things and leave. The guard does not say anything to the group that is praying.
>
> I don't know what to do so I sit on the cement ledge out of which the wire fence that encloses the prison has grown. I have my back to the prison. Someone has just turned off all the lights. I tell myself to breathe. I hear a rustle of leaves behind me. Not sensing any wind, I turn to see what might be afoot. And I find myself face to face with a large white cat. I can't imagine where this cat has come from. It is inside the fence and I am out—but it is staring at me. Our eyes are locked. The cat holds the gaze and I cannot look away. I speak to the cat: "What are you doing here?" The cat doesn't move. After several minutes the cat runs down the ledge on the inside away from me. It turns once more and looks at me then disappears into the night. I know then that Nadean is gone.

Notes

1 *Sound Tracks* produces innovative radio documentaries for National Public Radio profiling the lives of Americans living in communities often neglected or misunderstood.

2 Dick Pettys of the Associated Press narrated the execution of Alpha Otis O'Daniel by the state of Georgia, December 12, 1984.

3 Dick Pettys of the Associated Press narrated the execution of Alpha Otis O'Daniel by the state of Georgia, December 12, 1984.

4 Ordered by Justice Burton of the Florida Supreme Court. See www.openrecords.org.

5 News agencies profiling Karla included ABC News, American Friends Service Committee, The *American Statesman*, the Associated Press, The *Boston Globe*, The *Chicago Tribune*, The *Christian Science Monitor*, CNN, Court TV, The *Dallas Morning News*, *Denver Post*, *Fort Worth Star Telegram*, *Houston Chronicle*, MSNBC, The *New York Times*, the Miami *Sun-Sentinel*, *USA Today*, and the *Washington Post*.

6 Karla attributed her conversion to an organization called the "Family Life Training Center."

7 ABC's *World News Tonight*, CNN's *Burden of Proof* and *Larry King Live*, The *700 Club*, PBS's *News Hour with Jim Lehrer* and CBS's *60 Minutes* were among the programs that

provided coverage; Karla was also interviewed by talk-show host Sally Jessie Raphael, *Time* magazine, and London's *Daily Mail*. A Dutch evangelical TV station and the BBC attended her execution. Reuters, US *News and World Report*, The *New York Times*, and television stations from Italy, France, Australia, and Argentina made sure she was known worldwide.

8   CNN, *Larry King Live*, episode "Karla Faye Tucker: Live from Death Row," 14 January 1998. CNN Live Transcript #98011400V22.

9   ABC News, "A Closer Look: Women and the Death Penalty," hosted by Peter Jennings, 13 January 1998.

10 CNN, *Larry King Live*.

11 Ibid.

12 Ibid.

"Dealing with the Devil":[1] Karla Homolka and the Absence of Feminist Criticism

BELINDA MORRISSEY

[5]

Feminism's "Limit" Case

In 2002, shortly before Karla Homolka's proposed release from prison, an Internet site called "Karla Homolka Death Pool: When the Game Is Over, We All Win" was set up solely for the purpose of taking its visitors' bets on the exact date that someone would murder Homolka should her parole be granted.[2] One of the rules of the site stated that players were not allowed to influence the odds by killing her themselves or by arranging her death through any third party. Most of those who bet seemed to think she would live barely a month after her statutory release date. She was released from prison on 4 July 2005. There have been no known attempts on her life to date (June 2006), and the website has now been bought by the Canadian Coalition Against the Death Penalty and shut down. Several other Net sites have discussed the hour and manner of Homolka's death, although all proclaim they do not and will not condone violence toward her.[3] Karla Homolka has the honour of being one of the most hated female killers in the world. If the death sites are any indication, she has incited more people to want her dead and to be potentially prepared to commit her murder than any other woman still living. Yet, despite her notoriety, Homolka, like Myra Hindley before her, is ignored by most feminist critics writing about violent women; rather, she is subject what Helen

Birch has described as a "deafening silence."[4] This silence is certainly not due to a lack of popular interest. Mainstream discourses[5] have provided numerous and interminable representations that have covered the full spectrum of possible depictions, veering between the most likely condemnation of her as a monster and the least likely depiction of her as a masochistic victim under the control of an evil partner.

In this chapter I argue that the feminist silence surrounding this case has occurred because mainstream legal and media portrayals have frequently constructed Karla Homolka as a female sadist and, as such, not warranting feminist interest or involvement. Incomprehension and silence appear the only "appropriate" feminist responses to this sort of villainy.[6] Such silence, although hardly unusual (as I demonstrate shortly), is nevertheless seemingly at odds with the primary aims of feminist legal theory and analyses of cultural constructions of Woman and female gender performance. In the case of violent women, feminist legal theorists, in particular, have concentrated on breaking down the deleterious effects of the double jeopardy they face, principally through emphasizing contextual factors that may have influenced their actions and diminishing the importance of the conventional stereotypical ways in which women are usually represented. Often it is through subversion of traditional feminine roles and stereotypes that feminist theorists and advocates aim to promote understanding of individual women's case histories and, hence, to lessen discrimination against women in general. However, in so doing, they seem to have fomented a dichotomizing of cases acceptable to feminist intervention.

Women whose activities betray a feminist or autonomous perspective find themselves the subjects of further feminist legal analysis, as do those who have engaged in violent acts perceived as the consequence of previous abuse. So the selection of violent women acceptable to, and therefore discussed within, feminist legal theory depends upon whether they can inspire sympathy as victims or celebration as powerful avengers.[7]

The lack of response to women like Homolka, who have committed sexually violent crimes against other women, tells much, then, about the construction of the violent woman within feminist theory, particularly within feminist legal theory.[8] Homolka, and others like her, are not included in many feminist discussions of violent women because they cannot be made to fit feminist constructions of the violent female subject. Women who engage in violent crimes against younger women, therefore, form the "limit" cases of feminist theory on female violence.

"A Child Is Being Beaten (I Am Looking On)": The Beating Fantasy, Spectatorship, and Female Sadism

This chapter draws upon psychoanalytic theory to attempt to discover reasons for the particular treatment, or lack thereof, the Homolka case received from mainstream and feminist legal and media discourses. Psychoanalysis seems most apposite to the study of this case as several of the narrations of the behaviour of Karla Homolka echo Freud's articulation of female masochism—the beating fantasy. This fantasy provides a stock story upon which mainstream discourses base their denials of Homolka's agency. However, Homolka's unconscious reiteration of the beating fantasy in her own narrative of her behaviour also made evident that which is most threatening, and unwittingly unearthed the suppressed, in this fantasy. For this reason, it offers much to help explain feminist discourses' silence regarding Homolka.

Freud's essay "A Child Is Being Beaten," written in 1919, remains perhaps the most important individual work on female masochism.[9] In it Freud composes three-act dramas to explain the genesis of two varieties of masochism, labelled female and male, respectively.[10] The beating fantasy, which is of most concern in this chapter, is the female fantasy that Freud developed during his work with four female patients. The three phases of this fantasy run as follows:

Phase 1: "My father is beating the child (whom I hate)."
Phase 2: "I am being beaten by my father."
Phase 3: "A child is being beaten. (I am probably looking on)." (Freud 1978, 113–14)[11]

While the beating fantasy can be interpreted as an exercise in masochism, it can also be viewed as an articulation of women's culturally suppressed sadism. Its usage as confirmation of women's "natural" passivity and masochism is, therefore, debatable and indicative of the unstable foundation of these crucial characteristics of traditional stereotypes of femininity.[12]

The case of Karla Homolka is interesting to view through the lens of the beating fantasy as her own narrative of her behaviour corresponds very closely to Freud's three-act drama: Homolka claims to have watched her partner rape and murder young women. However, Homolka also actively participated in the "beating," raping the young girls herself. In this way, then, she embodies the terrifying potential hidden in the beating fantasy: that women will enact their sadistic desires on the body of someone less powerful than themselves.

Raping Virgins[13]

Karla Homolka, with her partner Paul Bernardo, was convicted of the abduction, rape, and murder of two teenaged girls, and of the drugging and rape of her younger sister, in St. Catharines, Ontario, in 1993. The couple first drugged Karla's sister, Tammy, with an anaesthetic and sleeping pills, and then raped her while she slept on 23 December 1990. Tammy accidentally died due to the overdose of drugs. During the next six months the pair continued to drug and sexually assault young girls. On 15 June 1991 Paul kidnapped fourteen-year-old Leslie Mahaffy. He and Karla sexually assaulted the teenager until Paul strangled her during the morning of 16 June 1991. Leslie's body was then dismembered, encased in concrete, and dumped into a lake, where it was found two weeks later. On 16 April 1992, Karla and Paul kidnapped fifteen-year-old Kristen French and kept her as a "sex slave" in their house until 19 April 1992, when Paul strangled her. Kristen's body was dumped in bushland and was not discovered until 30 April 1992. Most of the sexual assaults on all girls was videotaped.

Karla eventually left Paul on 5 January 1993, after a particularly savage beating at his hands. She negotiated an agreement with the police in exchange for her testimony, as at this time the videotapes of the assaults were missing. At her trial Karla pled guilty to all charges and, on 6 July 1993, was sentenced to two concurrent maximum sentences of twelve years for the manslaughter of Leslie and Kristen. She divorced Paul on 25 February 1994. The videotapes were finally handed to police by one of Bernardo's lawyers in February 1995. Paul's trial commenced on 1 May 1995. He was convicted of both murders and rapes and, on 1 September 1995, was given a life sentence with no parole for twenty-five years. He subsequently filed an unsuccessful appeal on 8 September 1995. Karla Homolka was released from prison on 4 July 2005.

Women Who Rape

This brief narration of the "facts" of this case depict Karla Homolka as, at the very least, a spectator of her male partner's rapes and murders of young girls. However, her own account attests that her involvement went far beyond voyeurism, making overt her active and sadistic participation.

The politics of Karla Homolka's specularity was a constant theme throughout Bernardo's trial, in which she appeared as the star witness for the prosecution. The question as to whether Karla actually witnessed events was vital to the case, but the implications of her having done so quickly became almost more important. For the look held the promise of her possible agency in, and therefore accountability for, the crimes, something she became increasingly desperate to avoid. Karla claimed, for instance, that she stood in a doorway and watched while Paul killed Leslie and Kristen. She claimed that she had watched him assault both girls and the other victims. Karla also claimed she helped him videotape the assaults but disagreed with him that they watched those tapes over and over again. Rather than admitting his assertion that the tapes were an essential part of their sexual fantasy life (J. Duncanson, N. Pron, and J. Rankin, *Toronto Star*, 22 August 1995), she insisted that she got no joy out of watching their repetition (*Bernardo v Queen*, 1 May 1995). Indeed, she stated that she had not even seen some of the tapes in police possession.

Karla's troublesome gaze was quickly neutralized through her assertion that, although she had clearly seen numerous horrific assaults on young girls performed both by herself and her ex-husband, she had developed a knack of looking but not seeing. Swaddled in this convenient "defence mechanism," she was then able to sit impassively through courtroom re-screenings of her rape of Tammy (Pearson 1998, 193) and through a video of the rape of a young friend of Tammy's, known only as Jane Doe, in which she "smiles for the camera and sticks her tongue out saucily…[even] employ[ing] one of the hands of the unconscious victim…to stimulate herself sexually" (K. Makin, *Globe and Mail*, 24 June 1995). As she observed to prosecutor Ray Houlahan: "I look at [such videos] and my eyes just stop seeing. It's not something I can control" (ibid.).

Karla Homolka's enjoyment of her activities with Paul Bernardo was nevertheless evident in hour after hour of those homemade tapes.[14] Apart from the very first such video of her sister Tammy, Karla never once flagged in her depicted enthusiasm for the sexual assault of helpless young girls. In tape after tape of assaults on Jane Doe, Leslie, and Kristen, Karla can be seen laughing lasciviously, waving gaily at the camera, licking her lips, actively engaging in her own rapes of the girls and aiding Paul's commission of anal and vaginal rapes (N. Pron and J. Duncanson, *Toronto Star*, 2 June 1995; S. Cairns and S. Burnside, *Toronto Sun*, 2 August 1995).

Due to the absence of incriminating video evidence at her trial, Karla Homolka was not convicted of the sexual abuse of any of her victims. Her extraordinarily light sentence reflected only her involvement in the two murders. At Paul's trial, Ray Houlahan stated that, had the tapes come to light earlier, Karla would have been tried for first degree murder along with her husband (*Bernardo v Queen*, 1 May 1995; K. Makin, *Globe and Mail*, 30 August 1995).

These statements and tapes would seem to provide evidence, then, that Homolka went beyond the voyeurism of the final stage of the beating fantasy and became a sadist herself. For her activities with her victims evidently demonstrates sexual pleasure that is "conditional on the humiliation and mal-treatment of the [sexual] object," which describes sadistic perversion (Bonaparte 1995, 432). Her evolution as a sadist suggests most powerfully, therefore, that the female beating fantasy is not entirely about masochism: Homolka's pleasure in causing pain makes overt the beaten's potential transformation into the beater.[15]

Sadist or Masochist? Voyeur or Victim?

Mainstream media and legal discourses responded to innuendoes of Karla Homolka's possible sadism in a typically hysterical manner. On the one hand, they vilified her, considering her inhumanly evil and more wicked than her male partner;[16] on the other hand, they hurriedly scrambled to rewrite her tale as one of loving self-sacrifice, or, in other words, to recast Homolka as a masochist.

The intense vilification that followed the conviction of Karla Homolka make evident the severity of her sins against heteropatriarchal society. The crimes she had committed were shown to far outweigh Bernardo's rapes, abductions, and murders for they included offences against "good" woman- and wifehood. Karla Homolka was presented as nothing but a façade, beautiful but vacuous, appearing to be the epitome of femininity with her neat suits and long hair, yet revealing "traditionally masculine" traits in her clear enjoyment of the rapes she performed on endless sex videotapes (M. Campbell, *Globe and Mail*, 2 September 1995). Indeed, she seemed to deliberately pervert classically feminine values, like nurturance and care, as she described how she anaesthetized some of her victims with a cloth doused in Halothane and then watched over them like a nurse while her male partner raped them (*Bernardo v Queen*, 1 May 1995).

Homolka was also persistently condemned for her lack of sisterly qualities. First, she had, by her own admission, offered her sister as a Christmas gift to Bernardo so that he could rape her and had then aided him in the rapes and murders of other teenaged girls. On one notorious tape, later titled the "fireside chat" video, made just three weeks after Tammy's death, Karla, dressed in her dead sister's clothes and engaging in sex with the girl's killer on her bed, offered to help Paul find and abduct virgins as young as thirteen so that they could rape them; and she stated that she enjoyed both her own and his rape of Tammy (N. Pron and J. Duncanson, *Toronto Star*, 2 June 1995; S. Cairns and S. Burnside, *Toronto Sun*, 2 June 1995).

Unsurprisingly, such revelations led to Bernardo's defence counsel, John Rosen, describing Karla as a "Venus fly trap" who lured young women for assault and rape (N. Pron, J. Duncanson, and J. Rankin, *Toronto Star*, 8 July 1995; *Bernardo v Queen*, 1 May 1995). Rosen's allegation neatly places the blame for the entrapment of these young women firmly on Homolka's shoulders rather than on those of Bernardo who, it is implied, would not have raped them had Homolka not provided them so conveniently for that purpose. This attitude is confirmed by a commentator on the trial, Christie Blatchford, who avers that, although both Bernardo and Homolka attacked the girls, "the betrayal…was Homolka's," and this was made worse by her gender as "what gives both deeds ringing cruelty is the fact that Homolka is a woman" (*Toronto Sun*, 8 July 1995).

Indeed, understanding Karla as a woman was impossible according to another commentator, psychologist Nancy Lands, who insisted that women found it impossible to "deal with" Karla Homolka because: "Women aren't supposed to do these things" (in M. Mandel, *Toronto Sun*, 2 July 1995). Specifically, as John Duncanson and Jim Rankin put it, "women just couldn't get past the fact she could serve up her own sister…to the sexual cravings of a psychopath" (*Toronto Star*, 3 September 1995). Even more worrying, however, were Homolka's admissions to police that she knew that if she ever had children with Paul, the girls would become his sex slaves and that any male foetuses would be aborted. Despite this, she still wanted to have his children, writing to a friend shortly after Kristen French's murder that she would get pregnant as soon as Paul finished the rap album he was writing (S. Cairns and S. Burnside, "The Illusion Is Real," *Toronto Sun*, 1 September 1995).

Needless to say, Karla quickly became an enigma for the media; the girl the court artists couldn't draw (J. Duncanson and J. Rankin, *Toronto Star*, 3 September 1995); the girl the psychiatrists couldn't pin down to a diagnosis; the girl who blithely crossed every boundary in the pursuit of her pleasure and that of her lover. In the words of one of her psychiatrists, Dr. Angus MacDonald, she was a diagnostic conundrum, as "despite her ability to present herself very well, there is a moral vacuity in her which is difficult, if not impossible, to explain" (cited in J. Duncanson and J. Rankin, *Toronto Star*, 3 September 1995). Karla was a "true mystery, both physically and psychologically," who left her secure, happy childhood behind and "went willingly" into Paul's world of rape, murder, dismemberment, and sadomasochistic sex (ibid.).

Despite his predations, Paul Bernardo, on the other hand, was generally considered a regular guy. His defence counsel, for example, told reporters that his client was "just like the rest of us," adding that "he may have his problems, but who doesn't?" (cited in S. Cairns and S. Burnside, "The Sooner, the Better for Crown," *Toronto Sun*, 1 September 1995). Even the redoubtable Christie Blatchford agreed, opining in her column, entitled, incidentally, "Icy Bernardo Chills Soul," that he "is one of us, a perfectly logical product of the modern age…self absorbed…needy…demanding of immediate gratification" (*Toronto Sun*, 16 August 1995). His indictment for twenty-eight rapes, performed during the early years of his relationship with Homolka, and his acknowledged sexual sadism in the rapes and murders of Tammy Homolka, Leslie Mahaffy, and Kristen French, were not sufficient to dislodge his claim to humanity. As journalist Judy Steed wrote, Paul "is not a freak from outerspace…[but] a product of this culture, conditioned in the shadowy underworld of porn… whose behaviour escalated from using it to doing it" (*Toronto Star*, 2 September 1995). Bernardo was merely a classic hedonist, with his pleasure being his only "raison d'etre and…guiding principle" (C. Blatchford, *Toronto Sun*, 19 August 1995). He, unlike Homolka, was not impossible to understand, for "his sociopathic behaviour practically leapt out like a check list from the pages of psychiatric manuals" (J. Duncanson and J. Rankin, *Toronto Star*, 3 September 1995).

Bernardo's wife battering was also somehow acceptable because, although he had clearly battered Karla just before she left him, there was some doubt as to whether he was really a *regular* wife beater. Karla's family, for example, failed to notice any of her injuries until the final few months of their relationship; family doctors supported this allegation. The couple were, for the most part, considered by friends and family to have been loving and happy together until mid-1992. Paul was viewed as rather dominant and controlling of his wife in public, but she didn't appear to take offence at this. Even Karla herself admitted that Paul's control of her, at least in the beginning of their relationship, didn't worry her as the things he asked of her were not terribly important to her and he reciprocated in kind (*Bernardo v Queen*, 1 May 1995). Indeed, Karla, in the words of *Toronto Star* journalists, appeared "made to order for Bernardo…everything he wanted in a woman: good looking, great body…someone he could control, dominate, and use as a sexual playtoy— and later enlist as a partner in his crimes" (J. Rankin, J. Duncanson, and N. Pron, *Toronto Star*, 2 September 1995).

Bernardo, then, was not entirely responsible for his acts as a sexual sadist; he was, rather, part of a team. Like Ian Brady (of Moors Murders fame) before him, Paul Bernardo needed Karla Homolka to take the final step from rape to murder (M. Campbell, 2 September 1995; K. Makin, "Risk of Bernardo's Killing

Homolka Rated 'High,'" *Globe and Mail*, 2 September 1995). Theirs was a "spiralling involvement" that really took off after the accidental death of Tammy (Pearson, cited in M. Campbell, *Globe and Mail*, 2 September 1995), ultimately creating "an awe-inspiring terror-and-rape machine, their blond good looks and toothy charm a ghastly contrast to the utter lack of mercy which, together and separately, they displayed to their captives" (C. Blatchford, *Toronto Sun*, 23 August 1995). Even Paul's eventual beating of Karla was explained using the team mentality: he bashed her, so journalists speculated, because she was panicked by the thought of arrest and he lost patience with her, considering her more of a liability than an ally (J. Rankin, J. Duncanson, and N. Pron, *Toronto Star*, 2 September 1995).

At the conclusion of his trial, Bernardo was presented not as evil but as sick; not as abnormal but as so usual that psychiatrists apparently had no trouble labelling him with the understated diagnosis of an antisocial personality disorder (J. Rankin, J. Duncanson, and N. Pron, *Toronto Star*, 2 September 1995), even though they considered his sexual sadism to be so extreme that he had membership in a group "populated by only 30 of 1000 killers analyzed by the FBI" (K. Makin, "Risk of Bernardo's Killing Homolka Rated 'High,'" *Globe and Mail*, 2 September 1995). So common were Bernardo's peccadilloes that they invoked a number of regular descriptive terms, such as paraphilia, sexual sadism, voyeurism, hebephilia, urophilia, coprophilia and narcissism (J. Rankin, J. Duncanson, and N. Pron, *Toronto Star*, 2 September 1995). Bernardo, it seems, was a perfect candidate for psychiatric investigation: a psychiatrist's dream.

Eventually, mainstream legal and media discourses were even able to recuperate Karla Homolka's troublesome narrative of sadism and cruelty through unconscious recourse to psychoanalysis. Following the stock story of Freud's interpretation of the female beating fantasy, these discourses "simply" rewrote both dramas as tragedies of masochism.

Karla Homolka's narrative of victimization and coercion was developed by none other than the prosecution counsel, Ray Houlahan, at her ex-husband's trial. He was helped in this endeavour by Karla herself, who, upon entering prison, became an avid reader of texts on the battered woman syndrome. Indeed, she even recommended Lenore Walker's book *The Battered Woman* to several of her friends and associates who were due to take the stand during the Bernardo trial (S. Cairns and S. Burnside, *Toronto Sun*, 2 August 1995; J. Duncanson and N. Pron, *Toronto Star*, 2 August 1995; K. Makin, "Bernardo Trial Told of Effects of Abuse," *Globe and Mail*, 12 August 1995). She also managed to convince no fewer than three court appointed psychiatrists that she had been regularly and severely beaten, although they were unable to agree on whether she had developed BWS (*Bernardo v Queen*, 1 May 1995; K. Makin, "Bernardo Trial Told of Effects of Abuse," *Globe and Mail*, 12 August 1995; "Crown Closes Its Case against Bernardo," *Globe and Mail*, 15 August 1995). Even if she had, however, almost everyone from the prosecutor to the psychiatrists concurred that this couldn't excuse her participation in the rape and murder of three young women (*Bernardo v Queen*, 1 May 1995; K. Makin, "Risk of Bernardo's Killing Homolka Rated 'High,'" *Globe and Mail*, 2 September 1995; S. Cairns and S. Burnside, "The Mystery of Karla Homolka," *Toronto Sun*, 1 September 1995; C. Blatchford, *Toronto Star*, 1 September 1995).

Ray Houlahan's portrayal of Karla Homolka was always going to stretch the public's concept of battering relationships. Her catalogue of the abuse she suffered and the control her partner exercised over her—which began with him choosing her friends and her hair colours and ended with daily beatings and him forcing her to eat his faeces—was extreme but not impossible to imagine. Certainly no one denied she had been beaten very savagely just before she left Paul Bernardo. However, Karla's complete inability to take responsibility for *any* of her actions during the entire five-year period of her relationship with Paul Bernardo was the sticking point for many watching the proceedings. For Karla denied her agency for every act she undertook, ranging from the innocuous, like her decision to send her partner hundreds of sexy cards and letters throughout this time, to the sinister, such as her theft from her workplace of the drugs necessary for the rapes and her determination not to free Kristen French or to help Leslie Mahaffy when she had the chance. As Rosie DiManno observed: "'He told me to'…was her mantra, her robotic response to query after query lobbed by Crown attorney Ray Houlahan" (*Toronto Star*, 20 June 1995).

Although heavily criticized in the media, this masochistic, nonagentic portrayal of Karla Homolka was eventually allowed to stand as the final word on her case. Accompanied by photos of her beaten face, the *Toronto Sun*, for instance, claimed in its last piece on the trial that Karla was under "the evil power of a sexual sadist" who had gradually conditioned her to total dependence on him, to the point where she so needed "the affection and connection" that she would "do anything to maintain it" (S. Cairns and S. Burnside, 3 September 1995). The *Globe and Mail* also summed up the case as that of a "combination of two complementary sexually deviant individuals with a more clearly dominant male and a compliant, masochistic female" (K. Makin, "Risk of Bernardo's Killing Homolka Rated 'High,'" *Globe and Mail*, 2 September 1995). Karla's potentially troubling agency, accidentally evidenced in her virtuoso verbal jousting with Bernardo's defence counsel, John Rosen, was subsumed under a flurry of articles stating that she was a passive, chameleon personality whose "future behaviour depends far more on whom she happens to meet than on anything within herself" (K. Makin, "Risk of Bernardo's Killing Homolka Rated 'High,'" *Globe and Mail*, 2 September 1995; J. Duncanson and J. Rankin, *Toronto Star*, 3 September 1995). She is presented here as a truly blank canvas, a tabula rasa waiting only to be written into being by her next lover. With a character analysis like this, it was hardly surprising that one of the letters to the editor commented wryly, "God help us if she falls in love again" (C. Carruthers, *Toronto Star*, 2 September 1995).

Without a submissive woman, a sadistic man would never act, but together the two may become a "lethal pair." This conclusion goes some way towards revealing the complexity of such relationships rather than merely reasserting the simple frame through which they are generally seen. Michelle Massé (1992, 44) argues, for instance, that sadomasochistic partnerships inhabit a "mutual and deeply problematic" relationship through which "both sadist and masochist define self and other." In her terms, these relationships blur the boundaries of activity and passivity, of agent and victim (43–44) as both are vital to the continued existence of the other and function together in mutual desire.

Yet, partnerships like those of Homolka and Bernardo need not be read as sadomasochistic dualities at all; rather, they might be understood as the union of two sadists, driving each other on, searching for the same unfulfillable desire. For, as Marie Bonaparte (1995, 447) states, the sadist too demands the impossible:

> Born of the lover's eternal but unattainable desire to unite with his beloved, this ambivalence craves the destruction of the subject in order that the vain, and thus painful, striving may end. Yet, though the great criminal sadist will at times partially devour his victim, true union with her is still withheld, as to all lovers. Then, only a destruction of that ephemeral plaything of his passion will establish a more enduring love which, for a time, assuages the sadist's torturing, unappeasable desires.

To act in concert so effectively, as this couple did, insists upon mutual need. For, other than following slavishly the wishes of the beloved, what are the pleasures for masochists in aiding their partners to destroy young girls that they, themselves, have also raped and violated? Could not the pleasure be more sadistic in origin, based on *both* partners' desire to dominate, to violate, and, finally, to possess utterly?

Moreover, Karla Homolka's narrativization as a masochist omitted an important element of her story. Any suggestion of her enjoyment of the crimes was buried in most media reports and trial proceedings under an avalanche of protestations regarding her devotion to Paul and her extreme emotional dependence upon him. None of these representations considered that women who team up with male sexual sadists might have issues of their own to work out via sadistic behaviour. An FBI profile of such killers, for instance, observed that their female partners all "fell" for them with remarkable swiftness. Yet, as Patricia Pearson (1998, 185) comments, this interesting fact is not considered further by the researchers, although it could easily indicate that the women may have been interested in such men because they had *similar* desires. Nor is their eventual violence towards children and young girls seen as the product of anything but coercion. The idea, as Pearson remarks, that "women can be strategically aggressive toward children, or that their violence isn't always personal, private, or impulsive, that sometimes it is…a means…of furthering an ambition…a vehicle to her own empowerment" (102) is never given the credence it deserves. Instead of viewing Homolka's attitude as a response to the "corrupting power of love" (179), we could just as easily view her as a predator who *wanted* to keep Paul Bernardo and who was happy to oblige him in any way he wished as long as she stayed firmly at the centre of his sexual universe (192).[17] This would not be devotion, but strategy; not coercion, but empowerment.

The mainstream depictions' rigorous suppression of Homolka's cruelty to and hatred for other women functions primarily, then, to negate female violence and female desire while reinforcing the autonomy of male desire and the prosaic nature of male violence. For portrayals of Homolka casting her as having killed "for love," to please her male partner, explicitly insist upon her lack of responsibility for her crimes. Like many of the women in Hilary Allen's (1987, 83) study of female offenders, Homolka is depicted as never having engaged in an intentional act in her life. The only desire she is presented as possessing is that of attending to the needs of men, any more active desire fulfilling *her own wants* being disallowed her.[18] The mass media audience was, thus, prevented and protected from having to countenance the possibility, indeed the reality, of female violence and female sadism.

Feminist Silences

The main impediment to a feminist consideration of the case of Karla Homolka proceeds from the unpalatable suggestion that she may have enjoyed her crimes. This distaste does not result from her transgressions of the stereotypes of good wife and woman, as these are rarely problematic in feminist legal or cultural studies theory. However, for such theorists, political exigencies do form a prime barrier to discussions of women like Homolka: it is harder to defend a person who has apparently willingly committed heinous acts of cruelty than one whose actions resulted from duress or oppression. Women who desire to do more than merely watch "a child being beaten" are not just castigated, it seems, but repressed out of conscious existence. In feminist theory this suppression has a lot to do with the original aims of the movement and the constraining/enabling power of identity politics.

In undertaking the primary feminist aim to expose and challenge female oppression within heteropatriarchal societies, it has been historically necessary to found feminist politics on particular feminist constructions of Woman. The two most important and enduring of these are the victimized woman and the nurturing woman. The victimized woman embodies the damage patriarchal oppression has inflicted upon women, and the nurturing woman demonstrates that women possess knowledges and modes of behaviour that, although developed as a response to oppression, nevertheless differ markedly and are considered preferable to those privileged under patriarchy.

Crucially, however, neither of these constructions of Woman acknowledge feminine potential for violence or sadism, which means that the actions of women like Homolka are effectively excluded from feminist representation. Furthermore, her media portrayal as the willing slave of a man is likely to be read in some feminist discourses as examples of "antifeminism" (Dworkin 1983, 195), where women's upholding of the injunctions of heteropatriarchal stereotypical good wifehood is considered inimical to a feminist dismantling of these very structures.[19]

Politically, then, it is relatively easy to determine the reasons for feminist legal and cultural studies theorists' silence regarding the case of Karla Homolka as it would not seem very useful in advancing the cause of female equality and freedom from oppression. Nevertheless, representations of women like these have much to tell about mainstream law and media's negation of female desire, violence, and agency. Such cases do have relevance for feminist projects relating to the representation of women in the media, the legal portrayal and sentencing of female criminals, and even for philosophical analyses of female agency and subjectivity.

Gender Performatives and Discursive Clashes

Further reasons for the persistent exclusion of cases like those of Karla Homolka from a feminist construction of violent female subjectivity lie in their unsettling of pretheorized notions of femininity. Her transgression rendered overt the constructed nature of both mainstream and feminist performatives of femininity. For when dominant legal and media "scripts" called for complete submission to the demands of Paul Bernardo, Homolka provided evidence of her own desire; when only her spectatorship was required, she gave allegations of her own abusiveness; when remorse was expected, she shed no tears; and, finally, when her partners' sadism, autonomy, and sole responsibility for the crimes was demanded, she demonstrated that the rapes and murders would and could never have taken place without her.

Likewise, Homolka clearly did not demonstrate the main requirements of feminist performatives. Female autonomy, independence, solidarity with other women and protection of children are all valued in feminist female gender performatives, and women's oppression and victimization by men are given sympathy and understanding. Homolka's autonomy was suspect as she acted in concert with, and perhaps under the jurisdiction of, Paul Bernardo; her independence was also debatable as she constantly professed her need to retain her partners' love; her solidarity with other women and her protection of children were evidently non-existent; and her victimization and oppression by men is also doubtful as, while she insisted she was coerced, her own narratives and video footage tell a different story.

The transgressive character of Homolka's femininity in both feminist and mainstream legal and media discourses is largely a symptom of a discursive clash as her performance of femininity as willing slave and older dominatrix of younger women is quite well established within the fictional discourse of pornography.[20] Homolka's insertion of her "real" activities into this already extant fictional role demonstrates the availability of such a role for women and the ease with which women in "real life" situations can assume it.[21] Nor is she the only woman to so do. Indeed, this role is particularly popular with women who kill and sexually assault in partnership with men.[22] Pornographic discourses provide convenient scripts in which couples like Homolka and Bernardo can situate and articulate their desires via particular representations that shape the form and content of their rapes and killings and, hence, the ways they come to understand them (Cameron and Frazer, 1987, xiii). As Patricia Pearson observes, "whatever the accessible cultural rationale is, we will borrow it to explain ourselves" (1998, 40).[23] This is not to suggest that Homolka consciously shuffled between discourses as fully formed selves to find the performative best suited to her activities. Gender performatives are not roles "which…express or disguise an interior 'self'" so much as acts "which construct the social fiction of (their) own psychological interiority" (Butler 1990a: 279);

rather, she learned to "feel" and to "be" a willing slave and a dominatrix by learning to act as them. The particular corporeal acts required by particular gender performatives reproduce the script while allowing for individual inter-pretations of any enactment.

Feminist incorporation of Karla Homolka's enactment of pornographic performatives is deeply problematic as the discourse of pornography itself has often been considered antithetical to feminism's general aims and values. The feminist critique of pornography instituted in the early 1980s by theo-rists like Andrea Dworkin, Susan Griffin, and Catherine MacKinnon, although subject to challenge in more recent feminist theory, is nevertheless still cited in popular debates,[24] which continue to argue that pornography somehow "causes" violent crime against women.[25] Karla Homolka's narrative of sexual sadism, therefore, could never be acceptable under feminism. For even the most broadminded feminist analyses of pornography rarely consider the slip from masochist to sadist, which is inherent in the beating fantasy and which is narrated so well in Homolka's tale;[26] instead, women like Homolka, who make violent pornography using non-consenting participants, are left to inhabit the unlivable body, or perhaps the unthinkable body, of feminist legal and cultural theory.

Mimetic Identifications

The very excessiveness of Homolka's transgressions raises the possibility of an alternative reading of her case based around Luce Irigaray's ideas on mime-sis. Through its deliberate and subversive assumption of the feminine role in discourse, mimesis aims to thwart the continued subordination of women. Irigaray (1985, 75–76), in using this technique to reveal and speak the often silenced feminine, explains its political purpose in her essay "When Our Lips Speak Together": "[Women] must, through repetition—interpretation of the way in which the feminine finds itself determined in discourse—as lack, default, or as mime and inverted reproduction of the subject—show that on the feminine side it is possible to *exceed* and *disturb* this logic."

Lynda Hart, citing Elin Diamond, asserts that Irigaray posits two sorts of mimesis that exist simultaneously. The first, "patriarchal mimesis," involves mere copying of the patriarchal ideal. The second, "mimesis—mimicry," sub-verts the first in its excessive production of "fake offspring," which threatens patriarchal order via simulacra that may *look* like the original but that, through their multiplicity, reveal a semblance indicative only of the non-existence, the lack of authority of that original (Hart 1998, 85–86). Through "playful repetition," then, mimesis might become a strategy that has the potential to reveal the construction of Woman by illuminating that which is supposed to remain invisible" (Bell 1999, 139).

Although Homolka heretofore appears representative only of the horror of a femininity so perverted as to turn against itself, she can also be interpreted as mimetically identified with the stereotypical role of the good wife. In pushing to their extreme limits the demands of passivity and selflessness typically made of women in heterosexual ideologies of love and romance, and especially in the role of good wife, Homolka subverts such fantasies and turns them inside out. The extreme passivity these roles demand is transformed into passive aggression as Homolka's enactment demonstrates that, in the end, lack of action becomes a form of acting and that spectators are never just neutral observers. She may not resignify the term "woman" in a way appealing to feminist theory, but she does make overt the monstrous limits of comforting heteropatriarchal allegories of obedient, loyal, and accommodating wives. In this sense, then, she has behaved mimetically, enacting this stereotype of wife so effectively that her performance becomes both criminal and terrifying.

A mimetic reading of Homolka's performance of conventional roles shows as well that agency is a product of the discursive regime that portrays it. Traditional stories of good wives and mothers generally reduce agentic representations so as to emphasize feminine passivity. Mimetic tales, however, such as this alternative reading of Homolka, stress female agency by presenting over-identification as a deliberate subversive tactic.[27] This interpretation does not diminish her agency or culpability; rather, it shatters the myths through which such a woman is represented. The full horror of her acts is therefore preserved rather than hidden, analyzed rather than ignored. Indeed, such analysis in effect forces recognition of the "ruse of reality," as Lynda Hart (1998, 203) puts it, where the Real is excluded in favour of the production and maintenance of culturally and socially acceptable "reality." The experience of female sadists is thus granted a moment, a place, an identity within "reality," which then allows female sadism to exist at all.

Conclusion

This chapter demonstrates some possible reasons for the absence of feminist criticism with regard to cases like Homolka's. In considering these, it becomes clear that cases such as this one operate as the "limit" cases for feminist female gender performatives and serve as good tests for the paradigmatic subject

models upon which feminist legal theory is premised. These models of subjectivity are necessary because they allow the discourse to speak generally
about women's representation and treatment within traditional legal discourse. Nevertheless, the silence surrounding this sort of case shows that these
narratives and performatives of subjectivity do not necessarily allow for even
an acknowledgment of certain violent women who radically transgress their
parameters. Feminist failure to publicly recognize the agency of women
involved in truly heinous crimes, and its disregard of the mainstream law and
media's vilificatory portrayals and later recuperations, denies the ramifications such representations have for all women.

The complexities of desire and agency operating in the case of Karla
Homolka needs means of feminist expression. As Lee Fitzroy (1997, 44–45)
has stated, we need to question and to challenge homogenous aggressive masculinity and passive femininity, even if it doesn't always seem immediately
politically expedient, for it is philosophically vital that we acknowledge violence as human rather than as solely masculine. In Patricia Pearson's (1998, 232)
terms, it is also important that we "develop a vocabulary of motive that incorporates concepts of female power and accountability," so that we don't undermine the rationality of some female aggression.

The non-agentic recuperations of female sadists produced in the
malestream law and media can no longer remain unchallenged. Certainly ana-
lytic difficulties are raised due to the moral repugnancy of the crimes, but to
ignore such cases is to allow their protagonists the refuge of the myth of female
passivity. Homolka's is an important case because, through her own narrative
of her crimes, she embodies the slip from masochism to sadism inherent in
Freud's female beating fantasy. She makes clear the false neutrality of spectatorship, in particular exposing the floating identification of the watcher from
beater to beaten, revealing the sadistic pleasures the one who watches enjoys
when she, too, finally begins to beat. Most significantly, she shows that women
possess the potential for sadism, even though this has been repressed, denied,
and submerged under an avalanche of protestations regarding the innateness
of female masochism.

Notes

This chapter is based upon and substantially revised from material published in Belinda
Morrissey, *When Women Kill: Questions of Agency and Subjectivity* (Routledge 2003).

 1 This was a phrase used by journalist Patrick Bellamy regarding the deal Karla Homolka
    made with the prosecution in her ex-husband, Paul Bernardo's, case, which allowed

her a much reduced sentence in exchange for testimony against Bernardo. See http://
www.crimelibrary.com/serials/bernardo/archive2.htm. Accessed 20 January 2003.

2   This site was found at http://www.geocities.com/byebyekarla/. Accessed 20 January
2003, but now shut down.

3   Details of these sites are described at http://www.crimelibrary.com/serial_killers/
notorious/bernardo/11.html?sect=1. Accessed 20 January 2003.

4   Myra Hindley, with her partner Ian Brady, raped and murdered five children and
buried their bodies on the Yorkshire Moors in 1963–64. During the twenty-seven
years since their sensational trial, Ian Brady has been largely forgotten in the public
imagination, spending his time in an asylum for the criminally insane. Myra Hindley, on the other hand, has been the focus of continued opprobrium and was, until
her death, frequently described as "the most hated woman in Britain" and as a sexual deviant with extraordinary powers of charismatic influence over others. (For further information see Birch 1993.)

5   "Mainstream discourses" here refers to the dominant news media and the court transcript of Paul Bernardo's trial. The dominant news media cover the major circulation
newspapers and commercial or government-funded television and radio channels.
Alternative newspapers and community radio and television stations and programs
are not considered to form part of the "dominant media," although at times their
material may well be similar to that of their mainstream counterparts. I use the term
"dominant" because, in terms of audience reach, the media so described are pervasive. Furthermore, the dominant news media work in a symbiotic relationship with
the mainstream legal institutions, covering legal material as it occurs in court and
usually repeating much of the verbiage used verbatim.

6   Crimes of sadism are usually considered "masculine," and sexual violence against
women is most often depicted as more commonly male than female behaviour. (See
Kirsta [1994] and Pearson [1998], for examples of such characterization.) Women
who do engage in sadistic acts of sexual violence against other women are considered
to transcend "common" villainy in their apparent motivelessness, their ferocity, and
their repetition as well as in their uniqueness, for women who murder and sexually
torture young women are relatively rare in the annals of crime (S. French 1996, 40;
Kirsta 1994 168–69).

7   These dual images of women correspond to two different varieties of contemporary
feminism. In Jane Gallop's terms, these are "victim feminism" and "power feminism."
Victim feminism has grown out of the politics and activism of second wave feminists and tends to emphasize the restrictions operating in women's lives under heteropatriarchy. Power feminism, on the other hand, is often promoted by third wave,
or postfeminists, and "explores women's potential," proposing that "what women
need is to recognize, enjoy and enhance our power" (Gallop 1997, 71).

8   Cases of other women who have killed and tortured children and young women,
such as those of Myra Hindley, Rose West, Martha Beck, and Patricia Moore, have all
suffered from this dearth of research. See Birch (1993), and Cameron and Frazer (1987)
for the only feminist work on Hindley; and Knox (1998) for the sole feminist analysis of Beck I could find. Amanda Matravers, from the University of Cambridge, has
recently completed a three-year study of female sex offenders in Britain, whose offences
ranged from indecent photography to sexual murder. Her findings are reported as similar to my own, and she concludes that "such offenders...challenge the dearly held

beliefs that women are incapable of sexual aggression," and that our cultural inability to acknowledge women's propensity for such crimes may prevent offenders from developing any sense of responsibility for them (A. Matravers, *Canberra Times*, 19 February 2001).

9 Kaja Silverman (1993, 48) describes it in her paper "Masochism and Male Subjectivity" as the "most crucial text" in understanding this phenomenon.

10 The sentence he uses to describe this beating fantasy—"a child is being beaten"—reveals the grammar of the fantasy and makes evident the modifications it must undergo before its final incarnation (Laplanche 1995, 118).

11 A full elaboration of the theoretical issues can be found in my book *Why Women Kill* (2003). It is important to distinguish this fantasy from the more commonly analyzed male fantasy, whose three acts are as follows:

> Phase 1: "I am being beaten by my father."
> Phase 2: "I am loved by my father."
> Phase 3: "I am being beaten by my mother." (Freud 1978, 126–27)

12 Freud's work has been enormously influential in modern Western heteropatriarchy and still grounds mainstream constructions of "good" womanhood. Freud's work is described in *The New Fontana Dictionary of Modern Thought*, for instance, as having "revolutionized the popular view of human nature in the West...and it has penetrated into almost every nook and cranny of our culture" (1999, 339). Nick Mansfield (2000, 25) agrees, stating that "the whole field of twentieth century culture...exhibits the fundamental insights of Sigmund Freud and his followers." Simone de Beauvoir (1949b, 70) analyzed the impact of his construction of Woman on Western thought in her groundbreaking study *The Second Sex*, arguing that, in terms of prestige and authority, psychoanalysis constituted the new Western religion. Many other more recent feminist theorists have also followed this line. For instance, Linda Hart (1998, 26) observes in her most recent text that, while Freud is not the "gospel on sexuality," he has produced "texts that have invaded Western culture's unconsciousness."

13 The information cited here was obtained from Bernardo's trial transcript notes, *Bernardo v Queen*, Ontario Crown Court, 1 May 1995.

14 Transcripts of the tapes, and descriptions of their content, is found in Bernardo's trial transcript and in coverage of the trial in the *Toronto Sun*, the *Toronto Star*, and the *Globe and Mail*.

15 Michelle Massé notes that, although the literature on beating fantasies insists that there is no correlation between the fantasy and the desire for actual abuse, some studies have found a correlation between sadistic fantasy and a desire to actually abuse. Interestingly, a link between masochistic fantasy and a desire for physical abuse was not found. It would seem, then, that sadists are more likely to seek out victims for actual abuse, while masochists are more inclined to prefer fantasy to reality (Massé 1992, 64).

16 Deborah Cameron and Elizabeth Frazer (1987, 25) also found in their examination of the case of Myra Hindley that women involved in sadistic crimes are seen as far more wicked than any man.

17 Mehera San Roque (1999, 47) critiques Pearson's thesis on violent women, arguing that she isolates each of the cases she analyzes from its socio-legal context, preferring to utilize a kind of gender blindness in her view that all violence is somehow equivalent.

I agree with this critique in general; however, Pearson's remarks on Homolka do have validity in terms of my argument regarding the possibility that Homolka's acts may well demonstrate willingness rather than being the result of coercion.

18 In Karla Homolka's case, for instance, the Crown went to a great deal of trouble to insist that she was not a lesbian, calling seven witnesses to the stand to attest to her lack of same-sex desire (*Bernardo v Queen*, 1 May 1995). Karla herself was so vehement in her own protestations of heterosexual loyalty that, eventually, Christie Blatchford felt the need to comment that the inscription "Karla Homolka: Not a Lesbian" should be written on her tombstone (*Toronto Sun*, 13 July 1995).

19 Andrea Dworkin's *Right-Wing Women* offers an extensive discussion of the meaning and implications of antifeminism for feminism.

20 The term "pornography" does not imply a specific form of sexuality but, rather, relates to representations of sex and to common stock stories or scenarios used to narrate sexual encounters, especially violent sexual encounters. "Pornography" functions as a discourse, or as several discourses, that provide particular representations or stock narratives of subjectivity and agency (see Kappeler [1986] and Lewallen [1988]). The roles of willing slave and dominatrix are common throughout the history of pornographic writing. Early examples, such as de Sade's *Justine*, written in the eighteenth century, include examples of both these roles. Sacher-Masoch's *Venus in Furs* includes a female sadist, while the later classic *The Story of O* concentrates primarily on the exploits of its passive female protagonist. Innumerable contemporary films and popular books also involve women performing both roles. Interestingly, these roles also appear in some lesbian pornography (see Califia [1993], [1994]; and some of the stories in Newman [1995], for only a few examples).

21 Although it can be argued that the mainstream discourses' depiction of them as having killed "for love" bears a marked similarity to the pornographic portrayal of "willing slave." Furthermore, as pornography is central to Western heteropatriarchal culture, Homolka's enactment of performatives from this discourse can be considered mainstream representations. Nevertheless, I wish to draw a distinction between mainstream legal and media discourses and pornography, even though in this case they show their aptitude for symbiosis. (For further discussion of the centrality of pornography to Western heteropatriarchy see Caputi [1988], especially 161–69.)

22 Myra Hindley, for instance, also inserted herself into this role, as did Martha Beck, one of the couple denoted the Honeymoon Killers, and Rose West. Their usage of pornographic discourses did not end with these self representations; most of these couples also chose to produce some actual pornography of their own. Brady and Hindley made audio tapes and pornographic photographs of some of their victims; the Wests took photographs, video and audiotapes; and Homolka and Bernardo, of course, made videotapes.

23 Tellingly, the Bernardo/Homolka legal case later attracted audiences because, as the *Globe and Mail* commented, it provided "stock fantasies—sex with schoolgirls, sex involving a threesome, sex with an unwilling partner…that have tempted us for decades' (K. Harvey, 7 August 1995). Bernardo's trial was partially "a trial about pornography," with the defendant depicted as a "stock character" who got off on the standard fare of sexual sadists—dog collars, death threats, ropes, handcuffs, pain, domination (J. Steed, *Toronto Star*, 2 September 1995).

24 In brief, this position holds that pornography evidences the innate aggression of male psyches and men's hatred of women. Pornographic representations objectify women, and women's experiences of objectification are the true core of their oppression.

25 Witness, for example, the continuing debate over the consequences of children's viewing of sex and violence on television, culminating in the introduction of the V-chip to allow parents to screen out all sexually explicit and violent material from the programs received.

26 Jessica Benjamin (1984, 292–311), for instance, considers "erotic domination," and in particular the masochistic fantasy *The Story of O*, in her work on the subject. Some feminists have undertaken work on sadomasochism and, in particular, female sadism; however, such studies remain relatively rare in the annals of feminist theory. Pat Califia, in particular, has written a great deal about the politics of s/m sex and her self-professed sadism. However, the sadism she speaks of remains strictly within the confines of consensual s/m scenes (see, for instance, several of her essays in *Public Sex*). Angela Carter's *The Sadeian Woman* (1979) is one of the classic studies of the Marquis de Sade's oeuvre and of pornographic fiction in general. Her study of de Sade's *Juliette* is particularly interesting in the context of this chapter; however, it necessarily remains an analysis of fictional sadism rather than a consideration of actual sadism such as that performed by Homolka. Gayle Rubin and Lynda Hart have also discussed s/m, particular lesbian s/m, but, as in the case of Califia, they analyze it as a consensual sexual practice (see Rubin's essay "Thinking Sex" and Hart [1998]).

27 This is not to suggest that Homolka was *herself* intentionally acting mimetically as the focus here is not on determining the "truth" by returning to the original "source" of the acts; rather, it is to provide only another possible method of reading and analyzing these cases as socio-cultural phenomena.

FIGURE 11 Prisoner ballet dancing at Kingston Prison for Women, 1950s (with permission from Canada's Penitentiary Museum Collection, Kingston, Ontario).

[section two]

Techniques and Technologies of Representing Violence

FIGURE 12 Kitchen at Kingston Prison for Women, 1961 (with permission of Canada's Penitentiary Museum Collection, Kingston, Ontario).

Pearls and Gore: The Spectacle of Woman in Life and Death

ANNETTE BURFOOT

[6]

Introduction

One of the main purposes of this collection is to explore the apparent difference between women who kill and women who are killed. It is the contention of the editors that the distinction between these two aspects of violence is less clear than commonly perceived and is carefully mediated through socialized representational practices. In this chapter I argue that eradicating women and the murderous feminine are interrelated and are well illustrated in examples of early modern medical imaging. I examine the scientific treatment of the female model within this historical context and compare it with contemporary debates concerning visualizing the body as a materialization of violence against the feminine and against women. I make the case for a direct comparison between the visual representations of femininity that appear in horror and science fiction, on the one hand, and those that appear in science, on the other.

Modelling Femininity in Life and in Death: The Horrific and the Ideal

The female body has long been a significant marker of the boundary between life and death. The Freudian psychoanalytic drama, for example, is based on the characterization of femininity as simultaneously nurturing and a fearful void. One of the ways this characterization has been explored in terms of representation is through feminist analysis of horror, especially the horror film. In her analysis of films such as *Alien*, Barbara Creed (1990, 135) describes how the characterization of the female-as-lack is presented within a context of a phallic economy and manifests as a primal fear of the archaic mother: "the dread of the generative mother seen only in the abyss, the monstrous vagina, the origin of all life threatening to reabsorb what it once birthed." The public spectacle of harnessing, suppressing, even killing this feminine über-assassin has been debated at great length in other feminist analyses of horror (Creed 1993; Clover 1992; Modleski 1986; Kristeva 1982). Carol Clover is best known for her analysis of the treatment of the feminine in slasher movies, that subgenre of horror that typically features a gaggle of teenagers trapped in a horrific experience where they are picked off one by one by some monster (usually a deranged adult male). The series of killings usually involves visible and gory attacks on the body with knives, blades, and chainsaws. The last teenager standing is often a young woman who manages to outwit the killer. Sometimes this cunning figure saves her on-screen male love interest as well. Clover focuses on this "Final Girl" as the psychic manifestation of masculine fears that focus on violation of the body by evoking bleeding vaginas and castration. The Final Girl, usually a virgin or at least not engaging in on-screen sex, safely serves as a male surrogate in a heterosexual setting and provides a release for male fear of the feminized body. This analysis of fear and the resulting transference, along with Creed's work on the archaic mother figure as arbiter of life and death, are relevant to medical visual culture and to our understanding of the binary function of the feminized body as killed and as killer.

Mary Ann Doane (1990) introduces another form of transference relevant to the analysis here; namely, that set up by a modern culture saturated with visions of uncharted and mysterious worlds generated by an increasingly socially dominant scientific and technological discourse. It is seen as no coincidence that the rise in science fiction occurs as industrialization, based on scientific endeavour and technological expertise, shifts into high gear. Doane examines Villier de l'Isle-Adam's story of *Tomorrow's Eve* (*L'eve future*, first published in 1886), and in particular the role of the robotic and man-made Eve named Hadaly (the Arabic word for "ideal"). She contends that the idealized feminine form, both good mother and mistress, being "opened up for dissection" is a masculine response to fear and uncertainty in the modern technological age (Doane 1990, 164). Technology is harnessed, the unknown is kept at bay, and men are made useful when the character Thomas Edison (a telling hero of the technological age) builds Eve. Although within the associated Fordist paradigm men's bodies are analogous to machines, the women's body literally becomes a machine (167). Nowhere is this more obvious than with the figures—one robotic, one organic—of Maria in Fritz Lang's 1926 film *Metropolis*. A confused film in terms of its treatment of science, technology, and gender at the height of the Industrial Revolution, it does make clear the demeaning effects of the capitalist-led mechanization of men's work. The sexualized and demonic robot Maria (created by the mad scientist character, Rotwang) and the caring, maternal organic Maria hover somewhat hesitantly around the central theme of capitalist exploitation of masculinity in the booming era of technological wonder captured in idealized and futuristic cityscapes. Doane's idealization of the feminine form as masculine transference clarifies the respective roles of the Marias in *Metropolis*: whereas Hadaly incorporates the Madonna-whore in an obviously artificial form, Lang splits these between the technological and the organic. By doing so he clearly identifies the fear of the technological and transfers it to a fear of unbound feminine sexuality (whereas in horror slasher films it is the fear of feminine sexuality combined with reproduction that figures in the feminine form). Ludmilla Jordanova (1989, 124) warns that it is a mistake to dismiss the robotic Maria as science fiction as her form "represents two different forms of danger—technological and sexual—riveted together." The robotic Maria (created to look identical to the organic one in order to confuse the revolting masses of male workers) performs a crazed sexual dance among a group of lustful and easily led men. Eventually burned "alive" at the stake, the sexualized, robotic Maria is eventually replaced on screen by the maternal Maria, who then mediates the class conflict between city manager and the leader of the underground workers in front of a traditional church. Technology and the futuristic city have, respectively, been violently dispensed with and removed from the landscape: all is well among the men and the safely idealized woman.

Laura Mulvey (1996), in a collection of essays on fetishism and curiosity, examines the iconographic representation of femininity in terms of curiosity and knowledge in the classical myth of Pandora. Pandora is the Greek mythical figure who is created by the gods to seduce men and bring them harm with her box of evils. Instructed not to open the box, her curiosity gets the best of her: Pandora opens the box and, like her Christian sister Eve, brings earthbound misery to man in the form of forbidden knowledge. Another important part of Mulvey's analysis of Pandora concerns topography, which embellishes notions of inside and outside with surface-as-secret. Pandora, Mulvey posits, does not simply carry the box secreting doomed knowledge; rather, she *is* the box and embodies the unknown as dangerous: "Pandora evokes the double meaning of the word fabrication. She is made, not born, and she is also a lie, a deception. There is a dislocation between her appearance and her meaning. She is a Trojan horse, a lure and a trap, a *trompe-l'oeil.* Her appearance disassembles" (Mulvey 1996, 55). As does the robotic Maria in *Metropolis.* And what gods and god-like mysteries put asunder, man creates to control, as with the idealized constructs of organic Maria and Villier's Hadaly.

An almost identical tension between and packaging of femininity feared and femininity idealized is found in early modern medical imaging.

Modelling Femininity in Modern Medical Science

Studies of contemporary visualizations of the human body in medicine, especially in the Visible Human Project, are relevant here (Cartwright 1998; Marchessault and Sawchuk 2000). Lisa Cartwright examines this digital representation of a male and a female body, fully dissectible and available online, in terms of the history of medical anatomical representation, and she concludes that this contemporary female representation is something of an innovation in a long line of male body forms presented as the human norm. In many ways, Cartwright's analysis contemporizes Londa Schiebinger's (1987) work on early modern medical illustrations of skeletons. Schiebinger concludes that sexual difference becomes of interest to the newly forming profession of modern medical science just as women begin to make moves towards political emancipation in eighteenth- and nineteenth-century European society. Anatomical drawings, one of the mainstays of early medical education, began including female skeletons in order to prove that sexual difference goes down to the bone, effectively inscribing this as natural law (typically in terms of smaller brains and larger pelvises), from which political decisions and social norms based on gender discrimination were formed. These, in turn, effectively denied women a place in much of public life and almost completely prevented their equal participation in (especially scientific) knowledge formation. Schiebinger and Cartwright mark the medical image as both a material and materializing object that mediates patriarchal principles and women's lives. When the principles of horror introduced above are applied to medical imaging, they reveal how modern medicine simultaneously constructs and violates the feminine.

Some of the earliest forms of the body-as-spectacle in modern Western medicine are the wax anatomical models developed in northern Italy and used throughout Europe between 1800 and the early twentieth century as didactic tools for the growing profession of medicine. The Visible Human Project that dominates gross anatomy today stems directly from these earlier models. The female versions of the early modern models (including real hair and pearls) are also gore-filled Pandora's boxes that mediate primal fears of death and disease with a particular mix of masculine desire and an emergent idealization of nature-as-woman. Below we explore these anatomical waxes as powerful visual materialization of the feminine as simultaneously deadly, desirous, and delivered into the Galilean universe of empirical rationality.

La Specola is considered the oldest public museum in the Western world and is located near, and connected via corridors to, the grand former Florentine home of the Tuscan dukes, Palazzo Pitti, the Uffizi (where the ducal treasures were housed) and Palazzo Vecchio (the seat of the duchy's government). It was inaugurated in 1775 as the Imperiale Regio Museo di Fisica e Storia Naturale (the Imperial Royal Museum of Physics and Natural History) and, from its inception, was open to all classes of the public. The site not only provided a public science education but it also became an institute of formal study and experimentation. Several years before its inauguration, La Specola (as it became commonly known once its Osservatorio Astronomica was added in 1780) housed a ceroplastic studio (where wax anatomical models were made). Around 1790 scientific subjects began to be taught at the site, and a science library was established. In 1923 it became the University of Florence, and the museum now contains the university's Department of Physics and Natural Sciences. Today only the zoological collection and anatomical ceroplastics remain at the original museum site (physics and astronomy were moved in 1869 to the nearby hill of Arcetri, where Galileo spent his last years).

The use of wax models for the study of the body can be dated back to the medieval period and Alessandra Giliani of Persiceto (d. 1326), who was a Bolognese prosecutor (an assistant to anatomists and surgeons whose business it was to dissect dead bodies in preparation for anatomical research or demonstration). However, wax modelling was not reserved to the emerging professions of medicine and modern science. Leonardo da Vinci and Michelangelo both created wax anatomical models of life-sized and "flayed" bodies (skin removed to reveal underlying muscle formations). This was a common activity for Renaissance artists in their attempt to passionately and realistically render the human body through stone and paint.

The collection of wax anatomical models at La Specola numbers in the hundreds and includes over a dozen full-scale models in various stages of dissection. The models are distributed throughout eight rooms and are in their original display cases and their original positions. The display is designed to start with the more superficial and gross (in terms of gross anatomy) aspects of the body (stance and structure based on skeletal and muscular aspects) in Room 1 and then to proceed to the more mysterious and functional aspects of the body (nerves, the endocrine system, internal organs, and reproduction) through Rooms 2 to 8. All models are made of wax, and some have additions of hair and eyelashes to heighten the realistic effect. The models (both full-body ones and parts) are accompanied by framed pictures of the model surrounded by radiating lines pointing to numbers that correspond to a typography of parts and function kept in small drawers under the glass cases. The rooms were designed to be visual and interactive aids for teaching medicine and science. One of the models, a gynecological life-sized model, has removable parts.

The proximity of this museum-cum-classroom to the ducal residence, the seat of power, and the prestigious art collections signifies the growing importance of the empirical sciences. Galileo's struggle with the papacy and eventual triumph over church dogma is beautifully illustrated in an altar-like room, La Tribuna di Galileo (the Tribute to Galileo), which is housed in the same building as is La Specola. Here we find visual testimony to the early modern scientist's triumphant gaze in a fresco depicting his presentation of a telescope and his account of the moons of Jupiter to the papal court. It is significant that, set in the centre of this chapel-like room, is a statue of Galileo but with no reference to divine intervention. Here it is evident that scientific rationality has replaced Christian dogma as legitimate knowledge. Also obvious is the priority of sight in this emergence of empiricism as a new world order. Presaging the Cartesian theory of individuated mental awareness of the material world, Galileo's success with the early telescope challenged the accepted and closely held Christian belief in the divine materialization of the world. Galileo was publicly and, most say, severely punished for the visual evidence he published in support of the Copernican theory of planetary movement (that the earth revolves around the sun and not vice versa) (Rowland 2001). By tracing the movement of the moons of Jupiter across the night sky with the scopic extension of the telescope, Galileo demonstrated that it was the earth that moved and not the sun. This was considered sacrilege as it went against scripture, which claimed that God created the earth with a sun that rose in the east and set in the west. This was the basis of Galileo's being subject to the inquisition of the Roman Catholic Church beginning in 1633.

You can look through one of Galileo's telescopes in the Museo di Storia della Scienza a Firenze (the Museum of the History of Science at Florence). In the rooms that follow you can also see a microscope that Galileo made (or had made). As a mathematician and astronomer, Galileo did little with the microscope and had little interest in biology and human anatomy. But for others, the invitation to enter the microscopic world lay wide open and was taken up: there is a surge in the publication of early modern medical texts in seventeenth-century Europe (Lippi and Baldini 2000, 419). It is also true that the visual entry into the body had started before the development and dissemination of the telescope and microscope, as is evident in the famous 1543 anatomical illustrations by the pathologist Andreas Vesalius in *De humani corporis fabrica libri septum* (Carlino 1999, 1). Human dissection, despite Christian belief in the sacred status of the body (also God-given, like planetary bodies, and thus immutable), was well under way throughout the Christian empire at the time of Galileo's trial. Here Galileo functions as a paradigmatic marker of a constellation of developments that represent a significant shift towards a visual mediation of the world—one that includes the human body as *prima materia* and that offers uncharted territory for a newly emerging medical scientific gaze.

Science as Cinema: Technologies of Violence

Unfortunately, it is very difficult today for the public to gain access to this tribute to Galileo, which is housed apart from the collection of zoological models (including the anatomical wax models housed one story above). The anatomical display of La Specola has always been open to all classes of the public (as long as they were clean and presentable). As such, this part of the museum in particular, but also the emerging visual culture of modern science in general, opened the new empirical world to venues that lay beyond the traditionally closed doors of its courtly and priestly patrons (Findlen 1996). Following the practice of dramatically displaying dissections (which were performed in semi-public "theatres"), the models of La Specola formed a contemporary popular culture (Carlino 1999). And one of its main draws was the exciting journey into the mysterious terrain of the body's interior, with the most exciting scene of all occurring in the gynecological room.

Ludmilla Jordanova, a critical museologist, has examined the models at La Specola in terms of gender stereotypes and the prevalent scientific epistemologies at the time they were created (1989). For example, she explores the concept of depth and how the relatively recent permission to enter the body surgically, dead or alive, relates to the overall project of science, whose purpose is to penetrate and reveal the secrets of Nature. Jordanova also points to the "erotic charge" (55) of being able to undress the dissectible model through levels of dissection to reveal—a five-month-old fetus. It is no coincidence that, at this time and for some time afterwards, Nature is commonly captured in a nubile female form sporting a veil. "The Doll," as La Specola's most famous dissectible wax model is nicknamed, could easily stand in for Nature—as well as for Hadaly, for Eve, or for either of the Marias. She, and other female wax models at La Specola, also relate to the combination of desire for and dread of the feminine, and the battle between the scientific rationalization of life and chaos.

The museum creates a sort of reverse cinema: the picture doesn't move but the people visiting it do. The eight anatomical rooms are designed to be walked through in a certain order: from the outward and visual manifestations of the human body (muscles and skeleton) to the inside and functional aspects (circulatory and nervous systems, organs, and reproductive systems). This distinction between the outer and the inner aspects of the body establishes a persistent distinction between form and function in modern medicine. It also draws significantly on dualistic and gendered assumptions regarding life and death, rationality and carnality, fear and desire, and presages Freud's and Lacan's interpretation of the primal scene as psychic catharsis and the formational, liminal divide between life and death.

Almost everyone walking into Room 1 (skeletal and muscle systems) recoils at the hyperrealism of the skinned models that surround and fill the room. Throughout the first three rooms of the intended route in this part of the museum, skulls perch atop rather elegant male figures that assume upright and animated postures. Other figures lounge horizontally, gentleman-like, in large glass cabinets with skinned faces resting on bony and sinewy hands and arms. The carefully crafted and coloured wax reveals every anatomical detail and provides a constant reminder of how time will treat our bodies—how death and decay will strip our mortality, layer by layer, to the bare bones.

But these models of the skeleton-as-gentleman that appear early in the display format are soon replaced by more horrific dissections in Rooms 4 and 5. Ironically, these later models have more to them than do the earlier ones in that they display the circulatory, nerve, and endocrine systems, so that you see the skeletal and muscular base covered with veins and arteries, glands and nerves (see fig. 13). Although this additional anatomical detail and more precise dissection draws us nearer to the moment of violation, or the cutting into the body, these figures remain more mechanistic and robot-like than organismic.

In contrast, a sense of edging towards the abyss is heightened as you move into Room 6, where three female models lie prostrate in their respective glass

FIGURE 13 "The Skinned Man," wax anatomical figure from La Specola, Florence, Italy, c 1785 (with permission of Annette Burfoot).

cases. Up until now, no full figure has much in the way of skin or hair and, as such, appears less like a human than like some form of organic robot or cyborg. Inversely, the female figures have plenty of signs of what we hold to be human. Designed to exhibit the internal organs and the digestive system, the models of the young beautiful women with long plaited hair lie with their torsos cut from clavicle to pubis and with the innards pulled out and draped over both sides of nubile torsos (see fig. 14). Their heads are tilted backwards exposing the neck and inviting the viewer in, as if in a scene that crosses between Dracula and Jack the Ripper. The female models' faces are masks of a sort of drugged rapture, their lips partially open and their beautiful but unfocused eyes gazing into the distance. Their hands are gracefully poised by their sides, with one of the figures holding her own plait.

This visual feast of gore and the erotic continues. Down the corridor from this large room is a much smaller room, Room 8, on the way out of the museum (resonating with the Bataillian notion of the dreaded lower half of the body as fecal exit, among other things) (Bataille 1962). It is the gynecological room containing Clemente Susini's "decomposable," or modular, female figure: "The Doll" (see fig. 15). This is a hands-on model that is designed to have the front panel of the torso removed to reveal four successive levels of dissection until one reaches the deepest level, which includes an opened uterus with a five-

FIGURE 14 "Woman Holding Her Plait," wax anatomical figure from La Specola, Florence, Italy, c 1785 (with permission of Annette Burfoot).

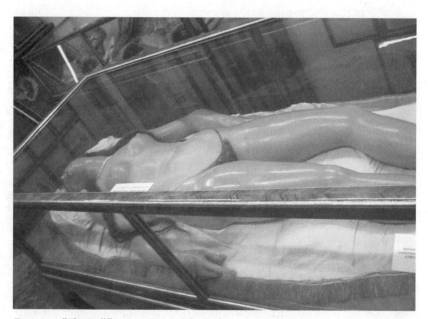

FIGURE 15 "The Doll," wax anatomical figure from La Specola, Florence, Italy, c 1785 (with permission of Annette Burfoot).

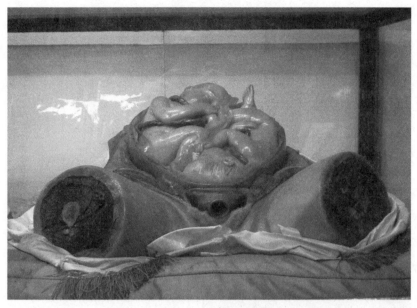

FIGURE 16 "Dissected Uterus with Twins at Term," wax anatomical figure from La Specola, Florence, Italy, c 1785 (with permission of Annette Burfoot).

month-old fetus inside. The model in its closed form is remarkably worked in that it is rendered as a beautiful and erotic female figure. The likeness is of a young woman, again supine, with her head tilted back and slightly to one side as if in some state of sexual ecstasy. Her young, firm breasts sport erect nipples, her lips are slightly parted, and she stares dreamily off into the distance. One leg is slightly bent, allowing us to look directly at her external genitals (rendered complete with pubic hair). This model is normally displayed closed, in its erotic rather than in its horrific form. The horrific is reserved for The Doll's surroundings.

The "Medical Venus," as she is also known, is surrounded by full-sized models of female uteri (heavily pregnant in most cases) with large amputated thigh stumps framing the external genitalia and the dissected womb. Skin, fat, and muscle are peeled back like a huge orange to reveal either a distended pregnant uterus or a well-developed fetus inside (see fig. 16). There are also cabinets containing a large collection of fetuses removed from the uterus in all stages of gestation (although the earlier models illustrate homunculism— fully formed miniature humans—rather than embryology as it is understood today). There is also a choir of dissected newborns, almost all male and positioned in a baby Christ-like pose with little arms reaching outwards to embrace and bless and with a slightly tilted head gazing down knowingly and forgiv-

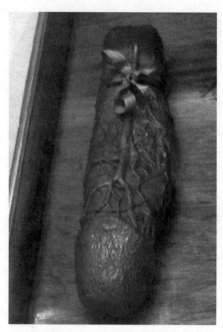

FIGURE 17
"Beribboned Penis," wax anatomical figure
from La Specola, Florence, Italy, c 1785
(with permission of Annette Burfoot).

ingly on the observer and the doll. Within this womb-like, small, and packed room, any mystery of anatomical femininity is exposed: there are no surprises left and the mystery of life itself softly glows in waxy realism that both shocks with the fear of death and delights with sexualized dissection. And off in a corner of the gynecological room is a beribboned phallus—a large penis separate from any other part of the male genitalia with a little bow wrapped around its base (see fig. 17). It lies at the foot-end of The Doll, near her genitalia, and serves as a phallic pointer within a patriarchal display of curiosity and fetish.

Conclusions: The Materialization of Violence

Mary Ann Doane points to the work of Annette Michelson and argues that the play of technological artifice, fear, and femininity moves feminist debates on representation beyond gender stereotyping and the "cinematic iconography of repression and desire" to a place where the feminized form is "the fantasmatic ground of cinema itself" (Doane 1990, 166) With the analysis of La Specola's wax models above, I argue that cinema and science are homologous. The prioritization of sight in the Galilean scientific revolution coupled with increased empirical scrutiny of the human body (and the modelling at La Specola based on such) set the scene.

Teresa de Lauretis states frankly that "violence is engendered in representation" (1987, 33). Hers is a critical Foucauldian perspective on sexuality as technology—a set of techniques for maximizing life so as to support eighteenth-century bourgeois hegemony and class survival by privileging various objects of knowledge, including the sexualization of the female body and the control of procreation. But she does not accept Foucault's erasure of the history of family violence: "Gender must be accounted for. It must be understood not as 'biological' difference that lies before or beyond signification, or as a culturally constructed object of masculine desire, but as a semiotic difference— a different production of reference" (48). Thus she, along with Doane and Mulvey, understand the production of femininity as a patriarchal materialization. Ludmilla Jordanova, who chooses a more modern feminist perspective as opposed to the poststructuralism of de Lauretis, applies similar notions to the models at La Specola themselves. I contend that the social constructionist argument she adopts with regard to the wax models can be updated to take into account the materialization of gender in early modern medical discourse.

Jordanova (1989, 55) also points to the obvious sexualization of the female models at La Specola, and she includes the concept of depth as sexualizing contemporary nineteenth-century femininity within an accepted, scientific context: "Of course these models were already naked, but they gave an added, anatomical dimension to the erotic charge of unclothing by containing removable layers that permit ever deeper looking into the chest and abdomen. It is certainly possible to speak of shared metaphors at work here, such as penetration and unveiling, which are equally apt in a sexual and in an intellectual context." This notion of the scientific delving into feminine mystique resonates with Doane's (1990, 164) reading of Hadaly as "opened up for dissection," as a masculine response to fear and uncertainty in the modern technological age.

Jordanova also responds to the violence in the representation of the feminine at La Specola, especially in the gynecological room. She refers to the "special kind of eroticism at issue here [that has] a further aspect not so far discussed: violence" (Jordanova 1989, 60). She describes three types of violence in medical representations of women: epistemological (i.e., Francis Bacon's call to scientists to wrest secrets from woman-as-Nature); actual (dissection of, surgery, and experimentation on the female body); and representational or "any literary or artistic device, or indeed any idea, which invites readers and viewers to collude with sexually aggressive fantasies and practices" (61). The models, although they reflect all three forms of violence, especially reflect the last. The gynecological models are butchered female forms, cut at the thigh and above the abdomen, gruesome platforms for the display of gravid pregnancies and female genitalia.

The "Little Venus," also by Susini (found at the Museum of the Poggi Palace in Bologna) and La Specola's Doll are both decomposable (as translated literally from the Italian *scomponibile*) and, as such, are considered among the more valuable of anatomical model types (there are others worldwide and are similar). They are also female, young and beautiful, and form elegant and erotic presents, packages, and Pandoras to be dived into. As we have seen, Mulvey uses the Pandora myth to illustrate feminine-as-fetish (the psycho-analytical reaction to profound and primordial fears); and she draws parallels to Trojan horses, the Christian myth of woman as the origin of betrayal and knowledge, as well as to modern robots and cyborgs (often beautifully feminine and bearing dangerous knowledge as technology-gone-amok). The eighteenth-century female wax figures of La Specola deserve to be included in the list. Their exterior exquisite beauty-as-feminine draws the eye into the terrifying interior of literally spilled guts. The mysterious lack-that-is-every-thing—the womb, the vagina—are laid out for rational comprehension and celebration over dark, deadly, chaotic nature. These models are also Carol Clover's (1992, 35) "Final Girl" (the feminized male figure that finally kills the feared monster) of the horrors of eighteenth-century Europe and today: fear of the material body (as disease and premature death) and fear of the metaphorical body (the feminine as mysterious betrayer of life and problem-atic site of origin). They act figuratively to express simultaneously the mon-strous embodiments of our fears of body-based fragility, chaos, and mortal-ity and the slaying of that monstrosity by the ordered and safe world of modern scientific rationalism.

These models form a logical extension of the scientific gaze associated with Galileo, who simultaneously explored the expanse of the heavens and the depths of once hidden anatomical knowledge. As eyes turned skyward, they entered the body and other uncharted territories, decrying dogmatic and mythic representations for the naked-eye truth. And the Grand Duke of Tus-cany Peter Leopold's (1747–92) decision to collect the scientific curiosities of the duchy in La Specola; to augment them with increasingly popular anatom-ical waxes, effectively making the museum a working medical school; and to open the display to the public both heralded the rise of empiricism as a new world order and provided the spectacle of its triumph over the horrific other. Rationalism takes an embodied anatomical form logically inscribing and con-taining the body even as it opens it up. Surfing the edge of this wave of mod-ern scientific ideology is the archaic, deadly feminine, tamed somewhat through scientific scribing and sexual objectification. But anxieties remain. Alignments of fleshed and desirous features with gore and the feminine as site of origin return us to primal fears of the generational matrix. I conclude with what Creed (1990, 140) argues: it is important to distinguish prescription from description. This display of killing women makes sense in terms of scientific rationality and profound fears of the feminine. But it need not. This materialization of femininity could also be resistant, and certainly it is potent. Cyborg-like, La Specola's Doll is not a sexual goddess of new science. She may be materialized as fleshy feminine trope by science, but she also materializes science and technology.

"I Am Awake in the Place Where Women Die": Violent Death in the Art of Abigail Lane and Jenny Holzer

LISA COULTHARD

[7]

In a commentary written for the art exhibit Scene of the Crime, Ralph Rugoff highlights what he sees in contemporary art as a fascination with violence and crime and, in particular, with the residues and traces that define the forensic scene of violent crime. Blood stains, bodies, and the debris of violence occupy a significant place in this often shocking and grotesque trend in postmodern art; but equally significant is the framing absence and pervasive sense of loss. It is the traces of crime and death, the absence of the human figure and the attention to the ruins of modernity that characterize this art. More than merely a formal characteristic or trope, Rugoff argues that, in its foregrounding of absence, this "forensic aesthetic" suggests a distinct mode of spectatorship, one based in detection and active investigation rather than in absorption or observation. The forensic spectator is thus asked to inspect and organize details and traces of action and, because the traces never construct a narrative whole, the spectator is led to recognize in his or her failure the incomplete and contingent nature of clues:

> Taken as a whole, this art puts us in a position akin to that of the forensic anthropologist or scientist, forcing us to speculatively piece together histories that remain largely invisible to the eye....As with any investigation, one of the difficulties of this task is the temptation to make things fit, to squeeze clues into

a coherent picture by highlighting some facts and excluding others. Any competent detective must be suspicious when evidence falls too neatly into a pattern. (Rugoff 1997, 62)

Looking carefully and obliquely for the clues and minutiae that might betray the narrative of violent crime, the investigative spectator becomes a suspicious agent, vigilant for the banal or missed detail. Merging the postmortem with the postmodern, this forensically obsessed art thus asserts absence as a positive value as the ignored and mundane traces and details of acts committed and lives lived become the focus of artistic and spectatorial inquiry.

In this chapter I consider two art works that use this forensic fascination with absence and evidence to examine the hidden and quotidian aspects of violence against women: Abigail Lane's Bloody Wallpaper and Jenny Holzer's Lustmord. Taking their cues from documented acts of the murder of women, these works do not explicitly represent the acts of violence addressed; instead, depicting violence obliquely or rendering it in written form, each of these works uses visual absence to approach acts of brutal murder. There are clues and traces in the images and stories of violence evoked in each work, but it is through visual absence that the spectator is invited to recognize the particular murderous events that prompted each work. In Lane this absence is evoked through a problematized visual representation that makes violence a feature that is only discovered slowly and through careful spectatorship; in Holzer, it is discovered through the negation of visual imaging in favour of letters and words shaped into austere, aphoristic statements. While viscerally descriptive, Holzer's aphorisms, like Lane's patterned images, are not immediately indicative of violence (letters printed in light or engraved in stone), and it is only through the active process of reading that the spectator gradually forms a narrative of brutal violence. In both works the violence referenced is distanced from forms of visual certainty, representation, or narrative clarity; the narrative of violence is one constructed by the viewer through careful engagement with, and investigation of, its traces and effects. In both works the fact that only traces or partial narratives of violence are given thus offers a commentary on the pervasive after-effects of acts of brutal violence and gives a sense of the particularly problematic visibility of forms of violence against women (battery, rape, domestic abuse)—forms that are often ignored, repressed, or disavowed as unverifiable, invisible, or culturally and legally ambiguous.

Because her installation pieces address crime scenes, found bodies, lost dogs, lost persons, and unknown events, British artist Abigail Lane's complex works have been linked to issues of memory, history, and the status and residue of evidence. Essays and books having to do with her work bear titles like "Missing Miss Lane," "Repeating the Unrepeatable," "Body of Evidence,"

"Stilled Lives," and "Apocalyptic Wallpaper," and several commentators have made direct connections between Lane's art and Freud's analysis of the uncanny, of the once familiar that has been estranged through repression: Iwona Blazwick refers to the *unheimlich* dread that resides in her domestic settings, Gill Saunders notes the *unheimlich* nature of the bottom and bloody wallpaper prints with their evocation of silencing and suffocating domesticity, and other critics hint at the strange and unfamiliar dread that surrounds her work. But more than merely defamiliarizing the familiar, Lane's uncanny images make what seems unfamiliar (violence, murder, blood, death), familiar and mundane through the attention to the details and traces of violent events. In this attention to detail, violence is everywhere evoked in Lane's work even though it may not be explicitly represented, and the viewer is brought into forensic reconstructions of scenes of trauma or murder in a way that highlights both the material traces of violence and the absence of full knowledge of events and experiences. As one reviewer noted in ARTnews (Feaver 1995, 143), "Her materials yield evidence to the forensic experts we imagine ourselves to be."

Although forensically themed, Lane's works do not always engage with violence, and many of the traces and clues are domestic, everyday, and often wryly humorous: in the images of ink pad bum prints (Bottom Wallpaper 1992; Blueprint 1992), fingerprints and footprints (Conspiracy Board Game 1992 and Making History 1992), lost bride posters, stuffed and concrete dogs, and domestic scenes with animal diorama spectators, Lane makes use of mundane materials that confront the viewer with seemingly innocent images. In this combination of a thematic concentration on clues and a formal use of everyday materials, these works, although placed in museum or gallery settings, counter any sense of the transcendence or permanence of art and utilize ephemerality to comment on the fleeting and inconsistent nature of evidence.

This attention to banal details is equally evident in those installations of Lane's that confront violent crime more directly: The Incident Room (1993) and Skin of the Teeth (1995). The Incident Room confronts the viewer with a partially buried, pale wax female figure, lit with photographic lights. The earth and the body create a mound in the installation space, and the photographic lights mark off and illuminate the body, which is only visible in parts through the brown earth (the body's head is slightly turned, her light hair visible, as is the whole one of her arms, one hand, and part of a foot). Without mess or obvious signs of trauma, the pallid and iridescent skin of the female victim contrasts with the richness of the brown earth, and the lights emphasize this contrast while reinforcing the sense of a forensic investigation: the edge of the crime scene is marked off by the presence of the lights, which in turn invite

us to look more closely for clues and details. In addition to the partially discovered body, the room contains an old brown table with a mock tabloid
newspaper called the "Express & Echo," dated Friday, 18 June 1993. The headline reads "The bride, the body, the mystery and its maker: ARTIST'S DEADLY
PLOT REVEALED" and a photograph of Lane on the run with a human female
arm in hand appears underneath. The story reveals the artist's plan to place
the installation (accompanied by posters reporting a missing bride) on-site in
a flowerbed at Killerton Gardens near Exeter. The mock paper decries the
gruesomeness of such an installation and suggests the problematic relations
between art, life, and reality: "'A lifelike model of a living mannequin would
have been acceptable,' the spokesperson continued, 'but a dead one was not.'"
As a mockery of the politics of death and representation, Lane's "missing
bride" implicates the public fascination with violent spectacle: the association between the model in the earth and the missing bride, and even with a
violent crime, are all conjectural, and the narrative of homicide is constructed
by the viewer or her/his surrogate, the Killerton Gardens spokesperson. The
work dares you to be offended and suggests that the minimal ingredients for
the construction of a narrative of intrigue, mystery, and violent murder are a
female body, some dirt, and a light or two. Cued by the familiar framing devices
of detection and criminal investigation, the spectator brings the narrative of
violence to the work—a work that, after all, is merely a collection of everyday
materials and objects.

Similarly concerned with crime scenes, Lane's Skin of the Teeth, conceived
for the Upper Gallery space of ICA (the Institute of Contemporary Arts), was
composed of several items with only loose connections between them.
Although composed of household objects (fireplace, dog, wallpaper) and common materials (wax, cement, paper), the work created an atmosphere of
intrigue and mystery that prompted one reviewer to describe the installation
as an "Edgar Allan Poe psychodrama, complete with heavy breathing beneath
floorboards and such memorable methods of disposal as an acid bath or stuff-
ing body parts down the drain" (Feaver 1995, 143). This reference to body parts
and hidden violent murder are confirmed when one considers the arrangement
of materials in the exhibition: Skin of the Teeth consisted of a room with red-
patterned wallpaper, a cement fireplace hearth, a red wax hanging head and
arms, a huge red wax ink pad with hinged zinc cover, the sounds of muffled
scratching, and a life-sized cement Jack Russell terrier, looking up at the viewer
with ears pricked in attention. Upon close examination the wallpaper reveals
a repeated motif of random splatters and the appearance of a handprint.
Information produced along with the exhibit explains that the pattern is mod-
elled on a New York police archive photograph of a homicide crime scene:

the patterned wallpaper is thus exposed as the blood splatters and desperate clamouring of a woman fighting to survive a violent murder. With this additional material and its traces of a coldly forensic process of investigation and detection, a scene of a bourgeois, domestic interior is transformed into a scene of violence and of evidentiary traces. In its repeated motif and deceptive simplicity and beauty, this bloody wallpaper offers a comment on survival (the handprint, the last traces of life fighting to live), on the banality of death (it can happen in the home, in an environment of supposed safety and harmony), and on the problematic visibility of violence (the wallpaper is not initially understood or seen as a marker of violence).

In addition to the disconcerting stain of the wallpaper is the presence of the pet dog, which also initially seems to offer comfort rather than threat, but which, like the wallpaper, upon close examination reveals its own stain. For the exhibit, Lane had a dog stuffed then cast in concrete; the dog's hair exists in trace form on the concrete surface and one is faced with the absent presence of the dead companion animal. As Lane comments, there is a confusion between inside and outside in the surface of the dog's skin, a confusion that is tied to the ambiguity set up by the presence of a dead dog in an animated pose: "I wanted to avoid making a perfectly carved dog. Instead I wanted something that still had energy but has been grounded because it's concrete. You get that sense as soon as you see its face, because the eyes are concrete. They're just dead. It's something that continues to interest me—where the line is drawn" (quoted in Flood 1995, 61). As confusion between interior and exterior, the hair of the inverted dog skin acts as an inverted and perverse echo of the blood on the walls. As cover, the wallpaper acts as another kind of skin, which replicates the disorienting liveness of the dog skin and draws attention to the sardonic twist of the exhibition title (these victims did not survive by "the skin of the teeth"). The blood on the walls of the domestic interior set up a connection between body and home that is violated in the act of murder; the blood becomes a kind of writing on the wall, and the wallpaper in its domestic resonance operates as a testament to the violence that occurred within a particular domestic space (the murder of a woman within her home) and a critique of the covering up of scenes of domestic violence that is a part of a society and culture that values the idealization of hearth and home.

Using material from a crime scene, Lane transforms the image of domesticity into a crime scene, but with the notable difference that without the detective, the clues are not guaranteed meaning or narrative closure and the viewer is left to assemble them him or herself. The wallpaper's violence is only perceptible in its repetition and in close investigation; the viewer is forced into a position of crime-scene investigator as he or she tries to piece together the separate elements of the exhibit in order to construct a narrative of events. The clues are disparate and all are shockingly mundane—banal figures (dog, room, fireplace, human body) and familiar materials (cement, wax, paper)—and all are equally deceptive or duplicitous: they are not what they first appear and it is only in their details that they are betrayed. The violence is manifest as much in its absence as its presence: there is no body, no kinetic, active, or disruptive sense of violence, only the clean and domesticated traces of an absence of life (paint blood, wax body, cement dog).

In its slow revelation of details, Bloody Wallpaper thus exposes the distorted truth of the scene of domestic coziness and harmony (the banal comfort of a nice patterned wall covering, a warm hearth, and the presence of the household dog): the reality of violent death is not hidden behind this image of home but, rather, is constitutive of it. Lacanian theorist Slavoj Žižek notes the disruption inherent in this kind of revelation. For Žižek (1991, 165), the horror of the real is not an underworld or hidden feature of life but its core, and the image of harmony is merely the fantasmatic idealization necessary for existence: "The kernel of reality is horror—horror of the real—and what constitutes reality is the minimum of idealization the subject needs to be able to sustain the real." When the real intrudes, it does so in the form of a stain or blot on an otherwise innocent image, thus marking the traumatic kernel, with a detail or clue.[1] In Bloody Wallpaper it is the detail—the handprint, the eeriness of the repeated abstract patterns, the hair on the cement dog—that renders the domestic home *unheimlich*. The blood of murder and the skin of the dead dog are uncomplicatedly viewed (at least initially) as familiar and banal instances of bourgeois home decoration; the disturbance comes from the ease with which the objects slip from one context to another and the impact is one of unsettling disorientation—home and homicide become too close for comfort.

In Lane's work as a whole, this stain of violence is often made concrete through the presence of animals, which in taxidermied or cast form occupy central places in her installation art and photography. The violence of Lane's animal figures is oblique, indirect, visible only as trace: hidden violence is both a part of the construction of the animal figures (where did she acquire the skins of the dogs for example?) and a part of their positioning within the forensic framework or narrative of her installations. For example, the dog in Bloody Wallpaper is frozen (cast in concrete) and seems strangely out of place and unrelated to the violence of the wallpaper, the eerie scratching at the door, or the screaming wax head. The dog is not party to violence but functions as its mute witness and curious bystander.[2] The pet dog, Lane seems to be suggesting, is as ambivalent as the bloody wallpaper, which is both a sign of domestic coziness and extreme violence, and is as dead as the photograph, which both preserves a moment and kills it through stillness.

This ambivalent domestic/wild is constitutive of Lane's more recent series, Still Lives (1997), which shows, not domestic pets, but people in domestic settings being watched by "wild," albeit stuffed, animals. The Still Lives are part of an exhibition entitled Whether the Roast Burns, the Train Leaves, or the Heavens Fall (1998), which also included the installation You Know Who You Are (a pair of smoking shoes that offers that image of disappeared, evaporated, or inchoate human form), and the video project The Figment (1998), which Lane has recently made (with the addition of The Inspirator and The Inclination into a three-part series entitled Tomorrows World, Yesterdays Fever (Mental Guests Incorporated) (2001). The Still Lives photographs (with titles like "Her Life Became Nocturnal," "His Values Were Personal," and "It Was on the Tip of Her Tongue" display humans going about daily (and not so daily) activities, oblivious to the world outside and to the animals watching them through the windows. The wild animals in the dioramas outside these scenes look on, curious yet strangely calm. The animals here are spectators: elevated on plateaus, lit with an ethereal, otherworldly glow, they are the viewers, not the exhibits. The domestic scenes range from the mundane (watching television, sleeping), to the disturbing (a woman on the floor is dead or unconscious), to the outright violent (a women tied to a chair). The animals are mute witnesses, psychic projections, and voyeuristic stand-ins to these domestic scenes, and they occupy a place at once familiar and yet otherworldly. Animals and spectators thus form the borders or mirror images for the viewed human dioramas, which come to occupy a place between our world and the imitation wild nature of the exterior world.

Two of these photographs stand out in the series for the implied violence of the frozen action: in "She Imagined She Knew the Future" (1997), a woman is gagged and tied to a chair in a living room, with a stuffed tiger prowling behind her outside the window, and in another, "She Didn't Need Her Eyes Open in Order to See" (1997), a woman in a housedress lies face down on the floor of a kitchen, lit by a glow from an open doorway and observed by a mountain goat. There is no outright violence represented in either scene (the bound woman is alone and the only ominous presence is that of the stuffed tiger) and the woman in the housedress is accompanied by signs of disarray (a fallen glass lies beside her) but there is no physical evidence of violent trauma. The violence is implied, felt, or sensed but not depicted, and the taxidermied animals, in their banality and transcendent positioning, are important clues in the scenes displayed.[3]

Like Bloody Wallpaper and Incident Room, the Still Lives offer not direct violence to the viewer but, rather, the clues from which she/he can, and is invited to, construct a narrative of violence. The animals are there as clues (the growling tiger invites the construction of a violent story to explain its presence) and as traces of human conquest and aggression (their reanimation signalling and recreating the occasions of their deaths). Through them the viewer is placed in a role of secondary witness (we are watching the animals watching the humans) and forensic investigator (the animals presence suggests a mystery, an action having occurred or about to occur that requires an observer or protector). They remind us of their own exhibition framework, their own death and reanimation in scenes of hunting, feeding, or wariness before the impact of the hunter's bullet, and we are left wondering if the frozen moments of the humans are significant ones (of threat or pursuit) or merely mundane quotations of typical human acts (human specimens in natural habitats), and we are left to reconstruct the corollary of their frozen animation: are these moments caught in the instant before the hunter's bullet strikes? In each the evocation of violence, and in particular of a masculinized violence of conquest and scientific inquiry, is implied in the museum frame of animal exhibition, and their attentive yet dead gazes suggest that we should view the frozen moments with care and attention. Like the killed and reconstructed growling tiger, the woman tied to the chair suggests the invisible violence to come, referencing the instance just after what we observe, the instance before her own violent death: she is frozen in this moment of impending doom, of anticipated violence, for the eyes of the curious spectator.

Similarly concerned with witnessing and piecing together the traces of violence, Holtzer's Lustmord series offers words rather than objects to represent the rape and murder of women. While the title refers to a generalized mode of sexual murder, the impetus for Lustmord was the reports of the rape and murder of Bosnian women during the war in the former Yugoslavia, a connection that was made explicit in the first incarnation of the work as a magazine edition, which used ink mixed with the blood of Bosnian women (volunteered donations for this express purpose) for the title page heading "I am awake in the place where women die." For Lustmord Holzer abandoned the ironic objective rationality of her aphoristic art (her series Truisms, for example, offered philosophical thoughts brought down to the level of cliché, which were displayed on everything from billboards to T-shirts and televisions) and approached the war horrors from three subjectively defined perspectives: the perpetrator, the victim, and the observer. The work is a series of statements from the perspective of each of the persons who are involved in the violent rape and murder of a woman. In its first incarnation, Lustmord appeared as a series of photographs of the phrases printed in capital letters on the skin of women. The surfaces are photographed in detail (you can see hairs, pores, variations in skin tones), and the parts of the body are anonymous and nondescript (the skin covers the whole area of the photograph and there are no images that would clearly identify a body part). Later versions of the work have involved the inscription of the phrases on marble benches, LED displays, red leather walls of a house interior, and printed silver bands around human bones.

In each incarnation the focus is on the words and the effects of the variation in modes are surprisingly consistent in so far as each focuses on traces: traces of writing (the impermanence of writing, whether on skin, including the tanned hides of leather, or with light) and traces of the body (skin, blood, bones). This focus on residue and remains is in keeping with the forensic statements that make up the exhibit and depict the scene of the crime from the perspectives of those involved. The statements are brutal, detailed, and disturbingly simultaneously concise and evocative: they are discrete speech acts that coldly describe events without adjectival qualification and are often without emotional response, but they stick with the viewer and resonate. This coldness is especially evident in the phrases ascribed to the perpetrator, of which there are twenty-seven, who presents his acts objectively and refers to his victim only as "her": "I WANT TO FUCK HER WERE SHE HAS TOO MUCH HAIR"; "SHE ACTS LIKE AN ANIMAL LEFT FOR COOKING"; "I FIND HER SQUAT-TING ON HER HEELS AND THIS OPENS HER SO I CAN GET HER FROM BELOW"; "SHE ROOTS WITH HER BLUNT FACE"; "SHE HUNTS ME WITH HER MOUTH"; "SHE HAS THREE COLORS IN HER EYES"; "I BITE HER CLOSED AGAIN." The phrases are notable for their simple brutality (both syntactical and descriptive) and for the cold breakdown of violence into discrete acts perpetrated on an observed but dehumanized victim. The perpetrator is given no psychology or motivation separate from his present acts on the victim, and there is no sense of remorse, passion, or even pleasure: the descriptions are clinical ("I STEP ON HER HANDS"; "I SPLAY HER FINGERS") and the victim is an object that appears to the per-petrator to be especially designed for these acts of brutal violence ("THE COLOR OF HER WHERE SHE IS INSIDE OUT IS ENOUGH TO MAKE ME KILL HER"). As Sabine Sielke (1996) notes, these acts are figured in terms of female excess ("TOO MUCH HAIR"; "HER BREASTS ARE ALL NIPPLE"), but it is interesting that this excess is defined only in the most vague and generic terms: the victim is merely hands, mouth, fingers, and breasts: there are no adjectival qualifications or descriptions that would personalize, define, or set this victim apart. This generic victimization is echoed in the artistic presentation, where all voices (perpetrator, victim, and bystander) are given the same formal qualities and the accumulation of discrete statements has an end result evocative of repetitive acts of violence. Although the piece offers a story of one victim, one perpetrator, and one bystander, the repetition of statements, the variation in form, and the generic violence of the statements work to extend the violence described beyond the particular subjectivities and beyond the impetus for the installation (the rape and murder of Bosnian women).

This generic quality is mitigated in the victim's statements, which are more personalized and which involve direct address: "MY NOSE BROKE IN THE GRASS. MY EYES ARE SORE MOVING AGAINST YOUR PALM"; "I HAVE THE BLOOD JELLY"; "WITH YOU INSIDE ME COMES THE KNOWLEDGE OF MY DEATH"; "YOU HAVE SKIN IN YOUR MOUTH. YOU LICK ME STUPIDLY"; "YOU CONFUSE ME WITH SOMETHING THAT IS IN YOU. I WILL NOT PREDICT HOW YOU WANT TO USE ME"; "I FEEL WHO YOU ARE AND IT DOES ME NO GOOD AT ALL"; "I AM AWAKE IN THE PLACE WHERE WOMEN DIE." In the shift from objective description to subjective response, the victim's statements have a more immediate, personal, and visceral impact. The focus shifts from acts to sensations ("YOU LICK ME STUPIDLY"), and towards the more subjective experiences of knowledge, prediction, and pain. There is an awareness of bodily boundaries and sensations ("I DO NOT LIKE TO WALK BECAUSE I FEEL IT BETWEEN MY LEGS") and an awareness of the other human presence: "YOUR AWFUL LANGUAGE IS IN THE AIR BY MY HEAD." Significantly, the victim's statements do not mirror the perpetrator's; there are fewer statements and they do not describe the exact same moments. This disjuncture between reports suggests the vast differences in the experiences of perpetrator and victim and works to expand the viewer's understanding or empathetic knowledge: we get distinct, separate, and additional information from the other side of violence. Moreover, the use of "you" implicates the reader/viewer in the role of perpetrator; in responding to these unspoken statements we are at once the "you" addressed and the witnesses who have been granted subjective access to the victim's thoughts.

The sense of being implicated in the acts of violence is furthered in the statements attributed to the Observer. As might be expected from a witness to traumatic violence, the Observer—who is presented as being the daughter of the victim ("I WANT TO LIE DOWN BESIDE HER. I HAVE NOT SINCE I WAS A CHILD.")—speaks in a voice that is ambivalent in its mixture of objective description and subjective horror and hurt: "I FIND HER TOWELS SHOVED IN TIGHT SPOTS. I TAKE THEM TO BURN ALTHOUGH I FEAR TOUCHING THINGS"; "SHE ASKS ME TO SLEEP IN THE HOUSE BUT I WILL NOT WITH HER NEW BODY AND ITS NOISES AND WETNESS"; "SHE SMILES AT ME BECAUSE SHE IMAGINES I CAN HELP HER"; "SHE IS NARROW AND FLAT IN THE BLUE SACK AND I STAND WHEN THEY LIFT HER." There is empathy, a sense of loss, and a desire to help, but there is also a recognition of powerlessness and an attitude of disgust. Personal threat, helplessness, and the bodily presence of the victim impinge on any sentimentalized or purely empathetic response to violence. The confrontation with the violence of rape, torture, and death thus becomes inseparable from the act of grieving, and both are abject, repugnant, and messy. This messiness means that the survivor does not merely live on with loss but lives on to clean up and remove the traces of death: "SHE FELL ON THE FLOOR IN MY ROOM. SHE TRIED TO BE CLEAN BUT SHE WAS NOT. I SEE HER TRAIL"; "HER GORE IS IN THE BALL OF CLEANING RAGS. I CARRY OUT THE DAMPNESS FROM MY MOTHER. I RETURN TO HIDE HER JEWELRY."

In language, attitude, and deed, the Observer finds herself in between the statements of the Perpetrator and the Victim: she uses the first person, more subjective voice of the victim ("I"), but the references to the victimized person are in generic and objective terms ("she," "her"). We are given more information about her, there is a suggestion of a past and an indication of a future; unlike the victim and the perpetrator she exists outside of the moment of violence. She is there to respond, to clean up, and carry on. As viewer and witness to violence, this voice acts as surrogate for the exhibit viewer: we are likewise observers and witnesses to violence and we are both caught up in the acts of violence and victimized by them. Significantly, though, this slippage is attenuated by the victim's discursive implication of the viewer in the acts of violence, and even the place of the observer is not an easy or unequivocal one as it is burdened by the contradictions and uncertainties of the survivor.

In respecting this ambivalence, Lustmord suggests the significance of its tripartite structure. The three perspectives of Lustmord do not purport to offer a complete narrative of a crime; the victim's and the observer's statements become additions, second and third layers of clues to construct a sense of the events, rather than offering different perspectives of the same event. Not only does the work give precedence to the traumatic experience of pain and violence through its attention to the often ignored statements of female victims and bystanders, but the nature of these statements prevents any easy incorporation into clear narratives of victimization, martyrdom, or sacrifice. The discrete and unconnected statements work to thwart or disrupt any sense of full knowledge as the events of violence described will only ever be known in the most partial, fragmented, and incomplete way. The addition of layers of statements offers not a full narrative but only more details and more experiences that, in their fragmentary nature, seem to recognize the impossibility of ever revealing a full story. Lustmord does not attempt to offer a full account or reconstruction of even one story of rape and murder, let alone represent the masses of stories of violence against women both during war and during peace; instead, the three perspectives suggest by their incompleteness the impossibility of ever fully knowing violence, its origins, its enactment, its experience, or its lasting impact of loss and trauma.

Moreover, as a response to the historical invisibility of the rape and murder of civilian women as a result of war, the partial and multivalent nature of the accounts addresses the very recent and still inadequate and limited recognition of rape as a war crime, while connecting this specific violence to the greater invisibility of violence against women in times of peace as well as war.[4] It is in its use of multiple perspectives (especially in the intrusion of the bystander into the usual dichotomy of victim/victimizer) as well as in its disjointed and repetitive nature that Lustmord is able to address violence against women in both a specific and general context without offering an overly harmonious, totalizing, or simplistic account of the act, experience, or effects of violence. There is no assertion of universalized victimhood but, instead, a sense of the fragmented and incomplete nature of the categories of victims, perpetrators, and bystanders and the narratives of violence that they are able to relay.

This partial knowledge is reflected as well in the materials used—discrete fragments of different skin surfaces, bones, LED displays that scroll by so quickly that they are almost impossible to read. The body and the corporeal experience of rape and torture are suggested but not offered in concrete or complete form: we see body parts (the skin or the bones) or the evocation of permanence and ephemerality (cement, light) that suggest both the lasting damage of violence, the disappearance of its victims, and the passing nature of its recognition and acknowledgment. Moreover, within the exhibitions that stress a more permanent nature (cement or silver bands) there is a disjuncture between form and content (restful benches or beautifully inscribed silver) that is analogous in effect to the stress on traces (writing in light or on skin) and forensic evidence (human bones that the audience is invited to handle): in each the audience only comes to piece together a story of violence slowly and through close investigation, and the disorientation of the contradictions in form and content (a place of rest) or the fleeting nature of the writing (in light or on skin) or the piecemeal separation of decontextualized and fragmented body parts (images of skin, bones) make this process of narrative reconstruction laborious and jarring. Each mode or combination of modes (the LED and the bones were part of the same installation, for example) attempt to increase audience awareness and engagement; the narrative requires the piecing together of parts of the story, invites active involvement, and the materials used in the exhibits (rapid light, handling of bones or of ink-blood in a magazine, placing oneself on a bench and only slowly recognizing what is there inscribed) reinforce this active, participatory engagement. The materials are familiar and banal, and even the bones are rendered mundane through the invitation of touch and made somehow pretty or feminized through the delicate silver bands (suggestive of bracelets or animal identification bands for scientific tracking but also evocative of shackles and forced confinement).

In Lustmord these mundane materials do not contradict but, rather, emphasize the extreme violence of the acts described. Similar to the contradiction of the stylistic simplicity of the aphoristic statements used to describe acts of torture, rape, and murder, the mundane materials render the violence clinical, even ordinary—and it is made all the more horrific by this. Like Lane's uncanny domestic interiors, the emphasis is on a familiarizing of what is perceived as unfamiliar, and the shock of this recontextualization, the radical desublimation of violence, and of sexual violence in particular, provides the basis for the power of the piece. In Skin of the Teeth and Lustmord violence is both shocking and banal, particular and general, and, while both make reference to real acts of violence against specific women or groups of women, this connection to actual violence is made non-specific and inclusive through an attention to the residue and traces of violent acts. Using discrete details of violent acts and repeating and recontextualizing them, these works suggest the range, breadth, and ubiquity of violence against women, while recognizing the representational limitations and complexities of depicting explicit physical violence; although connected to scenes of actual violence, neither work is limited to a particular incident of violent death, and, through its material forms, each suggests the problematic visibility of violence. Violence is not shown in action, only in its effects, and this is precisely the point: the viewer is not given a clear narrative of punishment or resolution based in character motivation and is not shown the spectacle of rape, torture, or beating. We are not subjected to the viewing of the battered female body in corporeal form but instead are given a fragmented and partial access to violence as an experience, as an act with after-effects and lasting traces. Violence does not punctuate a narrative trajectory or offer a shock effect but lingers with the spectator as trace experience and haunting presence. The recognition of violence in each work is a slow process that implicates and involves the viewer and contradicts any notion that to show an act of violence or to depict a battered, raped, or tortured female body is to fully reveal or communicate the nature, effects, impact, and traumatic implications of violence against women. Violence is revealed not as a known entity but as a persistent stain and lasting residue of brutal destruction and dissolution.

In the disturbing but muted traces of works like Bloody Wallpaper or Lustmord we recognize the banality, domesticity, and quotidian aspects of the forms of violence addressed, and through this we come to see the pervasive and repetitious nature of violence against women: violence against women is not something that happens only in war, only in Bosnia, or only in New York homes, and it is not something that occurs within a clear-cut narrative of disclosure and punishment. Many acts of domestic violence and rape are not reported or, once reported, are not recognized as violence at all. Lustmord and Bloody Wallpaper echo this cultural invisibility of violence against women by rendering the brutality and death as something that is only slowly recognized: Lane's and Holzer's works do not offer a narrative of violent events (there is no cause-and-effect chain, no lead-up, motivation, or explanation) nor do they place acts of violence against women as unique or exceptional occurrences. The violence is presented as already there, as having occurred, and the viewer is invited to piece together the ramifications and implications of these traces of a pervasive and ever-present violence against women. In this emphasis on a present haunted by traces of past events but not explained by them, these works engage the viewer in a process of detection and discovery that will only ever be incomplete, partial, and conjectural. The viewer is offered pieces, the clues and residues of stories of violence that metonymically stand in for the many other stories of violence that could have been told: the photograph of the bloody walls of a New York crime scene used by Abigail Lane could have easily been another photograph of another domestic murder, and the story of systematic rape and death in Lustmord is not limited to wartime or to Bosnia. In both Bloody Wallpaper and Lustmord repetition (of the handprint in Bloody Wallpaper, of the aphorisms in Lustmord) suggests recurring or reiterated scenes of violence against women. Thus, while the specificity of the violence is significant in Lustmord, its repetitions and its reincarnation as different modes of exhibition invite the spectator to extend the issues it raises to include all acts of violence against women.

In both Lane and Holzer it is the foregrounding of the spectator's role as investigative witness that indicates the importance of recognizing violence against women, even if only in the form of partial and unsettled understanding: in these works the scene of the crime is not contained and does not end in forensic discovery and disclosure but in the implied impossibility of closure. The spectator becomes a witness to violence but only in the partial and temporally staggered form of a forensic investigation; we are curious and attempt "to speculatively piece together histories that remain largely invisible to the eye" (Rugoff 1997, 62). However, in the end it is not absolute disclosure or a harmonious narrative that is the result but a recognition that there is no full knowledge of the kinds of violence experienced by women whether in times of peace or times of war. In each, the trace or the clue transcends its unique evidentiary status (as proof of *this* event) and becomes instead part of a collection of evidence that is never fully absorbed into any single, unambiguous narrative of cause and effect. Evidence thus offers the viewer an understanding and awareness that does not stop at aesthetic absorption or acceptance but forces him or her to recognize that violence against women is present even in its apparent absence and that it can be found in banal details of the home or in the disappearing traces of transparent words written in light.

Notes

1 Žižek (1991, 53) notes the importance of this uncanny stain in detective fiction, where the central is "a detail that *in itself* is usually quite insignificant…but which nonetheless *with regard to its structural position* denatures the scene of the crime and produces a quasi-Brechtian effect of estrangement—like the alteration of a small detail in a well-known picture that all of a sudden renders the while picture strange and uncanny."

2 Lane explains the dog's presence as follows: "When I first made wallpaper, I envisioned using a dog of some sort to go with it. Because pets, especially dogs, are man's best friends. They're 'domestic wild,' like a kind of domestic beast. In that way I thought it related to the photographic image for the wallpaper, because by taking a photograph of something you automatically make it actionless" (quoted in Flood 1995, 61).

3 As witnesses, protectors, companions, and elevated beings, the animals in Lane's installation and photograph pieces are ambiguously powerful and indicative of a kind of stability and permanence not conferred onto Lane's human figures. Unlike the fleeting imprints of shoes or bottoms, the animal figures are stuffed, cast in concrete, still, and solidly placed. The humans in their domestic settings thus become analogous to the pedagogical and scientific displays of the museum. The humans, not the animals, are in the foreground and are subject to the classificatory and disciplinary regimes of knowledge: the Still Lives series can in this way be seen as showing us humans in their natural habitat, a viewpoint that is reinforced by the generic "he" and "she"s of the titles (pronouns which could also be applied to the animal subjects of the photographs). The humans may not be stuffed or cast in concrete but they are frozen in the photographic moment and thus can be seen to occupy the same contradictory position between life and death, real and replica, as the diorama inhabitants.

4 In her article "'I HAVE THE BLOOD JELLY': Sexual Violence, the Media and Jenny Holzer's 'Lustmord,'" Sabine Sielke (1996) notes the relation of the work to media treatment of the war in Bosnia and is critical of the American reception of the work, which tended to downplay the specificity of the violence addressed in the work.

Women and Murder in the
Televirtuality Film

JACK BOOZER

[8]

Communication media dominate contemporary American life and have increasingly been recognized as constituting the most central issue in Western thought and culture. The power and influence of this media world have also been reflected in cinema, including an entire cycle of Hollywood products released between 1995 and 2000, which I have dubbed the "televirtuality film" (Boozer 2002). In the course of this discussion, I provide the derivation and meaning of this term and briefly apply it to the initial televirtual cycle, which includes *To Die For, Wag the Dog, Strange Days, The Matrix, Edtv, Pleasantville, The Truman Show*, and *Nurse Betty*. The sheer number and quality of these eight original movies within a brief six-year period shows an elevated popular awareness of the media's impact. But my emphasis in this discussion is on how the condition of televirtuality, as it is reflected in these films, appears to alter traditional notions of basic identity and gender construction, particularly for women, and specifically in the two films that feature female protagonists. The leading women in *To Die For* and *Nurse Betty* find themselves in troubling engagements with television and the televirtual, much as do the male protagonists in the six other films in this group. But the women in these two films attempt to use rather than to challenge its power over them.

Before proceeding to elaborate upon these two films, it is necessary to define televirtuality as it relates to basic identity construction. Given today's media-saturated environment, several theorists have called for a reconceptualization of the individual subject position. In Michel Foucault's discursive approach, individual identity is not potentially rooted in some universalist moral core à la Plato; instead, it remains open-ended but culturally contingent (Rorty 1992, 332). Social theorist Paul du Gay observes, more specifically, how the radical increase in socialization by commercial media spawns an entirely outwardly directed and decentred position that mocks any notion of personal autonomy. For Du Gay (1997, 289), contemporary subjectivity is "not an essentialist but a strategic and positioned one," an identity increasingly formed "extrinsically" by the sovereignty of media influences. Reflexive identity awareness was obviously increased in modernity through the representational tools of photography, radio, motion picture, and, eventually, television. But mechanical and electronic representation also placed the proverbial machine in the garden and living room, and the electronic image into the subconscious. In other words, the innocent notion of identity residing in the natural sensory body has been compromised by the invasive power of media images: direct sensory interaction gives way to the audio-visually extended body of electronic data immersion.

This technologically extended being no longer has the luxury of relying upon natural sensation and testing mechanisms within a complete personal body presence but, rather, must constantly assess its existence in relation to the many media forms in which it appears to be reflected. The newly sign-conscious self experiences life mainly in relation to electronic communication systems, which have their own political economic structure and tendencies. While these systems can expand an individual's informational horizon, they can also distract from and reduce opportunities for private processing, or for direct interpersonal encounters that are physically grounded in real space and time. All of this works against the kind of personal, self-motivated testing that might lend itself to the development of self-reliance in a sexed body. How is an independent, much less autonomous, self to be realized against the increasing thrall of electronic communications that constantly push products, people, infotainment, attitudes, and world views—a veritable deluge of data in both real time and cyberspace time?

Douglas Kellner's (1995, 35) *Media Culture: Cultural Studies, Identity, and Politics between the Modern and Postmodern* asserts that electronic media have fully colonized culture and that television is at the forefront of this colonization has become an intimate part of everyday life. It stands ready to feed our awareness at any moment of the day or night, and one of its largest audiences is the young. From the earliest stages of growth, a child's interpersonal intimacy is now significantly influenced by televisual systems and their constant direct and indirect demands for attention (Beatty 2002). In terms of immediacy and breadth of audience delivery, sheer volume of infotainment content, and direct political economic power through paid and unpaid promotions, television continues to hold its place as the most omnipresent, comprehensive, and hence powerful cultural tool ever created. Unlike the haphazard reading of print and the occasional patronage of theatrical motion pictures, both of which now constitute a secondary level of cultural experience, the ubiquitous and ceaseless presence of television and the computer-expanded televisual makes it the new world's primary totem and arbiter of social reality. Through its pervasive mediation of all aspects of present life, and increasingly of the past and the future, it has become the predominant consciousness and memory of public and private events. This has led to the development of the label "televisuality" (Caldwell 1995).

This term emphasizes television, however, without fully taking into account the effects of what communication systems in general have become through digital technology. This technology has linked the many forms of contemporary media and seamlessly joined digital representations of the real with hybrid and imagined images that have no direct relation to the real. Digital picture origination and manipulation have entirely altered photographic reproduction and established a flexibility in image-making that requires no precursor in the real world. And coupled with television's computer extensions into advanced, three-dimensional simulational imaging and experience, the sense of a televisual virtuality must also now be included in the nomenclature. As I have suggested, "The public reliance on reality that is joined in the 1990s by rapidly increasing attention to Internet/Web access and virtual effects [including video games] has created convergent systems of interactivity that have the further potential of complete simulational experience or 'virtuality'" (Boozer 2002, 200). A preferred term that preserves both the sense of televisuality and virtuality, therefore, would be "televirtuality."

Televirtuality presumes a true reflection of all reality even as it creates, selects, frames, edits, comments upon, and thus changes it. Televirtuality is also the entire image-driven landscape caught in a continuous circulation of new and recirculated and recombined images that now exist as a galaxy of signifiers detached from their "signifieds" (or reference base). This is the central characteristic of the postrepresentational, postalienation regime of "hypermedia" noted by postmodernists such as Jean Baudrillard (1983, 4), who describes its simulational status and affects:

> The age of simulation thus begins with a liquidation of all referentials....It is rather a question of substituting signs of the real for the real itself, that is, an operation to deter every real process by its operational double, a metastable, programmatic, perfect descriptive machine which provides all the signs of the real and short-circuits all its vicissitudes.

Baudrillard's definition is part of his larger metatheory, which asserts not only a technical, instrumentalist distancing from the real but also an active realignment of it. This "hyperreality," that results from "hypermediation," describes an omnipresent media condition fully determined by the modes of its sponsorship, production, and distribution.

A key aspect of this image world is certainly its promotional sponsorship, which seeks to accentuate audience fantasies of self-empowerment precisely where the individual is less and less in a position to imagine or to act in a self-determined way. Despite the appearance of an expanded personal authority via self-extensions through media, as Stephen Frosh (1987) has pointed out, a new kind of residual anxiety about locating the self in the welter of potent images arises. This existential dilemma is also leveraged by the individual's recognition of the increasing necessity for establishing the self in hypermedia terms. Because televirtuality implies a comprehensive reification of and reliance upon simulational images, its affect shifts not only the centre of experience but also the centre of desire from the personal body to an extrinsic domain. This shift leapfrogs immediate spacial experience in a constant vacuation of the real that further blurs the line between reality and simulated "reality." For Baudrillard, the hyperreality of media represents a condition in which the very "messages of the unconscious have been short-circuited," right along with cognitive processes relative to the symbolic and the imaginary.[1] This new, overall alignment of the self that is imposed by the hyperreal or televirtual may be seen, furthermore, to be an abiding assumption of all of the films in the cycle discussed here.

Viewed from a gender perspective, *Wag the Dog, Strange Days, The Matrix, The Truman Show,* and *Edtv* all feature adult male leads and a masculine orientation. They contain dilemmas of identity directly related to violent conflicts over contested territories that are both real and virtual. Hence, they largely follow the conventions of male drama and action cinema. These new versions of turf wars, however, are typically fought for the control and/or direction of entire simulational systems. The masculine televirtuality films thus assume that system alienation and resistance are still possible for the action hero. The women protagonists—Suzanne Stone (Nicole Kidman) in *To Die For* (1995), and Betty Sizemore (Renee Zellweger) in *Nurse Betty*—are challenged by the same prevailing systems, although their arena of confrontation is largely domestic and career oriented rather than systemic. (This is in keeping with the long and predominant tradition of women's leading roles in film, which have tended to focus on personalized perspectives that permit a fuller investigation of psychological and emotional development.) The characters Suzanne and Betty are enthralled from the outset by the world of television, and they strive literally to attach themselves to its seductive reality. One might inquire, therefore, whether their individual experience with the televirtual further reinforces women's traditional roles or whether it essentially alters their developmental self-perception and public positioning as women.

Director Gus Van Sant's *To Die For* was adapted for the screen by Buck Henry from a book-length story by Joyce Maynard, which is loosely based on a highly publicized murder in the New Hampshire town of Derry (called Little Hope in the film). The entire structure and documentary-like conception of the film, much like the book, is a reflection not simply on a fictionalized recreation of the primary character (Suzanne in the film version) but on her overwhelming experience of the televirtual.[2] The film's opening credits appear over a winter montage of journalists running through a snow-covered graveyard to reach a funeral, at which an attractive young woman appears to be the object of their frantic attention. Shown too in this flurry of images, but not fully comprehensible, are flashes of lurid press headlines referring to sex and death, and a shot of a frozen lake overshadowed by the sound of a scream. This is quickly followed by the brief view of a young man lying face up in a small pool of blood. Henceforth, the story predominantly unfolds either through apparent interviews with the primary characters, some of whom directly address the camera, or through dramatic representations of the events to which they refer. The film audience remains in the position of observing a journalistically edited viewpoint that, notably, is not occupied by any one particular character. In the impersonality of this enunciating position—which is invasively directive but remains disembodied and only half-conscious—is suggested the omniscient force of televirtuality.

To Die For has the appearance of a murder exposé in which certain peripheral characters comment on the events portrayed, although the constant self-consciousness about the use and effects of television reverberates onto another level of meaning. For example, the parents of the two main characters offer their views about their children on a television talk program called *The Laura Show* (the host is never shown or heard), which bears an uncertain time frame in relation to the events discussed. In addition to the many other interviews and dramatic segments that are re-presented in fragments and loosely specified times, the film continues to call attention to a rather arbitrary arrangement of different narrative elements that suggest the random collation that passes for media evidence. Near the film's conclusion, an interview scene with a young female character is literally broken up into more and ever smaller frames until someone calls "cut" and a slate handler briefly appears in the multiple images. This closing reminder of the frequent allusions to the constructed nature of the text irrefutably points beyond all the issues of story content to a comprehensively reflexive comment on the mediating process. The spectator is invited to become active in piecing together the collage of images in this version of a woman's life. The viewer's act of following the collection of these scenes into a larger narrative pattern not only imitates what Suzanne has done in her life but also recreates the way media participants come to formulate their own little parts in this ubiquitous domain.

The main storyline follows the grasping quest of the prim young Suzanne, who aspires above all things to be a star news reader. Her initial motivation towards performance results from early encouragement from her father, who is shown with her when she was about three years old in a black-and-white home movie. Later, following a junior college education, she has already come to the conclusion that "You're not anyone in America unless you're on TV. On TV is where we learn who we really are." This is more than a concept for Suzanne: she has built her entire identity around her passion for her career, which might appear to suggest a modern woman's independence and self-determination. She consistently presents herself in business clothes and speaks in the manner of a journalist reading a script. She takes a part-time position as a helper on a local community-access cable show and then, by sheer force of determination, moves up to hosting a low-tech, single-camera weather report. Her new boss laughs at her "gang-busters" over-seriousness, but he eventually yields to her willfulness, as do other men whom she targets as avenues to her success. The strength of Suzanne's position in the narrative owes partly to the fact that she is right about the social power of television, if not about the way individuals can make it serve their own agendas.

Early on, Suzanne marries the conventionally dull young Larry Martello (Matt Dillon) against the better judgment of his perceptive sister Janice (Illeana Douglas). Janice doubts Suzanne's sincerity and doesn't see how she fits with their family or Larry's position in his father's successful Italian restaurant. More important to Suzanne than Larry's financial security, however, is the fact that he is at first impressed by her career ambition. Suzanne takes this as carte blanche. For their honeymoon, she surreptitiously chooses a Florida city that is hosting a journalism conference, to which she constantly sneaks off while Larry is out fishing. Her pandering to the world of television includes having sex with the news personality who gives a speech at the conference, although their sexual escapade is suggested rather than shown. Suzanne also hosts a gourmet dinner for her and Larry's parents, which she falsely claims to consist of her own creations. For his part, Larry remains lovestruck, providing Suzanne with both a car and a puppy. Eventually, however, he insists that Suzanne corral her unrealistic dreams so that they can start a family. At the moment he speaks, he is framed from her viewpoint in a telescoped iris shot, complete with foreboding music that belies her indifferent facial expression. From that instant, Larry and his patriarchal family image becomes, in her mind, a decisive obstacle to her desire to become a celebrity.

Because Suzanne is so hyperbolic in her conviction that personal growth and success lie in the power of merely presenting her smiling face on television, she appears at the outset to be a hollow performer. To advance her status at the community access station, for example, she repeats a line delivered by the spokesperson at the convention to her boss: "TV joins together the global community, and the TV journalist is the messenger who brings the world into our homes, and our homes into the world." Closer to Suzanne's own attitude is her learned directive for evaluating personal experience: "What's the point of doing anything worthwhile if nobody is watching? As people are watching, it makes you a better person." Suzanne's religious devotion to the benefits of television, however, is hard for others to take in one so narrowly self-serving.

This explains why she ends up with gullible, underprivileged students when she tries to recruit at the local high school for help with her little TV documentary. She calls her project "Teens Speak Out," but she quickly turns her young helpers into followers of her own career crusade. She offers them calculated personal attention and assurances of rewards. The overweight Lydia (Alison Folland) is told she will become her media assistant as Suzanne climbs to TV fame. And Russell (Casey Affleck), the sexually frustrated misogynist, is promised money if he will help his buddy Jimmy. Suzanne devotes most of her considerable energy to the complete sexual and emotional seduction of the inarticulate Jimmy (Joaquin Phoenix). She manipulates him through sexual intercourse and lies about how Larry abuses her and will never let her go. Her techniques of seduction are hardly original, but the fifteen-year-old Jimmy is mesmerized by the attentions of this intended TV star of twenty-five. He gets swept up into the role she assigns to him as her beloved rescuer and future mate.

Hence, her real power with these youngsters and with her boss and her husband is exhibited less through any journalistic skill, much less personal authenticity, than through her performative skills in masquerade, her sheer ability to project an image—something that she has learned from her father and the televisual environment.

Suzanne imbibed at an early age the troubling conviction of idealism, which takes the literal form of honouring TV as her personal platform of celebrity. Television has made her not only into a religious convert to its power but also into a priestess of its validity. In her frantic career longing, she has made herself into the kind of talking doll she believes is required for TV, even as she misses the automaton quality in the image she projects to others. Her excessive self-centredness results in a lack of separation between her TV performances and her everyday self. She tries to be "on" all the time with or without the presence of a video camera. The well known traditional pressure on women to look and feel a certain way has been further exaggerated in the culture of image worship, and Suzanne signifies a very negative extreme of this. She has narcissistically devoted herself to become a TV icon, a position that she has misconstrued as comprising a complete life. Her devotion to self-image is such that she disregards inconvenient people and details, which make her gradual turn to homicidal intrigue an open book for the police. She fails to consider the way her lustful careerism creates an obvious motive in a still largely patriarchal and competitive economy.

While recognizing television's power, Suzanne's success drive is already misguided by her earlier media-trained egocentrism. This is highlighted in the one murder scene that the film does choose to exhibit. Jimmy's reluctant shooting of Larry Maretto is timed by Suzanne to correspond with her official absence from home. Van Sant sets this up through a series of cross-cuts between her live weather report, shown on her and Larry's living room TV, and the actual murder of Larry, which tales place in their home's adjacent foyer. Larry's murder is dramatically muted in wide shot, while the simultaneous TV presentation of Suzanne gains in significance. This imbalanced pairing of the televisual and a live event reflects her belief that being on TV will protect her since that will take precedence over anything not seen on TV. Suzanne views herself as an empowered spokesperson for television, but the life that she believes she is directing as a subject on TV soon turns her instead into its object.[3] As this story continues to reveal, televirtuality does not answer to individual desires except in so far as the individual acts according to its sign hegemony.

Suzanne exemplifies one who depends on the presence of cameras for self-realization. The need not only to attach herself to but also to be the image is a literalization of the desire stimulated in consumer advertising to find happiness through the product. Suzanne "Stone" incarnates the loss of self in the desire to become the publicly advocated image. This is not the result of a patriarchal ruse to objectify only women as performers but, rather, is a condition of televirtuality and the kind of exteriorized, contingent identity formation it creates for all. Suzanne's experience evidences the image identification process that is indigenous to televirtual culture. And this process does not offer personal fulfillment, except in image terms of exteriority and appearance; rather, it brings with it an insecurity that extends, in Suzanne's case, to the level of utter desperation. Her fundamental desire becomes a media dependency that demonstrates all the symptoms of addiction. It leads her to a state of disassociation that sets the stage for her manipulation of young people to bring about her homicidal plot. Since she feels that she is nothing without the confirming presence of TV cameras, anyone close to her who might enhance or block her access to them becomes an object or tool and, hence, deserving of how they are used.

This interpretation is reinforced by the events following Larry's death. The obvious trail of evidence left by Suzanne and her two male helpers certainly points to their legal conviction on charges related to the murder. But Larry's father, Joe Maretto (Dan Hedaya), seems unconvinced. Joe and what remains of his family watch as Suzanne claims to the television public that her husband was using cocaine supplied by the teenage boys who killed him. This drives Joe to destroy his TV with a baseball bat. When Suzanne proceeds, prior to her trial, to seek profit from the media for her story, Joe is finally driven to hire a killer of his own. This individual (David Cronenberg) poses as a media rep and has her meet him at a country lake, where she believes he will receive her self-produced, self-promotional videotape and make her a generous offer of TV work. But again her career self-absorption is such that she overlooks the details in one of her documentary videotapes, which is eventually seized by the police (and later picked up for TV broadcast). It shows her two boy groupies winking at her in the classroom in such a way as to further link them to her as the conspiratorial mastermind of Larry's death. This oversight hints again at the way Suzanne thinks of TV in relation to private behaviour. Like her miniskirted dance in front of her car headlights to seduce Jimmie, she wants him to believe that their performances of sex and violent conspiracy was part of the same thing—a private arrangement that will remain secret because it took place off-screen. As the film makes clear for all the characters, however, there is no free space to construct a private self outside televirtuality.[4] It has already short-circuited Suzanne's

resources for personal independence, along with any hope for a holistic gender identity.

Baudrillard (1988, 82–83) notes, in *The Ecstacy of Communication*, how
we can "no longer reconcile things with their essence...because they have
mocked and surpassed their own definition. They have become more social
than the social (the masses)...more real than the real (simulation), more
beautiful than the beautiful (fashion)." The move to a hypermediated state
of simulation, to the spectatorial consumerism of televirtuality, objectifies
the individual to the point that "the object [the sheer flood of data] has become
the subject's mode of disappearance" (97). This condition of self loss obviously
applies to both genders. But the disconnection from the sensory body and
from potentially self-confirming personal experience has additional consequences for women. The force that turns the nurturing and/or life-giving
aspect of womanhood into an objectified and eroticized taker of life in *To
Die For* is particularly egregious. The inference here is that televirtuality has
overwhelmed the intimate possibilities of subjective interpersonal support,
including presumably child care, and created instead, among other things, an
inverted maternal figure who sends children out to kill rather than to grow and
prosper.

Suzanne may not be aware of the cinematic image of woman as killer,
which has long been manifested in the figure of the femme fatale, but its history is instructive (Boozer, 2002). Suzanne's behaviour echoes that of Barbara
Stanwyck's Phyllis in *Double Indemnity* (1944) and of Lana Turner's Cora in
The Postman Always Rings Twice (1946), who marry for financial security and
then conspire through sexual involvement with another male to murder their
husbands out of a desire for social advancement. Suzanne's methods thus
appear to be a throwback to more regressive times of women's second-class
status in the 1940s. What is new here is the careerism and her belief that she
can control the image system. This is a bridge to the femmes fatales of 1990s
cinema, such as Briggit (Linda Fiorentino) in *The Last Seduction* (1994) and
Meredith (Demi Moore) in *Disclosure* (1994), who largely forego the help of
male co-conspirators and actively manipulate communication and legal systems. Their cynical application of televirtual tools (including online data
scams and virtual reality file thefts) also demonstrate more advanced technological skills and mental sophistication than is shown by Suzanne, whose
world is the 1970s. As highly promotional and sexualized figures of careerist
crime, Briggit and Meredith imply an increased indifference to gender norms,
except where convenient. In contrast to these two aggressive executive types,
To Die For's Suzanne has limited financial resources and is transparent in her

homicidal tactics. Her re-enactment of the classic femme fatale murder formula is hence anachronistic.

Following Joyce Maynard's book, Suzanne never makes it to trial, let alone
to the sale of her story or herself to big media. She never gets beyond the
frozen country lake that serves as the site of her notably unseen demise. Rather
than an eroticized death scene so common to films anxious to play up the
revenge on the socially transgressive femme fatale, the frame simply holds on
an empty ice-covered expanse in the late afternoon light. The film thus mit-
igates the sacrificial punishment of the over-ambitious career woman, which
has been used in the past to shore up masculinity and to reconfirm the patriarchal family. Suzanne's devotion to TV as a personal tool is clearly naive and
too obvious to be the point of the film's overall satiric irony. Even young Lydia
recognizes at last that TV cannot "make one better" if almost everyone is spending so much time watching it.

It is left to Suzanne's primary adversary, Joe Maretto, to reveal the film's
ultimate irony. When the phone call for Joe, who is waiting for it at his restaurant, comes in from the Italian-speaking killer of Suzanne, Joe shares a knowing glance with his unnamed wife. She looks up with a pleased expression as
she personally serves the table of the local detectives who have already gathered the evidence for the trial against Suzanne. This brief scene hints that
there will likely be no conclusive investigation of Suzanne's death. However
deserving Suzanne might be of Mr. Maretto's vengeance, his final decision to
take the law into his own hands has a specific cause: he mistrusts the trial
process under heavy media scrutiny and assumes, probably correctly, that
Suzanne will somehow survive her legal punishment and realize a media profit
from his son's bloodied name. Joe's ultimate motivation for retaliation is hence
lodged in a televirtual assumption.

As Joe previously demonstrated in his interview appearance on *The Laura
Show*, which it is now apparent was made after Suzanne's death, he is even
more personally invested in a public image than is she. Joe has learned to play
by the public and private rules of televirtuality, which require of him and his
business an awareness of selective sponsorship and audience targeting, as well
as of the "program" displayed. Suzanne has sought merely to give her life significance by becoming a TV celebrity while never fully grasping the media's
comprehensive power. Joe, on the other hand, has already perfected televirtual consciousness since his privileged social status allows him to hide
behind its prevailing ideology of law and consumer capitalism. Ironically, he
goes so far as to quote *The Godfather* in his TV interview. He means to show
his gracious Italian acceptance of the mythic American "melting pot" through

his son's marital choice of the Anglo-Saxon Suzanne. So long as the facade of business, the patriarchal family, and legal responsibility is sustained in simulational terms, then discreet forms of actual murder can be overlooked.

There is a tradition in satirical cinema of a gullible public accepting capital murder and useless wars. What is new in *To Die For* is the constant reminder of the artificiality of the televirtual process, even as it tends to mask its effects of personal displacement, consumer fetishism, and violence. The film's closing image suggests the ethical problematic in televirtuality. In this shot, Larry's sister Janice skates over the frozen surface of the lake where Suzanne is shown entombed behind nature's own translucent screen of ice. The televirtual world she would force to serve her has killed her instead. Suzanne's fate points to a hypermediated world's capacity not only to seduce but also to entrap her with its assurances of extrinsic fulfillment. This is revealed through the brutal victory of the older (mafia-connected) business and family man (Joe) over the young careerist upstart and confused murderer (Suzanne). Joe's conspiracy against Suzanne presents a greater social threat than was ever presented by Suzanne because his probable freedom will result from an institutional form of repression that hides the televirtual motivation that finally drives him. Hence, televirtuality's seductive spectacles and overlaid conventionalism become sedatives that serve the political economic regime that perpetuates it.

Televirtuality manifests itself as a comprehensive enactment of the real world. This hyperreal matrix that presupposes reflective truth, however, reflects most the interests of its sponsors, who seek the attention and resources of its mass audience. And it is a male-dominant business and political sponsorship that leads the controlling interests of vertical hypermedia. Joe Maretto is a lowly figure here and hardly a traditional villain, but he is associated with the conservative values of corporate greed and political power that thrive in and drive the commercial world of the televirtual. Televirtuality is invested in politicized commerce and media dependency, where real abuses involving class, gender, race/ethnicity, and even war are perpetually moderated through sponsors, including governments (*Wag the Dog*), who edit or promote in ways that reinforce the engines of simulation.

The cultural interrogation of televirtuality in *To Die For* also has similarities with the dark, satirical situation comedy *Nurse Betty* (2000), although the focus of the latter film is on one of televirtuality's innocent victims, Betty "Sizemore." Written by John C. Richards and James Flamberg, this Neil LaBute–directed project traces Betty's fate as a married Kansas diner waitress who loses the ability to distinguish her real world from the one that she has avidly followed on TV. Her loss of reality discrimination results from witnessing, while at home, the gruesome murder of her drug-dealing and two-timing husband Del (Aaron Eckart). This horror creates a clinical condition identified later as "post-traumatic disassociation." Because Betty is simultaneously watching a video of her beloved hospital soap opera star on *A Reason to Love* at the time of Del's demise, in her mind she somehow transmutes the TV actor into a real doctor, whom she suddenly wants to pursue, marry, and work beside as a nurse. She makes a car trip from Kansas in a dream state that is somewhat like Dorothy's in *The Wizard of Oz*. Betty's destination is the Oz of Los Angeles, and her wizard is the Dr. Ravell shown on daytime TV. Her sudden slide into an oblivious televirtuality then, while clearly motivated by traumatic shock, also suggests TV's function as a form of fairy tale escape from that which is painful or monotonous. The bleakness of her life with Del and her dead-end job at the diner are established at the beginning. Betty's disassociative condition, therefore, becomes a perfect metaphor for one form of televirtual experience. It can offer an exciting substitution—the jouissance of hypermedia action and fantasy—that appears to elevate the real while moving the individual further from it, as a narcotic drug might do.

Betty's story, more fully than Suzanne's, thus demonstrates women's desperate longing but continued victimization in televirtuality, which is initiated here through a TV fantasy. With a full-size cardboard cutout of her soap opera star folded in the trunk of one of her now-dead husband's better cars, and with no knowledge of the several kilos of cocaine Del has also hidden there, she suddenly drives off to find her dream doctor. At a fundraiser in Los Angeles she makes a direct romantic pitch to the man she recognizes as Dr. Ravell. The real George McCord (Greg Kinnear) is charmed by her ability to continue to see and talk to him in the character of the doctor, as if she were also an actor on the daytime soap. Meanwhile, in the parallel story structure established throughout the film, Del's killer Charlie (Morgan Freeman) and his son Wesley (Chris Rock) have not succeeded in locating the cocaine and suspect that Betty has made off with it. They guess that she is headed to her family home in Oklahoma and travel there in pursuit of her.

Charlie learns a little from Betty's folks about her innocence and goodness, and he becomes quickly enamoured of his idea of her identity and of her photograph, which he places in full view on his car's dashboard. Charlie's photo of Betty, like her big cardboard cutout, connects them in their mutual practice of visual idealization. These images also serve as reminders of the distance between the media artefact and the associations that spectators may project onto them. Charlie, for example, plans after this one last job to retire from his enforcement role in the illegal drug business, which apparently doesn't fit his personal inclination towards beautiful sunsets and pure and innocent people. Charlie is so drawn by his enlarged fantasy of Betty's goodness that he wants, against Wesley's better judgment, to see and talk to her about what she represents for him. This assassin's romantic longing is as off-kilter as is Betty's attachment to the TV doctor, and both of these twisted desires confirm the power of televirtual suggestion.

In Los Angeles, Betty has continued to live in her disoriented state, despite the efforts of her Latino housemate Rosa and of the actor George to bring her out of it. George partly misreads her intentions and believes she's potentially a great actor who wants to perform on the soap opposite him. When he introduces her on the set of *A Reason to Love* and gives her test lines to act out, Betty's disassociative condition suddenly falls away and she runs off in a state of shock. At this juncture George and Betty have already realized a mutual attraction, albeit within the context of their misunderstandings. Meanwhile, Charlie and Wesley invade Rosa and Betty's house and hold them hostage, along with Betty's sheriff and journalist friends from Kansas. A shootout ensues that leaves Wesley dead and Charlie wounded.

Charlie has had no intention of killing Betty, nor does he want to give the police the satisfaction of shooting or capturing him, which would ruin his image. Instead, he takes control in the only way he deems possible: he steps into a closet and shoots himself. Betty's goodness is shown to be dangerous in its naiveté, and she appears incapable of rescuing others. *Nurse Betty* thus exemplifies the distortions and unpredictability of televirtual influences: romantic longing spins quickly beyond the control of even the most well-meaning individual. Ironically, the many forms of obsession that surround Betty—including her husband's philandering, dope dealing, and gruesome death—seem closer to "normative" televirtual behavior than do Betty's goodness and Charlie's longing for redemption. The latter impulses, in fact, manage to seem out of touch and even pathological. The basic instincts of all of these characters get distorted in the hypermedia world that constantly displaces their essential reality testing with the formulations of commercial media experience. Not only are personal growth impulses superseded in the systems of symbolic representation but the entire process of personal identity construction is turned inside out.

Following the genre conventions of comedic satire, Betty is eventually forced to give up her psychotraumatic fantasy just as the older Charlie finally puts a stop to the degraded reality he has chosen. The satire ends hopefully for the kind-hearted and now more clear-eyed Betty, although her survival within televirtuality has been mainly a matter of sheer luck. In the end, she is hired as an actor on *A Reason to Love* because her final experience with Del's killers has attracted news publicity for the show and made her into a curious celebrity. The next scenario has her seated in a diner with George as they try to sort out their confused feelings for one another. This scene is suddenly modulated into a video version of the soap opera—an almost mimetic recreation of the actual event. The televirtual again exploits what little remains of personal reality. Betty's implausible road to career fulfillment through television suggests the absurdity of its easy promises and solutions.

Hence, the career desires and identities of Suzanne and Betty are literally defined and determined by the televirtual, as are their brushes with death. All of this suggests an extension rather than an abatement of female problems in televirtuality, which consistently cuts across history and meanings with newly sponsored opinions and styles of the moment but continues to play on easy stereotypes and spectacles of violence as part of its shorthand. Suzanne and Betty find themselves drawn towards televisual idealizations, which determine their formulations of both their self-image and their goals. That they are both lower middle-class provincial women also suggests a class stereotype regarding TV's most gullible audience, although televirtuality should be recognized as a condition in which class can be manipulated as an image force as readily as can gender. In any case, the absence of self-determination and autonomy in these two characters causes them to react to their world exactly in the objectifying way they are treated—that is, as having validity only in their reflected images. For women who have already experienced a long history of oppression and objectification, televirtual experience offers at best an increased visibility and even mobility. What it does not offer is an increased self-realization. It does not alter essential class or gender attitudes, which remain in the service of an appearance-oriented consumerism. Instead, the all-pervasive world of the simulacra offers to women a continued distraction from and discouragement of a personally developed self-confidence and purpose. Suzanne and Betty appear already doomed as they fall back into extreme forms of regressive behaviour and either kill or are surrounded by violence. Since women have historically not been the primary instigators of violent confrontationalism, this trend in televirtuality can hardly be read as a positive sign.

The overinvestment in the spectacles of sponsored signification that characterizes televirtuality clearly undermines personal independence and nurturing tendencies, which Western culture has traditionally looked to women to ensure. This is also reinforced by the oppositional character pairings of both Suzanne and Joe (who become killers) and Nurse Betty and Charlie (who are perversely idealistic). The desperate attempts by Suzanne and Betty at personal confirmation through television-related dreams follows directly from their loss of interior rootedness. Thus, in the cinema of televirtuality, where women now appear almost as likely to be instigators as victims of violence, the potential for self-understanding, much less systemic resistance, seems remote. Nor is the image of woman as seducer/murderer or as romance addict any longer to be read simply as a patriarchal excuse for masculine domination. Under televirtuality, the sex wars become merely another tool in the larger media co-optation of personal and sexual autonomy. Across the landscape of hypermediation, therefore, which flattens gender difference even as it reinforces traditional stereotypes and performative sexuality, the already twisted nurturing tendencies of women appear increasingly to be tied to patterns of exteriorization, objectification, and escapist fantasy. Suzanne and Betty's utter desperation, which either invokes or unintentionally contributes to violence in the televirtual film cycle, therefore, becomes a dire warning of what is being lost in the current regime of displacement.

Notes

1 Baudrillard (1998, 184) expresses this as an essential new understanding: "To the famous categories of the real, the symbolic and the imaginary, it is going to be necessary to add the hyperreal, which captures and obstructs the functioning of the three orders."

2 While Joyce Maynard (1992) explains in the Author's Note in her book that she has used the real story of the highly publicized murder "in a novelistic way" to show how our thoughts "are created and manipulated by television, movies, popular music and magazines," she doesn't explain her main diversion from the real story, in which the murderer is convicted and sent to prison. The fictional name Suzanne Stone is no less ironic than is the name of the actual person, Pamela Smart, particularly given the transparent nature of her actual plot with fifteen-year-old boys.

3 Baudrillard carefully opposes the passions of the subject with those of the Object, which are "indifferent" and "inert." For the Object, "the ironic passions of cunning, silence, conformity, and willing servitude are opposed to passions of liberty, desire, transgression, the passions of the subject" (Baudrillard, 1988, 93).

4 See, for example, Andrew Wernick (1991, 195): "Once we are communicating at all, and especially in public, and therefore in a medium which is promotional through and through, there is no going outside promotional discourse."

"I'm in There! I'm One of the
Women in That Picture!"

MARGOT LEIGH BUTLER[1]

[**9**]

I'll bet you've pictures of yourself, maybe images of yourself from throughout your life, photos lying loose in a box or pressed behind plastic sheets in
spiral-bound albums. What if you received an invitation to donate one of
your photos to an exhibition in honour of women who'd been murdered in
your area, an invitation to stand in and be pictured with one of their names?
Imagine rifling through your photos, seeing yourself as you've been photographed while imagining yourself in a harrowing narrative in which you've
been murdered. Susan Orlofsky, a teacher who donated her photograph for
this exhibition, said:

> It was kind of a scary thing to realize, OK, if I give them a photo, what that
> means, because I thought, well I could be one of these dead people as well. But
> I decided that it would be an honour to put my photo in their show, so I got my
> high school graduation photo, pretty dated and I look a little different cause it
> was quite a few years ago, but that's how I was hung in the show.[2]

The exhibition was called NHI—No Humans Involved, and it was one part of
a public art project in San Diego, California, in 1992. Five artists—Deborah
Small, Elizabeth Sisco, Carla Kirkwood, Scott Kessler, and Louis Hock—produced this work to address the unsolved, and largely uninvestigated, sexual

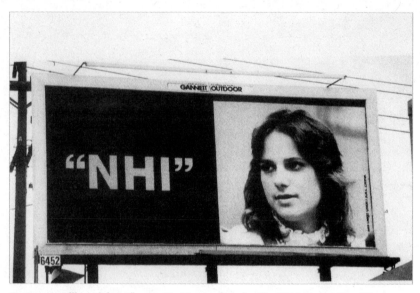

FIGURE 18 Billboard from "NHI—No Humans Involved" artists' project, San Diego, 1992
(with permission of Deborah Small, Elizabeth Sisco, Carla Kirkwood, Scott Kessler,
and Louis Hock).

assaults and murders of forty-five San Diego women between 1985 and 1992.
NHI—No Humans Involved artist Elizabeth Sisco states:

> The goal of the project was to pay tribute to the murdered women, raise pub-
> lic awareness about the series of murders and the botched police investigation,
> and relate the local reaction to the crimes to larger social attitudes toward gen-
> der violence....The purpose of NHI was to humanize the victims and demon-
> strate that violence against any woman is unacceptable. (Sisco 1993, 42 and 45)[3]

The project takes its name from a derogatory term that, according to a San
Diego police source, is used by police for what they describe as "'misdemeanour
murders' of biker women and hookers....Sometimes we'd call them 'NHIS'—
no humans involved" (*Sacramento Bee*, 7 October 1990).[4] By using this "in-
house" police phrase as the title of their project, the artists announced a hidden police narrative and shaped the language and focus around which the
story of the unsolved murders and police investigations would be publicly
discussed, widely debated, and contested.

    NHI—No Humans Involved was launched with a billboard bearing the
letters "NHI" and a photograph of a young woman, Donna Gentile, a sex-trade
worker and police informant whose testimony against the San Diego police was
nationally televised and who was, soon afterwards, murdered. The artists'
project[5] also included a performance called MWI—Many Women Involved; a

FIGURE 19 Gallery installation from "NHI—No Humans Involved" artists' project, San Diego, 1992 (with permission of Deborah Small, Elizabeth Sisco, Carla Kirkwood, Scott Kessler, and Louis Hock).

public panel composed of community members, experts, and the mother of one of the murdered women; an information booklet on the murders, police investigations, and media coverage; and the gallery exhibition[6] of photos of the women who were killed, or, when their photos weren't available, those of stand-ins like Susan Orlofsky, quoted above.

Influenced by the artists' methodologies, this chapter shares the politicized desires that I understand constituted NHI—No Humans Involved, and which continue to shape my own research on this artists' project. I've published work on the NHI—No Humans Involved project (Butler 2001a), written a chapter about it for my doctoral dissertation (Butler 2000), and discussed it in diverse academic and activist contexts in Europe, the United States, and Canada. In the fall of 2001 I presented NHI in the Downtown Eastside of Vancouver as part of an alternative education program called the Humanities Storefront 101. At that time forty-five women were "missing"[7]—unaccounted for[8]—in this area, and the police had just decided to treat the disappearance of thirty-one of these women as murders. So, though the NHI—No Humans Involved project had taken place almost ten years earlier, in another city and in another country, the circumstances seemed chillingly similar.

Halfway through my talk, when I was showing a slide of the NHI gallery exhibition (see fig. 19), a young woman came in, walked through to the back of the room, sat and looked at the slide and called out, "I'm in there! I'm one of the women in that picture!" It later turned out that Megan had misrecognized the image on the screen, thinking it was documentation of an artist's photo-series she's part of, a series called "Heroines," which is made up of images of Downtown Eastside women pictured as heroin addicts.[9]

But in the meantime, as we tried to sort out Megan's confusion, mine increased: it was as though one of the women in the NHI documentary photographs—women whose faces I'd been looking at for years while researching and writing about NHI, women who'd become so familiar to me, without my ever having met them—had stepped out of her context (and mine) and into this room in the Downtown Eastside. Megan stayed for the rest of the session, discussing the police (whose main station is so close by) and telling us about her drug addiction and work in the sex trade, and how she'd been trying to quit and move away but kept getting drawn back in.

Megan's "I'm in there! I'm one of the women in that picture!" voices and interpellates the women labelled NHI by the San Diego police, and the photo-donors who turned—or, as the artists say, "humanized"—the phrase "no humans involved" in their public art project. "I'm in there! I'm one of the women in that picture!" may also voice the missing and murdered women from Vancouver's Downtown Eastside and from the Lower Mainland, whose photographs appear in newspapers, on websites,[10] in friends' and families' photo albums, in police files and artists' photo-series, and at the memorial site at the Pickton farm in Port Coquitlam—now an excavation site, where some evidence of their presence is being found. In 2002 Robert Pickton was charged with the first-degree murder of fifteen women: Tanya Holyk, Sherry Irving, Helen Hallmark, Inga Hall, Jacqueline McDonell, Georgina Papin, Brenda Wolfe, Jennifer Furminger, Patricia Johnson, Heather Bottomley, Heather Chinnock, Andrea Josebury, Sereena Abotsway, Diane Rock, and Mona Wilson. By the beginning of his trial in January 2006, Pickton had additionally been charged with murdering Sarah de Vries, Angela Jardine, Cindy Felkis, Debra Jones, Marnie Frey, Diana Melnick, Tiffany Drew, Andrea Borhaven, Wendy Crawford, Cara Ellis, Kerry Koski, and an unidentified woman referred to as Jane Doe. At the memorial site at the Pickton farm, women's photographs, pressed behind plastic sheets, are placed with poems, tributes, flowers, feathers, candles, wreaths, medicine wheels, sweetgrass, and mementos.

I think that Megan's exclamation "I'm in there! I'm one of the women in that picture!" articulates a kind of implicatedness that can be seen as a way of noticing, marking, paying attention to what we're "part of," in and across time and place, and within relations of power. Implicatedness is a concept, practice, and method—an approach to felt, involved and involving, lived politics that can shape who we take ourselves to be and what we might do. Implicatedness is good at raising questions about relations between "me" and "we," between personal and collective selves.

I draw on Donna Haraway's (1991b, 193) work on subjectivity, which argues that "the knowing self is partial in all its guises, never finished, whole, simply there and original; it is always constructed and stitched together imperfectly, and therefore able to join with another, to see together without claiming to be another."[11] Equally relevant is her version of figuration: "A figure collects up the people; a figure embodies shared meanings that inhabit their audiences" (Haraway 1997, 23). I work with figurations of implicatedness that are visual and vocal: a figure of vision called the "focalizer," which narratologist Mieke Bal (1995, 158) sees as an agent of vision in a work that represents vision, and thereby offers positions of viewing to the real viewer;[12] and the "parrhesiastes," a figure of frank, courageous speech in the face of danger, who risks speech when s/he could have kept silent. In his book *Fearless Speech*, Michel Foucault (2001, 18) describes parrhesia as truth-telling in situations where "the parrhesiastes is always less powerful than the one with whom [s]he speaks."[13] Following the work of feminist epistemologists and situated knowledges that work with questions about "who knows," about "truth claiming" and power, I stretch parrhesia beyond its epistemological legitimacy (as traced in Foucault [2001, 14–15]) to figure Donna Gentile, and others, as a parrhesiastes who risked frank speech and its implications in dangerous situations.

> The point is to make a difference in the world, to cast our lot for some ways of life and not others. To do that, one must be in the action, be finite and dirty, not transcendent and clean. Knowledge-making technologies, including crafting subject positions and ways of inhabiting such positions, must be made relentlessly visible and open to critical intervention. (Haraway 1997, 36)

Figures of vision and speech see and say, show and tell, they focalize and vocalize. And the relations between seeing and saying are subtle, entangled, mutual, and variable: like the embodied, breathed relations between the assonant words "focalizer" and "vocalizer." Figurations of implicatedness vocalize and focalize in language and images that are present, implied, imagined, unseen, and so on. This chapter takes up the relations, these permutations of seeing and saying, through genre, approach, experience, and inhabitation.

"I'm in there! I'm one of the women in that picture!" is set in five parts, which inhabit the felt, involved and involving inflections of the figures of implicatedness included above (and more). Together, they take us through different standpoints and partial perspectives "pausing at sites of available viewing,"[14] and cultivating different relations with photography which trouble separations between personal and collective selves, what's imagined and what's actual, between representation and reality, between the semiotic and the material.

Photographers, Seen and Imagined, of Photographs Seen and Unseen

> This subject of vision, the focalizer, is often used to stage the position of the outsider as photographer. That position is a condition of the production of the snapshot....This position matters; it is crucial for our understanding of the mode of vision at stake. (Bal 1996b, 142)

Photographers, seen and imagined: everyone who took each of the pictures of each of the women contributed to the NHI—No Humans Involved gallery exhibition and documentation—such as friends, families, court reporters, artists, school photographers (say "cheese" or, cheekier, say "sex"). Everyone who's not seen, who's in front of the women and behind the camera; who's part of these modes of vision, these technologies; who's not seen yet can be made "relentlessly visible."[15]

> Focalization is the relation between the vision narrated and the object represented. The inflection the telling or showing subject brings to the perception of the object. (Bal 1996a, 71)

Photographers situate the relation between the vision narrated and the "object" represented; and the inflection that the telling (vocalizing, parrhesiastic) or showing (focalizing) subject brings to this perception.

> We may be talking about an artefact, but we are also talking about ourselves in the terms the artefact has delineated for us. (Holly 1995, 83)[16]

Photographers, seen and imagined, of photographs seen and unseen: we're imagining those who took photos in genres like snapshots (caught unaware, surprised, unprepared, relaxed); portraits (staged photos taken in studios, during a court appearance, at hallmark occasions, in urban locations, at scenic viewpoints [step back]); establishing shots (at a party, in the sunshine, next to a river, on a bed); alone and with others (focalizing "I want you who're looking at me to want me," or, with only the edge of an arm remaining after some body's, some memory's, been cropped out [the place where someone used to be]). Did the women who donated their own images for the NHI exhibition put them, later, back into boxes and albums, the next time saying to their interlocutors: "I don't think I ever told you, but this photo—it's a self-portrait and I lent it, I lent my face, for an art show. My photograph went with the name of a woman who'd been murdered. I didn't expect to get it back."

In front of the photographers (seen and imagined) of images in the NHI exhibition, the women (the subjects of vision, the focalizers) look posed, serious, happy, sexy, surprised, wholesome, enigmatic, disappointed, proud. These aren't actual or staged "crime scene" photographs—facing their photographers, the subjects represented are very much alive, the women still alive beside the women who were killed: Jane Doe #1, Donna Marie Gentile, Tara Mia Simpson, Patricia Smith, Marsha Shirlene Funderburk, Djuna Demetris Thomas, Linda Joyce Nelson, Linda Kay Freeby, Deborah Ann Stanford, Trina Carpenter, Jane Doe #2, Cynthia Maine, Michele Riccio, JoAnn Sweets, Jodell Jenkins, Carol Jane Gushrowski, Theresa Marie Brewer, Jane Doe #3, Sophia Glover, Nancy Allison White, Jane Doe #4, Cindy Jones, Kun Yueh Yeh Hou, Melissa Gene White, Juliana A. Santillano, Volah Jane Wright, Rosemarie Ritter, Rhonda Lynn Hollis, Anna L. Varela, Sally Ann Moorman Field, Sara Finland Thornton, Diana Gayle Moffitt, Jane Doe #5, Cheri Lee Galbreath, Melissa Sandoval, Janet Moore, Sandra Cwik, Mary Wells, Diana Ampura Luna, Cynthia Lou McVey, Linda Christine Marler, Denise Marie Galloway, Hena Nicolette Frye, Margaret Orozco Jackson, and Felix Abarca.[17]

About half the women whom the police referred to with the phrase "no humans involved" were "known" sex trade workers: they also worked as beauticians, waitresses, and homemakers; there was a nurse, a word processor, a stock supervisor, a grocery clerk, a hospital kitchen aid, and a writer; seven of the murdered women were African-American, seven were Latina, one was Asian-American, thirty were Caucasian, and five were unidentifiable;[18] and at least eleven were mothers—yet the police and the media coverage of the NHI project overwhelmingly referred to them as "prostitute murders."[19] Grouping these different women as NHIS ("'misdemeanour murders' of biker women and hookers" [*Sacramento Bee*, 7 October 1990]) contributes to the myth that good girls are safe and that bad girls get what they deserve. Linda Barker-Lawrence of the National Victims Center in Dallas, Texas, was quoted in the *San Diego Union* (12 February 1989) saying: "Most people think of prostitutes as someone who is hard-core, and that she asked for what she got. But the last time I looked, the sentence for prostitution is not execution."[20]

In Vancouver and the Lower Mainland many of the unaccounted for and murdered women are First Nations;[21] together, along with and between all of the women, they are overridingly being publicly described and pictured as prostitutes and drug users, or else they are shoehorned into various mobile stereotypes of the "bad girl" who's in the wrong place, in the wrong company, doing the wrong work, living the wrong lifestyle, wearing the wrong clothing, doing the wrong thing at the wrong time—just being wrong, just being all or any of the above. You get the picture. The inflection.[22]

So, when I see a bar running across the top of the page in the newspaper, a bar that holds the beginning of a grid, another grid, of photographs of more missing and murdered women, a row of photographs cropped to look like mug shots such as appeared in the *Vancouver Sun* on 26 July 2002, the day that I was writing this sentence, with each

WOMAN'S FULL NAME in bold capitals followed by

Last seen: on this date and

Reported missing: on this date;

or when I see in the newspaper a map of the Lower Mainland with inserted photos and brief, stereotyped, effective descriptions of forty more women murdered whose "cases" are unsolved (*Vancouver Sun*, 23 November 2001);[23] when I see this artefact delineating the terms by which we talk about ourselves, about each other, I find myself imagining the photographers who took these pictures.

Implied Viewers of Photographs, Seen or Unseen, in San Diego, the Lower Mainland and in *Killing Women*

> The space of the museum presupposes a walking tour, an order in which the dioramas, exhibits, and panels are viewed and read. Thus it addresses an implied viewer—in narratological terms, a focalizer—whose tour produces the story of knowledge taken in and taken home. (Bal 1996a, 18)

Photographs imply viewers; they imply relations between photographers, viewers, and photographs; and (focalizing and vocalizing) relations between the vision narrated and the object, the subject, represented. Site-specific public art projects like NHI—No Humans Involved imply viewers by unexpectedly, carefully, cannily, locating artwork in public sites. For instance, by installing one NHI billboard so that it faced the San Diego County Administration Center, and the other near the San Diego Police Headquarters, where police likely would have had to engage with it regularly and would have been faced with their own term "NHI" being made public.

Photographs, seen or unseen, imply viewers. Widespread media coverage of NHI billboards was facilitated by the artists' press release sent out on the day the billboards were launched; in it, they solved the mystery of the letters "NHI" and identified the woman pictured as Donna Gentile, whom the audience may have remembered having seen on television in a court appearance giving testimony against the San Diego police years before. This information would have been seen by anyone watching the evening news or reading the newspaper, who then may have gone to see the billboards for themselves, if they hadn't seen them already. Thus the order in which the NHI artists' works were viewed and read may have produced different "tours" and "stories" for many implied viewers.

Further, "implied viewers" includes anyone who participated in the NHI exhibition, such as families and donors who gave photographs; anyone who went to see the exhibition deliberately or by chance, who perhaps sat on the couch (like the two focalizers pictured in the documentary image on page 157), which implied their presence before they ever entered the space; and anyone who went to other NHI events at the gallery. And when the project's documentary photographs are included in a videotape (*No Humans Involved* 1993), presented to an audience, or printed or discussed in a newspaper,[24] on a website (http://crca.ucsd.edu/~esisco/nhi), in a journal (Simonds 1994), or in a book (Pincus 1995), then implied viewers are readers like you, of books like this one, "whose tour produces the story of knowledge taken in and taken home" (Bal 1996a, 18).

> The focalizer is an agent in the work who represents vision, and thereby offers positions of viewing to the real viewer....Such a reading mediates between sender and receiver by *pausing at the sites of available viewing positions*....[T]he narrativization of the viewing process it entails inserts the mobility, the instability and the time-consuming process of reading sequentially. (Bal, quoted in Melville 1995, 158, emphasis mine)

Installed in the NHI gallery, hung before many implied viewers, the photographs became figurations ("A figure collects up the people" [Haraway 1997, 23]) for the families and friends who turned the gallery into a place of respect and commiseration, as well as a space in which to contest the silence and invisibility of these murders and of social practices of violence against women. Cheryl Lindley, a performance artist who donated her photo for the exhibition, said:

> The part about the project I liked the most was the gallery where all the photos were hung....The families of the victims started showing up and bringing flowers and having picnics. It took on its own life and the gallery became like a holy spot or something, and it was the only time for a lot of these families that their loved one had been treated with dignity and respect, and for a lot of people it was the first time they had some closure with it all.[25]

I imagine that the "implied viewers" of the NHI exhibition all had differently attenuated and inflected experiences: for instance, how might it have been for the slain women's families and friends to see their picture in this exhibition, or to see another woman's picture with their loved ones' names?[26] for NHI audiences to see images of women they knew?[27] or for the donors to see their photos with the names of women who had been murdered? Correspondence between face and name, between image and text—especially inside a grid format that promises control of the order of things (Foucault 1994)— is usually, seamlessly, ideologically, secured by a textual function that Roland Barthes (1988, 39) calls "anchorage": "Hence in every society various techniques are developed intended to *fix* the floating chain of signifieds in such a way as to counter the terror of uncertain signs: the linguistic message is one of these techniques." (There were five "Jane Doe"s found murdered in San Diego between 1985 and 1992; and how much uncertainty in the Lower Mainland, how many more "Jane Doe"s?)

The photographic convention of the text anchoring (otherwise uncertain) visual signs was "turned" when the NHI artists invited community women to contribute their photographs to go with the names of murdered women; in this way, they troubled separations between personal and collective selves— "me" and "we"—what's imagined and what's actual, between representation and reality, between the semiotic and the material. And placing these image-texts in a grid unsettles another photographic convention: the sense of security and certainty guaranteed by the orderly, ordering grid itself ("an order in which the dioramas, exhibits and panels are viewed and read" [Bal 1996a, 18]). In this way, the artists offered implied viewers, focalizers, a chance to re- or de-narrativize "the story of knowledge taken in and taken home" (Bal 1996a, 18).

Yet what if this non-correspondence between faces and names laid out in a grid, elsewhere and at another time, occurred "by mistake"? What narratives might arise? What could the implications be for subjects, for implied viewers and for (imagined) photographers of these images, and of images as yet unseen, as yet untaken? On 25 July 2002, the RCMP–Vancouver Police Department Joint Missing Women Task Force issued a press release on their website headed "Change of Order of Images," which stated: "Please note the images of the missing women posted at 1:32 pm were posted with the incorrect corresponding names. The names corresponding to the photos were corrected at 1:55 PM."[28]

In the meantime, for those twenty-three unaccounted for, unaccountable minutes, the women's pictures became stand-ins for and with each other. Did any become Jane Doe while lending their names to other women? Who looks on this website—who are its implied viewers—and how frequently, apprehensively, hopefully do they check? For them, what happened during those twenty-three minutes? For viewers who looked at the website during that time and didn't notice the oversight, how implicated are the grid layout and the practice of stereotyping women from the Downtown Eastside in this form of truth-claiming? How was the mistake, the misnaming of missing women, recognized—was it by an (imagined) photographer of one or more of the photographs? by everyone who took each of the pictures of each of the women in many genres, later labelled and arranged on this police website?

> Focalization is the relation between the vision narrated and the object represented. The inflection the telling or showing subject brings to the perception of the object. (Bal 1996a, 71)

Earlier, an implied viewer, prefigured before she arrived, walks into a (site-specific) public presentation on art about violence against women held in the Downtown Eastside of Vancouver, misrecognizes herself "as if" she's in a photograph from another time and place, and shouts out "I'm in there! I'm one of the women in that picture!"[29] Then a focalizer becomes a vocalizer who tells the audience about her own experiences with drug addiction and sex trade work—someone who could be, but one hopes never will be, classified by the disrespectful term "NHI"—yet by calling out "I'm in there!" she became a stand-in for the women in the NHI project and implicated herself with them. Megan's best friend was the second woman "missing": Donna Gentile was the second woman murdered during that time in San Diego, and her picture is projected on a slide screen in front of the presentation audience, right then, right now, and on page 156. The picture that Megan referred to when she called out "I'm one of the women in that picture!" is also, simultaneously in her mind's eye (from the perspective of her [imagined] photographer), another photograph that is, as yet, unseen by implied viewers who are readers of *Killing Women: The Visual Culture of Gender and Violence*, who've not yet seen Megan, posed, pictured, and posted on "Heroines" photographer Lincoln Clarkes's website—not named but listed by number—standing in front of a funeral chapel in the Downtown Eastside.[30]

Photographs imply viewers; they imply relations between photographers, viewers, and photographs; and (focalizing and vocalizing) relations between the vision narrated and the object, the subject, represented. Pausing at the site of viewing a (previously stable) documentary image of women from another place and time, Megan became a figure who "embodies shared meanings that inhabit their audiences" (Haraway 1997, 23). She voiced and interpellated the implicatedness, instability and mobility, and the partiality of implied viewers.

As discussed so far, figures of implicatedness—who see and say, focalize and vocalize, show and tell what we're part of—amplify the epistemological and ontological relations between personal and collective selves, what's imagined and what's actual, between representation and reality, between the semiotic and the material. All this inflects "an implied viewer (in narratological terms, a *focalizer*) whose tour produces the story of knowledge taken in and taken home" (Bal 1996a, 18).

Donnas Gentile

> A figure collects up the people; a figure embodies shared meanings that inhabit their audiences. (Haraway 1997, 23)

> The commitment involved in *parrhesia* is linked to a certain social situation, to a difference of status between the speaker and her audience, to the fact that the *parrhesiastes* says something which is dangerous to herself and thus involves a risk, and so on....*Parrhesia*, then, is linked to courage in the face of danger: it demands the courage to speak the truth in spite of some danger. And in its extreme form, telling the truth takes place in the "game" of life or death. (Foucault 2001, 13, 16)[31]

There are a few words to read aloud. Donna Gentile in a prison cell in the Las Colinas women's jail, serving a prostitution conviction, four months before her death, making a tape recording that her lawyer will release to a television reporter after her body is found:

> I have no intention of disappearing or going out of town without letting my lawyer know first. Because of the publicity I have been given in the police scandal, this is the reason I am taping this....I feel that even someone in uniform and a badge can still be a serious criminal. This is the only insurance I have.[32]

It didn't work, this insurance. I want to know what else she said, or is written about her. I look for Donna Gentile on the Internet and find mainly articles that discuss her and also statements by other Donna Gentiles who I want to have been her. On the website of coyote (a prostitutes' advocacy group), which doesn't yet talk about the many women missing from the Vancouver area or the evidence of some of their murders, I find:

> One prostitute who did file a corruption report against a police officer in San Diego was murdered shortly after the report. [Donna Gentile] Serial murder of prostitutes has become a major problem in this country. In the last three years, more than 100 women have been murdered on the West Coast by no more than three men, none of whom have been caught.[33]

On another I read:

> 22-year-old Donna Gentile. Gentile, an alleged prostitute, was found in 1985 off Sunrise Highway in East County and her mouth had been stuffed with stones. She had recently testified at a police civil service hearing against two officers who were disciplined for engaging in improper conduct with a prostitute. One officer, Larry Avrech, was fired and the other, Lt. Carl Black, demoted. According to Gentile Avrech provided her with confidential police information in return for sexual favors. Some investigators interpreted the stones in her mouth as meaning she had been killed in retaliation for her testimony.[34]

She went on the stand and later her mouth was stuffed with gravel and stones. She went on the stand (pictured [*focalizing*] on the stand, on national television, *later on the billboard looking at the letters* NHI *with her mouth closed*) and her (*parrhesiastic*) mouth was stuffed with stones and gravel.[35]

There are more Donnas: a "donna" is a woman, more than one donna is donne, to give is donner, to donate. Gentile means gentle, dear. Dear Woman Donna Gentile: a Donna Gentile writes condolences to another Donna online, and I'm drawn to read it:

> Donna,
> This is such a blessing to me. I miss _____ dearly and I am thankful that _____ had the foresight to capture _____ on tape and video…it is so refreshing to be able to hear _____ again…
> Let not your heart be troubled!
> Love always, Donna Gentile[36]

And meanwhile another Donna Gentile is at a funeral in Cleveland:

> An estimated 3,000 police officers, from departments across Ohio and the country, attended the service. Afterward, people stood and watched as the long line of cars with flashing lights made its way through downtown streets. A dozen sheriff's deputies stood at attention in front of the Justice Center, saluting as the gray hearse…passed by. Across the street, a woman stood with one hand above her heart, as though saying the Pledge of Allegiance. "It's so sad," said Donna Gentile, an administrative assistant at Cuyahoga County Domestic Relations Court. "I just can't get over how quiet it is," said Gentile, one of hundreds of people watching the slow procession on Lakeside Avenue [for Patrolman Wayne Leon who was shot on duty]. "It's like everyone went quiet as soon as it started."[37]

It took eleven days for Donna Gentile's body to be identified. There were forty-four more, and then there were more women's bodies found and more women nearby and elsewhere, missing and missed,[38] seen, unseen, last seen[39] continuing

Photo Donors

Which photo donors are there, here? Can you see others?

1. Those who have pictures of women who may be missing or murdered.
2. Are these pictured women, themselves, ourselves, photo donors?
3. Whoever donates photographs of the women "last seen" who were named at the Women's Memorial March in Vancouver (February 14, 2003) and here on page 176.
4. Each of these women?
5. Maggie de Vries whose donated photos of her sister Sarah de Vries are published in *Missing Sarah: A Vancouver Woman Remembers Her Vanished Sister.*
6. Is Sarah de Vries a photo donor?
7. More women nearby and elsewhere who donate their photos.
8. Are the forty-five women murdered in San Diego, named on page 161, photo donors?
9. Those who didn't look at or put forth the photographs they had (seen) of Donna Gentile during the eleven days her body lay unidentified.
10. Those who look for, hoping to find and see and perhaps show, images of Donna Gentile and find Donnas Gentile. Here, are they "knowing selves"? "The knowing self is partial in all its guises, never finished, whole, simply there and original; it is always constructed and stitched together imperfectly, and therefore able to join with another, to see together without claiming to be another" (Haraway 1991b, 193).
11. The Donna Gentile who's verbally pictured standing "with one hand above her heart, as though saying the Pledge of Allegiance," not in court but at the well attended funeral of a police officer killed on duty.
12. The writer who attended this funeral and spoke to and described and quoted Donna Gentile, and the newspaper that printed the article, perhaps with a photograph.
13. The audiotaped words and videotaped images donated between grieving Donnas.
14. The name [Donna Gentile] pressed between square brackets that looks like a partial photo frame, printed on the COYOTE website.
15. Donna Gentile testifying against San Diego police officers, photographically documented. Were her parrhesiastic words also recorded and so, in a sense, donated?
16. Those who photographed and printed and continue to reprint the image of Donna Gentile testifying: state authorities and civil servants, artists,

writers, academics, filmmakers, journalists, website producers, editors, publishers....Does it raise questions about photographic and associated practices if they are all considered to be implicating themselves, ourselves, as photo donors?

17. Vancouver photographer Lincoln Clarkes.

18. Are the 10—of 125 unnamed and numbered—women pictured as heroin-addicted "Heroines" on Lincoln Clarkes's website, photo donors?

19. Donna Gentile, the second of forty-five woman murdered in San Diego between 1985 and 1992, as a stand-in for Megan's best friend who she said—while looking at Donna Gentile's photograph—was the second woman missing from the Downtown Eastside.

20. Megan.

21. All the photographers, seen and imagined, of donated photographs of unaccounted for women posted on RCMP–Vancouver Police Department Joint Missing Women Task Force websites. And those involved in the sites' production and maintenance.

22. Are the women whose photographs stood in for each others' for those twenty-three unaccounted for, unaccountable minutes photo donors? The women referred to as Jane Doe?

23. The women whose donated photos could have been "anchored" with the name Jane Doe in the NHI—No Humans Involved exhibition.

24. Dick Lewis—head of the San Diego Metropolitan Homicide Task Force set up to investigate the women's murders and the police corruption involved—who publicly stated that he "chose to withhold the women's photographs"[40] from the NHI—No Humans Involved exhibition is not a photo donor.

25. Ashley Phillips.

26. The sister of Margaret Orozco Jackson.

27. The mother of Linda Christine Marler.

28. Cheryl Lindley.

29. Those who donated self-portraits to the NHI—No Humans Involved exhibition.

30. Implied viewers of photographs, seen or unseen, in San Diego, Vancouver, and the Lower Mainland and in *Killing Women* who are also photo donors.

31. Those who donated the photos printed in the *Vancouver Sun* of the forty women murdered whose "cases" are unsolved—photographs that someone at the *Sun* inserted into a map of the Lower Mainland, with brief stereotyped descriptions of the women.

32. Are these forty women photo donors?

33. Publishers, editors, designers, technicians, writers, reporters and photographers who work at newspapers, magazines, journals, books, and so on that include photos of the women missing and murdered in Vancouver and the Lower Mainland. Does considering whether they are photo donors raise questions about the conventions—of layout, of subjects' consent—involved in their work?

34. Photographers, seen and imagined, of donated photographs seen and unseen.

35. Are photographers of "crime scenes" actual and staged—police, photojournalists, ambulance chasers, photographers, artists, film and video makers, and so on—photo donors in other contexts?

36. Those who place women's photographs at the memorial site at the Pickton farm on Dominion Avenue in Port Coquitlam.

37. Are the women named on page 158, whose presence, whose absence, has been located at the Pickton farms in Port Coquitlam, photo donors?

38. Those who took and/or donated pictures of women missing and murdered in Vancouver and the Lower Mainland which appear in newspapers, on websites, in photo albums, in police files, etc.

39. Are all of the women who are part of the photographic series "Heroines" photo donors?

40. Megan, when she called out "I'm in there! I'm one of the women in that picture!"

41. When the NHI project and documentary photos are included in public presentations, videotapes, printed, or referred to in information booklets, in newspapers, on broadcast news, on websites, in journals and books, are all those involved—who show and tell the NHI project, such as Margot Leigh Butler is doing here—photo donors?

42. "MWI—Many Women Involved" photo donors.
    People on the NHI—No Humans Involved "town meeting" panel, who spoke up, vocalized, who looked towards and addressed the audience and cameras under the focalizing "unseeing eyes" of the women's photographs:

43.   Cynthia Bernee, community educator and trainer in the area of violence against women.

44.   Norma Jean Almodovar, author of *Cop to Call Girl* and Prostitutes' Rights Advocate.

45.   Catherine Spearnak, local journalist whose 1987–88 stories for the *Escondido Times-Advocate* and *San Diego Magazine* led to the formation of the Metropolitan Homicide Task Force.

46. Douglas Holbrook, professor of political science and business law, San Diego State University, and attorney for Donna Gentile.

47. Pat Riccio, mother of slain Michele Riccio.

48. San Diego police photographers of photographs, seen and unseen, of women they referred to as NHIS.

49. Donna Gentile.

50. The NHI artists when they gave permission for their documentary photos of the gallery and the billboard to be reprinted in *Killing Women*.

The NHI artists who, through donating their own images and through this project, were focalizers and parrhesiastes, engaging practices and figurations of implicatedness:

51. Deborah Small.

52. Elizabeth Sisco.

53. Carla Kirkwood.

54. Scott Kessler.

55. Louis Hock.

56. Those who donated photographs of the women who were murdered— such as Pat Riccio who donated an image of her daughter Michelle, and Margaret Orozco Jackson's sister, and Linda Christine Marler's mother— and the women (such as Ashley Phillips and Cheryl Lindley) from many different San Diego communities who donated their own photos to NHI— No Humans Involved as stand-ins for many of the forty-five women who were sexually assaulted and murdered, and whom we can see in the printed photograph on page 157.

57. Susan Orlofsky.

58. If you've found a picture of yourself that you'd like to donate, slip it in here, between these pages. Maybe the person(s) to whom you lend this book to will do the same.

Notes

1 Many people made invaluable contributions to this work: Megan, Anne Stone, my family, Susan Lord and Annette Burfoot, Marika Sandrelli at PACE (Prostitution Alternatives Counselling and Education Society) Vancouver, and the NHI—No Humans Involved artists Deborah Small, Elizabeth Sisco, Carla Kirkwood, Scott Kessler, and Louis Hock.

2 Susan Orlofsky interview, San Diego, 2 August 1996.

3 Further to the police investigations of the women's murders, Sheriff Jim Roache stated in 1991 that "Ninety-five percent of the task force resources were going to (investigating) police corruption. Nothing was happening with the killings" (*San Diego Tri-*

bune, 18 July 1991). Nevertheless, on 25 March 1993 (a year after the NHI—No Humans Involved project) this task force was declared to have been "the most successful serial killer task force in US history" (District Attorney Edwin L. Miller Jr., quoted in the *Los Angeles Times*, 25 March 1993), closing twenty-six of the cases, although sixteen of these did not have enough evidence to bring criminal charges. NHI artist Deborah Small has noted that the man accused of the bulk of these crimes made an easy "target" for police scapegoating since he was "in a sense a male 'NHI,' he was a person who was homeless and had no family to defend him...he had a similar profile to the [murdered] women" (Deborah Small, interview, San Diego, 2 August 1996). Please note that all of the cited newspaper articles about NHI—No Humans Involved are from the NHI project archive.

4 Archived NHI—No Humans Involved information booklet, 5.

5 Some background information on this kind of art practice: some public art projects, like NHI—No Humans Involved, are produced collaboratively and are temporary and site-specific. This genre is part of conceptual art practices that were politicized through the influence of anti-war protest; identity politics (especially feminisms); attention to divisions of labour; critiques of existing art practices; criticisms of the modernist "white cube" and expansion of what's seen as possible art installation sites, art materials, and subjects; and desires for wider audiences and community involvements and so on. This practice appeals especially to artists who enjoy working collaboratively and non-hierarchically, and are interested in how the materiality, timeliness, and situatedness of an artwork contributes to its meaning, politics, and audience engagement.

6 The NHI exhibition took place in a rented storefront in downtown San Diego between 22 February and 22 March 1992.

7 In Vancouver now, the word "missing" turns too easily into the phrase "missing women"—a phrase that has been shaped into a trope that has personal and political meanings and effects. For instance, when police press releases cite the numbers of "missing women," community groups, like the Downtown Eastside Women's Centre, contest them, estimating much higher rates of violence against women than officials have recognized. See the Downtown Eastside Women's Centre's press release from 8 February 2002 at http://www.rapereliefshelter.bc.ca/issues/eastside_women04.html and the Prostitution Alternatives Counseling and Education (PACE) Society's report "Violence Against Women in Vancouver's Street Level Sex Trade" at http://www.vcn.bc .ca/pacekids/report/. Accessed 21 March 2006.

8 Further, the tropic use of the phrase "missing women" is highlighted, and I think contested, with alternative words and phrases: for instance, on the commemorative pamphlets distributed by the Women's Memorial March Committee, 14 February 2003, before a march led by First Nations elders through Vancouver's Downtown Eastside, "missing" women's names were listed with "Our prayers remain with the women who are still unaccounted for."

9 This work by Lincoln Clarkes can be seen at http://www.highway99.com/lclarkes/ heroines/index.html, and many of the photographs have been published in his book *Heroines* (Clarkes 2002). Accessed 21 March 2006.

10 For a sister's tribute, see http://www.angelfire.com/wa3/missingsister/index.html. For an artist's tribute to the missing women, see http://orcagirl.com/missingwomen. For a personal Webpage dedicated to compiling information about the missing women, see http://www.dlganz.50megs.com/index.html. For a mainstream media site, see

http://cbc.ca/news/features/bc_missingwomen.html. See also the Attorney General of British Columbia's "Reward for Information" Poster posted on the Vancouver Police Department's Website at http://www.city.vancouver.bc.ca/police/news/missing/poster.pdf, and labelled photographs of the women on http://www.missingpeople.net/investigationturnsupmoremissing.htm. Accessed 21 March 2006.

11 In Haraway's (1991, 183–201) work on "vision"—on seeing together, on optics as a politics of positioning, and so on—vision is always mediated, and perspectives are partial, situated, non-innocent, accountable, critical, and mobile in the hopes that "in this way, we might become answerable for what we learn how to see."

12 The terms "focalizer," "focalize," and "focalization" are contested and invested concepts for talking about "vision" in contemporary narratology. Here, vision is seen looking—a preoccupation in contemporary visual theories—and slight shifts render important partial, perspectival, epistemological, ontological, and phenomenological registrations. I draw primarily on Mieke Bal's work, which theorizes focalization inside texts and also, increasingly, in visual work. For a composite of passages from her key essays on focalization, see "Dispersing the Gaze: Focalization" in Bal (2001).

13 I have regendered this quote, both to remain in the spirit of Foucault's influence and to amplify some contemporary desires for parrhesia as a technology in the care of the gendered self: "Responding to a student's question, Foucault indicated that the oppressed role of women in Greek society generally deprived them of the use of parrhesia (along with aliens, slaves, and children). Hence the predominant use of the masculine pronoun throughout" (Foucault 2001, 12n4). Clearly, parrhesia may be a technology in the care of many contemporary and historical "othered" selves.

14 This phrase is from a quote that is worked with in the next section: "The focalizer is an agent in the work who represents vision, and thereby offers positions of viewing to the real viewer....Such a reading mediates between sender and receiver by pausing at the sites of available viewing positions....[T]he narrativization of the viewing process it entails inserts the mobility, the instability and the time-consuming process of reading sequentially" (Bal 1995, 158).

15 "The point is to make a difference in the world, to cast our lot for some ways of life and not others. To do that, one must be in the action, be finite and dirty, not transcendent and clean. Knowledge-making technologies, including crafting subject positions and ways of inhabiting such positions, must be made relentlessly visible and open to critical intervention" (Haraway 1997, 36).

16 This quote, which discusses the relations between art historians and the work they study, carries on: "What the discussion of the gaze in works of art has taught us is that perception always involves a circulation of positions, a process of movement back and forth that will forever undermine the fixity of the two poles, inside and outside" (Holly 1995, 83).

17 Archived "NHI—No Humans Involved" information booklet, 25–28.

18 Ibid., 15.

19 This is a paraphrase of Sisco (1993, 43).

20 Archived NHI—No Humans Involved" information booklet, 15.

21 See "Native women missing and/or murdered in Canada" at http://www.geocities.com/waabzyi/native.html and http://www.turtleisland.org/news/donnajoe.htm. Accessed 21 March 2006.As well, here is an excerpt of a statement issued by Faye Blaney of the Aboriginal Women's Action Network at a press conference on 8 February 2002: "When

Aboriginal women's lives are dispensable, then the likes of Gilbert Paul Jordan and Robert William Pickton can come out and perform without fear of any consequences. I urge you, the media to report, in a more accurate fashion, to move away from the victim blaming that pervades your stories on the 'Missing Women' and the 'Memorial March.'" http://www.rapereliefshelter.bc.ca/issues/eastside_women02.html. Accessed 21 March 2006.

22 Here's an example, from an article headlined "If the Girls Had Been Dogs the Police Would Have Done More," which ran in the *Guardian* on 27 February 2002:

> Kathleen Hallmark-McClelland's daughter, Helen, disappeared in August 1997, aged 31, after years as an addict and prostitute in the Downtown Eastside. Hallmark-McClelland bombarded the local police with desperate phone messages but heard little in return. "The police didn't show up or call. It took a month and a half for the detective to come out to see us. He actually suggested my daughter could have moved to Florida and changed her identity but most of them don't have the price of a bus ticket downtown. If six dogs from the neighbourhood had disappeared, there would have been more done," says Hallmark-McClelland who now works for a community magazine called *Lookout*, dedicated to tracking down the missing. The police even appear to have been given numerous specific tip-offs about Pickton. "Farmer Willie" was apparently a familiar figure in the Low Track [Downtown Eastside], regularly picking up women and taking them back to Port Coquitlam. Moreover, he had been charged in 1997 with stabbing a prostitute at his farm. The charges were eventually dropped, apparently due to lack of evidence to corroborate the woman's version of events, but there was no dispute that she had run out of the Pickton farm screaming and covered in blood. (http://www.guardian.co.uk/g2/story/0,3604,658519,00.html. Accessed 21 March 2006)

23 This map is prefaced with "Since 1980 in BC, there have been 40 unsolved murders of women who either worked in the sex trade or were vulnerable to predators because they used drugs, lived on the street, hitched rides with strangers, or earned their living as exotic dancers" (*Vancouver Sun*, 23 November 2001).

24 For instance, when discussing the NHI artists' request for photographs of the women for the exhibition, Dick Lewis—head of the Metropolitan Homicide Task Force set up to investigate the women's murders and the police corruption involved—said that the task force "chose to withhold the photographs out of respect for the victims' families. 'These are unsolved murders, by and large, and I don't see the advantage of giving photos to an art exhibit. I don't think it's appropriate. If your mother or sister were murdered, I don't think you'd like to see her in an art exhibit'" (quoted in the *San Diego Union-Tribune*, 28 February 1992). This remark is in stark contrast to a statement Lewis had made earlier: "These women by and large are transient, don't have family ties, they're drug abusers, in fact, many families, although they knew they were gone, were really glad they weren't coming around any more" (*No Humans Involved* 1993).

25 Cheryl Lindey interview, San Diego, 2 August 1996.

26 Two of the families of murdered women—the mother of Linda Christine Marler and the sister of Margaret Orozco Jackson—offered photographs once they'd seen the exhibition. This was written in the Comments Book at the gallery: "It means a lot to us to know that there are people like you to donate your time in all that is taking

place in this project. We truly appreciate you. Family of Margaret Orozco Jackson, one of the slain women."

27 For instance, San Diego University lecturer and photo donor Ashley Phillips told a reporter that one of her students saw her photograph in the exhibition and was afraid she had been murdered: "That's what makes the exhibit powerful. People are going to say 'I know that woman,' and that will make them think 'What if she had been murdered?'" (*San Diego Union-Tribune*, 28 February 1992).

28 http://www.rcmp-bcmedia.ca/pressrelease.jsp?vRelease=1562 and see http://www.rcmp-bcmedia.ca/pressrelease.jsp?vRelease=1560 for elaborations. Accessed 21 March 2006.

29 All sorts of different relations between subjects and subjectivities, between images and texts, and between seeing and saying and showing and telling could be drawn out if Megan's engagement was theorized through the theme or trope of Lacanian "misrecognition" and through Braidotti's work on the practice of "as if": "What I find empowering in the practice of 'as if' is its potential for opening up, through successive repetitions and mimetic strategies, spaces where alternative forms of feminist agency can be engendered" (Braidotti 1994, 7). Megan could also be figured as a Harawayan "mutated modest witness" (Haraway 1997, 267). Elsewhere, I have theorized Donna Gentile and the NHI artists and photo donors through this figuration: "Witnessing is seeing; attesting; standing publicly accountable for, and psychically vulnerable to, one's visions and representations. Witnessing is a collective, limited practice that depends on the constructed and never finished credibility of those who do it, all of whom are mortal, fallible, and fraught with the consequences of unconscious and disowned desires and fears" (Butler 2001a, 394–98).

30 This photo is posted at http://www.highway99.com/lclarkes/heroines/index.html. Accessed 21 March 2006. Along with many other photographs of Downtown Eastside women pictured as drug addicts, it has been published in Lincoln Clarkes's book *Heroines* (Clarkes 2002). See Butler (2004a) for a lengthy critique entitled "The Hero of *Heroines.*"

31 Again, I have regendered this quotation.

32 Archived "NHI—No Humans Involved" information booklet, 22.

33 http://www.freedomusa.org/coyotela/what_is.html#top. Accessed 21 March 2006. Note that I haven't added "[Donna Gentile]": she was already there.

34 http://www.mayhem.net/Crime/greenriver.html. Accessed 21 March 2006.

35 "The commitment involved in parrhesia is linked to a certain social situation, to a difference of status between the speaker and her audience, to the fact that the parrhesiastes says something which is dangerous to herself and thus involves a risk, and so on" (Foucault 2001, 13).

36 This letter, in its original form, was posted on the Internet sermons website of Lutheran Pastor Roger A. Robinson, addressed to the pastor's wife Donna http://www.internetsermons.com/robinson.htm. Accessed 1 June 2004.

37 "Memorial Will See Another Name," *Sun Newspapers*, 6 July 2000 (http://www.sunnews.com/news/2000/0706/WMEMORIAL.htm). Accessed 21 March 2006.

38 *Missing Sarah: A Vancouver Woman Remembers Her Vanished Sister* (Penguin, 2003) is the name of the book written by Maggie de Vries about her sister Sarah de Vries. Robert Pickton has been charged with her murder. For a review of this book, see Butler (2004b).

39 At the Women's Memorial March through Vancouver's Downtown Eastside on 14 February 2003, women who have been murdered and women who are unaccounted for were commemorated. In the commemorative pamphlet, some women's names are followed by 'LS,' which means Last Seen, while 'M' means Murdered: Angela Arseneault (5/20/77 LS 1997), Andrea F. Borhaven (1972 LS 1997), Ann Wolsey (12/20/72 LS 1/1/97), Catherine L. Gonzalez (9/27/68 LS 3/95), Catherine M. Knight(5/5/66 LS 4/95), Cindy L. Beck (4/17/65 LS 9/97), Dawn L. Cooper (5/4/64 LS 1996), Dawn M. Crey (10/26/58 LS 11/1/2000), Debra Jones (12/31/57 LS 12/21/2000), Diana Melnick (8/26/75 LS 12/21/2000), Dorothy A. Spence (8/6/62 LS 7/30/95), Elaine Allenbach (4/6/62 LS 7/30/95), Elaine P. Dumba (3/12/55 LS 89), Elise Sebastian (1/1/52 LS 10/16/92), Francis Young (1/7/60 LS 4/6/96), Ingrid Soet (7/13/59 LS 8/28/89), Jacqueline M. Murdock (1/28/71 LS 8/14/97), Janet Gail Henry (4/10/61 LS 6/25/97), Julie L. Young (7/17/67 LS 10/98), Kerri Koski (8/14/59 LS 1/7/98), Kathleen D. Wattley (10/20/59 LS 5/18/92), Laura Mah (3/23/43 LS 8/1/85), Leigh Miner (3/24/58 LS 12/21/93), Linda Grant (3/18/53 LS 10/84), Lillian J. O'Dare (1/8/94 LS 12/12/78), Marcella H. Creison (6/2/78 LS 12/98), Maria Laliberte (11/7/49 LS 1/1/97), Michelle Gurney (2/11/69 LS 12/11/98), Nancy Clark (2/29/66 LS 8/22/91), Olivia G. Williams (1/19/75 LS 12/6/96), Rebecca Guno (5/25/60 LS 6/22/2001), Richard (Kellie) Little (3/12/69 LS 4/23/97), Ruby A. Hardy (3/23/65 LS 1998), Sheila C. Egan (8/4/78 LS 7/96), Sheryl Donahue (7/4/63 LS 5/30/85), Sherry Lynn Rail (9/8/56 LS 12/96), Stephanie Marie Lane (5/28/76 LS 1/10/97), Tanya C. Emery (M) (10/6/64 12/1/98), Teresa L. Triff (8/17/69 LS 4/15/88), Teressa A. Williams (2/14/73 LS 7/1/88), Tiffany A. Drew (1/31/75 LS 12/31/99), Violet Delores Heman (2002), Wendy L. Allen (12/10/45 LS 3/30/79), Wendy Crawford (4/21/56 LS 11/99), Yvonne M. Abigosis (11/23/57 LS 1/1/84), Yvonne Boen (11/30/67 LS 3/16/2001). There are many more women's names commemorated, without 'LS' or 'M'; and another heading which says "Women's DNA found": Andrea Joesbury (M) (11/5/78 LS 6/2001), Angela R. Jardine (6/23/71 LS 11/20/98), Brenda Wolf (M) (10/20/72 LS 2/1/99), Cindy Feliks (M) (12/12/54 LS 1/18/97), Diane Rock (M) (9/2/67 LS 10/19/2001), Georgina Papin (M) (3/11/64 LS 3/2/99), Heather Bottomley (M) (8/17/76 LS 4/17/2001), Heather Chinook (M) (11/10/70 LS 4/15/2001), Helen M. Hallmark (M) (6/24/66 LS 8/97), Inga M. Hall (M) (1/25/52 LS 2/26/98), Jacqueline McDonnell (M) (6/6/76 LS 1/16/99), Jennifer Furminger (M) (10/22/71 LS 3/30/2000), Marnie Frey (8/30/73 LS 8/97), Mona Wilson (1/13/75 LS 11/23/2001), Patricia Johnson (M) (12/2/75 LS 2/27/2001), Sarah de Vries (M) (12/5/69 LS 4/14/98), Sereena Abotsway (M) (8/20/71 LS 4/14/98), Sherry Irving (M) (3/19/73 LS 12/96), Tanya Marlo Holyk (M) (2/8/75 LS 10/29/96).

40 As has been stated in note 24 in relation to the NHI artists' request for photographs of the women for the exhibition, Dick Lewis said that the task force "…chose to withhold the photographs out of respect for the victims' families. 'These are unsolved murders, by and large, and I don't see the advantage of giving photos to an art exhibit. I don't think it's appropriate. If your mother or sister were murdered, I don't think you'd like to see her in an art exhibit'" (quoted in the *San Diego Union-Tribune*, 28 February 1992). This remark is in stark contrast to a statement Lewis had made earlier: "These women by and large are transient, don't have family ties, they're drug abusers, in fact, many families, although they knew they were gone, were really glad they weren't coming around any more" (*No Humans Involved* 1993).

Killing Time: The Violent Imaginary of Feminist Media

SUSAN LORD

[10]

Introduction

From the first feminist murder fantasy in cinema, Germaine Dulac's *The Smiling Madame Beudet* (1923), to the ugly realism of Coralie Trinh Thi and Virginie Despentes's nihilist millennium-closer, *Baise-Moi* (1999),[1] cinema by women, not surprisingly, imagines its violence as vengeance, as a just-cause response to the exploitation of the body, the burden of sexual difference, and/or psychic violations of everyday life under patriarchy. Feminist media have been studied for both their narrative content and their politics of form—that is, for their attempt to articulate sexual politics as also a problem of the form any representation takes (most notably in writings by Laura Mulvey [1975], Teresa de Lauretis [1984], and Mary Ann Doane [1988]). In feminist media practice, this problem is worked through both in terms of specific issues related to representation (such as, how does one photograph the female body?) and in terms of the aesthetic or formal traditions of the medium being used (such as, in cinematic terms, how does one create a sequence of images that does not reproduce gender binarisms?). Underlying both of these concerns is the entanglement of and the tension between aesthetics, ethics, and politics. What is (perhaps not surprisingly) rarely discussed is the fact that the feminist film canon is strewn with corpses, imagined or literal, male and female, depicted or described. Most often the violence is performed by the women in the film, but in films such as those by Marlene Gorris (*A Question of Silence* [1982], *Broken Mirrors* [1984], and *Antonia's Line* [1994]) violence against women is also explicitly represented as a condition in which the characters live and enact violence. Rapists, johns, cruel husbands, shop clerks, and even plastic surgeons are given their comeuppance in the canon, sometimes with guns but also with domestic tools or shopping carts. There are also acts of violence without recipients of violence (Martha Rosler's *Semiotics of the Kitchen* [1974]; see fig. 20]) as well as reflections on the violent imaginary itself (Maya Deren's *Meshes of the Afternoon* [1943]).

Rather than focusing exclusively on the plots and the moral and political issues the films raise, I want to think about the act of violence and its motivations in terms of a politics of time, therefore looking at the temporal imaginary that subtends the act of violence and its formal embodiment. This politics of time comprises at least four temporal registers: the time of the form of the work of media art, the time of the represented acts and their environment, the time of the viewer, and, most interestingly, the time of the agent herself. With regard to the latter, the agent's age and subjective development and/or acts within the story world or visual space of the piece can be—and

FIGURE 20 Scene from *Semiotics of the Kitchen*, 1974 (with permission of Martha Rosler).

often are—of a different temporal register than is that of the other characters, events, and environments represented. This difference between the female agent and the world(s) that form her social, historical, and/or aesthetic context constitutes the bad timing (or mistiming) of the violent imaginary.

The films enact a rupture in the chronometric time of linear history by giving priority to the felt body; and this rupture is given form through the performance of violence. This chapter draws on feminist phenomenology and film theory to elaborate upon that with which the films themselves are concerned. I first trace the violent imaginary as that which develops in response to the conflicting temporalities that form the context for female subjectivity in modernity. These connections between temporality, violence, gender, and modernity are elaborated by working through three key moments of the feminist film canon produced largely in Europe and North America. I then anchor the feminist theory and history to (chiefly) three films that correspond to these three eras of feminism. In these three films, and others that I reference, violence is a manifestation of a temporal crisis in the relationship between technologies of modernity and the body—specifically, the female body as a prize commodity shared by the scientific and entertainment industries. This crisis has two interwoven registers of significance: the women in these films are aging; and, formally, the films reflect upon temporality, technology, and the body. The films express that felt body, giving an aesthetic form to what Vivian Sobchack (1994, 85) describes as follows: "We often experience the changes of aging as somehow alien to us, as if the 'real self' is frozen in time, imprisoned somewhere within the aging body."

The three films that I use as keys to, or anchors for, this experience are: Germaine Dulac's *The Smiling Madame Beudet* (1923), Chantal Akerman's *Jeanne Dielman, Quai du Commerce, 1080 Bruxelles* (1975), and Kim Derko's *The Book of Knives* (1996). In 1923 French director Germaine Dulac's character Mme Buedet loads a gun with real bullets in the hope that her insufferable husband will shoot himself and bring to a close the excruciating and endless boredom of her married life. The film is structured like a repeating loop, without resolution, mirroring the repetition of daily habits of bourgeois heteronormativity. In Belgian filmmaker Chantal Akerman's 1975 film *Jeanne Dielman, Quai du Commerce, 1080 Bruxelles*, the minimal plot also focuses on the domestic life of a middle-aged, middle-class woman, Jeanne; however, unlike Dulac's character, Jeanne is a prostitute who, towards the end of the film, kills a client. Her actions are given formal and dramatic equivalence in real-time, whether she waits, peels potatoes, drops a fork, or kills a john. Over twenty years later, in *The Book of Knives*, a short experimental narrative film by Canadian filmmaker Kim Derko, Iris Campbell, a character whose frozen image as a medical commodity has not been permitted to age since 1905, kills her plastic surgeon in 1995. The film is structured as a series of case studies, and the technologies of imaging are central to the medical diagnoses to which Iris is subjected, functioning both as structural and dramatic elements of the film's form and content.

Waves and Themes

Following the productions of feminist visual culture from the first wave of Western feminism in the 1910s and 1920s through the second and third waves, we are able to see reflected the issues dominating the feminist counter-public sphere at particular moments: bourgeois domestic troubles and the struggle for a public life are present in the story worlds and their formal presentations in the early cinema of Lois Weber, Alice Guy Blanché, and Germaine Dulac; the struggle over the meaning of femininity in the 1940s and 1950s films of Maya Deren and Dorothy Arzner becomes in the 1970s and 1980s a more direct and confident interrogation of the oppressive conditions and cultural production of sexual difference, as exemplified in Akerman's *Jeanne Dielman* (1974), Martha Rosler's *Semiotics of the Kitchen* (1974), Sally Potter's *Thriller* (1979), Anne Claire Poirier's *Mourir à tue-tête* (1979), Marlene Gorris's *A Question of Silence* (1982) and *Broken Mirrors* (1984), and Lizzie Borden's *Born in Flames* (1983). The mid-1980s through the 1990s sees a shift from sexual difference to gender and cultural difference: Leslie Thorton's *Adynata* (1983), Anne Wheeler's *Loyalties* (1986), Tracey Moffatt's *Night Cries: A Rural Tragedy* (1990), Pam Tom's *Two Lies* (1990), Ngosi Onwurah's *Body Beautiful* (1990), and the films of Trinh T. Minh-Ha (most notably for this context: *Sur Name Viet, Given Name Nam* [1989] and *A Tale of Love* [1995]).

Given that technologies of the reproducible image, from photography to digital mediations, as well as those technologies of seeing related to biomedical systems, function as tools of containment, invasion, surveillance, and control of the female body and the female subject in dominant Western culture, feminist visual culture has long critiqued, transgressed the uses of, and attempted to reimagine the limits of these technologies. Hence, while technology is cited as a problem in terms of processes of representation throughout most of the canon, the 1990s also sees direct feminist critical engagements with issues related to cybernetic and biomedical technologies as instruments of identity construction and containment. These concerns are central to both Tom's and Onwurah's investigations of cultural difference as well as in Kathy

High's *Underexposed: The Temple of the Fetus* (1993), Yvonne Rainer's MURDER *and murder* (1996), Kim Derko's *The Book of Knives* (1996), Janine Marchessault's *The Numerology of Fear* (1999), and the work of Shu-Lea Cheang and other digital artists (such as Nell Tenhaaf). While not all of those listed address violence in a direct way, most of them do reflect on violence as a formative condition for female subjectivity and as a pervasive condition of life for women in modernity.

We can see the exercise of violence as the means by which to effect a momentary and often unspectacular break or rupture in a time loop of repetitious acts and deadly boredom (*The Smiling Madame Beudet*). Or it is an act temporally structured to function as equivalent to other acts—thus commenting on the culture of violence against women as naturalized and habitualized in the routine of daily life and its visual culture (*Jeanne Dielman*). Or it is a direct assault on the visual culture of gender containment (*The Book of Knives*). Or, more conventionally, it brings closure or cessation by functioning as the climax (*Broken Mirrors*).

In the majority of these films and tapes, the agent of violence is decidedly middle-aged. Mothers and/or sex workers and/or wives and/or patients: the conflict between aging and not having autonomy as a temporal subject is a central dramatic and/or formal tension that gets expressed as violence and even murder. There is also a specific issue relating the medicalized, aging body as a site or agent of violence. In Kim Derko's *The Book of Knives* (1996), which is exemplary of this subgenre, the felt body is prioritized over the body as object of measure, spectacle, or erotic attraction. Here the logic that links technology (medical and visual), chronometric time, and the spatial and temporal confinements of the female image are disrupted. This rupture, I argue below, in the chronometric time of linear history comes about through the emergence or prioritization of the felt body; and it is often enacted in feminist cinema through the performance of violence.

One thread joining various feminisms throughout the twentieth century is the struggle for temporality—for its emergence through praxis from modernity's production of time (Lefebvre, 1991) and technological subordination of time to space. In other words, we are dealing with a struggle against the particularly modern form of time that uses imaging techniques and technologies to freeze women out in space.[2] Central to the last twenty-five years of feminist analyses of the image of women in modern visual culture is Laura Mulvey's oft-cited insight that "women are simultaneously looked at and displayed, with their appearance coded for strong visual and erotic impact so that they can be said to connote *to-be-looked-at-ness*...her visual presence tends to work against the development of a story line, to freeze the flow of action in moments of erotic contemplation [for the imagined male viewer]" (Mulvey 1975, 10). This understanding of the image of woman as that which is associated with the stilling of time, with the space and not the narrative of cinema, with arrest rather than development, is what I refer to when I discuss the spatial freeze of modern femininity. This condition of the Western social imaginary is central to feminist culture's critique and alternatives. While this condition of spatialization has a long history in Western culture (see Burfoot in this volume; as Julia Kristeva [1981]; Susan Bordo [1987]; and Rosi Braidotti [1991 and 1994]), the marriage of capitalism, biomedical science, and technologies of the reproducible image create a condition within which the detemporalized and endlessly reproducible image of woman circulates as the shared and prized commodity. The rationalization of vision, as discussed by Susan Bordo (1987, 23), is the "nightmare of the infinite universe transformed into the well-lighted laboratory of modern science and philosophy." Such spatial revelation is coextensive with the pursuit of the kernel of time, time's essence; that is, the representation of time as progress and without loss, a standard time, with direction, purpose, and so on. And, according to Elizabeth Ermarth (1992, 30),

> Historical time, and the consciousness coextensive with it, is at least potentially interchangeable among individuals because it is consciousness of the *same* thing: an invariant world, one that changes according to certain laws that do not change. Any individual perspective is only arbitrarily limited; it is only the "accidents" of language, nationality, gender, and so on that obscure this potentially cosmic vision. But this condition notwithstanding, if each individual could see all of the world (so the representational convention of time goes), all would see the *same* world.

She continues this ironic statement by remarking that, "the triumph of historical time entails a perpetual transcendence of, one might even say flight from, the concrete, and because of this, it offers no assistance to those who must deal with material limitation, including the ultimate material limitation of death" (30). We may well understand time as artefactual, as plastic, as made (as is evident when we consider that time is structured differently in different cultures), but the view of time as progress, as always on its way to the next place in line, is an order of time well suited to, in fact made to order by, the marriage of capitalism and science. Hence, making time otherwise appears to be only in the interest of those for whom this form of historical time "offers no assistance." The time of use, aging, and death for female subjects whose sociocultural (i.e., objective) value had been guaranteed by a time that doesn't want to know death—the image, frozen in space—is culturally coded as useless time (i.e., without function or future). This view is reproduced and intensified by biomedical technologies and their chronometry.

To deprive the body of its time and to deprive time of the body by rendering it as only a spatial object is to create the condition of a double suffering. That body cannot live its time; and, unable to live its time, it is deprived of its historicality and its mortality. Of course, the forms of time in the everyday and in representational worlds are not the same; but the embodiment of representation—the psychic leaning upon the body and the body's adoption of postures of being—produces the imaginary of and in the everyday. Hence, among the many implications of this condition of the spatial frieze for subjectivity and, therefore, for society is the elimination of futurity as a collectively created, and creative, experiment in and with time. In the films I analyze, the murders and other violent acts by women function as formal enactments of disparity and dissension within the patriarchal spatial economy of the image. As well, these murders function as momentary thresholds and limits of the concrete and collective suffering of detemporalization that continually appear in the exercise of power. In nearly all cases, the moment of violence is reflected upon as being connected to the technologies that form, inform, or extend from the social and aesthetic production of these problematic spaces. For example, the technologies are interrogated by some gesture of filming that works to obscure vision and its hold on the framing of the world or through a direct action that either narratively or metaphorically turns the technology into a useless or differently used object.

In many films from the period of the 1970s to the 1990s there is a heightened engagement with turning the dead gaze of imaging technology upon itself by, in Laura Mulvey's (1975, 18) words, "[freeing] the look of the camera into its materiality in time and space and the look of the audience into dialectics, passionate detachment." While this is arguably present in the work of the previous decades, feminist cinema of the 1970s and 1980s confronted the problem of producing a space of representation reflective of the socio-historical relation of women to modernity's dichotomous arrangements of power and knowledge. This practice was correlative with—and often a companion to—feminist theoretical and political investigations into the material conditions that produce gender and sexual difference. In this way, we can perhaps best understand feminist cinema as participating in social discourse through its response to that which the discourse cannot speak—or to the silences and absences the discourse, however critical, produces.[3] The theoretical and practical questions converged with the concern over the ethical and political stakes of representing the female body within a cultural context where economic and symbolic power pivots upon the investment, circulation, and marketing of the sexed body as a consumable entity. The structural impossibility of film and photography to not re-present the female body as already sexed, as always bound to the position of "to-be-looked-at-ness," was a condition that could not be "overturned by a contemporary practice that is more aware, more self-conscious" (Doane 1988, 140). Elaborating on Mary Ann Doane's summary of this impasse, the dichotomy articulated in theory between essentialism and anti-essentialism (which underwrites the proliferation of binaries named above) had as its correlation in practice two equally "inhibiting and mislead-ing" positions: (1) full presence of an untrammelled body—a position that preassigns transparency to technologies of mechanical reproducibility and thus presupposes the technologies' inherent ability to offer verisimilitude; or (2) absence of any depiction of that body—a position that presupposes that symbolic capital is so thickly embodied by imaging technology that the nega-tion of any realism is the only aesthetic response. These two positions repeat the founding problem rather than offer another syntax for representability: in the first position, female identity is not only adequated to the body, it is ontol-ogized; that is, the truth of identity is equated with being via appearance (i.e., appearance = essence), the foundation of which is nature. In the second posi-tion, this biological determinism is understood as a construction of knowledge, and, due to the technological determinism that drives this analysis, technol-ogy itself is ontologized. Ontologized technology is thus projected onto the body in its absence. Based on this summary, we can see that both positions emerge from the problematic inheritance of modernity's ocularcentrism, which equates vision with truth—a vision that becomes inextricable from technologies that process the world as information, organize it as a spatial image, and construct nature as that which exists to be dominated.

Murderous Thoughts: Madame Beudet, Jeanne Dielman, and Iris

The reflection on violence and the spatialization of femininity—of being locked into an image and frozen out of time—was undertaken in two foun-dational films of the feminist canon: Dulac's 1922 silent French film *The Smil-ing Madame Beudet* and Maya Deren's 1943 *Meshes of the Afternoon*. While the differences in context and film form are important, these films both produce a homology between violence and the atemporal image; and for both, the mise-en-scéne of the domestic sphere is used to signify menace and containment. Thus, these films can be understood as the origins of the feminist gothic in cinema. Where Deren's experimentalism permits a series of image–concept relations to be directly reflected upon (the shattered mirror and the dead woman, the window as frame, the mirror shard and the shape of the knife, and so on), Dulac's short narrative reflects on the atemporality of and in the domestic sphere at the level of narrative structure, making it particularly interesting for our purposes here.

Madame and Monsieur Beudet live in the provinces and, as the closing titles tell, are "joined by habit." M Beudet relieves his boredom by taunting his wife with the possibility that he will shoot himself with the gun he repeatedly pulls from a desk drawer, flails around, and points to his temple, laughing uproariously (see fig. 21). Mme Beudet lives with her boredom by playing the piano and reading popular magazines from which she conjures dream lovers (see fig. 22). One evening M Beudet goes to the opera, locking his wife's piano before leaving her at home. She spends the night reading and fantasizing about a young tennis player, whom she animates from the still images in the advertising pages of her magazine. However, these fantasies are repeatedly interrupted by phantasms of her ghoulish husband. So, before going to bed, she loads his gun and replaces it in his desk drawer. After a restless sleep in which she dreams about signs of confinement (domestic objects, the "House

Figure 21 Scene from *The Smiling Madame Beudet*, 1923 (with permission of M. Yann Beauvais).

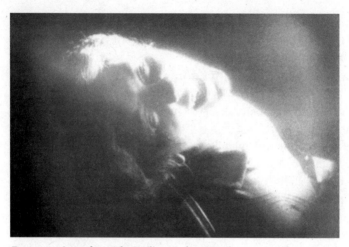

FIGURE 22 Scene from *The Smiling Madame Beudet*, 1923 (with permission of M. Yann Beauvais).

of Detentions and Corrections," and nightmare images of her husband—all of which are structured around an intertitle "Always the same horizons…"), she is confronted in the morning with her husband's rantings against women ("Women: do you know what is to be done with them?") and his performances of violence: he crushes a doll's head in his fist, pulls out the gun, aims it at his temple and then, before pulling the trigger, swings the aim toward her. The gun goes off, just missing her but shattering a vase of flowers. He interprets her attempted murder as intended suicide, for which he consoles her. The consolation is parodied by the appearance of puppets in the upper portion of the screen performing a melodramatic resolution. The film then ends as it began, with a dreary view of Chartres and a shot from behind the couple as they walk up a cobbled street, passing a priest on the way, with an iris-out (blackening out of the frame from circumference to centre) closing the screen to black. The opening title is repeated ("In the provinces…") and added to with the words: "In the quiet streets, without horizon, under the heavy sky.…Joined together by habit." This leaves us with a sense of infinite repetition, suggestive of the entrapment of women not only in an array of social institutions but also within representation itself: a film loop through which her objective and subjective conditions are mediated, measured, and repeated.

The mise-en-scène and theme of menace and danger *within* the home can be followed through several other films in the canon to form a type of subgenre of the feminist gothic. Arguably, there is a politics of time within this subgenre, as is evident with Deren's *Meshes*, Sally Potter's *Thriller* (1979), Anne Wheeler's *Loyalties* (1986), Tracey Moffatt's *Night Cries: A Rural Tragedy*

(1990), and Jane Campion's *The Piano* (1993). Patricia Mellencamp (1995), Laleen Jayamanne (2001), and I (Lord 2006) have taken up the theme of the feminist gothic and its particularly colonial birth. For our purposes here, I need only point to the fact that the forms of violence, the intimations and acts of murder, are manifestations of the *Heimlichkeit* (familiarity, or homeliness) being a space of its opposite—the uncanny. The home (domestic and national) is viewed in these films as a place haunted by the violent history of silenced women and colonial others. Within these spaces and narratives we also find violence between mother and daughter (*The Piano, Night Cries*). These damaged dyads form the thematic centre of other films, such as Pam Tom's *Two Lies* (1990).

Films dealing with sex work and/as domestic labour form another feminist subgenre central to the politics and aesthetics of the canon. One film that reflects directly on the violent imaginary and its particular temporal order is *Broken Mirrors* by Marlene Gorris. In this film Gorris uses a thriller format to explore two seemingly separate narratives. The first is of a man who kidnaps women, photographs them with a polaroid camera at each stage of their psychic disintegration and physical degeneration, and murders them. He affixes the photographs in sequential order to the wall of the room he uses to contain the women, leaving each series up for the subsequent woman to see as she is held captive. The second narrative thread is about a woman who becomes a prostitute and who, with her colleagues, frees herself from the brutality of being a sex worker. But the two stories mirror each other and eventually intersect: a john who turns out to be the killer is killed by the sex worker. Breaking the mirrors of "man-made" containments is the final victory (see fig. 23).

This overt and heavy-handed use of symbols of confinement and emancipation has a more subtle and complex reflection in Chantal Akerman's *Jeanne Dielman*—a film that is foundational to the last three decades of feminist media and that is of particular relevance to the issues of time, technology, and the body. The film makes use of elements that register the cinematic and social conditions of women's suffering: domestic containment, social fantasies of woman as automaton and as prostitute, the scenarios of melodramatic time, and boredom. For 198 minutes we observe three sequential days of Jeanne's almost obsessional routine of making beds, cooking, eating, having sex with a john, stabbing the john, cleaning, and so on. Slowly, the melodramatic sense of "bad timing" enters the frame, with inert objects seemingly animated by some external force. And with the melodramatic, the uncanny and the unfamiliar slip into and defamiliarize and denaturalize the most mundane of gestures.

FIGURE 23 Scene from *Broken Mirrors*, 1984, directed by Marlene Gorris.

> Jeanne performs the murder as if it were one more necessary action within a series of routine timed gestures. Redesigning drama, Akerman purposefully skips the representation of causes. For motives she substitutes a series of automatic, alienated gestures, all with a similar effect. (Margulies 1996, 93)

Akerman tropes on the sublime machine of the modern feminine-automaton, making of and through Jeanne a fold or question in time and timing: teleological accumulation *and* inertia, temporal sequence *and* suspension, self-determined *and* moved by external forces.

Ivone Margulies, in her book *Nothing Happens: Chantal Akerman's Hyperrealist Everyday*, argues that, in the "hyperreality" of Akerman's films, a "corporeal weight" is derived through duration, repetition, and the seriality of simplified forms to the effect of bleeding the temporal register of the filmic into the viewers' experience of watching the film.[4] And while it is certainly true that in *Jeanne Dielman* the repetitive, automaton-like acts of the female "character" have a political content (representing the work of prostitution and domestic chores in real time, for instance), the little "disasters," the minimalist accumulation of change, also register boredom as "constitutive of impatience and anguish" (Margulies) and illuminate the fragility of order.

The temporality of her films works within the conditions of modernity's order of time in order to turn it back on itself, to make it examinable by the viewer as a condition shared by women in Western culture. In the film, time is nearly stilled in order that the space of containment within the screen and the mise-en-scène can be read: the physiognomy of women's spaces (kitchens and bedrooms) and the singular texture of everyday life. However, this everyday life and these spaces are rendered strange, unfamiliar, almost uncanny through small inversions of banality as well as through temporal strategies that blur animate/inanimate, motion/stillness. Of major importance, then, are the non-events: the long takes, the camera that hardly moves, the cuts that rarely occur, and so on. These are techniques by which the "action" is expressed. That action is boredom—Akerman did, after all, choose "sloth" as her sin in the omnibus film *Seven Women, Seven Sins*.

In her essay "Historical *Ennui*, Feminist Boredom," Patrice Petro (1996, 197) makes the following argument *for* boredom:

> It is perhaps not surprising...that so much feminist work over the past decades...has involved an aesthetics as well as a phenomenology of boredom: a temporality of duration, relentless in its repetition, and a stance of active waiting, which, at least in their feminist formulations, allow for redefinition, resistance, and change. For women modernists, aesthetic and phenomenological boredom provide a homeopathic cure for the banality of the present—a restless self-consciousness...very different from the ideal of disinterestedness.

In Akerman's work boredom and repetition are companions that, through the use of long takes and real time, bring difference into existence. Real time dominates but, due to the habits developed in viewing conventional films, there is no time that moves more slowly. The time it takes to watch Jeanne wait, for instance, can become a time endured or a time for scrutiny and reflection on hidden forms of violence of everyday life—or both.

In this final section I turn to the 1990s and to the discourses of violence in terms of time, through aging and medicalization, by considering a film wherein the aging female body meets medical technology as a chronological enforcer. Toronto filmmaker Kim Derko's *The Book of Knives* provides a time and, thus, a desire for the aging body, a body generally abandoned to abject spaces. *The Book of Knives* is a short experimental-narrative comprising seven chapters, or case studies, that chronicle episodes in the history of women's treatment by psychiatric medical experiments. And while a lobotomy and an electroshock treatment are among the medical experiments depicted, the use of technologies of mechanical reproducibility are understood as being fundamental aspects of the treatment and are themselves under constant interrogation by the film. The present tense of the film concerns a woman in her thirties, Iris Campbell, who is undergoing psychiatric evaluation as a result of

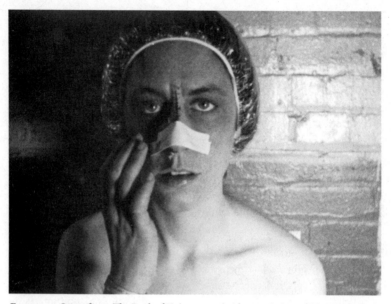

FIGURE 24 Scene from *The Book of Knives*, 1996 (with permission of Kim Derko).

her having murdered a plastic surgeon. She appears as the patient in each of the seven case studies in the chronicle, beginning in 1905 with Walter Greenough Chase's (a doctor who made early medical films) epilepsy biographies, and ending in 1995 (the year the film was made) with a yet-to-be written chapter of Iris Campbell's treatment by a Dr. Shaw—a fictional female psychiatrist whose book of case studies are the textual double of the filmic episodes. Significantly, Iris commits suicide in one of the cases. I suggest that much of the affective and connotative value in the film emerges from the crisis undergone by the time of the lived-bodies when they confront the chronometry of the medical gaze, diagnosis, and treatment. This order of time, the view of history from which it emerges, and the role played by commodification is a nexus that abhors and makes abject the aging female body.

The discursive, historical, and technical construction of aging can explain a great deal about why such bodies are situated as a ruin of representation and, thus, why abjection seems to be the only discursive field to contain such bodies. But the constructionist approach gives us little means by which to understand the desire and temporal self-understanding of its subjects. Given that the medical treatments undergone by the subjects in the film effect most evidently the surface of the body (its morphology and its skin), the attempt to represent aging here is also an attempt to produce an image of sentience—that aspect of being to which the knowledge of life (the science, technology, and

FIGURE 25 Scene from *The Book of Knives*, 1996 (with permission of Kim Derko).

economy) is inimical. In other words, by giving temporal priority to the complex experience of aging and medicalization, the specular body—as scientific object and as the cultural scene of abjection and disuse—is subordinated by the felt body. What Kathleen Woodward (1991) describes as a phantasm of the felt body as the immobile/companion, empty, or fragmenting body is relevant here as well. The felt body in the film is, thereby, not a fullness or completion. And the disunity is not merely reflective of the fact that the film deals with multiple issues or offers multiple time zones for such issues; rather, the two terms—aging and medicalization—become incompatible in the same time, indicating that, for the female subject, these experiences are radically inconsistent with her coextensive assignment by medical discourse and treatment. One ghosts the other. And that incompatibility is expressed as violence.

The Book of Knives initially appears not to be about aging because the central character is young. But the issue of aging is pervasive—Iris Campbell as a medical subject is not permitted to age, she is static, a record, frozen in the chronometric space of medical imaging. The film also contains—in the double sense—a tremendous violence: discursive, symbolic, and physical violence done to and embodied by the women, and a moment when the psychic mechanism of interring trauma breaks apart. Iris's murder of the plastic surgeon is, on the one hand, a heavy-handed symbolic act; on the other hand, it is the only act that frees her into time.

Doubled violence is discussed by Vivian Sobchack (1994) in her article "The Revenge of the Leech Woman: On the Dread of Aging in the Low-Budget Horror Film." While she is clearly working with quite a different cinema, her discussion is illuminating nonetheless. The aging woman is, according to Sobchack, scared and scary: "Subjectively felt, she is an excess woman— desperately afraid of invisibility, uselessness, lovelessness, sexual and social isolation and abandonment, but also deeply furious at…the double standard of aging in a patriarchal culture" (Sobchack 1994, 82). She goes on to modify Kristeva's (1982) theorization of abjection, which comes from within (pregnancy and cancer), to argue that the proliferation and splitting of cells, the changes in volume, the indomitable growth of the Other within the body causes the bodily changes of the figures in these horror films. "Within the transformed, monstrous, and visible bodies of these women divided against themselves in desperation, anger, and self-loathing, there is indeed an 'other.'" By working the popular cultural image through a phenomenological perspective on the felt body, she formulates that "we often experience the changes of aging as somehow alien to us, as if the 'real self' is frozen in time, imprisoned somewhere within the aging body" (85). The films thaw or animate this "time of the other."

The device of using the same actress/character suggests two interwoven points: it serves as a critical commentary on the medical standardization of women, a standardization homologous to commodification—the always-the-same in countless number and the ever-new. And, extending from this point, the standard of the medicalized female functions representationally as a form of cryogenics: frozen in the discursive and pictorial spaces as the medical commodity, Iris has no time. Present-day Iris, having had botched plastic surgery, embodies this history of the yoked ideals of youth and beauty as female, but the containment of such ideals breaks apart and she becomes the "scary" woman Sobchack refers to. Unlike Sobchack's Leech Woman, however, Iris's morphology is unchanged—she doesn't physically age or become physically monstrous—although the first shot of Iris is post-operative, stitched, and swollen. In fact, she remains well-composed and taut throughout—her skin as unsagging as her discourse as she interrogates the psychiatrist. Those previous generations of Iris documented in Dr. Shaw's medical history text are animated by Iris as she reads agency into the subjects of those case studies; in turn, these other Irises become companion bodies that temporalize Iris's own subjectivity.

Conclusion

In Derko's film the priority given to the temporality of the aging body has the effect of "unnaturalizing" the historical and chronometric laws that under-write scientific and cultural value. And with the three films focused upon here—*The Smiling Madame Beudet, Jeanne Dielman*, and *The Book of Knives*—the critique is accompanied by an alternative: the felt body, as desiring not just more time but a different time, an other time, is given a representational complexity and a reflexive mode for temporal self-understanding through acts of violence. As with Madame Beudet and Jeanne, Iris's aging body's incom-patibility with the ideologies of femininity and the commodification of the female body produces a moment for reflection upon the dominion of a techno-logic of time and the forms of violence that the confrontation with this form of time engenders for women. Through the production of counter-images and counter-temporalities in the feminist public sphere, this confrontation is expressible as a cultural engagement rather than as private suffering. As I have attempted to do here, feminist media can thus be analyzed as a form for and an externalization of the violent imaginary embodied by women in their nego-tiations with or refusals of the narratives, images, and time zones of moder-nity.

Notes

1 I have elected not to include a discussion of Coralie Trinh Thi and Virginie Despentes's *Baise-Moi* because it does nothing to extend or add to the reflections on screen vio-lence undertaken by a century of women filmmakers and video artists. In other words, it does not extend the feminist counter-public sphere. The postfeminist aura with which it was received would categorize it with other female action films, from *La Femme Nikita* to *Lara Croft: Tomb Raider*; alternately and more productively, it could be read within the framework of the new screen violence of French postnational cul-ture. It is worth noting that, to date, only one woman—Bérénice Reynaud (2002)—has written a review of this film. I concur with her conclusion that the film does not provide any insight into the violent imaginary of women—though this may have been the intention of the filmmakers. The other thirty reviews of the film that I read were written by men. The most thoughtful of these is Scott MacKenzie's (2002) report on the censorship controversy surrounding the film.

2 Central to the last twenty-five years of feminist analyses of the image of women in modern visual culture is Laura Mulvey's (1975, 10) oft-cited insight that "women are simultaneously looked at and displayed, with their appearance coded for strong visual and erotic impact so that they can be said to connote *to-be-looked-at-ness*...her visual presence tends to work against the development of a story line, to freeze the flow of action in moments of erotic contemplation [for the imagined male viewer]." This understanding of the image of woman as that which is associated with the stilling of

time, with the space and not the narrative of cinema, with arrest rather than development, is what I refer to when I discuss the spatial freeze of modern femininity. This condition of the Western social imaginary is central to feminist culture's critique and alternatives.

3   This is part of larger debates about the modernity of feminism and the privilege enjoyed by linguistic-based analyses of film.

4   I rely on Margulies for providing the best analysis of Akerman's well-known equivocations about feminism, which are often cited in writings about feminism and film. The following passage covers many of the infamous statements and makes important feminist sense of them.

> Akerman's work…is in the best tradition of feminism, an "irritant" to fixed categories of "woman." It is in this spirit that she has expressed her distance from an essentialist feminism: "I think it is poor and limiting to think of my films as simply feminist. You wouldn't say of a Fellini film that it's a *male* film….When people say there is a feminist film language, it is like saying there is only *one* way for women to express themselves."…"I won't say I'm a feminist film-maker….I am not making women's films. I am making Chantal Akerman films."…Akerman's approach to type takes [the notion of representativeness] to task…Akerman's characters, I argue, go beyond the neutralization of individuality present in constructions of allegorical or "average" types. The question underlying her novel conceptions is that of creating a potentially plural representation that nevertheless does not attempt a totalized status. (Margulies 1996, 12, 15, 18)

FIGURE 26 Prisoners' glee club, Kingston Prison for Women, 1955 (with permission from Canada's Penitentiary Museum Collection, Kingston, Ontario).

[section three]

National Trouble: Gendered Violence

FIGURE 27 Mills Eisert escape site, Kingston Prison for Women, 1961 (with permission from Canada's Penitentiary Museum Collection, Kingston, Ontario).

Dario Argento's *The Bird with the Crystal Plumage*: Caging Women's Rage

FRANK BURKE

[11]

Introduction

It is no secret that Italian cinema is heavily masculine. If we look at middle-to highbrow Italian film (the work best recognized internationally) we find that, until recently, there have been only two women directors of note, Lina Wertmuller and Liliana Cavani, from the immediate postwar period up until the late 1980s.[1] Moreover, women characters have tended to be secondary, reflecting only male characters, male attitudes, and male values. Even the work of Wertmuller and Cavani can be criticized from a gender perspective. The former has tended to enact a structural critique of power relations that, at best, places women within male roles or role-emulations and, at worst, within regressive, passive, "typical" female behaviour. The latter, particularly in a film such as *The Night Porter*, carries out a psychological critique of power that leaves its woman protagonist with *only* the possibility of regression and, worse still, self-degradation.[2] If we turn to lowbrow Italian film—the genre or subgenre films such as the sword-and-sandal epic, the spaghetti western, the *giallo*[3] (or thriller), and obviously the sexploitation flick—the situation is even worse: no women directors and consistently problematic constructions of women.

The one place where women have consistently achieved centrality and representational power is in the Italian horror film, particularly through the persona of Barbara Steele during the heyday of Italian horror in the 1960s. It is arguable that this centrality constitutes merely a misogynist projection of male anxiety along the lines suggested by Barbara Creed (1993, 7) when she says: "The presence of the monstrous-feminine in the popular horror film speaks to us more about male fears than about female desire or feminine subjectivity." However, it is also arguable that, in individual instances, the Italian horror film may offer woman's "monstrosity" not just as male projected horror but also as a consequence of women's rage, grounded in and justified by women's experience of violence and oppression. In fact, I would argue that Dario Argento's *The Bird with the Crystal Plumage* (1970) presents its female protagonist-killer not merely as a projection of the author's or the horror genre's male angst but as part of a comprehensive critique of the condition of women in a male world.[4]

Making claims for a serious reading of *The Bird with the Crystal Plumage* may seem a bit of as stretch. Leon Hunt (2000, 326) claims, "if Italian horror has been an extreme case of the [horror film's] outlaw status, it is also difficult to imagine a 'progressive' reading of Dario Argento's films." However, as Chris Gallant (2000, 7) notes at the outset of *Art of Darkness: The Cinema of Dario Argento*, Argento's films "invite analysis" at least partly because they situate themselves "between the European art cinema and a genre labeled 'Exploitation.'" Argento's films establish themselves as something more than a mere reproduction of genre "pulp" partly through referencing more self-reflexive practitioners of horror: Alfred Hitchcock, Michael Powell in *Peeping Tom* (1960), and one of the quintessentially "serious" filmmakers of the 1950s and early 1960s, Michelangelo Antonioni (see Gallant 2000, 11–19; Newman 2000, 108; Thrower 2000, 129). Moreover, they do so in terms not just of style but also of socio-political issues and, even more so, issues of masculinity.

"Seriousness" aside, it may also seem wrong-headed to proffer a pro-feminist reading of Argento. Critics such as Barbara Creed (1993) and Carol Clover (1992), though opening up significant new possibilities for reading recent Hollywood horror films in the context of gender, have made it difficult to see them, in the final analysis, as anything other than a reinscription of patriarchy and masculinity.[5] However, recent analyses of Argento's work (see Knee 1996; Gallant 2000; Balmain 2002; Shaviro 1993; *Kinoeye* 2002a, 2002b) have drawn different conclusions by focusing on issues such as identity, subjectivity, and the fluidity of cinematic signification in his films.

A pro-feminist reading of Argento must also confront his own most frequently cited comment about gender: "I like women especially beautiful ones. If they have a good face and figure, I would much prefer to watch them being murdered than an ugly girl or man" (Jones 1983, 20). In fact, Argento's words (a provocative reaction, I suspect, to the usual restrictive line of questioning imposed by the interview format) are belied by his films, which repeatedly subvert the conventional duality of male-fetishizing-assailant and female-fetishized-victim. As Adam Knee (1996, 215) notes:

> While Argento's work does tend to have more female victims (two of his films are even set in schools primarily for women), he nonetheless includes quite a few male victims and often dwells on their deaths at some length. Argento's protagonists are themselves fairly evenly split between male and female. Moreover, where Clover sees the killer as being male in most slasher films...Argento's killers, in their variety and obscurity, tend to frustrate...such generalizations about gender.

In addressing Argent's "gender bending" I seek not only to provide a new reading of *The Bird with the Crystal Plumage* but also to situate that reading within the film's historical moment: 1969 Italy. I suggest that Argento's film reflects the increasing self-expression and visibility of women in postwar Italy that led to the women's movement—a phenomenon that arose virtually at the moment *The Bird with the Crystal Plumage* appeared. And I link the film to manifestations within Italian postwar cinema (despite its masculinist bias) of women's growing strength in Italian society as well as to growing representations of violence in the 1960s, which provide a context for Argento's linkage of women's self-expression, political protest, and violence.

The Bird with the Crystal Plumage

The Bird with the Crystal Plumage stakes its claim to seriousness from the outset by foregrounding important themes, many of which were central to oppositional culture of the 1960s: the domination of nature and man's (I specify gender advisedly) alienation from it; an obsession with possessions or, in the film's scheme of things, collection; the exteriorization of inner life and a consequent radical split between inside and outside; and, finally, as a mode of relating to the world that encompasses all the above, colonization.

The film's title, recalling Hitchcock's *The Birds* (1963), implies the first theme. Man's dominion over the natural is revealed (along with the relevance of Hitchcock's film) early on by rows and rows of stuffed birds in glass cabinets at the Fondazione Wilkinson, for whom the male protagonist Sam has written a manual on the preservation of rare birds. Later on, a race track and zoo prove important to the plot, as does the painter Consalvi, who keeps cats in cages in order to fatten them up and eat them. The motif of caging comes to encompass virtually all the urban imagery in *The Bird with the Crystal Plumage*, including the high-rise apartment building in which Ranieri and Monica live, and Sam and Julia's apartment. Moreover, caging seems virtually internalized within the film's figures themselves. The crystal plumage ("like glass" we are told at one point) means that the bird of the film's title is self-encased. And the two killers in the film, Monica and Ranieri, dress head-to-toe in patent leather, likewise caging (and effectively denying) their bodies in "plumage," dissociating them not only from their world but also from themselves.

The fundamental alienation from nature implied in the motif of caging is perhaps most strikingly conveyed by Consalvi's painting. Accurately described by the antique store owner as "naïf but macabre," it depicts a young girl being attacked by a man in a snowscape that is strangely distorted. It is as though the act of aggression has violated the natural order, rendering it grotesque, or as though, in the contemporary world, man can see nature only as "macabre." Consalvi himself lives on a farm where he has managed to seal off all access except for a second-story window, from which he lowers a ladder if he so chooses. (As he puts it: "Nobody gets inside unless I want them to.") The plumage of glass and patent leather or vinyl "skin" of the killers also seal off the figures they encase, while transforming the natural (skin) into something artificial and "macabre."

Caging bespeaks collection, and in addition to ornithological foundations, zoos, and Consalvi, the film focuses on an antique store and, most centrally, an art gallery. The police obsessively collect and analyze information via the usual forensic apparatus, plus tape recorders and a hilarious computer data bank and information processor. Sam and Julia have littered their apartment with paintings, posters, busts, and other paraphernalia that are ultimately eclipsed by a photograph of Consalvi's painting that Sam "collects" from the antique store. Julia, a model who does little but look pretty and lie around the apartment, is clearly a collectable for Sam; and Monica, who is many years younger and seems to have little in common with her husband Ranieri, is apparently there to fulfill his need (reflected in his career as an art gallery proprietor) for exquisite objects.

Of course, *The Bird with the Crystal Plumage* is not an analysis of colonization per se; its allusions to historical instances tend principally to underscore a habitual mode of relating to the world (conquest, possession, projection of

self onto other) that characterizes the present as well as the past. This coloniz-
ing relation is not only violent in and of itself within the film, it also evokes
extreme alienation on the part of those living colonized lives (compartmen-
talized, objectified, split off from themselves). Consalvi is the clearest case in
point, but indicative as well is Caucaso, the "bird with the crystal plumage":
"They have to keep it isolated. It can't get along with the other animals. They're
going to have to move him....He can't even stand the smell of them." It is this
alienation that gives rise to the violence in *The Bird with the Crystal Plumage*.
Moreover, the violence (as well as colonization) represents both a critique of
masculinity and an analysis of women's response and perpetually renewed
oppression in the face of it.[6]

As may already be clear, there is an implicit critique of alienated masculinity in the film's representation of Consalvi and Caucaso. Sam is both
alienated and hollow, a classic American extravert come to Italy because he has
lost his ability to write. His dependence on external stimulation is partly what
draws him into the murder investigation, and his involvement in the investigation becomes a means of detaching himself from everything else, including
Julia. Inspector Morosini is just as vacuous as Sam, focused entirely on the
outer world of crimes and clues, with no life apart from his job, no home.
When the case is "solved" and he has no more external stimulation, he falls
asleep—on television, no less! Ranieri is aloof and unpleasant at best.

The film's critique of masculinity extends far beyond mere character defi-
ciencies. Most important is Monica's assault by a man when she was a young
girl. Male violence against women is the original sin, the fall from grace, with
the Biblical overtones underscored by Consalvi's edenic (albeit "macabre")
rendering of the attack. Moreover, this event is just the most blatant one in
which men substitute violence for intimacy. Morosini and his profession are
an obvious case in point, but so is Sam. The first time we see Julia and Sam
together (she has returned from a modelling trip and he from witnessing an
apparent attack on Monica at the art gallery), he keeps ignoring her affectionate invitations to bed. He then "dreams" of Monica, covered in blood,
once Julia finally persuades him to make love. This is only one of a number
of occasions in which Sam shows little or no interest in lovemaking or in
reciprocating Julia's affection, obsessing instead on Monica, the painting of her
assault, and the serial killings.

This, in turn, is part of a more profound disregard for Julia on the part
of Sam, Morosini, the police, and Sam's friend Carlo, which can only be interpreted as systemic misogyny. As Morosini drags Sam deeper into the investigation, he blatantly ignores Julia's passionate and justified objections. Far

worse is the treatment of Julia when Sam receives a phone call that threatens not only him but also her. The phone call is taped and, five times thereafter, is replayed, three times by the police and twice by Sam for Carlo. Morosini shows no interest whatsoever in the threat made to Julia, and in fact he and his colleagues fail to even replay that part of the conversation. Sam does replay it, but he and Carlo ignore it. (Argento insistently juxtaposes the words relating to Julia with the utterly indifferent expressions on the faces of the men.) Consistent with this, Sam goes off to visit Consalvi (a fitting union of two self-absorbed males) and leaves Julia alone in the apartment, where she ends up under terrifying siege. Julia's fundamental lack of significance for Sam is underscored in Monica's study near the end, as Julia lies bound, gagged, and barely conscious on the floor. Sam remains oblivious to her presence throughout the lengthy scene.

Julia's subjection to chronic disregard is a milder, more subtle version of the assault on Monica. Both derive from being female in a male world. Monica responds to her abuse with rage and becomes a serial killer. Julia responds to hers with frustration and, at a couple of points, even anger, However, her anger remains contained, female, even "cute," while Monica's rage is lethal, male-identified, and thoroughly threatening to a world in which violence is a male prerogative. It is for this reason that Julia is allowed to continue at large in a male world (her insignificance, or "trivialness," is her greatest asset), while Monica is ultimately incarcerated and explained away with facile psychological analysis (doubly "caged").

While the psychiatrist's explanation contributes to the film's unmasking of masculinity and misogyny in its ultimate effacement of Monica, it also allows the film to make some interesting moves regarding her (i.e., women's) agency. We are told: (1) that Monica was assaulted as a young girl; (2) that the effects of this traumatic event remained repressed for ten years, until by chance she saw Consalvi's painting; and (3) that "strangely she did not identify herself with the victim but with her attacker," turning her awakened rage against women rather than men. First of all, this account historicizes Monica, placing her experience and, more important, her experience of male sexual violence, at the source of the film's action. I want to emphasize this in contradistinction to critics such as Creed and Clover who, I feel, dehistoricize by addressing films and their female characters in universalizing Freudian and post-Freudian terms, which make representation only and always the reproduction of patriarchy/masculinity without the possibility of also being about women experiencing violence. Second, it allows Monica to choose a position of empowerment in response to her victimization. Third, it implies (and here

I do dovetail with Clover) that women can only be empowered by becoming male identified. In this respect, it also reproduces women's victimization in the female objects of Monica's awakened rage: but we will see that this gets addressed in the final scenes of the film in a manner that the psychiatrist, quite symptomatically, refuses to acknowledge.

In fact, the complex linkage between Monica's agency and masculinity complicates the issue of gender in ways that promote productive critique. The film pushes Monica's male identification to the point where she possesses the male gaze: ogling young women, taking their photographs, spying them through binoculars, and so on.[7] On the one hand, this is a clever *giallo* trick, aligning our gaze with what appears to be a man's and thus fooling us into making gender assumptions about the killer. On the other hand, it contributes to the distinction between Monica's "unacceptable" ability as a woman to assert her identity while and by remaining unseen (i.e., to exist beyond representation) and Julia's, who as a model repeatedly shot passively in close-ups, occupies the classic "acceptable" female role of object-of-the-gaze. (As we have seen, this classic form of visibility is, paradoxically, a form of invisibility in its reduction of women to profound insignificance.) Moreover, by resituating the gaze, the film encourages us to question our own tendency to make knee-jerk gender assumptions.

When the principal male characters make such assumptions, it can be read as an ideologically induced misreading of the situation. Sam assumes from the start that what he saw at the art gallery was a man attacking Monica. (We are told at the end it was the reverse.) Morosini and his band of assistants blithely assume that they are looking for a male killer. In light of the film's representation of men and its juxtaposition of Monica and Julia as the unacceptable versus the acceptable woman, it makes sense to read this not just as a failure to see what is really there but also as an inability to acknowledge women's rage because to do so would be to accept women as genuinely other. This, I would argue, is the crux of the matter in terms of a gender rereading of *The Bird with the Crystal Plumage*.

This reading becomes particularly tempting in light of the insistent elimination of women's anger and acting out in the film's final scenes. Even Julia gets "disciplined" for her aforementioned moments of anger that, though far more cute than menacing, are still not to be tolerated. In fact, she ends up thoroughly neutralized in the first scene in which she appears after having thrown flowers and a vase at Sam as he yet again renounces intimacy for his now largely private murder investigation. In her next appearance, she is, for the only time in the film, wearing black, the colour identified with Monica's rage.[8] (It is Monica who chooses to adorn herself in black for her killing sprees, though Ranieri, we are told, comes to appropriate her garb as well as her violence.) Moreover, the "Black Power" poster that has been visible on the wall in earlier scenes takes on prominence as a commentary on Julia's anger. However, it also becomes a reflection of the impossibility of that anger. For in this scene, as Julia is under siege, the poster is repeatedly juxtaposed with her terror, not her "power." Moreover, though she resists and even wields a knife at one point, suggesting Monica-like power and rage, she ends up traumatized. She collapses on the floor, pulls herself up weakly onto a table calling out "Sam," then collapses again. (Sam's arrival has scared off the assailant, thus saving Julia.) The next morning she is in bed, restored to whiteness (mostly naked, with some sheeting gathered around her), extremely fearful as she looks around her and again calls out "Sam."

While Julia's ultimate helplessness is central to the film's critique of classic gender logic, her extreme distress is also significant, helping prepare for an extraordinary moment that briefly unsettles this logic. As the film reaches its crisis point and Sam enters Monica's dark study (ignorant of where he is and who he is about to encounter), we can hear on the soundtrack a subtle but unmistakable series of sighs and moans, connoting extreme dis-ease, angst, and desperation. The sounds are clearly female, and most important, they are extra-diagetic. We might want to assume they originate only from Julia, bound and gagged on the floor. However, the first time we see her, she is unconscious and silent. Moreover, the sound echoes in a way that emphasizes that it is non-ambient. Nonetheless, it certainly speaks in part to her experience of being attacked and traumatized, now twice within some twelve minutes of film time. But it can also be identified with Monica since it functions as the "soundtrack" for her study, the place where we have seen her carefully preparing for her acts of violence. In fact, through its lack of differentiation and, even more so its narrative excess, I would argue that the sound makes the study the space of women's (not just one woman's) angst, and grounds what has emanated and is about to emanate from the study in that pain, giving it exceptional credibility. This credibility is heightened by the fact that the sound does not exist at the beginning of the scene, a shot from within the study with Sam still outside. It only begins upon Sam's entry, suggesting that women's pain is inaugurated by man's "penetration."

The study sequence reflects Sam's utter and comic incompetence, while his inability to sense Julia's presence reveals his utter lack of connectedness to his environment. At the same time, the sequence highlights Monica's "black power." (She appears in her vinyl/leather garb towards the end of the sequence.)

Though an extremely thin and fragile figure, she has managed single-handedly to capture Julia and Carlo, bind and gag the former, and kill off the latter. Moreover, apropos of her links to a gallery, her power expresses itself as art. She has propped Carlo in a chair, thus staging his death and confirming her status (evident earlier in her photography) as not just a killer but as an artist of death. She thus combines the physical violence of her original assailant with the violent aestheticism of Consalvi.

Most important, in terms of the film's representation of women's rage, this sequence marks a radical turning point in Monica's behaviour and one that exceeds dramatically the bounds placed on her by the psychiatrist's ensuing analysis. Despite his claim that Monica has identified (only) with her assailant, turning her aggression against other women, Monica here clearly shifts her focus. She does not kill Julia, just incapacitates her. In fact, Monica has now aligned her rage with its appropriate object: men. Having killed off Carlo in literally spectacular fashion, she focuses her impressive powers of creative mayhem on Sam. She lures him into the art gallery, where again she seeks to turn murder into spectacle or, perhaps more accurately, installation art. She seeks to make the invisible visible, turning on the bright gallery lights (she, not Sam, is the true finder of the light in these scenes). And she seeks to make visual art of the best kind—that is, aesthetically powerful, culturally signifi-cant images. With extraordinary dexterity and timing she loosens the ropes on a huge piece of sculpture, at the same time she turns on the lights, so that the sculpture lands and clamps down on Sam. Possessing numerous sharp pro-truding blades, the sculpture is a massive vagina dentata, around and upon which Monica dances, poking a knife at Sam's nose and gleefully imaging cas-tration, as she prepares to do him in. She thus reenacts the primal scene under-lying the film: the substitution of sexual aggression for intimacy. However, she does so from a woman's point of view, swallowing up, with her vaginal instrument of revenge, Sam-the-prick. No option here to disengage from "lovemaking"!

Clearly, seen in the context of the narrative specifics of *The Bird with the Crystal Plumage*, the vagina dentata is not only a manifestation of male anx-iety in a male-directed film within patriarchy, as Barbara Creed might argue, but also an instrument of women's self-assertion and empowerment. However, taking into consideration the fact that Monica only employs, rather than fash-ions, this sculpture, and speculating that it may indeed be the work of a male, we could see Monica-the-artist bodying forth for us yet another cultural truth: the restriction of women to appropriation rather than creation in a male world. She thus visualizes for us the real limits to women's self-assertion and empowerment, prophesying her downfall. To the extent that this sculpture might be, in Creedian fashion, a purely male construct, we could also see Monica visualizing for us ground zero of male sexuality: a puny dissociated head grafted onto a body that is, in fact, only a projection of that puny little head. In other words, masculinity/patriarchy is men just fucking themselves.

Unfortunately, from a feminist perspective, Sam does not truly get fucked. Two men arrive to "ejaculate" him from the vagina dentata, as Monica, who has been pounded on the head, makes moaning sounds that seem clearly to voice the sado-sexual frustration of murder interruptus (sounds that recall the distressful moans in Monica's study but without the pure desperation and angst of the latter). Instead of Monica's poetically just payback/copulation, we get Sam and Morosini hugging next to the prematurely evacuated fanged womb, with Morosini making the sexually suggestive comment: "I'll help you up."[9]

Ultimately, then, women's rage, or the expression of that rage as a factor signifying individuation or autonomy, is impossible in a male world. The final sequence of the film presents the normalization and exteriorizing of the institutional world as it seeks to eliminate all traces of women's rage, women's self-representation, and women-centred meaning. The sequence begins in a television studio where a commentator and a psychiatrist undertake to "explain" all that has occurred. Their words reward close analysis:

> TV Commentator:
> The final curtain has fallen at last on this tragic affair, which has kept the whole city in a state of shock. Monica Ranieri, hopelessly insane, is in custody at the psychiatric hospital. Her husband, who loved her not wisely but too well, lost his life in a last attempt to turn suspicion away from his wife.

> Prof. Rinaldi:
> Ten years ago, Monica Ranieri, who had already evident paranoid tendencies, was brutally attacked and suffered severe trauma. Nevertheless, she recovered sufficiently to return to a normal life. Her mental disturbance remained dormant for ten years until she came across the painting which depicted the horrible scene of which she had been the protagonist. Her latent madness came to light, violent and irresistible. Strangely she did not identify herself with the victim but with her attacker. In order to explain the behaviour of her husband, who attempted murder on various occasions to protect his wife, we must assume he suffered from an induced psychosis. He was influenced by his paranoid wife to the point of becoming homicidally psychotic himself.

Both the commentator and Rinaldi trivialize Monica's experience by turning it into theatre and, more specifically, into the consummate genre of disavowal—

melodrama ("the final curtain has fallen on this tragic affair," "the horrible scene of which she had been the protagonist"). The commentator dismisses Monica as "hopelessly insane" while he elevates Ranieri to the status of hero, even though he has presumably committed the exact same kinds of crimes, copycatting in order to "protect" her. Rinaldi effaces all sociological causes and of course all gender analysis as "severe trauma," "mental disturbance," and "latent madness" stand in for male aggression and the oppression of women. In short, Monica's justified rage against men is replaced by insanity, and he even undercuts the importance of her having been attacked by prefacing his reference to the attack with the claim that she "had already evident paranoid tendencies." His unwillingness to acknowledge her rage is implicit in his claiming only that she identifies with her assailant and in his failure to see that her violence ends up thoroughly reoriented towards men. He also ignores corollaries to his theory that might threaten male centricity, such as the fact that Monica's presumed identification with her assailant raises the possibility of her attraction to women and makes her violence quite possibly a suppression of lesbianism. (In fact, Sam is told by the antique owner that Monica's first victim was "said [to have] preferred women.")

Not only does Rinaldi minimize the effects of male violence on Monica, but he also makes Monica the cause of male violence with the preposterous notion that Ranieri "suffered from an induced psychosis...[and] was influenced by his paranoid wife to the point of becoming homicidally psychotic himself." Moreover, the exoneration of Ranieri on the part of both the commentator and Rinaldi flies in the face of what we do and don't see in the film. For one thing, in the two scenes in which we see Ranieri and Monica struggling with the knife, there is no conclusive evidence that Monica is attacking him. What we do know, however, from the police investigation is that, during the first scene, Monica receives a wound attributable to a left-handed person—and we soon discover that Ranieri is left-handed.[10] Perhaps most telling, during that scene we see a black glove–clad hand, undoubtedly that of Rainieri, pushing the button that cages Sam between two glass doors, preventing him from seeking out assistance for the seriously injured Monica. Why would Ranieri do this if he were merely the victim, as the police psychiatrist maintains, ever seeking to protect his wife?

More important, we see a left-hander—that is, Ranieri—killing the young woman who had been targeted at the race track, in a highly skilled and sexualized act. He is not just some haplessly devoted husband clumsily or perfunctorily trying to kill women in protective imitation of his wife. Moreover, prior to the "kill," we see him brandishing his knife and taking his inspiration from the same painting in the study that has presumably set Monica on her path to violence. In other words, he kills with premeditation as well as relish. If we couple this with his general unpleasantness and weirdness we are forced to question (1) whether his involvement in murder was solely to protect Monica or, rather, to satisfy his own sadistic sexual desires, and (2) whether he has not, in fact, been trying to kill Monica as well as other women. It is clear at the very least that he has appropriated Monica's rage for ends very different from hers—a kind of violence or at least violation in and of itself— and that he is far from the innocent victim and saviour Rinaldi would have us believe him to be.

The final sequence also undercuts Rinaldi's efforts to normalize matters by crosscutting his words with the departure of Julia and Sam from Italy. We seem to have the classic happy ending as the "good" couple are reunited, the horror now surmounted, and are on their way "home" (to his, though, not hers). However, the shots of the airport and airplane emphasize only disjunction and dissociation. Julia and Sam are emphatically "getting out"—thoroughly rejecting all that has gone on "inside" Italy. Moreover, the film ends not with the plane arriving at its destination "home" in the United States but, rather, leaving the ground and, in the final seconds, breaking the frame in mid-air. Sam and Julia end up lost in space. Moreover, as Rinaldi begins to declaim upon Monica's supposed madness, his words are intercut with joltingly disconnected shots of the airport runway: fragmented images of different types of planes from different airlines whirling about in different directions violating the "180-degree rule" of consistent screen direction. This whirling outside world of the runway becomes increasingly and again joltingly intercut with the calm inner world of the plane's cabin, of Sam and Julia's safe space. In short, "normalization" is actually blindness to chaos achieved through retreat into what is probably the most confining and isolating human "cage" in the film.

The suggestion that normalcy has not triumphed is further implied as the crosscuts from the TV studio move from outside to inside the plane and create more gender-specific implications. On the one hand, Julia seems to represent the perfectly contained "ideal" female in male society—demure, placid, passive, and happy. Gone are all signs of black as she is dressed in white and, even more "reassuringly," pink. However, she first appears in juxtaposition with the Rinaldi's words: "her latent madness came to light, violent and irresistible." She appears again as he says, "strangely she did not identify herself with the victim but with her attacker," and for the third time as he says, "in order to explain the behaviour of her husband...." Then, Sam appears in juxtaposition with the words "who attempted murder on various occasions." Moreover, on the phrase "induced psychosis" there is a cut from Julia looking up, to Sam moving quite unnaturally in her direction, creating a sense of unease if not menace. And as Rinaldi says "to the point of becoming homicidally psychotic himself," there is a cut to Sam appearing from behind a partition, again moving towards Julia. In short, the story of Monica and Ranieri gets reenacted with Julia and Sam becoming its protagonists, by association, implying strongly that underneath the seeming normalcy of their relationship lies the potential for the same homicidal violence that characterized the other couple.

There is even a wonderfully suggestive return of women's "black power" during the closing moments in the figure of a nun, in her habit, seated across from Julia. While this seems to represent the consummate containment and institutionalization of women (much like Julia-in-pink), it might also be read as the inevitable "effect of blackness" generated by women's containment. At the very least, it suggests that the power of blackness has not disappeared entirely. We can perhaps hope, particularly given the superimposition of the Monica–Ranieri story on Julia and Sam, that Julia may one day awaken within her patriarchal cage and bring her own "latent madness" to light in a revolution in consciousness and action far more effective than Monica's.

In sum, *The Bird with the Crystal Plumage* requires us to evaluate very carefully what we are told in light of what we are or are not shown. Though much of what we see remains inconclusive,[11] this very inconclusiveness lends itself to far more gender-critical assumptions and conclusions than those provided by the television show. The film suggests, among other things, that the only "evolution" that has occurred within the male world of the film is from blindness in the face of women's rage and its origins to acute misrecognition of that rage as "insanity." This of course mirrors society's reaction to the women's movement and the rise of feminism, which were so often dismissed as hysterical overreactions with no real basis (i.e., contradictorily, as "reactions" to "nothing"). As far as Monica's "evident paranoid tendencies" are concerned, I find them a sign of extraordinary mental health for any woman caught in the world of *The Bird with the Crystal Plumage*.

Contextualizing *The Bird with the Crystal Plumage*

While a pro-feminist rereading of a film such as *The Bird with the Crystal Plumage* may be useful for rethinking signification in the film itself, in Argento's corpus, and, to some extent even in the post-Gothic (Italian) horror film, it becomes much more meaningful if inserted into a social and ideological context that helps render it plausible—that is, within the story of women in the years leading up to *The Bird with the Crystal Plumage*. In sketching that story (albeit briefly, given its role as conclusion rather than substance of this chapter), I focus at times on the historical and at times on the cinematic representation, as befits Argento's cultural formation.

Although the role of women has been and continues to be highly restricted in Italian culture (the number of women in Italian politics, for example, is woefully low in comparison with other Western countries), there have been moments of notable strength in the past fifty years. The one that comes to mind most readily, particularly in relation to a film released in 1970, is the women's movement formed in the wake of 1960s student protest and the "hot autumn" of Italian labour discontent in 1969. However, because the movement, for the most part, succeeded rather than preceded the making of *The Bird with the Crystal Plumage*, its "prehistory" is more relevant to the film than is the movement itself.

In the early postwar period this prehistory is reflected in (at least) two types of filmic representation that confer power or validation upon women. The first is the neorealist[12] woman worker and "warrior," symbolized by Anna Magnani, who struggles (though not always with success) against the harsh socio-economic realities of an Italy emerging from the devastation of war. This figure is grounded in the powerful role played by women in the Resistance, which, in turn, gave rise to *L'Unione donne italiane*, an association formed in 1944 that, as a wing of the *Partito communista italiano*, was instrumental in obtaining the vote for women (first exercised in 1946) and remained active throughout the postwar period in the pursuit of equality for women (see Birnbaum 1986, 51–65, 198–21; Hellman 1987, 217–20).

This figure was relatively short-lived, disappearing long before *L'unione donne italiane*, which dissolved in 1984. It gave way to the 1950s international star figure best represented by Gina Lollobrigida, Sophia Loren, and Claudia Cardinale. This figure is not nearly as validating as is the Magnani figure, reflecting less the power of women in Italian society than the Americanization of Italy—the "objectification" of Italy-as-woman in an increasingly mass-mediated world—as well as the colonization of Italian cinema by Hollywood. (Because of the huge number of Hollywood productions and personnel present in the Eternal City in the 1950s, Rome came to be dubbed "Hollywood on the Tiber" by American entertainment journalists.) Yet even though the strength of the Italian starlets derived much less from the characters they played than from their largely orchestrated star quality (see Buckley 2000), each of them did, at various points, bring strong Italian female characterizations to the screen, thus rendering visible certain aspects of women-centred Italian culture that otherwise would have remained in the shadows.

It would be difficult to argue that the resistant warrior or the Italian glam queen have direct links to *The Bird with the Crystal Plumage*, but they do form a significant part of the cinematic environment in which Argento was raised. Directly relevant, on the other hand, is a third female figure, who appears in the late 1950s and throughout the 1960s:[13] the bourgeois or bourgeois-aspiring protagonist seeking or forced to seek a new identity as woman in an Italy experiencing unprecedented prosperity, industrialization, and modernization.[14] Argento's bourgeois, urban, self-employed, and pathologically self-directed Monica, in an anything-but-conventional marital/family situation, has clear ties with this third figure.

Although the socio-cultural context that gives rise to this figure has not been a subject of extensive research,[15] we can posit a number of contributing factors. As Luisa Passerini (1991, 168) notes, women experienced "profound changes in everyday behaviour...in the 1950s"—changes that could be characterized as "informal emancipatory movements." More specifically,

> These included the adoption of new behaviour patterns, above all regarding consumption, by very large numbers of women who were "on the move," often literally through emigration....The changes in consumption concerned the body, the home, and transport. The changes also involved the modification of women's lifestyles and their self-representation in everyday life: going out, walking in public, traveling, smoking, and the questioning, in part not yet translated into action, of sexual mores. (168–69)

Paul Ginsborg (1990, 244) notes that, while more Italian women than ever became housewives in the 1960s, they also became "individuated" and targeted within consumer society: "The women's magazines and the television advertisements of the time exalted...the modern Italian woman." In short, there was a significant shift, even within the role of housewife, from submission and sacrifice to self-gratification, which, in turn, reflects a growing urge for self-expression.

Concomitantly, the 1960s saw a significant change in attitude even with respect to family or marital roles. Conducting research as early as 1961, Lieta Harrison noted signs of rebellion among younger women in Italy, and in research conducted in 1964-65 among over 1,000 teenaged girls from various parts of Italy, she found that 62 percent did not want to get married (Marwick 1998, 93-94, 386-87). In terms of emerging intellectual discourse around women, Simone de Beauvoir's *The Second Sex* appeared in Italy in 1961 (it was published in France in 1949), while Betty Friedan's *The Feminine Mystique* appeared in 1963. The debates that developed around these books formed part of the intellectual background for Italian feminism of the 1970s.

Within Italian cinema, changes in women's attitudes and roles are prophesied by the Ingrid Bergman/Roberto Rossellini heroines of the early 1950s, though the Bergman phenomenon is anomalous in terms of Italian culture because of her status as outsider, exacerbated by the scandal her relation with Rossellini provoked in the conservative Roman Catholic environment of the times. They are more thoroughly embodied in the work of Antonio Pietrangeli through the 1950s to the mid-1960s,[16] which treated a variety of displaced and alienated heroines from both the provincial proletariat and the urban bourgeoisie trying to survive in an Italy in social and economic ferment. (Passerini's comments above are particularly relevant to Pietrangeli's provincial heroines.) During the same period, Italy's premier woman screenwriter Suso Cecchi D'Amico helped craft a variety of strong female characters, working with directors such as Luchino Visconti and Michelangelo Antonioni.[17]

The strongest links between new 1950s and 1960s Italian cinematic figurations of women and the work of Argento lie in the films of Antonioni and Fellini. I earlier noted Argento's tendency to cite Antonioni in his films. Intriguing in this respect is the fact that the actress Monica Vitti is the principal embodiment of the Antonioni bourgeois alienated, heroine (*L'avventura* [1959], *L'eclisse* [1962], and *Red Desert* [1964]), and Argento's heroine in *The Bird with the Crystal Plumage* is named Monica. Even more intriguing are the links between *The Bird with the Crystal Plumage* and *Blowup* (1966), the Antonioni film whose traces appear most frequently in Argento's work.[18] Like *The Bird with the Crystal Plumage*, *Blowup* is a *giallo* in which the protagonist becomes obsessed with the photographic representation of a violent event: the photo of Consalvi's painting in the former, the protagonist's own photos (which imply rather than depict a crime) in the latter. More important, in each case, the principal female figure (bourgeois, alienated) is initially viewed by the male protagonist as a victim, only to turn out to be much less innocent. In *Blowup*, the power of the female is not expressed through a visible artistry of violence; however its very invisibility and indefinability makes it uncage-able, allowing it to operate more powerfully and to culminate in the profoundly evocative dissolution of the male figure (masculinity/patriarchy?) in the final moments of the film. In Antonioni's next film, *Zabriskie Point*, released in the same year as *The Bird with the Crystal Plumage*, women's violence will be far more in evidence, if only on an imaginative level when, in the penultimate scene, the heroine Daria envisions the apocalyptic "blow-up" of a house in the desert near Phoenix, representing, among other things American patriarchal culture.

The link with Fellini is clearest in terms of the latter's *Juliet of the Spirits* (1965), a portrait of a bourgeois woman's journey to independence and individuation, and a film whose traces are everywhere in evidence in Argento's 1977 *Suspiria*. The anger and violence of women that we see in *The Bird with the Crystal Plumage* and *Suspiria* are, in Fellini's work, as in *Zabriskie Point*, expressed largely in symbolic terms, through Juliet's flashbacks, dreams, and vision. However, it is clearly there, making *Juliet of the Spirits*, in many respects, a woman-centred horror film rooted in childhood abuse both cultural and religious.

I would also argue for a link between Argento and another major Italian director, Marco Ferreri.[19] In some ways the evidence is more tenuous here because there is no obvious citation of Ferreri in Argento's early films. (For one thing, as a younger director than Antonioni or Fellini, Ferreri lacked the corpus, in the 1960s, to draw upon.) Yet the link might well be as strong or stronger, in that Ferreri had strong pro-women politics of which Argento was directly aware. By 1967 Ferreri had made two films dealing with the exploitation of women, *La donna scimmia* (1963) and *L'harem* (1967). As a film reviewer for the daily newspaper *Paese Sera*, Argento knew Ferreri's work and noted in print his desire to meet with him (Della Casa 2000, 31). In fact, he did interview Ferreri in connection with the *L'harem* and, inevitably, on the theme of women. Describing *L'harem*, Ferreri tells Argento:

> E' la storia di una donna che non è aiutata da nessuno. Vede, viviamo in una società maschile dove si fa un gran parlare della donna, della libertà della donna, dell'emancipazione della donna, della parità della donna. Ma nessuno veramenta auita la donna. Perché è una società maschile. Le donne sono l'ultima colonia. (Della Casa 2000, 32)

> It's the story of a woman who is not helped by anyone. You see, we live in a male society where a lot is made of women, of the freedom of women, of the emancipation of women, of women's equality. But no one truly helps them. Because it is a male society, and women are the last colony. (Translation mine)

Ferreri then displays a clear awareness of contemporary proto-feminist discourse: "La donna a quaranti anni è finita. Ella passa per i quattri stadi: prima è la fidanzata, poi l'oggetto sessuale, quindi diventa madre, ed è finita" (Women at the age of forty are finished. They pass through four stages: first there's the girl friend, then the sex object, then they become a mother, and then they are finished [Della Casa 2000, 32, translation mine]).

In fact, *L'harem* is a brutally frank film, particularly for an Italian male director, about a woman who seeks to express her sexual independence, only to be ganged up on by the four men in her life, reduced to a housewife, and ultimately killed. Its treatment of violence against women, women's containment in traditional roles, and their punishment outside those roles clearly links up thematically with *The Bird with the Crystal Plumage*.

The woman-centredness of Antonioni's, Fellini's, and Ferreri's work from the late 1950s to the late 1960s (or 1970, if we include *Zabriskie Point*) combine a growing desire for individuation and independence; a growing ability for self-expression, at times, violent; and a growing sense of victimization and resentment that reflect perfectly a climate in which women are becoming more alienated, political, separatist, and expressive. These films anticipate but also, in many ways, instantiate a world in which women's discussion groups (originating in 1969) will evolve into more political affiliations, such as *Rivolta femminile* and *Movimento della liberatione delle donne italiane* (1970) and *Lotta feminista* (1971–72), which, in turn, will contribute to the organization of successful referenda on divorce and abortion in the 1970s and to an awakening far beyond the confines of feminism itself to women's issues. (Unfortunately, as suggested earlier, this awakening has not translated itself into any radical increase in women's involvement in Italian public life.)

These films also, of course, represent an environment in which Argento's abused and enraged heroine Monica becomes ideologically possible and perhaps necessary, even if she remains unrecognizable to her male pursuers, both professional and amateur. The one factor Argento adds to the work of his three Italian contemporaries is a degree of explicit violence that reflects not the women's movement but, rather, a (masculine) 1960s climate of dread and bloodshed grounded, among other things, in the Cold War, American aggression in Vietnam, campus and urban violence in the United States (to which the Black Power poster in *Crystal Plumage* alludes), Third World revolutionary guerilla warfare, and, in Italy, the endorsement of violence as an acceptable strategy on both ends of the political spectrum, leading to the right-wing bombing in Piazza Fontana (Milan) in 1969 and acts of right- and left-wing terrorism throughout the 1970s. Cinematically, the 1960 ethos of violence is reflected, with strong critique, in the work of American directors such as Sam Peckinpah and Arthur Penn and, with less critique, in the Italian horror film and, more important, in the spaghetti western cycle initiated by Sergio Leone.

This conjunction of masculine violence with women's political resistance provides an appropriate note on which to conclude this analysis and contextualization of *The Bird with the Crystal Plumage*. The very same sort of conjunction has created what I have argued to be a misunderstanding and under-estimation of Argento's film. His intermingling of violence and gender resist-ance, though necessary in terms of the film's signifying strategies, has ren-dered it extremely difficult for horror critics (and, we may assume, the public) to separate the latter from the former and, far more important, to give the latter its due.

Notes

1 In recent years, women directors have become more visible in Italy. Often they are the daughters of postwar directors and producers, such as Cristina and Francesca Comencini (Luigi) and Fiorella Infascelli (Carlo). The most important feature-film director of the past fifteen years has been Francesca Archibugi, who has directed a film nearly every two years while scripting several others.

2 Although this is not the place to argue the point, I find both Wertmuller and Cavani strong woman directors with an informed sensibility on gender issues (albeit criti-cal rather than emancipatory).

3 *Giallo* is the Italian term for "thriller" and is derived from the colour of the paperbacks that introduced the thriller as a literary genre in the 1930s.

4 Strictly speaking, Argento's work is often a composite of *giallo* and horror, *The Bird with the Crystal Plumage* being a case in point. However, the strong horror compo-nent of his work has led him, rightly, to be considered principally a horror director.

5 Creed emphasizes not just male dominance in the horror film but also the power of a "monstrous-feminine," and along with this a complexity in spectator identification that exceeds the traditional theoretical equations male = sadism, female = masochism, in classic Hollywood plot and spectatorship. Nonetheless, as my quotation from Creed suggests, the monstrous-feminine is ultimately a product of patriarchal signification. Clover emphasizes the undecidability of gender construction in recent horror sub-genres (such as the slasher film), likewise dissolving the opposition between sadistic and masochistic viewing pleasures. Nonetheless, Clover's principal concern (and jus-tifiably so given the focus of her analysis) is how this undecidability operates in rela-tion to a male viewer.

6 I will, for the most part, use terms such as "masculinity" or "male world" rather than "patriarchy." The latter has rather specific connotations in terms of feminist histor-ical and feminist psychoanalytical theory. Ultimately, of course, *The Bird with the Crystal Plumage* could be read within those theoretical bounds. However, I am more interested here in addressing the workings of the film in relation to gender without reference to the theoretical apparatus involved in patriarchal critique.

7 I refer shortly to the fact that Monica's interest in women could be read as lesbian, something that the film's classically male interpreters of her behaviour cannot pos-sibly admit. This might open up the possibility of reading Monica's "scopophilia" in terms of the lesbian gaze. However, the moments in the film in which she owns the gaze over her potential victims are so brief and so difficult to detach from Ranieri's copycat behaviour that such an analysis seems a bit beyond the scope of my reading of *The Bird with the Crystal Plumage*. However, given Argento's love for playing with

the gaze elsewhere (most notably in *Opera* [1987]), an analysis of the (potential) lesbian gaze in his corpus would be most welcome.

8   Julia wears almost exclusively light colours. She is often seen wrapped in white bed sheets, and at various times she wears a white bathrobe and a white rain coat. The one exception to her light garb prior to her scene in black is, appropriately, the scene in which she gets annoyed at Sam for paying an informer to get him some information and then is targeted, after the informer has left, by the threatening phone call. Here she wears an orange blouse.

9   Reading this as a double entendre may be stretching it (another double entendre) in terms of Argento's probable grasp of English. However, the film was shot largely in English (certainly the English-speaking parts were), and Argento had worked on numerous projects, prior to *The Bird with the Crystal Plumage*, such as spaghetti westerns, intended for an English-speaking audience.

10   The fact that Sam decides in the study, when confronted with Monica, that he had really seen her assaulting her husband in the art gallery proves nothing. It is not corroborated by what we see, and there is no reason to believe that he is any less wrong or stupid at the end of the film than he has been all along. In fact, it is he who uncovers for us the fact that Ranieri is left-handed, when he throws him a pack of cigarettes and Ranieri catches it with his left hand. But he does not even seem to recognize the importance of what he and we have just seen.

11   For instance, I do not mean to suggest that we can determine the assailant to be Ranieri and the victim to be Monica in the first art gallery scene, just that there are contradictory versions that lead us to question not just who did what but on what basis we make assumptions and draw conclusions.

12   Neorealism was the name given to Italian filmmaking of the immediate postwar period that focused on the socio-economic realities of an Italy devastated by war but also struggling with pride born of the Resistance to refound a nation devastated not just by the war but also by the moral and political catastrophe of Fascism.

13   Here I create a category whose broadness satisfies the needs of this chapter but that would prove inadequate to a more concentrated analysis of women in postwar Italian cinema. For instance,

   • the Rossellini/Bergman figure merits discussion on its own because of the cultural factors involved in this relationship both personal and artistic;
   • there tend to be significant socio-economic differences between the heroines who achieve some form of individuation and those who remain in crisis or come to a tragic end;
   • the films of Pietrangeli differ from those of Ferreri in that the former are socio-economically oriented and the latter gender oriented.

14   This period in Italy's history is generally referred to as the "Economic Miracle" or "The Boom." Strictly speaking it occurs between 1958 and 1963, but the transformation of Italy that crystallized in those years was under way well before and was felt long after.

15   Rebecca West (1998, 169) notes that "there is an obvious lacuna in scholarly work devoted to women's culture…in…the two decades or so following the Second World War."

16   In particular: *Il sole negli occhi* (1953), *Nata di marzo* (1957), *Adua e le compagne* (1960), *La parmigiana* (1963), *La visita* (1963), and *Io la cononsceva bene* (1965). Pietrangeli died

at the age of forty-nine as the result of an accident at the end of the shooting of *Come quando perché* (1969).

17 See Brunetta (1998, 284–87) for a summary of D'Amico's contributions to Italian cinema and its representation of women. (Unfortunately, Brunetta's positive comments are undercut by gender stereotyping as he refers to D'Amico within the brief space of little more than a page as a "Great Mother," "vestal virgin," "angel," and "nurse," whose script work resembled crocheting and who created "the atmosphere and the working and emotional conditions of family writ large" [285–86, translation mine].)

18 Most blatantly via David Hemming's starring role in *Deep Red* (1975).

19 Ferreri, far less appreciated internationally than Antonioni and Fellini, was born in 1928 and died in 1997. Most of his films were ferocious critiques of masculinity and the victimization of women. In addition to those cited above, his principal gender-centred films are: *L'ultima donna* (1975), *Ciao maschio* (1977), *Il futuro è donna* and *I Love You* (1986), and *La carne* (1991).

How Positively Levitating! Chinese Heroines of *Kung Fu* and *Wuxia Pian*

SUZIE S.F. YOUNG

[12]

Introduction

The martial arts film continues a long Chinese literary tradition of fighting women who leap and somersault in perfect, trained weightlessness; unbound from the hearth and the altar, they venture forth to protect, avenge, challenge, and offend. This chapter considers some martial arts heroines of the *kungfu* film and *wuxia pian*,[1] whose aerialism distinguishes them from the weightier representations of "action heroines" such as the big-breasted comic-strip heroines (Barbarella, Wonder Woman), the sexually exaggerated or perverse criminal femme fatale (the Bond girls), or the hysterically phallic and muscular mothers whose generative bodies will make (Sarah Connor, played by Linda Hamilton) or break (Ripley, played by Sigourney Weaver) humanity's future (the *Terminator* and *Alien* series, respectively). In particular, I focus on the different ways in which the "aerial sublime" (Russo 1994, 11) is valued in *Wing Chun*, made in 1994 and directed by Yuen Wo-ping, and Ang Lee's more recent *Crouching Tiger, Hidden Dragon*, made in 2000.[2]

In the majority of American big-budget action movies action heroines are not the leads but the sidekicks or supportive romantic interests; when women star as heroic fighters, they are avenging mothers or grief-inspired daughters contained within stereotypes such as "feisty heroine," "tomboy," and "butch."[3] If the woman warrior has reached symbolic exhaustion in Hollywood's blockbusters, spawning only sequels and series, she has also launched the receptive overdrive that greeted Ang Lee's *Crouching Tiger, Hidden Dragon* (2000), in which three fighting women defy gravity as well as stereotypes and social expectations. Yu Shulien (played by Asia's once highest-paid action queen, Michelle Yeoh) is a superior martial artist who displays an equanimity that epitomizes grace, strength, and compassion; Jen (Zhang Ziyi) is a bureaucrat's daughter who shows fire that amounts to lightning, all flash and courage and reckless nerve; and Jade Fox (played by Zheng Peipei, a veteran of the *wuxia pian* since the 1960s) is a passed-over student of *kungfu* who becomes a formidable and deadly foe. At a time when any modicum of feminist sensitivity makes it difficult not to cringe at the idea as well as the actual film of *Charlie's Angels* (2000), Lee's *Crouching Tiger, Hidden Dragon* (hereafter, *Dragon*) offers, instead, heroines whom we admire not for their figures, hairdos, clothes, or body (bawdy) humour but, rather, for their cultivated fighting skills, their moral deliberations, and their strength of conviction.

It would be a mistake, however, to assume that the fighting heroines in *Dragon* are the products of a millennial feminism. In fact, women warriors have always been integral to the *wuxia pian*, where they are judged not for the misogynist "feminine honour" of the chaste or coy "butterfly" but, rather, for their honour on the battlefield, their love of justice, and their courage in the face of evil; in these primary poetics of the genre, the women—as often as not—lead the men.[4] Yim Wing-chun (Michelle Yeoh), the subject of the second film (*Wing Chun* 1994, dir. Yuen Wo-ping) in this chapter, is an excellent example as she sidesteps gender traditions to defend herself, her family, and her village against macho bullies, fighting nobly and bravely, and leaping higher and faster than the robber chiefs who terrorize the countryside.

When fighting women control the narrative trajectory as they leap, vault, bolt, hurdle, and fly, how far do they push the limits of cinematic femininity in neoconservative culture? In what follows, I seek out the occasions for feminist pleasure in *Wing Chun* as well as critique the ersatz feminism in *Crouching Tiger, Hidden Dragon*. I do not suggest that those who trumpet the progressive in *Dragon* have it all wrong—certainly, all the female protagonists are active and capable women, and in their many battles they give at least as good as they get.[5] However, *Dragon*'s women are consistently given only mutually exclusive choices—for Shulien, it is honour or love; for Jade Fox, duty or self-respect; for Jen, family or freedom—so that, in the end, each of them is stripped of their freedom to choose. They battle each other fiercely, but still each loses everything she has fought for: Shulien, who had postponed love for too long for the sake of honour, loses the man of her dreams to the poisoned dart of Jade Fox, who had initially killed out of self-respect but then forfeits that virtue when she kills out of convenience and jealousy; Jen, who had defied her parents and refused all obligations in order to seek and express absolute freedom, in the end leaps from the mountain for an eternal flight that is, if not death in fact, at least a kind of death. In contrast, the women in *Wing Chun* are "odd boundary creatures" who move tactically with their talents to help themselves and each other, and to contest enforced hierarchies; they are, to borrow Donna Haraway's words, "signs of possible worlds" (Haraway 1991a, 22). In *Wing Chun* the women are introduced to us by the things they say, the actions they take, and the desires they have (individually and collectively), unlike in *Dragon*, where the women are introduced by their backstories of men they have loved and lost, as heroines in a fantasy of the lost phallus. When evidence of care, generosity, and mutual admiration among the women occasionally escape to the threshold of the visible in *Dragon*, the film becomes a hysterical text "in which the weight of the not-said…threatens to capsize the work's literal meaning"[6] (Modleski 1991, 137). *Dragon* works hard to concentrate on friction by dramatizing the women's unending conflict and continual antagonism, whereas *Wing Chun* delights in the three women's differences and complementarities.

Flight

For as long as I can remember, martial artists in the movies have been defying the laws of physics, breaking boulders with their fists, knocking down giant trees with their feet, and slicing through steel with their swords, battling on—for good or for evil—until some slight advantage that the virtuous possesses reveals itself to triumph over the sins of greed and the forces of irresponsible power. Those were the movies of my childhood and youth, and the magic swords and extrakinetic abilities of the heroes and heroines seemed no more ridiculous to me then than lightsabres and Jedi "force-lightning" seem to fans of the *Star Wars* films now. But what raises the greatest indignation and even the ire of some is that the martial artists *fly*. Why do they have to fly? The answer is surprisingly reasonable: a primary goal of *wushu* (martial arts) and of its sister art, meditation, is harmony between the inner and the outer worlds, wherein neither the contingencies of the human nor the forces of nature would (pre)dominate. Levitation—moving through the air with ease—is a logical outcome when an equivalence and interchangeability exists between the human world and the natural world.

Flight has always been a part of the Chinese martial arts novel, and the earliest swordplay films in 1920s Shanghai were already fantastic spectacles of superhuman locomotion. But aerialism as an asset in the martial arts genres is not intended to escape earthly connections. Whereas Socrates used flight to portray the nature of the soul as superior to the body—the charioteer's horse that is "fine and good and of noble stock…moves on high and governs all creation" as the soul, but the other horse, which is "opposite in every way," sheds its wings and "falls until it encounters solid matter…and puts on an earthly body" (Plato 1973, 50)—Laozi elucidated a requisite complementarity in which flight (exploration) is possible precisely because of rootedness (stability): "high and (be)low lean upon each other."[7] The problem, for modern audiences, is that levitation is easily assimilable to the Socratic kind of disembodied freedom reinforced in the late Victorian era, when bodies were simply not admitted into existence. This is not the aim of the women of *wuxia*, who do the work of the world and want the things of the world (including being with each other and with the men they love). The freedom they enjoy is that of mastering their actions so that these become magical—the *wuxia* heroines grow invisible wings to conquer all odds.[8] Mary Russo (1994, 11, 29) calls it "the aerial sublime,…a realm of freedom within the everyday" but also "an embodiment of possibility and of error." Yuen Wo-ping's *Wing Chun* has faith in the quotidian, in risk, and especially in the complementarity of flight and rootedness; in contrast, Ang Lee's *Crouching Tiger, Hidden Dragon* alternately laments the failure of one and then of the other.

Female Triads

Crouching Tiger, Hidden Dragon (2000, dir. Ang Lee)

The women of *Crouching Tiger, Hidden Dragon* fly high, fast, and far. The film is ostensibly about freedom, particularly feminine freedom, so it is worth noting that the three female protagonists live entirely outside the feminine mainstream of Chinese society—of that or any time. Women's freedom is shown to exist only in binary opposition to the ties of family and is revealed most often as irresponsible and randomly hurtful or even deadly to others. It is equated either to isolation and self-sacrifice, at best, or to adolescent tantrum and mad vengeance, at worst. But when the price of freedom—whether of speech, action, or desire—is beset by loneliness, interminable deception, and even murder most evil, it is at least equally as compelled (obliged) a state of being as is that of submission and obedience, suggesting not a viable alternative but, rather, a poverty of choice. This is not a vision of feminist freedom.

The film begins when Yu Shulien (Michelle Yeoh), an extraordinarily gifted swordswoman and experienced security courier, must deliver a sword named "Green Destiny"[9] to Sir Te (Lung Sihung) on behalf of Li Mubai (Chow Yun-fat), the greatest swordsman of his generation. Mubai—whose name suggests an unsettled heart (*mu*) yearning for clarity (*bai*)—is giving his valuable sword away because he has chosen to withdraw from *jianghu* (the world of martial arts) and to forsake his duty to avenge his *wushu* (martial arts) master, who was murdered by Jade Fox (Zheng Peipei). The sword is delivered safely—prompting Sir Te to compliment Shulien for carrying on her *father*'s business so well—but it is stolen that first night. There is brief combat but the masked thief escapes easily, using the patrolman's head to vault into the air and to fly with incredible speed across the rooftops. Much inferior in the martial arts, the guard is incapable of chasing into the air, but Shulien hears the commotion and at once takes up pursuit, flying after the thief, leaping from rooftop to rooftop with dazzling speed and accuracy.[10]

At last Shulien is able to ground the thief by ingenious footwork that blocks the latter's levitations, but suddenly another rooftop assailant shoots a dart at Shulien and, in this split-second of reprieve, the thief gets away. Shulien deduces the identity of the thief, and the next morning she goes to visit Jiaolong (Zhang Ziyi), Governor Yu's daughter (hereafter referred to as "Jen" to follow the film's English subtitles), to confirm the suspicion. At Sir Te's the day before, Jen had ever so demurely marvelled at the "heaviness" and the "beautiful scabbard" of the Green Destiny Sword, as though she were a weakling with no knowledge of the martial arts and no appreciation of the sword as a superior weapon. The truth is that she has been training in the Wudang style of *wushu*—as a child she was taught by the infamous Jade Fox disguised as an ordinary governess, but, more substantially and effectively, she secretly studied the manuals that Fox had stolen from the Wudang master who took her into his bed but not into his school. Jen hid her superior abilities from the governess, just as she was outwardly calm about her betrothal (made to fortify her father's political power) to the son of a wealthy family. However, excited to meet a swordswoman by trade, Jen—almost forgetting her masquerade as ingénue—confides in Shulien that she would rather roam the *jianghu* and participate in its affairs and thereby be free. Shulien offers a different perspective by sharing stories of flea-infested beds and long journeys without baths, and by disclosing her history of loss—a murdered fiancé and a subsequent repressed love for another in order to observe, in her words, "a woman's duty."

In contrast to Shulien's restraint, Jen—it is revealed to us in a lengthy flashback—once transgressed the confines of family and tradition by loving and living with a bandit, Luo Xiaohu (Cheng Chen), otherwise feared as "Dark Cloud" (hereafter referred to as "Lo" to follow the film's English subtitles). The exquisite cinematography in the wild northern desert, together with Yo-Yo Ma's performance of Tan Dun's solo cello composition, invite a romantic spectator(ship) so that when Jen returns to her parents and lives the seemingly sheltered life of a governor's daughter, we appreciate that, in her heart, fiery excesses grow. Lo—whose name ("Xiaohu") means "little tiger"—is the titular "crouching tiger" that awaits their reunion.

Jen's name—"Yu Jiaolong" in Chinese—means "delicate/pampered jade dragon."[11] Hard and smooth and believed to have protective qualities, jade was a royal gem in China and it continues to be used as a symbol of love and beauty. Dragons are the supreme symbol of strength, intelligence, and authority; they are fierce and they expect to be pleased—content dragons bring rain for the crops but disgruntled dragons cause immense floods. Dragons are shapeshifters: they can change to any colour or size; they appear and disappear in a flash; they live in the mountain caves and in the ocean depths, ruling the skies in the spring and the seas in the fall; they preside over the seasons as over life itself. Jen (or Yu Jialong) is the titular "hidden dragon" for whom the tiger waits.

On the surface Jen is smooth as jade, having refined her social graces not only as an accomplished calligrapher (one of the seven arts of a classical Chinese education) but also as a consummate liar, hiding her thief's heart from her two mentors (she betrayed her governess for half of her young life and deceived her new friend Shulien with perfect equanimity). She wants first what Fox has (fighting skills and a fighting heart), then what Mubai has (the Green Destiny Sword and superior *wushu*) and what Shulien has (freedom of self-determination), but instead of mutuality and camaraderie, her mimetic desire degenerates into rivalry and destruction, stubbornly reiterated in the narrative and underscored by an omniscient camera's frequent close-ups of her belligerent face.

Living up to the dragon of her name, Jen is an exceptional fighter whose celestial body presides in the skies as comfortably as on the ground, but this *jiaolong* (pampered dragon) is both naive and self-indulgent. Discontent with her life, she shapeshifts—now a coquette, now a ninja, now a fighting scholar named *Long* (dragon) who travels the *jianghu* for adventure—and she lashes out with half-formed ideas, with the result that chaos ensues wherever she treads (or, more accurately, flies). Her self-centred desires supported by superior martial skills cause havoc and mayhem and broken bones, whether they be to steal a sword or to pick a fight in a relatively peaceful inn. The damage she does—to friends and enemies without distinction—is reckless and ego-tistical, like the deluge released by an irate dragon.

While the dragon is headstrong and irascible, the fox is sneaky and long-suffering. Chinese mythology has many fox-spirits who appear in human form but they are usually represented as female and they seduce men to steal their strength, just as Jade Fox apparently did when she slept with Li Mubai's master and then killed him and stole the Wudang *wushu* manual.[12] While her anguish over the master's sexism—"he thought me good enough to sleep with but not good enough to teach"—has feminist potential, unfortunately it is largely passed over unsympathetically by the film, which chooses, instead, to dramatize her deception, deviance, and heartlessness: to her pupil Jen, as pre-viously to her teacher the Wudang master, Fox dispenses poison after love. While she does suffer injustice, she is portrayed as consistently making choices that aggravate rather than amend or heal an inveterately unjust society. Thus her life is essentially over when she chooses to avenge herself on the man who casts her aside on serious matters: she is caught, animal-like, in a trap of her own devising. She is the least "aerial" of the three women warriors, or, more accurately, the film is considerably less interested in displaying her aerialism than that of the other two heroines. Perhaps it is not just Fox's villainy but the origins of it—sleeping with the Wudang master but wanting even more—that prompt the camera's reluctance to spectacularize her body in flight.

While typically the women of the *wuxia pian* choose to defuse or instruct (as Shulien does in her battles with Jen) rather than to kill, there are Medeas, too, who will not limit their violence. Fox's method of attack is a surprise ambush of needles and darts laced with poison—hardly a heroic choice of weapon or assault—but even worse is her willingness to harm not only her ene-mies but also, just as readily, those she loves (she pretends to burn healing herbs for Jen when she is really burning poison). Certainly, her constant threat from off-screen and her typical violent entries from the frame's edges filmi-cally locate her as the error that history has produced but has not yet eradi-cated.

Virtue in the *wuxia pian* is recognized in those who contain their anger—not so as to turn it inward (like Madame Bovary, who poisoned herself, or Anna Karenina, who jumped in front of a train) but to decline its claims on the flesh and to redress it through self-training (to become consummate in both art and understanding [in this case, the art of *kungfu*]) or through pedagogy (Shulien tries to teach Jen by discourse and by example). This transforma-tion of anger from reaction to action both avoids the stunted understanding and cyclical, poisoned life of Fox, and creates at least the potential for community. It is in this sense that Shulien remains finally human; but, unable or unwilling to resist the seductions of melodrama, the film ensures that she becomes even more so as her life is fully rounded by tragedy. Shulien's gentleness and strength of character ironically create the preconditions of the film's tragic elements: out of respect and loyalty to her lost betrothed, she abstains from giving her love in its fullness to Li Mubai; thus, when he dies, their love is unconsummated and she faces a long life of loneliness and regret. Still, there is no hardness, only grace, in her last words to Jen, who brought her and Mubai to this sad pass. She does not turn on the girl—whom she likes—but speaks from a place of calm and serenity.

Shulien, as I've shown, is always full of grace. In fact, her name means "graceful lotus" and, like the lotus, with its roots deep in the soil and its long, gracefully undulating stalk topped by a magnificent flower that releases ambrosial perfume, Shulien is well rooted—connected to the earth—which gives her aerialist *kungfu* a suppleness and her person a purity and beauty that cannot be surpassed. For the Chinese the lotus has a strong iconic association as the Buddha is often seen sitting upon or surrounded by the petals of a lotus, and his *boddisatvas* (enlightened ones) are referred to as "lotuses." Although rooted in mud, the lotus rises to a place above the waters to display its unparalleled beauty and fragrance, and it purifies the very water in which it grows, improving life for all the creatures in the pond. So it is with Shulien, who remains true to herself and whose discretion heals the hurts of history. For example, in her investigation of the theft of "Green Destiny," she takes care to save Jen from public exposure, and during her fights with the impetuous young woman, she pulls her sword thrusts to spare her even as she bests this cantankerous attacker. However, in addition to the frenetic narrative insistence that each of the three female protagonists is made by a man she loved and lost, the film further eclipses lesbian erotic interest by compulsively substantiating a logic of maternal instinct: the good woman (Shulien) has it no matter how impetuous the daughter (Jen), but the bad woman (Jade Fox) does not.

While it is true that Shulien lives beyond the traditional confines for women, she fails to find fulfillment because, to a great extent, life is indifferent to female desire. But, lest it be said that what is needed is less feminism and more of Shulien's sort of ideal womanliness, consider the price she pays in repression, in lost opportunities, and in remorse. In order to live the life that is hers, she must travel always, be alone always, be trained and on edge always—not bad things if they are really what she wants, but everything in the film, from the very first scene to the very last with Shulien and Mubai, tells us that she does not want them, or, at least, that she does not want them more than she wants him. She may be a capable and respected *wuxia* in *jianghu*, but the major chord of her life is sadness and aloneness, loss and heartbreak. She is honourable in all things—she gives and forgives; she is a marvel of self-control, never indulging in self-pity or selfish desires; she loses the most without being in the least guilty of ever behaving badly. But this portrait of mature womanhood raises the question: who needs feminism if it simply delivers us back into a prefeminist world of self-sacrifice and repression? Ultimately, Shulien fails as a model of progressive feminism because she is returned to the stereotype of maternal sacrifice—chaste, discrete, and unfulfilled.

Wing Chun (1994, dir. Yuen Wo-ping)[13]

Wing Chun is a style of *kungfu* that is only a few generations old; its historical record is well, if variously, documented. A popular version has it that, during the Qing Dynasty (1644–1911), when oppression and cruelty were a daily norm, abbess Ng Mui from the Shaolin Temple was forced in 1674 to take refuge in the White Crane Temple on Mount Tai Leung after Emperor Kangshi had the Shaolin burnt to the ground. There she met Yim Wing-chun, the daughter of a *tofu* (bean curd) merchant, who was being harassed by a local bully. Taking pity on the young woman, the abbess taught her how to best an opponent who is larger and stronger—by borrowing his energy (redirecting his strength and brute force) to use against him, by positioning herself for close-range combat so that the far-reaching limbs of the taller and larger opponent are rendered useless, and by being calm, precise, and efficient in her movements. Yim Wing-chun successfully discouraged the bully from bothering her again, but she continued to practise and to refine her techniques, which she later taught to her husband Leung Pok-to and others so that they might defend themselves against intimidation and persecution by the corrupt Qing government.

Around this historical core, director Yuen Wo-ping grows a very odd apple by adding elements of low comedy and cheap romance, taking the film perilously close to *The Three Stooges* at one moment and to a cartoon version of *Rebecca of Sunnybrook Farm* at another. Unfortunately, a good portion of the clever humour is language-based and untranslatable into English subtitles. For example, because Chinese has no phonetic distinction between "he" and "she," the mistaken identity subplot (in which Wing-chun is mistaken for a man) is more sophisticated than it must appear to non-Chinese-speaking audiences. Nonetheless, the actors' performances are, for the most part, exemplary, and so, despite the silliness and romantic dross, there are veins of gold.

The main protagonists are women: Yim Wing-chun (again Michelle Yeoh), dressed always in men's *kungfu* clothes until the film's final act; her aunt Fong, nicknamed "Stinky-Mouth" and "Abacus" (Yuen King-tan); and the beautiful widow they rescue, Charmy (Catherine Hung-yun). Together, they form a transgressive triad that gives immense viewing and critical pleasures to feminist audiences.

Fong has two nicknames: the first, "Stinky-Mouth," is a double-entendre since she not only dines on fermented *tofu*—a pungent delicacy—but she also always speaks her sharp mind. For example, she advises the soon-to-be-married sister of Wing-chun to immediately leave her husband and return home if he should beat her. She rejects the reprimand from her brother, the father of the bride, by pointing out that she was simply looking out for her niece. He is exasperated by her unrelenting directness about gender relations, and he identifies her friendship with Wing-chun as the cause of the latter's "manliness."[14] Fong's second nickname, "Abacus," arises from another kind of shrewd judgment: she is materially driven, sharp in commerce, and decisive; she derides the slowness and indecision of the merchants (who are no match for her business "killer instincts") as well as the government-appointed and apportioned Scholar Wong (Waise Lee Chi-hung).

Though neither physically nor intellectually wanting, Fong's rejection of timidity, diffidence, and muteness as "feminine," and her refusal to be coy, coquettish, feeble, or withdrawn, result in her being passed over as an object of desire. That, however, does not discourage her from being the desiring *subject*, with her own distinct tastes and plans. In the first half of the film Fong leads Wing-chun to trick the wealthy Scholar Wong into paying out Charmy's debt, which was incurred from her husband's burial, and in the second half of the film she tricks him into marriage by first "compromising" him (she initiates and consummates sexual relations with him by letting him think he is actually with Charmy) and then by coercing him to marry her.

Foul-breathed and foul-mouthed, Fong indulges in fermented *tofu* to satisfy her connoisseur appetite, calls a spade a spade to rebuff the machismo lies, drives the sharpest deals to build her family's business, sees through gender-relations to both appease and dupe the slow-witted male population of the village, and picks and gets the husband of her dreams. Because the audience (i.e., the camera) is located to share Fong's point of view in these scenes, we may giggle, laugh, or shake our heads at her projects, but we are never invited to shake a finger at her.

At first the beautiful widow Charmy appears to be too conventional to suggest transgression. She is a good wife, risking all to save an ill husband and then, in accordance with Confucian principles, selling herself to pay for his burial. The oddness arises when she dresses in Wing-chun's discarded clothes in one of Fong's manoeuvres to drum up business for the *tofu* shop (Fong reminds everyone, "nowadays, everything depends on the packaging"). Indeed, Charmy goes on to consciously and playfully assume the position of spectacle for the villagers, thereby contributing significantly to the *tofu* business of the family that took her in; she also introduces to Fong and Wing-chun a frankness concerning erotic play and feminine pleasures, exceeding the role of passive wife or grief-stricken widow.

On this first day when Charmy emerges from the bedroom in pretty maidens' clothes that used to be Wing-chun's, the looks exchanged between them— but especially the *gaze from* Wing-chun—are charged with textual turbulence. At the most obvious level, it is an erotic gaze at an object of beauty. From the narrative we already know that Charmy is extraordinarily beautiful and that men in the village line up every day to buy more *tofu* just to indulge in another stare. A typical textual strategy is to extend the erotic interaction to the film's audience by a two-shot sequence, first of the beholder (whose gaze the film's audience shares) and then, in a reverse-shot, of the spectacle (to complete the narrative circle and to pander to the audience's own scopophilia). But this small film, in a bold move, puts Charmy *off*-screen as she poses in her new elegance and, instead, zooms in—swiftly, without attempt at self-effacement, from a medium shot that frames head to waist, to a close-up of head to collarbone—on Wing-chun, whose unblinking gaze is the image over which extradiegetic music begins to play. No one who watches the film can miss this unusual move, but it is especially refreshing when we recall, in contrast, *Dragon*'s persistent disavowal of lesbian interest and the unrelenting filmic efforts to infuse every look from its heroines with jealousy, malice, or maternal compassion.

An additional (not alternative) interpretation is that Wing-chun encounters her "lost femininity." Seeing this beauty in her (i.e., Wing-chun's) old clothes, Wing-chun must feel simultaneous recognition and misrecognition; in fact, we can reasonably compare her experience to that of the Lacanian "mirror stage" in which subjective experience of the self is comparatively more blemished than the vision of beauty before her eyes.[15] In an early and important translation of Lacan's work, Anthony Wilden (1968, 74) characterizes this sighting of the more ideal self as "a vision of harmony by a being in discord." Michelle Yeoh's virtuoso performance makes this clear, but there is still something else—momentary nostalgia—for Wing-chun knows the "anterior future," that "future catastrophe" that has already occurred (Barthes 1981, 96). The screenplay temporarily privileges this interpretation as Fong immediately begs Wing-chun's pardon and explains that she "didn't mean to"—that is, Fong didn't mean to remind Wing-chun of her passage (the "future catastrophe") from feminine beauty and charm. Significantly, however, Wing-chun does not concede to the misogyny that underlies the fear of "losing one's femininity"; instead, she teases her aunt for being "brainless"[16] and they share a laugh at the village men who would return tirelessly for another scoop of *tofu* and another gaze at her—that is, for another gaze at the "*Tofu* Beauty" that she used to be before she threw off women's clothing in exchange for men's garb, *wushu*, and independence. Now, as Fong candidly points out, the "bumps" that are supposed to be on her chest have gone to her biceps and those on her behind have gone to her thighs.[17] Although "musculinization" is presented as the reason Wing-chun lost her status as "*Tofu* Beauty" of the village (therein revealing the conventional desires of the village men), the film never argues that she has thus become less of a woman; instead, we see that Wing-chun "emerges as a de-formation of the normal," suggesting "new political aggregates…and refus[ing] to keep every body in its place" (Russo 1994, 16).

Wing-chun rescues Charmy three times from the mountain-bandits, defeating their leaders and foiling their plans; when their Second Commander tries to abduct Charmy in the night, his heated loins become literally so when Wing-chun throws flames at him from atop a fence post. This brings the First Commander into the fray and, thanks to his amazing "cotton belly" (which sucks in any kicking foot or offending fist and pulverizes it—his very own vagina dentata, if you will),[18] he fights the high-kicking, light-as-air, leaping and punching Wing-chun to slightly better than a draw. Shaken by her first near-defeat (she is beaten but not vanquished), Wing-chun seeks advice from her teacher, the abbess Ng. The aging nun gives her the final key to the technique—the famous "whipping action," which uses the opponent's strength and weight against him—and, with this, aerial Wing-chun is able to defeat the First Commander.

Much of the fighting in this film's narrative is the result of what I put forward as the other side of the Freudian penis-envy paradigm: womb anxiety. The womb is something both left behind and sought, both denigrated in language and venerated in secret. In *Wing Chun*, it is the ultimate outrage. The bully who cannot even meet Wing-chun's challenge to smash the *tofu* had started off by telling Wing-chun to "go home and make babies": he wanted to put this lofty, offending womb back in its place. Her fight with Second Commander ends significantly, not just casually, in his castration; thereafter, he is a self-confessed, self-pitying insomniac because he can never have children.

In the first duel between First Commander and Wing-chun, he agrees to give up Charmy if he loses; in the second and final duel three days later, the stakes are apparently higher: *he must call Wing-chun "Mom" if he loses.* Wing-chun wins the first duel when she meets his challenge and successfully pulls out the long, heavy spear that he had, with brute force, "implanted" at nearly roof level into a stone wall; but he is strong and she sustains internal injuries in their combat. Wing-chun arrives at the second duel dressed—for the first time in the film—in *women's* clothes: *pink* women's *kungfu* clothes. She chooses a set of short swords to fight against First Commander's long, heavy spear. Again he is strong, but she is light on her feet while he is weighed down by his weapon. She leaps and kicks and both gives and takes several hits, until he pursues her into a hut; there, his long spear immediately becomes a burden, getting caught first in the doorway and then in the ceiling. "Length is useless," she shouts at him! The double-entendre is clear and it is amusing, but what is most pleasing is the film's portrayal of her indifference to his weapon (let us not forget that, in enormous contrast, all three women in *Dragon* fetishize the hero's precious sword). Instead of usurping it when First Commander loses his spear (it's stuck, this time inadvertently, in a wall), Wing-chun throws down her swords too and they continue their fight with empty hands. He attacks with strength and throws fast and hard punches, but Wing-chun bends and dodges and leaps out of harm's way. Like the mosquitoes that she earlier observed perching on the soft mosquito net that gives way to every punch thrown at it, Wing-chun is precise in her flexibility and she is not harmed by her opponent's brute force. In the end, when he has exhausted himself, it is her turn to attack, and she defeats him easily.

Since the strength of Wing Chun *kungfu* lies in its philosophy of using the opponent's weight and momentum against him, it is more deadly in proportion to the opponent's strength and force. But the body count in the film is exactly zero, in spite of Wing-chun's victories against the bandits and kidnappers; in fact, the worst that she does is to castrate Second Commander, which is symbolic not only of a woman defeating a man but also of how this particular style of *kungfu* bends the phallus back upon itself. Significantly, the film's final battle does not end in a phallocentric exhilaration that erects a singular authority: in apparent paradox, Wing-chun uses her *kungfu* (i.e., her labour and her martial arts skills [see Note 1]) to defend the non-hierarchical character of her community.

Wing-chun is the most thematically important part of the "transgressive triad." Unlike the schoolgirl transgressions of Charmy or the wheeling-dealings of Fong, Wing-chun (and Michelle Yeoh, who plays her) is constantly in forbidden territory (at both the diegetic and extradiegetic levels): she cross-dresses, she fights, and she is as quick and as comical as any Jackie Chan character when she challenges a local strongman to smash a flat of *tofu* (the *most* smashable thing of all); amazingly, he fails (because of her marvelous acrobatics, which repeatedly jockeys the *tofu* out of his reach). The film ends with her wedding: dressed in her bridal finery, she makes a spectacular leap onto her horse some distance away: she has obviously not abandoned either her aerialism or her love of *kungfu*. Wing-chun marries her childhood sweetheart, finds a freedom that suits her and fits her world, and goes on to become the legend that every Chinese schoolgirl knows. The historical Wing-chun is arguably the most famous teacher of *kungfu* in modern Chinese history; the style is, of course, named for her.

Positively Levitating

While murder is not unknown in martial arts films, it is not synonymous with (or the ultimate aim of) the violence in the films' narratives and spectacles. Skill and virtue—including the all-important virtues of diligence and humility in the practice of one's *kungfu* skills—are traditionally what will triumph, for the goal of perfecting martial arts skills is to become simultaneously superior in terms of justice, mercy, understanding, and the ability to teach the benighted world (as the Buddha did upon his return from ultimate enlightenment). Violence thematically serves a higher purpose, vanquishing the truly murderous who are trapped within a hellish world of their own fears and jealousies.

The three women in Yuen Po-wing's *Wing Chun*—a small but expansive film—are self-defined as well as mutually supportive. Yim Wing-chun is perhaps the ideal portrait, but both Fong and Charmy strike me as equally progressive for, even though they live in a society that is not kind to women (to say the least), they manage to be true to their yearnings and consciences. Despite the film's humble special effects, the women in *Wing Chun* soar high; they manage to be more elevated precisely because they are so much more grounded. By its obvious esteem for the three female protagonists, Yuen's film insists that there are many kinds of femininities. In contrast, the fighting women in Ang Lee's *Crouching Tiger, Hidden Dragon* are entirely desperate, two of them lacking the humility required to defuse the ego-wielding evil-doers of the world. If this makes them more contemporary, it is at the cost not only of tradition but also of depth: they come off as shallow (Jade Fox) or immature (Jen) characters controlled entirely by what they do not have—by their lack. In the end, they are shrill, distraught, desperate. Whereas Lee's fighting women are the dragon, the fox, and the lotus who fetishize the master's weapons—his sword (of "luck and destiny") and his words (the Wudang manual)—Yuen's fighting heroines, named after and known by their own cultivated abilities (Abacus/Stinky-mouthed Fong, Charmy, and Wing-chun), are the producers of discourse and creators of destinies.

Wing Chun cost a fraction of the budget and made a fraction of the box-office intake of *Crouching Tiger, Hidden Dragon*, but in my view the portrait of the fighting woman is eminently more conducive to feminist pleasure in Yuen's casual comedy than in Lee's solemnly gender-focused film. In part this is facilitated by the more quotidian nature of the problems faced by the women in the smaller film as opposed to the aristocratic anxieties of Jen and the almost mythically evil responses of Jade Fox to all and everything in the bigger film. Whereas Shulien, Jen, and Fox's machinations take them away from home and community on flights more splendid and exhilarating, Wing-chun's flight originates from, and is grounded in, her community. Yim Wing-chun fights by first cooperating with her opponent's strength before sending it back through him, and even though she steadfastly declines the conventions of femininity, she does not reject or forfeit womanhood. It is this universe of opposites that gives *Wing Chun* a charm and a feminist philosophy sadly absent from the visually stunning but ideologically conservative *Crouching Tiger, Hidden Dragon*.

Notes

1 *Wuxia* is a transliteration from Mandarin for the "errant martial artist" and *pian* is 'film.' *Kungfu* has a literal meaning of both 'labour' and 'practice'—so that one could say "it was a lot of *kungfu* to carve that sculpture"—but it is also a vernacular expression that refers to the practised skills of *wushu*, the art (*shu*) of fighting (*wu*), or the martial arts. Although "*kungfu* film" and "*wuxia pian*" are often used interchangeably, in my view a more precise consideration would specify *wuxia pian* as a subset of *kungfu* films that is set in historical times and populated mostly by martial artists who accept a subjectivity defined by, and a daily life inextricably linked to, the martial arts; put another way, the *wuxia* is a martial artist (*xia* connotes a chivalrous rescuer, though of course there is always the antithesis) whose raison d'être is to fight (literally) to right wrongs and to protect the common folk. Although morally self-directed, the *wuxia*'s activities are necessarily determined in part by the actions of the other *wuxia* and are open to their scrutiny. The *kungfu* film, on the other hand, can have modern, even contemporary, settings, with characters for whom *kungfu* is a means—one among others—to other ends in their lives. The distinction I make between a *wuxia* and a *kungfu* fighter becomes especially helpful to our understanding of the psychosocial struggles of the fighting women foregrounded in *Crouching Tiger, Hidden Dragon*, a *wuxia pian*.

2 In the rest of the essay, directors are referred to by their family names ("Yuen" and "Lee") and characters by their given names (such as "Mubai" and "Shulien" and "Wing-chun").

3 For examples of women as girlfriends/sidekicks in action films, see *Cliffhanger* 1993, *Executive Decision* 1995, *Bad Boys* 1995, and *Fair Game* 1995. Some examples of action films with female protagonists are *The Long Kiss Goodnight* 1996, *Twister* 1996, *Terminator 2* 1991, and the *Alien* series 1979, 1986, 1992, 1997. For an excellent discussion of women in the action genres, see Yvonne Tasker (1993), "Action Women: Muscles, Mothers and Others" in *Working Girls: Gender and Sexuality in Popular Cinema.*

4 Long before Michelle Yeoh there were Yu SoChau, Lam Fung, Suet Nei, Fung SoPo, Connie Chan PoChu, Josephine Siao FongFong, and many others in Hong Kong's Cantonese swordplay films (tremendously popular in the late 1950s and early 1960s) as well as Zheng PeiPei (who also plays Jade Fox in Ang Lee's *Dragon*), Li Jing, Pan Tingzi and others in the Mandarin-dialect swordplays (mid-1960s to early 1970s) of the Shaw Brothers' Studio. Two immensely popular Cantonese films, *Yuloa Sunjeung* [Buddha's Palm] (1964) and *Bakgwud Yumyeung Geem* [White-Boned Sword] (1962), had four and five sequels, respectively (and hundreds of imitations), featuring heroines who not only defended the weak (including men) but also set the high moral standards of the dramas. Some diverse examples of recent fighting heroines of Hong Kong films are the characters of "Wonder Woman" (played by Anita Mui), "Invisible Woman" (Michelle Yeoh) and "Thief Catcher" (Maggie Cheung) in *The Heroic Trio* and its sequel, *The Executioners* (both directed by Johnny To and Ching Siu-tung, 1993), "Wolf Girl" in *Bride with White Hair, I* and *II* (dir. Ronny Yu and David Yu, respectively, both 1993), and "Snow" in *Deadful Melody* (dir. Ng Min-kan, 1994).

5 The buzz on the street during the Toronto International Film Festival (2000) was that this was the first truly feminist martial arts film. Film critics seem to agree. See, for example, the reviews of Amy Taubin in *Village Voice* (6–12 December 2000) and of Lisa Schwarzbaum in *Entertainment Weekly* (29 November 2000). Taubin classifies Jen as "feminist desire for freedom," while Schwarzbaum gushes that *Dragon* is "soaring and romantic, wild and serene, feminist and gutsy…one of the best movies of the year."

6 Tania Modleski (1991, 135–63) illustrates the homophobic hysteria in *Dead Poets Society* (dir. Peter Weir, 1989) and *Lethal Weapon 1* and *2* (dir. Richard Donner, 1987 and 1989) by systematically tracing the films' strategies of repression and disavowal of "unspeakable" homoeroticism and male masochism.

7 The phrase is *gao xia xiang qing*, in Chapter 2 of the *Dao De Jing* (or *Tao Te Ching*, c. 600 BCE)—literally, the scripture (*jing*) of the way (*dao*) of virtue (*de*)—attributed to Lao Zi (or Lao Tse).

8 In *Heroic Trio*, fighting women save the day for the mostly inept police. "Wonder Woman" somersaults on the electrical wires high above the street lamps to fight "Invisible Woman," who steals babies from the maternity wards and scales tall buildings to get away; "Thief Catcher" also defies the laws of physics as she and her motorcycle travel through the air to chase after criminals—for a fee. In *Bride with White Hair I* and *II*, "Wolf Girl" becomes the "White-Haired Witch" (Brigitte Lin) who deploys, among other weapons, her long hair to first battle her evil masters in order to be with the man that she loves and then battle him in order to defend her honour and punish his lack of faith in her. In *Deadful Melody*, "Snow" plays literally deadly tunes on

a lyre to avenge her murdered parents; she dresses as a man, speaks in a male voice, and mysteriously appears without any apparent method of travel.

9   The name for the sword in Chinese is *Yun bao jian*, which means "precious sword of destiny and/or luck"—*yun* is the word for both "destiny" and "luck."

10   Yuen Wo-ping's action choreography is unrivalled and unforgettable, while Peter Pau's cinematography follows and flies behind the fighters with an agility as nearly remarkable, showing not only the combatants but also the richness of the environment. But, always, it is the apparent weightlessness, the levitations and the flights, that impress us. Yuen is a veteran director with an impressive filmography, including *Tai Chi Master* 1993 (starring Jet Li), *Fire Dragon* 1994 (Brigitte Lin), *Iron Monkey: The Young Wong Fei Hung* 1993 (Donnie Yen) released as *Iron Monkey* in the United States in 2001, and of course *Wing Chun* 1994, the second film discussed in this chapter. He is also well known for his action choreography in American films such as *The Matrix* trilogy 1999–2003 and *Kill Bill, Vol. 2* 2004. Pau also has a venerable filmography, including *The Killer* 1989 (dir. John Woo), *The Swordsman* 1990 (dir. King Hu), *The Bride with White Hair* 1993 and *The Phantom Lover* 1995 (both dir. Ronny Yu), *The Promise* 2005 (dir. Chen Kaige), and American films such as *Double Team* 1997 (dir. Tsui Hark) and *Wes Craven Presents: Dracula* 2000 (dir. Patrick Lussier).

11   "*Yu*" is Mandarin pinyin for "jade" and "*jiao*" is Mandarin pinyin for "delicate/pampered." Both words are common in names for women. On the other hand, "*long*" is "dragon," and it is typically used in male rather than female proper names to suggest potency and success. For example, Bruce Lee is "*Li Xiaolong*," which means "little dragon Lee," and Jackie Chan is "*Chenlong*," which means "becoming [a] dragon."

12   Foxes are also said to hide in the attics of large houses and surreptitiously help themselves to whatever they want. True to her name, Jade Fox helped herself at both her *kungfu* teacher's house and later at Governor Yu's house.

13   Yuen is the director, action director, and composer of *Wing Chun*, his first film with a female lead.

14   Later, when Leung Pok-to—Wing Chun's childhood friend and fiancé returns to town after being away for six years, he does not recognize her but, instead, mistakes her for a man.

15   See Lacan (1977). Between the ages of six and eighteen months, the infant (with help from his mother) first experiences a sense of self-identity by recognizing and internalizing his mirror stage. However, "still sunk in his motor incapacity and nursling dependence," the child judges that he *looks* far more coherent than he *feels* (2).

16   The exact words translate as "without brains." I am not using "thoughtless" because the word suggests being uncaring or unkind, whereas Wing Chun means to acknowledge that Fong is simply impetuous and imprudent. Their relationship of mutual trust, respect, and love is one of the most satisfying elements of the film.

17   This is my translation. The English subtitles eliminated all the details, saying only that Wing-chun is muscular.

18   Readers familiar with David Cronenberg's *Videodrome* (1983) will recall that Max Renn (wise-guy porno pusher, played by James Woods) also develops a vagina right in the middle of his abdomen; in fact, he loses his gun into it. In both cases (Renn and First Commander), what has always been pushed down turns up to embrace the man and become a part of him.

The Madwomen in Our Movies: Female Psycho-Killers in American Horror Cinema

[13]

Come with me into the tormented, haunted, half-lit night of the INSANE....Let me take you into the mind of a woman who is MAD. You may not recognize some things in this world. And the faces will look strange to you. For this is a place where there is NO love. NO hope. In the pulsing, throbbing world of the INSANE MIND, where only nightmares are real. Nightmares of the DAUGHTER OF HORROR.
—Narrator/Demon (the voice of Ed McMahon) in the 1957 rerelease
of John Parker's *Dementia* (1955), entitled *Daughter of Horror*[1]

Lady Killers

In terms of sheer quantity, it is clear that male psycho-killers have dominated the tradition of what has come to be known as "realist" horror cinema in the United States—a tradition popularized by Alfred Hitchcock's *Psycho* (1960), in which the impossible, supernatural monsters of earlier horror films were replaced by antagonists of an apparently (or at least loosely) human ontology.[2] And with rare exception, male sociopaths, psychopaths, schizphrenics, and sexual deviants have also proven a great deal more (in)famous in American horror films and thrillers than have their female counterparts. For every Danielle Breton (Margot Kidder in *Sisters* [1973]), it seems there are twenty Robert Elliotts (Michael Caine in *Dressed to Kill* [1980]); for every Dorine Douglas (Carol Kane in *Office Killer* [1997]), at least fifty Hannibal Lecters (Anthony Hopkins in *The Silence of the Lambs* [1991] and *Hannibal* [2001]).

Moreover, and to the dismay (or is it the delight?) of those who would accuse the genre of a conventionalized if not inherent sexism, for every dumb male jock or clueless stoner dude to get sliced and diced in your average slasher movie—one highly codified subgenre of realist horror cinema, initiated in 1978 with John Carpenter's *Halloween*—it is practically guaranteed that two or three young women depicted as either bimbos or bitches will suffer a death that is both more protracted and more sadistic at the hands, knives, or worse of the killer. This holds true even in the more recent, supposedly innovative and self-reflexive, examples such as *Scream* (1996), *I Know What You Did Last Summer* (1997), *Halloween H2O* (1998), and *Valentine* (2001).[3] As Carol J. Clover (1992, 80, 82) notes of the slasher film, "Where once [the victim] was female, now she is both boy and girl, though most often and most conspicuously girl.…[E]ven in films in which males and females are killed in roughly even numbers, the lingering images are inevitably female." Although this last claim might seem self-evident to fans and scholars of such movies, it is worth providing some empirical support. According to Stephen Prince (2003, 246), "in a content analysis of the ten biggest-grossing slasher films, James Weaver found that the average length of scenes showing the death of male characters was just under two minutes and those showing the death of female characters was just under four minutes, and that these lengthy intervals were accompanied by expressions of fear, terror, and pain."[4]

When it comes to realist horror cinema, then, at least in the United States, it would appear that men (mostly) do the killing while women (mostly) struggle simply to survive. This bias towards male killers is nowhere more succinctly alluded to than in *Scream*'s memorable and frequently parodied opening scene, in which a wiseass Gen-X psychopath forces high-school beauty Casey Becker (Drew Barrymore) to play a twisted game with him on the telephone: answer correctly three slasher movie trivia questions or else die a horrible death. Casey has no problem with the first two, but then makes a fatal mistake, claiming that the hockey-masked murderer in *Friday the 13th* (1980) is Jason Voorhees when, in fact, it is Jason's *mother*. For a self-proclaimed fan of the genre to get this "trick" question wrong by confusing the killer's gender—assuming that it was a *he* rather than a *she*—is something to which *Scream*'s viewers clearly could relate.

Of course, the above observations are rendered more than a little problematic by the fact that so many male killers in the slasher subgenre, and in realist horror cinema as a whole, are depicted as cross-dressing, homosexual, impotent, or otherwise and variously "feminized." Clover (1996, 92) draws particular attention to this point in her groundbreaking 1987 analysis of the slasher film: "The killer's phallic purpose, as he thrusts his drill or knife into the trembling bodies of young women, is unmistakable. At the same time, however, his masculinity is severely qualified: he ranges from the virginal or sexually inert to the transvestite or transsexual, is spiritually divided...or even equipped with vulva and vagina." Taking the male killer's conventional feminization in conjunction with the *masculinization* of the slasher film's surviving female, the so-called "Final Girl"—usually depicted as tough, tomboyish, aggressive, and often given a male name (e.g., Marti, Terry, Stevie, Sidney)—Clover argues for the subgenre's characteristic emphasis on cross-gender identification. Prince (2003, 248) usefully summarizes her position as follows:

> The essential viewing dynamic that these films instigate in viewers is one marked by an oscillation between subjectivities marked as "male" (active, aggressive, empowered) and "female" (passive, unempowered, victimized) in terms of their cultural coding. These "positions," according to Clover, do not correspond in any fixed way with the gender of the viewer, in part because the films in question collapse and combine gender categories by featuring a killer who is a feminine male and a main character (the "Final Girl") who is a masculine female.

Although she goes on to ask "why, if viewers can identify across gender lines, are the screen sexes not interchangeable? Why not more and better female killers...?" Clover (1996, 92) effectively drops this line of inquiry in favour of an extended investigation into why the vast majority of slasher film *survivors* are female rather than male (among her answers: this representational strategy provides male viewers a degree of emotional distance from the Final Girl's abject terror; and it allows for these viewers to experience the thrill of playing with gender identity).

The closest she comes to answering the above question concerning the relative lack of female *killers* comes on the last page of her essay:

> The fact that we have in the killer a feminine male and in the main character a masculine female...would seem, *especially in the latter case*, to suggest a loosening of the categories, or at least of the equation sex equals gender. It is not that these films show us gender and sex in free variation; it is that they fix on the irregular combinations, of which the combination masculine female [i.e., the Final Girl] repeatedly prevails over the combination feminine male [i.e., the feminized male killer]. (Clover 1996, 106, emphasis mine)

Clover's qualification in the first sentence ("especially in the latter case") can be interpreted as indicating, if not a reluctance on her part to make any conclusive statements about slasher movie killers as opposed to survivors, at least an interest in concentrating on the latter rather than on the former.

Nevertheless, following Clover, one must acknowledge the extent to which the killer in slasher movies in particular, and in realist horror cinema in general, has been variously depicted as feminized or effeminate for this is clearly a convention in its own right—from *Psycho* and *Dressed to Kill* up through *Cherry Falls* (2000) and *Dahmer* (2002). Also, we should not overlook or underemphasize the sexual "truth" of these psychologically disturbed characters, a truth that usually (though not always) serves to confirm the killer's biological *maleness* even if not his enculturated/gendered *masculinity*.

Having said all this, the history of realist horror cinema in the United States, an otherwise fairly heterogeneous collection of films, has thematized, often to terrifying effect, the trials and tribulations of women psycho-killers. In what follows, I survey and analyze depictions of female madness in the horror and thriller genres, with an eye towards answering the following questions: (1) are the sorts of traumas attributed to the madwomen in these movies specifically gendered? (2) how does the particular manner in (and means by) which these madwomen kill function to code them as simultaneously empowered and subjugated? and (3) is there an essential connection between the sexual identity of a realist horror film's psycho-killer and the generic conventions that film seeks to employ, subvert, or transgress?

Although I hope to show that, in the case of both male *and* female psycho-killers, the motives for their murderous behaviour are usually traceable back to early childhood sexual abuse and trauma (even if this is only hinted at in the narrative), I also argue that the nature of the resulting psychopathology is manifested and portrayed differently for women than it is for men. Whereas the latter typically exhibit a gender confusion signified by the killer's possession of both masculine and feminine attributes, as Clover has revealed, the former give body to an anxiety intrinsic to patriarchal notions of femininity: namely, that the safe, nurturing, maternal female bears hysterical, possessive, violent impulses within her very soul. Thus my overarching thesis is that the representation of mad killer women in the horror genre differs systematically from that of mad killer men, with the former serving to reify patriarchal gender norms. In part because such norms hold sway across a diversity of cultures, in part because Freudian (at least pop-Freudian) themes and symbols are often self-consciously employed in the texts in question, a socio-historical index is less relevant to the present, characterological analysis than is the psychoanalytic approach adopted here.

In a sense, this chapter attempts to provide a brief history—more like a guided tour—of female madness in American horror-thriller cinema; the aim is not to provide a comprehensive list but, rather, to demarcate the topic and pave the way for a future taxonomy in (sub)generic terms. Along the way I stop to compare and contrast the depiction of biologically female psycho-killers with those who are (or else who turn out to be, as in *Psycho, Dressed to Kill, Sleepaway Camp* [1983], and *Cherry Falls*) biologically male. Moreover, I extend female psycho-killers as they are depicted in American realist horror to those found in other national cinemas—for example, in films such as *Repulsion* (UK, 1965), *The Bird with the Crystal Plumage* (Italy, 1970), *The Damned House of Hajn* (Czechoslovakia, 1988), *Heavenly Creatures* (New Zealand, 1994), *The Stendhal Syndrome* (Italy, 1996), *Tell Me Something* (South Korea, 1999), *Audition* (Japan, 1999), and *Freeze Me* (Japan, 2000)—to indicate the surprising degree to which these depictions cross socio-cultural lines.

Murderous Motives

Come, let me take you by the arm and show you the bed of EVIL you sprang from. Let me take you back to when you were a little girl. Let me show you—your father. Let me show you—your mother. Marked! Marked forever, DAUGHTER OF HORROR.

In his essay, "Lady, Beware: Paths through the Female Gothic," Adrian Martin (2001)identifies Maya Deren's avant-garde masterpiece *Meshes of the Afternoon* (1943) as "probably the first film to make the indelible link between a woman's experience of coming fatally unglued—splintered into multiple personalities, plagued by visions, slipping between alternate realities—and the sunny spaces of a daytime home environment, its every tiny but determining facet magnified, from the slope of the lounge room staircase to the bread knife on the kitchen table."[5] (Arguably, Germaine Dulac's *La Souriante Madame Beudet/The Smiling Madame Beudet* [1922] is the true initiator of such cinematic representations.) After looking at some earlier attempts by scholars, such as Thomas Elsaesser, Dana Polan, and Joanna Russ, to define "Female Gothic" cinema—by which they have in mind primarily the 1940s cycle of "wife-in-peril" suspense films and melodramas (beginning with Alfred Hitchcock's *Rebecca* [1940] and including *Suspicion* [1941], *Gaslight* [1944], *Experiment Perilous* [1944], and *Secret beyond the Door* [1948])—Martin (2001, 11) opts for a more flexible and open-ended formula than his predecessors; namely, "a woman voyages through a menacing, male dreamscape."

While allowing that "such voyages and dreamscapes can take on starkly different appearances and contents," Martin (2001,) argues that the variegated genre of Female Gothic depicts "the narrative, psychic and emotional confusions" of women in films where

> victimisers and victims, abusers and abused, dream lovers and demon lovers, those who can manipulate hard reality and those who succumb to wild, ravishing fantasy, can find themselves trading places in a hallucinatory, vertiginous instant. The Female Gothic is, at its core, a genre based on instability, ambiguity and ambivalence, in relation to the very status of reality as much as to questions of identity politics.

As Martin delineates it, the Female Gothic overlaps significantly—though not completely—with female psycho-killer films in American horror cinema. On the one hand, like the Female Gothic, female psycho-killer cinema focuses on women who are *both* "victimisers and victims, abusers and abused"—women whose grasp on reality is tenuous at best and who frequently "succumb to wild, ravishing fantasy." On the other hand, unlike the Female Gothic, female psycho-killer cinema does *not* include "persecuted woman" films such as the 1940s wife-in-peril cycle or the late-1980s "intimacy thriller" cycle (including *Thief of Hearts* [1984], *Call Me* [1988], *Blue Steel* [1990], *The Silence of the Lambs* [1991], and *Cape Fear* [1991]), in which a "dream-guy (usually a stalker or serial killer)…simultaneously menaces the heroine and leads her towards higher planes of ecstasy or self-knowledge)."[6] Although the lead woman in female psycho-killer films is frequently a victim of male aggression, she is never *just* a victim, and her murderous acts are never construable simply as self-defence or justifiable (even if only just barely) homicide. Indeed, it is the very excessiveness, irrationality, and/or misdirectedness of the woman's violence that renders her a monster in psychological terms, regardless of whether the cause of her psychosis is shown to lie primarily in childhood abuse, sexual molestation, or some form of traumatic experience. Finally, situated right at the border between persecuted woman and female psycho-killer films is the late-1970s cycle of American rape-revenge movies (including *Lipstick* [1976], *I Spit on Your Grave* [1978], *Mother's Day* [1980], and *Ms. 45* [1981]), followed by its mid-1980s revival (*Savage Streets* [1984], *Violated* [1984], *Naked Vengeance* [1985], *The Ladies Club* [1986], *Extremities* [1986], *Shame* [1987]) and foreign examples such as Takashi Ishii's *Freeze Me*, since in these narratives it is the very fact of persecution in the woman's adult life that proves productive of psychosis and retaliatory violence.[7]

In *Meshes of the Afternoon*, the female protagonist's violence is ultimately self-directed, the short film ending with Deren's character apparently dead from a suicide attempt. A similar plot development, in which suicide (whether successful or not) is effectively presented as a distinctly female response to either unrequited heterosexual desire or inescapable male domination, can be found in such later films as *Play Misty for Me* (1971), *The Haunting* (UK, 1963), *The Damned House of Hajn*, and—perhaps most emphatically—in the original, shelved version of Adrian Lyne's *Fatal Attraction* (1987).[8] In this version's alternative ending, the obsessive and psychopathic Glenn Close character commits suicide by solemnly running a knife across her neck to the strains of Puccini's *Madame Butterfly* playing on the stereo; the male object of her affection, Dan Gallagher (Michael Douglas), is then arrested on suspicion of murder.[9]

Without wishing to deny for a moment the wide-ranging influence of *Meshes of the Afternoon*, thematically and historically speaking, it is probably more accurate to label John Parker's *Dementia* (1955)—itself clearly indebted to Deren's work in its focus on conveying female subjectivity and its treatment of domestic spaces as claustrophobic and oppressive[10]—the foundational text in American female psycho-killer cinema. This independently produced cult film liberally and not always coherently mixes together expressionistic set design, surrealistic symbolism, and an experimental, dreamlike narrative in telling the story of an unnamed "gamine" (Adrienne Barrett) who pushes an obese rich man off a balcony after he forces himself on her sexually; in a thinly veiled castration sequence, she then cuts a hand off the man's corpse when she realizes that it still clenches the brooch he pulled off her neck on the way down. Although the film's 1957 re-release under the title *Daughter of Horror* sporadically inserts male voice-over narration in a misguided and largely unsuccessful effort at making the gamine a figure of disgust and loathing, *Dementia* (again like *Meshes of the Afternoon*) has no dialogue. In rendering her, if not literally mute, at least metaphorically silent, the film fixes a key convention for female psycho-killers, whose primary mode of self-expression typically occurs through spontaneous rages and hysterical bodily performances—frequently accompanied by infantile, inarticulate noises (shrieks, screams, squeals, and the like) rather than through words or arguments—hyperbolic gestures and embodied forms of communication that are common to the film melodrama as well).[11]

This stands in stark contrast to two popular strains of male psycho-killer cinema. In the first (e.g., in *Psycho, Prom Night* [1980], *Angst* [Austria, 1983], and the *Halloween* [1978–] and *Friday the 13th* [1980–] series), the male murderer's disconcerting silence during moments of vicious slaughter is, in the end, more indicative of his robotic, inhuman nature than of any psychological deficiency. In the second (e.g., in *The Silence of the Lambs* [1991], *Man Bites Dog* [Belgium, 1992], *Seven* [1995], and *The Watcher* [2000]), the verbose, often quite witty male serial killer goes to great pains—and is given plenty of screen time—to explain to the hero (and the audience) what he believes, rightly or wrongly, is the motivation behind his crimes. Thus, whereas male psycho-killers tend to be depicted as either arational or in some sense hyperrational, female psycho-killers are almost always depicted as *irrational*. The murders these women commit can usually be interpreted as crimes of either passion or obsession, and their simultaneously frightening and frightened cries while performing spontaneous, messy acts of violence—one thinks of such figures as Evelyn Draper (Jessica Walter) in *Play Misty for Me*, Danielle Breton (Margot Kidder) in *Sisters*, Alex Forrest (Glenn Close) in *Fatal Attraction*, and Hedra Carlson (Jennifer Jason Leigh) in *Single White Female* (1992)—reveals their status as *both* empowered victimizers and pathetic victims, and helps us to understand their capacity to shock and disturb viewers.

Not long after *Dementia*, Robert Aldrich directed a pair of campy but compelling "pseudo" female psycho-killer films, *What Ever Happened to Baby Jane?* (1962) and *Hush...Hush, Sweet Charlotte* (1964), in both of which male-directed homicidal mania ultimately takes a backseat to the psychological torture inflicted by one woman upon another (although the latter film's memorably gory opening murder scene is eventually revealed to be a crime of passion committed by a jealous wife against her unfaithful husband, replete with meat cleaver and yet another lopped-off hand). Like *Meshes of the Afternoon* and Robert Wise's *The Haunting* before it, and like Rob Reiner's *Misery* (1990) and Bernard Rose's *Candyman* (1992) after it, *Hush...Hush, Sweet Charlotte* in particular seeks to approximate the experiential quality of a distinctly feminine form of psychosis, whereby melodramatic conventions and icons of courtship (flowers, mirrors, swelling music, 360-degree swish pans) metamorphose into lethal weapons (knives, guns) or objects of disgust (body parts, insects). Saccharine dreams of heterosexual union and domestic bliss thus turn into horrible nightmares of spoiled romance and phallicized death symbols, with insanity the assumed or intended cause.

Numerous other female psycho-killer films, including *Dementia, Sisters, Office Killer, So Evil, My Sister* (aka *Psycho Sisters*, 1972), *Natural Born Killers* (1994), and *The Sky Is Falling* (2002), as well as prominent foreign examples such as *Repulsion, Heavenly Creatures, The Stendhal Syndrome*, and *Tell Me Something*, all contain sequences that purport to grant some form of subjective access to the woman psychotic's "inner life." For the most part, however, these sequences focus less on romantic fantasies that turn horribly wrong than on expressionistically (sometimes psychedelically, as in *Natural Born Killers*) distorted recollections or reconstructions of childhood traumas—sexual molestation, physical abuse, emotional cruelty or neglect—suffered at the hands of a monstrous parent figure.

This finding is at odds with Clover's (1992, 77) analysis of the slasher subgenre, according to which,

> Female killers are few and their reasons for killing significantly different from men's. With the possible exception of the murderous mother in *Friday the 13th*, they show no gender confusion. Nor is their motive overtly psychosexual; their anger derives in most cases not from childhood experience but from specific moments in their adult lives in which they have been abandoned or cheated on by men (*Strait-Jacket* [1964], *Play Misty for Me...*, *Attack of the 50-Foot Woman* [1958]).

Although Clover's stated focus is on the slasher movie in particular, and not on horror cinema generally, by parenthetically citing *Strait-Jacket*, *Play Misty for Me*, and *Attack of the 50-Foot Woman* she *does* appear to be extending her argument to films outside the conventionalized strictures of the slasher subgenre. She thereby opens herself up to a degree of criticism. For example, with respect to the female killer's "reasons for killing," Clover misses the significance of *Strait-Jacket*'s disturbing denouement. Here it is revealed that the madwoman going around chopping people up is *not* recently released axe murderer Lucy Harbin (Joan Crawford), who went crazy twenty years earlier upon finding her husband in bed with another woman, but, rather, Lucy's daughter Carol (Diane Baker), who watched her mother slaughter her father when she was just a little girl.

In short, and somewhat surprisingly, there is no firm distinction to be drawn at the level of convention between male and female psycho-killers in American horror cinema when it comes to the suggested motivations for their crimes. Just as plenty of female murderers are shown to act (out) in displaced and possibly unconscious response to childhood traumas experienced at home (e.g., Diane in *Strait-Jacket*, Dorine in *Office Killer*, Mallory Knox [Juliette Lewis] in *Natural Born Killers*, and Angelica [Joanne Verbos] in *The Sky Is Falling*), a number of male slasher movie killers seek bloody revenge for traumatic events suffered in their adolescent or adult lives (e.g., Kenny Hampson [Derek McKinnon] in *Terror Train* [1980], Alex Hammond [Michael Tough] in *Prom Night*, and Adam Carr [David Borneaz] in *Valentine*). Even in the case of films such as *Play Misty for Me*, *Black Widow* (1987), and *Basic Instinct* (1992), in which the female killer's history and psychology remain shrouded in mystery throughout—these women may be caught, punished, even tamed (e.g., *Basic Instinct*'s Catherine Tramell [Sharon Stone]) in the end, but they always remain enigmas—we cannot conclude that their anger "derives...from specific moments in their adult lives in which they have been abandoned or cheated on by men" (Clover 1992, 77). The most we can say is that such moments serve to trigger violent episodes in the present, violence that is just as likely to have its roots in these women's childhoods as in their recent pasts.

Consider two examples that would seem to offer stronger evidence in support of Clover's generalized conclusions than either *Strait-Jacket* or *Play Misty for Me*; namely, *Fatal Attraction* and *The Hand That Rocks the Cradle* (1992). The backstories in both of these films indicate that miscarriages suffered by the respective female psychopaths, Alex and Peyton (Rebecca De Mornay), in their adult lives play a significant role in the genesis of their current mental and emotional disorders. Upon closer examination, however, both narratives also invite speculation as to the presence of more primitive, quite possibly psychosexual motives as well. Although these motives are not overt (to that extent, Clover is correct), their existence nevertheless serves to complicate and undercut any straightforward understanding of the women as formerly well adjusted, "normal" adults who have cracked under specifically patriarchal pressures.[12] In the case of *Fatal Attraction*, when Dan breaks into Alex's apartment to try to find some information he can blackmail her with (so that she will leave him alone and not tell his wife of their affair), he sifts through newspaper clippings concerning the unexpected death of Alex's father from a sudden heart attack several years earlier. There is a clear suggestion here—even if it is left unconfirmed in the narrative—that Alex had something to do with her father's death. Assuming for the sake of argument that she killed him, and even granting that she would have been an adult at the time of his murder, the very fact of her victim's identity raises the question of what her father did to Alex (in reality or in her imagination; following Freud, it may not really matter) to warrant such vicious retaliation.[13]

Teaching Daddy a Lesson

> Run, DAUGHTER OF HORROR, run from your crime. But behind you the policeman with the face of your father, the face of your first victim. Pursuing you relentlessly through your haunted dreams. Hunting you mercilessly through the twisted corridors of your TORTURED mind. The HORROR that will track you down! The HORROR that will destroy you! Run. Run. Run. Guilty. Guilty. GUILTY! Nowhere to run. Nowhere to hide. If you could only wipe out the CURSE of your guilty past. If you could only become somebody else before it is too late.

By setting up stark and compelling oppositions between his two leads in both *What Ever Happened to Baby Jane?* (Joan Crawford and Bette Davis) and *Hush...Hush, Sweet Charlotte* (Bette Davis and Olivia de Havilland), Aldrich deserves a fair share of the credit for fortifying what would become a new trend in female psycho-killer cinema, one that is hinted at as far back as *Meshes of the Afternoon.* Aldrich's tactic, also employed by William Castle in *Strait-Jacket* and Reginald Le Borg in *So Evil, My Sister*, is to eventually turn the tables on his viewers, showing the "crazy" woman to be sane (at least relatively speaking) in comparison with the seemingly/superficially "normal" woman, who is exposed towards the end as the killer.[14] (In *Meshes*, Deren uses innovative camera tricks to show multiple visions of herself as the protagonist/antagonist.) Brian De Palma gives this convention perhaps its most creative treatment in *Sisters*, by making it appear that "bad twin" Dominique is the murderer when, in fact, Dominique has been dead for years and "good twin" Danielle suffers a form of schizophrenia in which she adopts Dominique's primitive mannerisms and homicidal tendencies during sexual encounters with men. Previously, Roy Ward Baker had experimented with collapsing the "good girl/bad girl" dichotomy in the "Barbara and Lucy" segment of his 1972 British anthology horror film, *Asylum*. Unlike De Palma, however, Baker strives to blur the boundaries between supernatural and realist horror by providing numerous "objective" shots—mostly eyeline matches—of Barbara's (Charlotte Rampling) projected double Lucy (Britt Ekland), shots that function to validate Lucy's existence "independently of Barbara's hallucinatory visions" (Schneider 2002a, 127).

At least on the surface, it would seem that most female psycho-killer films strive to take the ideologically easy way out by leaving unambiguous the "good girl/bad girl" character dichotomy, according to which a dependable, sensible, sexually conservative, attractive but not stunning wife, girlfriend, or daughter (Tobie Williams [Donna Mills] in *Play Misty for Me*, Beth Gallagher [Anne Archer] in *Fatal Attraction*, Sylvie Cooper [Sara Gilbert] in *Poison Ivy* [1992], Claire Bartel [Annabella Sciorra] in *The Hand That Rocks the Cradle*, Amy Miller [Shiri Abbleby] in *Swimfan* [2002]) is paired off against her virtual opposite—a sexy, promiscuous, uncontrolled and out-of-control mystery woman with few if any meaningful family ties and an obsession with getting rid of her competition for the affections of a particular man. This same basic formula, with minor twists, can also be found in *Basic Instinct, The Crush* (1993), and *Hush* (1998). Although the love-triangle plots effected in these films via the inclusion of a doubly desired male lead may at first viewing seem like a straightforwardly sexist wish-fulfillment narrative, it is crucial to recognize that the men in question are usually portrayed as distinctly unheroic and frankly unsympathetic: more often than not they are lying fathers, cheating husbands, unreliable co-workers. Though Hollywood convention may see to it that these men survive in the end, even attaining a measure of forgiveness from their unrealistically understanding spouses and children, they never escape their flings unscathed. While the madwomen usually wind up dead, institutionalized, or in jail, the men are left contrite, grateful to still have their families and, presumably, more fully domesticated than ever before.

Just as important, it should be pointed out that what initially looks to be a clear separation of these films' female leads into wholly separate psychological and experiential spheres is frequently undercut by the narratives in which they appear, thereby tapping into a powerful male anxiety that, lurking inside even the most tranquil and nurturing women is the capacity for uninhibited, irrational, uncontrollable violence. In films like *Play Misty for Me*, *Fatal Attraction*, and *Swimfan*, the progression (or rather, the deterioration) of the female psycho-killer's mental state goes from a cheerful acceptance of casual sex with a "taken" man to an "understandable" and frankly flattering desire for intimacy and commitment, and only from there to episodes of stalking, jealous rages, and eventually attempted murder.[15] And in films like *The Hand That Rocks the Cradle*, *Hush*, and *Fatal Attraction*, the seemingly (stereotypically) perfect mother/girlfriend/wife finally succeeds in summoning the requisite anger and spite to engage in direct physical or psychological battle with her competition, who comes across less as a wholly unfamiliar Other than as the "return" of her own repressed self.[16]

It may be tempting to conclude in these latter cases that what we have is simply a variation on the "Final Girl" character from conventional slasher movies—a masculinized female who, as Clover has shown, enables heterosexual male viewers to experience at least a momentary thrill of cross-gender identification. But to take such a stance would mean overlooking or ignoring the fact that, as opposed to the paradigmatic slasher movie Final Girl, the women in question are not portrayed as masculine (where this is understood by Clover, Prince, et al. as "active, aggressive, empowered") *throughout* the films' narratives; rather, they arrive at this state of being only after things have gone terribly awry, and only after they have broken free of their enculturated domesticity. And so, it would seem that much of the potency of female psycho-killers in American (if not international)[17] horror cinema stems from the various ways in which they give nightmarish expression to the "flip side" of patriarchal femininity, whereby passivity becomes possessiveness, vulnerability is replaced by viciousness, and maternal love is transformed into maniacal, passionate hate.[18]

Notes

1 *Dementia* was originally released without any voice-over narration. See Erickson (2002).
2 Note, however, that "monstrous humans have *always* had a place in the horror genre; among the many...examples to choose from here are Cesare the somnambulist (Conrad Veidt) in *The Cabinet of Dr. Caligari* (1919), child-killer Hans Beckert (Peter Lorre) in *M* (1931), raving lunatic Saul Femm (Brember Wills) in *The Old Dark House* (1932), and corpse-stealing cabman John Gray (Boris Karloff) in *The Body Snatcher* (1945). Nevertheless, human evildoers in post-1960 horror cinema have tended to come across as more 'real' than their predecessors in the sense that no obvious signs of physical deformity, simplistically signifying moral corruption, are made available to the viewer, hero, or victims for the purpose of immediate identification" (Schneider 2002b, 3).
3 See Schneider (2000).
4 The study Prince is referring to appears in Weaver (1991).
5 See also Elsaesser (1987), Polan (1993), and Russ (1973).
6 Martin (1994) coined the phrase "intimacy thriller."
7 See Clover (1992, 114–65) and Read (2000).
8 Compare *The Haunting of Julia* (aka *Full Circle*, 1978) and *Candyman* (1992), in both of which the female protagonist's ambiguously depicted suicide at film's end has more to do with concern for a surrogate child than with anxieties centring on an adult male.
9 In the commercially released version of Lyne's film, considered more palatable for mainstream American audiences, Douglas's wife (Anne Archer) gets to shoot Alex (Close) in the chest from close range. The problem with the original version evidently wasn't Alex dying, or even dying at her own hand—after all, she slashes her wrists earlier in the released version and cuts herself again later on—but, rather, in the possibility that the "good" Mrs. Gallagher might wind up a single mother with a young daughter to raise all by herself and that the "bad" Alex could possess the power to effectively take Dan with her.
10 As Martin (2001) puts it, "In Deren's vision, it is the terrain of the everyday, and the domestic, that lays the meshes that ensnare, complicate and traumatize a woman's life."
11 See Williams (1991).
12 In the case of rape-revenge films and higher-brow slasher-influenced fare such as *The Silence of the Lambs* (1991) and *Thelma and Louise* (1991), Clover argues that the unstable female leads may not be "cracking" so much as taking matters into their own hands.
13 It also raises the question, who was the father of Alex's miscarried child anyway?
14 Paul Verhoeven has it both ways in *Basic Instinct* by first making it seem that "good girl" Beth Garner (Jeanne Tripplehorn) is the killer, only to suggest in the end that original "bad girl" Catherine Tramell set Beth up for the latter's fatal fall. A similar, though less ambiguous, series of plot twists occurs in Bob Rafelson's *Black Widow*.
15 Takashi Miike's *Audition* offers an interesting parallel to these films within the context of contemporary Japanese society.
16 This is in line with Robin Wood's (1986) influential analysis of the American horror film.

17 This is not to deny the presence of certain socio-cultural particularities when it comes to the portrayal of female psycho-killers in other national cinemas. See, for example, Frank Burke's chapter on Dario Argento's *The Bird with the Crystal Plumage* in this volume.

18 I would like to thank the editors of this collection, Annette Burfoot and Susan Lord, for their helpful comments and suggestions on an earlier draft of this chapter.

Reverence, Rape—and then Revenge: Popular Hindi Cinema's "Women's Film"[1]

JYOTIKA VIRDI

[14]

The academic interest in popular Hindi cinema's dramatic reinscription of women as avenging daredevils, although belated, is welcome. The increasing popularity of these films in the 1980s and 1990s is accompanied by some turmoil over how to read this move (Ghosh 1996; Gopal 1997; Gopalan 1997).[2] Persisting complaints about static two-dimensional portrayals of women as victims or vamps, madonnas or whores, suffering mothers or pleasing wives, are now replaced by the charge that these women, figured as retaliating rape victims, are merely grist for the Hindi film mill furbished by and for male fantasies. The question is, do the victim-heroines masquerade as avenging women or do they indeed represent a politics of transformation and agency, dare I say a feminist one? Feminist anxieties around the eroticization of rape might, I argue, shift our focus away from other pernicious aspects of women's representation.

Taking my cue from the literature on film history, or rather films as history, I look back at Hindi cinema's record in dealing with what I designate the "women's film" genre. I use the term loosely to signal film narratives centring on a female protagonist. If literary and artistic representations are part of public discourse refracting the context within which they are produced,

251

then popular Hindi films too, contrary to conventional wisdom, are indexical referents, records of that discourse. One strategy then is to track the trajectory of the woman's film over time and examine its discourse before the arrival of the avenging heroine to assess discursive shifts, or the genre's transformation.

To plot this transformation I discuss three films, *Teesri Manzil/Third Floor* (1965), a thriller (though not strictly a woman's film); *Aradhana/Prayer* (1969), an exemplary maternal melodrama;[3] and *Insaaf ka Taraazu/Scales of Justice* (1980), which inaugurated the avenging heroine subgenre. Shifting representations of women circle metonymically around rape in each of these films. They reflect a discursive history in which revenge ultimately displaces the repression and erasure of rape, or reverence for the female protagonist's suffering. I suggest we view the impact of shifting discourses on women's representation, particularly feminist anxieties about their overdetermined and increasing eroticization, in terms of specific transactional changes in stereotypical female figures, which complicate the recent history of that representation. And within an international frame this representational shift resonates with other scenarios discussed in this anthology: Frank Burke's analysis of women in Italian horror films (chap. 11) and Suzie Young's description of women in the Hong Kong martial arts genre (chap. 12). This representation shift is a response to the pain of real women who have suffered violence, pointed out by Zoey Michele, and acknowledges Dorit Naaman's argument that figurations of violence against women in the postcolonial state encapsulates tensions in women's subjecthood.

Reverence for Victims

Shakti Samanta's *Aradhana*, faithful to the tradition of the maternal melodrama, is a narrative of excess: a woman's acute suffering, her sacrifices, and— a favourite theme in Hindi cinema—her intense love for her son. The film begins with passionate arguments in court, where the female protagonist, Vandana (Sharmila Tagore), is on trial. As the credits end, we hear the prosecutor's concluding statements. "Your honour," he says,

> in the eyes of the law, there is nothing more grave than the murder of a human being. And when the one who gives birth to human beings, a woman, murders a man, the crime becomes even more heinous. I therefore plead with the court that the defendant not be spared because she is a woman. She should be punished severely so that people learn from this precedent and justice is served.[4]

As Vandana, dressed widow-like in austere white clothes, is incarcerated, the camera tilts up to the barred window, and in a protracted flashback, the diegesis unfolds.

Vandana returns from college to live with her widower father and falls in love with air force pilot Arun (Rajesh Khanna), who dies just before they are to marry. Vandana discovers she is pregnant, suffers rejection from Arun's family, endures her father's death, and after further misadventures gives up her son to a childless couple, Ram Prasad and Anita. She gains employment as the boy's governess, but her happy years as a surrogate mother end abruptly when Anita's brother visits. He propositions Vandana but is killed accidentally in a scuffle with her and her son, Suraj, who intervenes to help her. To protect Suraj, Vandana assumes full responsibility for the death, and only after twelve years of incarceration is she released from prison. Several coincidences later she meets the adult Suraj (played again by Rajesh Khanna) now an airforce pilot. A war breaks out and Suraj is wounded in action, but during his convalescence, in the final denouement, he discovers Vandana's identity. To everyone's surprise within the narrative, in the last scene he introduces Vandana as his mother and declares her the co-recipient of his gallantry award.

In keeping with the demands of evolving genres there is something new in the film, despite the repetition. As a portrait of a suffering woman, it derives from the Indo-Anglian literary tradition developed in the shadow of eighteenth- and nineteenth-century Orientalist canons and Victorian norms (Tharu 1989). Sexual restraint, the control of libidinal energy, is intrinsic to this representation. While popular films absorbed principles of female chastity, *Aradhana* broaches heterosexual love as having a palpable sexual compulsion and explicitly associates romantic love with sexual desire. Yet, harking back to chastity principles, it also shows the ruinous consequences of extra-institutional sex for women.

There has long been a puzzling taboo on explicit sex scenes in Hindi cinema, with song-and-dance sequences standing in for them. The introduction of Eastman colour in the early 1960s led to abandoning the studios in favour of outdoor locations, especially for romantic sequences and their critical incumbent "song picturization," as it is known in the film industry.[5] Heroines stretch languorously across the landscape as though innocent of the camera's gaze and their own sexualized bodies. *Aradhana's* opening follows this new trend in depicting the wonders of "falling in love." Yet it somewhat daringly disrupts the sexual sublimation by negotiating heterosexual love outside social and familial sanction (i.e., marriage) in the course of the couple's courtship. Caught one day in an unexpected downpour, Vandana and Arun take shelter in a motel and, in an unusual moment for Hindi cinema, succumb to their sexual desire. The sequence is memorable for its elegance, skillfully addressing the censor board's and Hindi cinema's own curious prudery on matters of sexual intimacy.

Yet the entire film exhibits the "cunning" of the maternal melodrama that operates on two levels—both condemning women's victimization and punishing her for a reckless moment of sexual passion, the "sin" for which men go scot-free (Viviani 1991, 178). Bereft of a man's protection when her lover dies, she distances herself from her son to avoid the ignominy of unwed motherhood, hands over her rights and recognition as a biological mother,[6] and, worst of all, becomes easy prey to strange men. Though Vandana wards off an imminent rape, its upshot—the death of her rapist—drives the narrative forward. Through this and her voluntary incarceration to protect her son, her severance from him is complete. Typical of the genre of melodrama there is

> a constant struggle for gratification and equally constant blockages to its attainment. [The] narratives are driven by one crisis after another, crises involving severed family ties, separation, and loss.…Seduction, betrayal, abandonment, extortion, murder, suicide, revenge, jealousy…are…the familiar terrain of melodrama. The victims are most often females threatened in their sexuality, their property, their very identity. (Landy 1991, 14)

Despite the film's powerful rendition, it betrays a disconcertingly conservative strain. At the end of the film, instead of the "cathartic trial scene" that rehabilitates the mother, we get an exaltation by the state as the son shares his success with his mother, or at least deflects his glory onto her. In this, *Aradhana* resonates with several other films, from *Mother India* in 1957 to *Deewar/Wall* in 1975. These films share the theme of a suffering mother finally apotheosized by the state.[7] This veneration reinforces suffering as a value in itself, monumentalizing it, rather than resisting patriarchal norms. The suffering woman is held up as a model of womanhood, idealized, honoured, and decorated. In a fantastic and wholly fabricated gesture, the films have the son/state recognize the mother's martyrdom, making her suffering "worth it all." I see this move as particular to Hindi cinema and distinct from the 1930s Hollywood versions of such narratives, which show women's miraculous rise to power, fame, success, and money, returning them on an equal footing to the society that once rejected them. In turn, the 1930s Hollywood films reverse the European maternal melodramas in which the outcast mother sinks into anonymity and oblivion (Viviani 1991, 173).

Aradhana spawned several films on the same theme in the 1970s, becoming a virtual woman-victim subgenre—*Kati Patang/Falling Kite* (1972), *Amar*

Prem/Eternal Love (1973), and *Julie* (1975) are among the most popular. The narratives recuperate all kinds of "fallen women," deifying them and their suffering, and setting them up as objects of reverence. While the representation of women as abject but idolized victims (*Aradhana*-style) became the dominant mode for such women's films, a decade later, with the arrival of the avenging heroine, another subgenre replaced them.

Rape and the Rape Threat[8]

I now take a quick detour from Hindi films to representations of rape within a broader cultural milieu, particularly *before* the transformative moment of the second wave of the Indian women's movement. Lynn Higgins and Brenda Silver (1991, 2–3) note that representations of rape in myths and literary texts are at once a structuring device and a gaping elision: "an obsessive inscription—and an obsessive erasure—of sexual violence against women (and by those placed by society in the position of 'woman')….Over and over…rape exists as an absence or gap that is both product and source of textual anxiety, contradiction, or censorship." Classics, such as Samuel Richardson's *Clarissa* and E.M. Forster's *A Passage to India,* are cited most frequently as examples. With the arrival of the women's movement in the United States, signifying rape displaces its erasure. As Carol Clover points out, what mainstream Hollywood glossed up to Oscar standards in films like *The Accused* (Jonathan Kaplan, 1988) had already been said a decade earlier in the lowly horror/slasher genre, only "in flatter, starker terms, and on a shoestring." She suggests a temporal lag between high and low culture's representation of rape; and in folkloric terms, "a motif graduated into a tale-type" (Clover 1992, 20, 137).

The silence, elision, the gap to which Higgins and Silver allude was as much a mark of popular Hindi cinema's tradition, notwithstanding its "obsessive inscription" of rape.[9] Before 1980 Hindi cinema too dealt with rape covertly. *Teesri Manzil,* ostensibly a murder mystery, exemplifies this simultaneous inscription and erasure by using rape as a structuring narrative device and then adeptly repressing it. An entertaining 1960s thriller[10] with a superb cast, excellent pacing, and an enthralling storyline, it differs markedly from later films (like *Insaaf ka Taraazu*) in how it stages rape (or, rather, the rape threat) and represses it.

As the opening credits roll, a car pulls up in the darkness of the night. The camera tracks a woman's footsteps as she runs up several flights of stairs, jumps from the third floor, and dies. When the main narrative begins, Sunita (Asha Parekh) announces her resolve to avenge her sister Rupa's death and travels to Mussorie, the hill resort where her sister, she believes, was murdered the year before. Reconstructing Rupa's letters as evidence, Sunita is convinced that Rocky, the rock'n'roll musician at the hotel there, is responsible for her death. Sunita meets Anil (Shammi Kapoor), enlists his support for her mission, and the two fall in love. Anil conceals his alias—Rocky (his band name)—and the fact that he knew Rupa, who was once his admirer (an infatuated fan). When Sunita discovers his chicanery she rejects him. Meanwhile, several abortive attempts on Anil's life compel him to get to the bottom of the mystery. Sexual intrigue among Rocky's admirers and Ruby, the night club dancer, intensifies this mystery. Rocky single-handedly finds his assailant, the villainous Kunwar Sahib, and as he uncovers the connection between the deaths of Rupa, and later Ruby, and the attempts on his own life, another subplot unfolds. Rupa, accidentally an eyewitness to a murder implicating Kunwar Sahib, was pursued to her death, and Rocky, a suspected eyewitness to that death, becomes the next target.

The rape threat is an unmistakable subtext of *Teesri Manzil*. Sunita's goal to avenge her sister's death motivates the action in the first half of the film. Convinced that her sister was raped, her goal is to find the perpetrator. The text is, however, equivocal about the exact circumstances of Rupa's "rape" and death. This equivocation stems partly from the fact that the crime is reconstructed through second- and third-person accounts a year after Rupa's death. Apart from the prologue, which establishes the crime scene—a long shot of a woman running up stairs, her fatal fall, followed by a cut away to a man's footsteps fleeing the crime scene—the scenario surrounding her death is revisited several times in the film. *Rashomon*-style, we get varying accounts of the event: we are given Sunita's version twice, Anil's fragmented description once, and, in the denouement, the villain's nameless lover's tale fills in the missing pieces.

The difficulty is in fixing, and naming with certainty, what happened to Rupa. Sunita's reconstruction, along with other narrative accounts, move restlessly between explanations of unrequited love, a spurned lover, desire, shame, honour, homicide, suicide—and rape. Sunita infers from Rupa's account—wrongly, it is later proven—that Rupa was driven to commit suicide. Rupa's own letter, apart from expressing her desire for Rocky, is ambiguous. Rocky's later account quite plainly states that he consistently rebuffed Rupa's overtures. But one thing is clear according to Sunita: when a girl transgresses boundaries she must die. Rupa, Ruby, and Kunwar Sahib's nameless mistress all meet this fate. When Ruby dies, she lies in Rocky's arm and says: "My only crime, Rocky, has been that I have desired you."

There are moments in the film when the rape threat buried within the subtext is openly enunciated. Sunita's initial discomfiture with Anil when she journeys with him (to locate Rupa's killer) turns into romantic love after he makes short shrift of a marauding gang threatening to rape her in the woods. In an earlier scene Meena, Sunita's friend, is accidentally separated from Sunita and Anil on the same journey. The camera tracks Meena's lonely figure walking through the woods, tightening the frame around her as she looks fearfully beyond its edges—a classic cinematic signification of the rape threat.

Yet the quest for Rupa's rapist, which initially propels the narrative, stops abruptly, changes course, and becomes a tale of the accusation and redemption of an innocent man. Certainly the female protagonist, Sunita, is no defenseless woman. She sets out from her home as a woman with a purpose, a mission, to avenge her sister's death. *Teesri Manzil,* however, becomes an exploration of male anxieties of wrongful accusations—anxieties that constitute the founding principles of English common law transferred to the Empire's colonies.[11]

The Sexed Body and Ocular Pleasure

Before turning to the charge of masculine subterfuge employed in depicting rape scenes, I want to make an observation about the figure of the vamp—a liminal figure, favoured for decades in Hindi cinema, that significantly attenuated in the 1970s and had disappeared by the 1980s, coinciding with the emergence of the avenging woman. In a film about mystery and intrigue, the chicanery Sunita and Anil perform differ only in degree from the subterfuge in which Ruby engages. Yet Ruby is singled out as Sunita's opposite: the vamp. Ruby, a nightclub worker, makes a living as a vaudevillian. The "difference" between Ruby and Sunita is that Sunita, because of her feminine status, is the object of desire. Ruby, however, transgresses the line: a sexualized subject with a desire of her own, she aggressively pursues the man she loves. She appropriates "phallic power" and must pay for it with her death.

The actress Helen, who plays the Ruby-like figure in scores of films, is iconic of the vamp. In the roles she repeats again and again, Helen portrays not so much the "wicked" woman as the naughty, sexually alluring, immodest one—coded by her erotic, nimbly performed dance numbers—a wonderful medley of flamenco, jazz, modern, and belly dance movements set to adaptations of rock 'n' roll or jazz rhythms. Located in the public sphere, in the world of men, she is somehow bereft of a man of her own. Desired by all, yet loved

FIGURE 28   Scene from *Teesri Manzil/Third Floor*, 1965 (with permission of *Screen*).

by none, she inevitably—as in *Teesri Manzil*—zeroes in on the hero in her search to be loved by one man.

Yet within the pleasures and dangers of a liminal but exciting nightlife experienced by the privileged few, Helen is the "bad" undomesticated woman. For this she is punished with death, always an accidental act of "fate." Not altogether insignificant are the communal overtones of Helen's off-screen minority status as a Christian. Perceived as part of the Anglo-Indian community, an "impure" breed that could never gain legitimacy in a society acutely conscious of "origins," Helen plays with the pleasure and anxiety that the otherized Western lifestyle elicits.

Double-Speak about the Body

Between the moral authority of the state's censor board and preoccupation with women's bodies through strategic camera angles and movement is the gratification and scopic pleasure that filmed bodies, especially those of the vamp, offer to both male and female viewers. The vamp is presented as the sexualized woman, craving men and their attention by inviting their gaze upon herself, her body, her eroticized gestures and movements. This exhibitionism,

.pleasurable to the audience, is simultaneously condemned as immodest, pruri-
ent, and "bad." Thus one can enjoy the visual pleasure, the spectacular and
erotic dance numbers, while airing moral indignation by condemning the
woman in unison with the narrative in which she is inevitably punished.

This doublespeak is evident not only in films but in the entire discursive
culture surrounding films. It operates no differently in associated texts such
as the film magazines. During my search for secondary sources on films and
film history in the Indian National Film Archives at Pune, I was struck by one
preoccupation in film magazines through four decades of post-independence
cinema. The industry positions itself as demanding freedom of expression
and opposing censorship. At the heart of this wrangle is the contentious issue
of how much the films can show—a debate that is really about nothing more
than the right to show and see the woman's body. In magazines that reproduce ad nauseam stills, centrefolds, pin-ups, shots from films, and close-ups
of physical details of the female stars, the accompanying written text virtu-
ously repudiates the industry and the film stars for their declining values.
The visuals show the reader what is being decried. Such doublespeak continues in the films' texts, which invite us to see and then condemn the "bad"
woman.

Culling a few candid moments from the discourse in the film magazines,
I cite a film fan, who, in an unusually plain-spoken way reminds us of film's
nature—intrinsically and organically linked to the pleasures of voyeurism and
scopophilia. In the 1940s this fan wrote unselfconsciously to the magazine
Film India about his admiration for a new actress, Begum Para. He marvelled
at her diaphanous sarees, which enabled him to gaze at her magnificent breasts.
In a similar vein, Pandit Indra makes a case against the puritanical censorship advocated by *Film India*'s editor and the state. The open depiction of sex
and the body are, he argues, part of India's classical poetry. He quotes at length
from various Hindu poets, including the fourth-century poet Kalidasa's poems
in *shringaar rasa*,[12] full of descriptions of gods and goddesses, their bodies,
details about their lovemaking, and frequent references to the breasts and but-
tocks of the amorous women. Analogously, he goes on, films "without romance
will be as tasteless as food without salt!…The editor should not try…to destroy
the sweetness of our life leading us towards [the] darkness of so-called purity"
(P. Indra, *Film India*, July 1947).[13]

While the discourse on the extent to which films can or should "show"
(women's) bodies continues to this day, the figure of the vamp has become con-
spicuous by its absence. We can only speculate about the changes that prompted
this. The distance travelled can be graphically measured by the extent to which

the heroines substituted for the vamps. As the Helen-type figure atrophied in Hindi films during the 1970s, the female lead by the 1980s was transformed from a childlike innocent to a sexually alluring creature. In short, if heroines could satisfy what Begum Para's admirer sought in the movies, the vamp was redundant. Much of this had to do with changing boundaries within rules governing sexuality: the boundaries "good" women could occupy expanded slightly. Eroticizing the heroine marked a new trend; the vamp's figure thereafter was banished from Hindi films.[14]

Women's Rage

Feminist anxieties about constructing vengeful heroines through rape-revenge narratives in the 1980s circle around eroticizing rape scenes and, hence, perpetuating a victim syndrome while masquerading the revenge as female agency.[15] I propose that a historical approach might be helpful here. Comparing these films to their antecedents—the classic *Aradhna*-style victim, or the inscription erasure in *Teesri Manzil*—not only plots elements of continuity and change underscoring the industry's obvious generic impulse for repetition and difference but, more important, accounts for a broader discursive context of which these films are a part. Reverence no longer serves as sufficient compensation for the suffering victim woman.

Insaaf ka Taraazu[16] is indeed, as Lalitha Gopalan argues, the "inaugural moment" in rape-revenge films. She, among others (Rajadhyaksha and Willemen 1995, 416), points to the Mathura rape trial as structuring the context of *Insaaf ka Taraazu's* reception. In 1979 the Supreme Court overturned a High Court ruling and freed two police constables accused of raping Mathura, a minor, in police custody. In 1978 a Muslim woman, Rameeza Bee, was raped in police custody in Hyderabad, and her husband, a rickshaw puller, was murdered for protesting about it. In 1980 Maya Tyagi was raped in Baghpat, Haryana, then stripped naked and walked through the streets by the police. The "rape bill"—the upshot of public shock and women's rage—became the Anti-Rape Act in 1986 (Kumar 1994, 127–42; Kannabiran 1996, 32–41),

I wish to stress that context is central to understanding the avenging women subgenre. The Mathura rape trial marks the resurgence of the women's movement in India, dormant since pre-independence. In this phase women organized spontaneously, not under male leadership; a "grassroots female militancy" (Ehrenreich 1995, 85)[17] forced itself onto the national agenda, using rape as a powerful trope in a national discourse on women's subjugation by individual men and institutions. Nationwide agitations by women coalesced

to demand changes in the "rape laws." The concatenate effect of this historical moment shapes the latter-day woman's film.

The maker of *Insaaf ka Taraazu*, B.R. Chopra, a reigning auteur in the
film industry since the 1950s, has carved a special niche in Hindi cinema in his
explorations of gender politics through the vicissitudes of heterosexual love.
Chopra's films often trace the liminal social space women occupy, questioning permissible moral boundaries, even as he might carefully reinstate them.
His other films that stand out in this respect are *Gumrah/Deception* (1967),
Dhund/Fog (1973), and *Pati Patni aur Woh/Husband, Wife and the Other* (1978).
Insaaf ka Taraazu, hot on the heels of the demand to reopen the Supreme
Court's judgment in the Mathura trial, bears more than an incidental relation to the public discourse the verdict set off. Historically, the event marks the
beginning of the (re)entry of a discourse on women's place in the private and
public spheres framed in terms of women's *rights* (not reform, "uplift," or the
need to nurture special "feminine virtues").

The nation underwent a long consciousness-raising process as women
challenged and rewrote discriminatory laws on domestic violence, rape, dowry,
and the growing incidence of "dowry deaths." Family courts—instituted solely
to relieve conventional courts from the burden of family disputes—and the
soaring divorce rates were testimony to the serious "gender trouble" stirred up
by women's grassroots militancy. This ferment in gender relations features in
popular films. Women, albeit feminized and sexualized, were once revered for
their suffering. As the decades go by, however, they are increasingly capable of
violence and taking control.

Insaaf ka Taraazu was released while the debate was still under way on
new legislative measures to punish rape offenders and to replace rape laws
first established during British colonial rule. The film's heroine, Bharati[18]
(Zeenat Aman), winner of the "Miss India" title, is an independent career
woman, working as a model and making good money to support herself and
her schoolgirl sister, Nita (Padmini Kolahpure), in an apartment in Bombay.
The film begins with Bharati winning a beauty contest determined by popular mandate (i.e., the audience within the film). The man who awards her the
highest score, Ramesh Gupta (Raj Babbar), receives the honour of placing the
crown on her head.

Ramesh, a long-standing admirer of Bharati, uses his wealth to his advantage and makes casual efforts to be with her, while she, self-absorbed and pre-
occupied with her fiancé Ashok, obliges Ramesh in the routine fashion that a
star obliges fans. Slighted by her lack of interest one day when he visits her,
Ramesh barges into her room and, in a protracted sequence, attacks her, ties

FIGURE 29 Scene from *Insaaf ka Taraazu/Scales of Justice*, 1980 (with permission of *Screen*).

her down, and repeatedly rapes her. Bharati falls unconscious, and somewhere towards the end of this sequence her sister Nita comes home, sees Ramesh on top of Bharati, and flees the house, fearful and confused.

When Bharati reports the incident and presses charges, her lawyer warns that loopholes in the anti-rape laws make it virtually impossible to prove the rapist's guilt. In fact the defendant's lawyer easily reinterprets the sequence of events, casting severe doubts on her lack of "consent," the critical issue in all rape litigation. Bharati loses the lawsuit even though her lawyer is a committed and competent woman, and despite the trial's widespread publicity. Shunned by advertising companies that can no longer afford to have her name associated with their products, and by her prospective in-laws, who cannot cope with the adverse publicity associated with her, Bharati leaves Bombay.

Dispirited and depressed, she relocates with her sister in Pune (a city close to Bombay) and takes a low-paid job as a secretary in a store selling firearms. Nita, meanwhile, interviews for a job with a prestigious firm, but the interview turns into a nightmare when the firm's proprietor, the interviewer, is none other than Ramesh, who traps her in a room, humiliates her, and rapes her too. When Nita returns home and collapses, Bharati responds by taking a gun from the store, following Ramesh to his office, and killing him at close range, in cold blood, and in full view of his colleagues.

Bharati is arrested and tried. She refuses to hire a lawyer, choosing instead to defend herself. The court fails to recognize her due to the transformation in her appearance. In an impassioned speech about the miscarriage of justice for women, she reminds the court that she is Bharati, the model who was once raped by Ramesh Gupta. The failure to punish her rapist then, she argues, had only encouraged him to victimize another woman. In a dramatic end to the court proceedings, the judge, impressed by Bharati's arguments, sets her free.

In *Insaaf ka Taraazu* the victim becomes vengeful and victorious not only against the man who victimizes her but also against the entire misogynist juridical system. The film examines the ramifications of rape: the fact that it is nothing but an assertion of male aggression and power; that the rape gets rehearsed both literally and figuratively in a court trial meant to punish the rapist; that the rapist gets off due to lack of conclusive evidence; that the victim faces social ostracism along with acute depression and trauma in the aftermath; and that the crowning act of injustice is the court setting the rapist free. The film truly centres on the woman's narrative: the rapist's character is not elaborated beyond the fact that he is a well-to-do, "normal," even pleasant person, someone whose violence leaves an unsuspecting Bharati and the audience shocked and dismayed.[19]

The narrative structure explores two possible responses to rape that popular films have deployed. First, recourse to the legal process turns out to be a farce that leads to yet another woman becoming a rape victim. Second, the film valorizes a wonderful revenge fantasy: direct action and punishment followed by success in court. In the first courtroom proceedings, *Insaaf ka Taraazu* is unequivocal in condemning the juridical-legal system. As the woman lawyer tells Bharati at the outset: "It is very hard to establish rape. That is why so many rapists go unpunished. And whether or not the rapist is punished, one thing is certain, the woman definitely gets a bad name.…You may not know this, but for a woman, a court case involving rape is not very different from rape." At the same time the lawyer invokes "shame" and "honour," qualities at stake for the *shareef aurat* (good woman).

Bharati's response is firm—"I now neither care about society, nor about getting a bad name"—but she is less tough than she thinks. The defence attorney's reinterpretation of her as a model, along with a photo series of her with Ramesh, resembles Barthes's principle of writerly texts (1974, 3–9).[20] Her photographs, he argues, demonstrate the inner logic of an alluring sex object and a "modern" woman's permissive lifestyle. The defendant's lawyer badgers her for her "improper" conduct, which is demonstrated by her choosing a profession in which she displays her body. When Ramesh is set free for lack of sufficient evidence, Bharati sinks into a depression, unable to cope either with the publicity following the debacle in court or with a job requiring her to suffuse consumer products with her charm.

It is the second time around, when Nita gets raped by Ramesh Gupta for daring to testify against him in court, that Bharati takes direct action. Nita, making a career as a stenographer, is no model selling her body. As Bharati's lawyer states before she takes up the case, "A woman has to stand up some day and say she has the right to say, 'No,' and no man can touch her without her consent." Yet the first half of the film obfuscates this point, particularly through Ramesh's lawyer's vociferous argument in court. By posing extraneous issues such as Bharati's professional career as a model and the sexualization of her body that inheres to that career, the film implies a difficulty in demarcating consent from a woman's prior conduct (Balasubrahmanyan 1990, 107–53; Kannabiran 1996, 32–41).[21]

Compared to both Bharati's and Nita's brutal rapes, involving terror, pain, humiliation, and a tortured aftermath, Bharati's swift action against Ramesh seems painless. The film does not escalate the horror and cruelty in which Hollywood slasher films and, to a lesser extent, latter-day rape-revenge Hindi films indulge.[22] What the film carefully implants, however, is a woman character, once a victim but now ready to fight back. It is she (initially through a female lawyer) who takes up the fight, not her boyfriend, the police, or her father. It is worth noting that Bharati's maternal vengeance here is on behalf of her sister.

The weakest point in the film is the last sequence, in which Bharati makes her impassioned speech in court against rape. She likens women to temples of worship: each time a woman is violated, she says, a religious shrine is desecrated. In the montage of visuals that accompany her soliloquy, we witness a church, a Hindu temple, and a mosque crumbling. The allusion to women as symbols of (men's) religious communities is disconcerting, if not downright dangerous. While the film text elsewhere attempts to undermine patriarchal ideology, here it suddenly falls into the trap of rejecting rape not because it is a uniquely perverse assertion of men's power but because women, the victims, are likened to religious shrines. The film suddenly and unexpectedly concludes with an insidious thesis on rape. Rather than laying bare the connection between rape and patriarchy, it ends up invoking extant patriarchal discourses within Hindu tradition that place women in binary positions as the *devi* or *dasi* (goddess or slave). Holding women up as objects of reverence is posited as a counterpoint to rape rather than as a continuum within patriarchal discourse. This aspect of the film is more reprehensible than is the depiction of rape that Indian feminists protested, which I discuss later.

Clearly, despite the film ending with a tirade about reverence for women, what was new in *Insaaf* was that the woman, a victim such as those in the genre of Hindi films from *Mother India* to *Aradhana*, turned into a vigilante. In the 1980s the avenging woman figure became a trend: the "angry woman," replacing the "angry man" of the 1970s. Carol Clover (1993, 76), in the American context, points to the appearance of "rape-revenge" films as popular culture's response to the women's movement—feminism's gift to popular culture: "The marriage of rape to revenge was made in movie heaven....Ironically enough, it was a marriage for which the matchmaker was the women's movement, for in terms more or less explicitly feminist, rape became not only a deed deserving of brutal retribution, but a deed that women themselves (not cops, boyfriends, or fathers) undertook to redress."

It was perhaps this innovation, the introduction of rape to the revenge schema, already a staple of popular Hindi cinema, that made *Insaaf ka Taraazu* popular, spawning a veritable new subgenre. It led the way to fusing themes of sexual violence/rape—a handy (though not exclusive) trope[23] with which to excoriate and expose the pervasive violence (between classes) and corruption (within institutions) that humiliated heroines avenge. Although rape appeared in earlier films it was never at the centre of the narrative, and even when it was salient, allusions to its reality were carefully repressed. The rape *threat*, hovering in the margin of pre-1980s films like *Teesri Manzil*, is seized upon and made central in the 1980s. Women exterminating men appeared in earlier films, such as *Mother India* and *Mamta/Maternal Love* (1966) (Thomas 1989).[24] However, in these films women's fury and power service conservative patriarchal ideals apotheosizing motherhood. Here women are objects of reverential fervour rather than agents exacting revenge in the name of womankind.

Judged by its production values, *Insaaf ka Taraazu* is unusually poor, which comes as a surprise, given that the film was made by B.R. Chopra, a seasoned director. Aman's method acting, meant to convey a post-rape depressive stupor, lacks credibility. The song sequences fill out a parsimonious storyline, in contrast with Hindi cinema's usual multiple subplots that weave together during three hours of screen time. Furthermore, the long takes, virtually static camera, and flat three-key lighting make the film visually uninteresting.

Showing Rape: The Double Victim

As feminists we are caught between a rock and a hard place: the erasure of rape from the narrative bears the marks of a patriarchal discourse on honour and chastity; yet showing rape, some argue, eroticizes it for the male gaze and purveys the victim myth. How do we refuse to erase the palpability of rape and negotiate the splintering of the private/public trauma associated with it? *Insaaf* came under fire from Indian feminists because the fictional representation of rape elided the reality of underclass women's rape by the state (police or warring armies). Further, a (commercial) filmmaker's intervention in a discourse forced upon the nation by women was viewed as opportunism, which feminists found particularly odious. Equally, feminists who had seen (or not seen) the film roundly declared that the filmic depiction of rape could only titillate and entertain male viewers.[25]

Some of these criticisms are valid; still, too much gets thrown out with the bath water. It is no accident that *Insaaf* chose an up-market model as the victim of rape. By showing a woman voluntarily "selling" herself in the world of advertising, the film operates through the same doublespeak discussed earlier. Popular cinema in general focuses on the lives of the rich and famous, just as alternative cinema is conversely obsessed with portraying the lives of the poor, the subaltern. By focusing on Bharati, played by Zeenat Aman (who herself won the "Miss Asia title" in 1969), the film plays on extratextual information that the audience has about the star and situates itself in the space between Aman's real life and the character she plays on screen. *Insaaf,* unlike *Teesri Manzil* or *Aradhna,* set the new trend of eroticizing the heroine's body. Bharati's job of striking poses, openly flaunting herself before the camera, centres attention on her body. The centrality of Bharati/Aman's body (mis)leads the audience into drawing incorrect conclusions regarding beauty, desire, lust, and rape. The subtext of this is the most insidious of rape myths: "she asked for it." While such a critique rings true, it is equally pertinent that the film's second half subverts the argument of the first half.

When a humdrum, low-paid existence replaces Bharati's glamorous lifestyle after the courtroom fiasco, her little sister Nita gets a hard-won interview with a prestigious firm. It is of course a set-up, an occasion for Ramesh Gupta to assert his personal vendetta against Nita for testifying against him in court. If initially the film makes confused connections between lust, desire, and rape, on the one hand, and women's culpability on the other, this latter part of the film clearly deflects such a thesis. Nita represents the position of millions of women in lowly, underpaid positions, acutely vulnerable to men with power.

Regarding the rape scene's imbrication in representations of the already (sexually) coded woman's body, I disagree with Indian feminists who argue that the rape sequence in *Insaaf* is titillating. Although protracted, it conveys nothing but pain, horror, and naked male aggression. The rape is unquestionably gruesome. When Ramesh enters Bharati's bedroom he intimidates her and his intentions are soon clear. As she protests, "No, no," Ramesh taunts, "Yes, yes…beauty queen….Now kiss me." Bharati first fights back, then breaks down and finally passes out. She lies on the floor on the other side of the bed; in view are her feet tied to the bed, her head thrown back in an expression of terror that turns to numbness from exhaustion as Ramesh Gupta stays on top of her.

Mary Ann Doane (1988, 216) discusses the impasse confronting feminist filmmakers (or theorists for that matter) that stems from a "theoretical discourse that denies the neutrality of the cinematic apparatus itself. A machine for the production of image and sounds, the cinema generates and guarantees pleasure by a corroboration of the spectator's identity…[an] identity…bound up with that of the voyeur and the fetishist." She points to essentialist and anti-essentialist theories wherein the former presume and aim to restore representation of the female form in "images which provide a pure reflection of woman" (225), while the anti-essentialist refuses "any attempt to figure or represent that body," since the female body is always already and inescapably coded, written, overdetermined.

In her attempt to go beyond this impasse Doane (1988, 226) identifies the stakes involved as "not simply concern[ing] an isolated image of the body…rather, the syntax which constitutes the body as a term." In *Insaaf,* the rape scene's mise-en-scène, attacked so vociferously by feminists, frustrates, refuses to indulge the voyeur's fetishistic gaze, *without* neglecting to "show" the brutality of rape. Its "syntax" distances it from the "mandatory rape scenes" reviled in Hindi films. Displacing elliptical references to rape in the Richardson/Forster tradition, pushing rape into the public domain, and refusing its status as a private matter are unequivocal gains made by the women's movement.[26]

Yet scopophilic pleasure in rape representations is still a tangled issue. Linda Williams offers a psychoanalytic explanation of melodrama (weepies), horror, and pornography, three "body genres" that she classifies by their convulsive impact on the body—tears, fear, and orgasm, or the "tearjerker," "fearjerker," and texts "some people might be inclined to 'jerk off'" to. Williams draws attention to the perversions that these genres draw upon: masochism in melodrama, an oscillation between sadism and masochism in horror, and sadism, at least in the anti-pornography group's perception of pornography. Williams (1995, 148), however, urges us to see

> the value of not invoking the perversions as terms of condemnation. As even the most cursory reading of Freud shows, sexuality is, by definition, perverse. The "aims" and "objects" of sexual desire are often obscure and inherently substitutive. Unless we are willing to see reproduction as the common goal of sexual drive, then we all have to admit, as Jonathan Dollimore has put it, that we are all perverts. Dollimore's goal of retrieving the "concept of perversion as a category of cultural analysis," as a structure intrinsic to all sexuality rather than extrinsic to it, is crucial to any attempt to understand cultural forms...in which fantasy predominates.[27]

Invoking Clover's reading of the horror genre, Shohini Ghosh (1996, 176) points to the difficulty of fixing (gender) identification among viewers, and Lalitha Gopalan (1997, 53) concedes the viewer's oscillation between masochism in rape and sadism in revenge sequences. Even if we do admit to a variety of permutations and combinations in the masochistic/sadistic viewing positions—masochistic identification with rape, sadistic identification with revenge, a masochistic identification with rape and revenge, or a sadistic incitement in the rape and revenge sequences—it is not clear what is at stake for us as feminists. What are our anxieties about the effects of spectatorial arousal?

We might reconsider our own anxieties about the rape scene and focus instead on various other moments in the first half of *Insaaf* (especially the advertising agency's filming) that fetishize the female body as an object of the male gaze. The onus of such a construction shifts to a different filmmaking mode—advertising—and its recipients, the generalized consumer's scopophilic gratification, rather than the male's gaze. Bharati's post-rape depression interrupts her ability to glow for the camera and infuse consumer products with her radiance, motivating the second half of the film. Racialized beauty myths and proliferating beauty pageants (C. Chopra and F. Baria, *India Today*, 15 November 1996), offering women dramatic upward mobility from India's small towns to metropolitan penthouses, are aspects *Insaaf* clairvoyantly signals. This naturalized body/beauty myth combines far more pernicious aspects of patriarchy, capital, and commodification.

I draw a distinction here between the fetishization and sublimation of women's bodies for consumer commodities in advertising, and felicitations of the body as a site of intimacy, pleasure, and desire. In the 1980s the sexualized Hindi film heroine was no longer punished as was the phallic vamp for satisfying specular desires to see women's bodies, as Pandit Indra candidly states. Previous female stars' feigned lack of awareness about their bodies gave way to consciously teasing the limits of, and the pleasure in, "showing." In the 1990s bawdy film songs further pushed the boundaries of sexualized public discourse. Playing off the ribaldry in the *rasiya* tradition, these songs celebrate the risqué once associated with the peasantry and folk music. Displacing earlier decades of film music's lilting poetry fashioned by a refined urbane sensibility, these tongue-in-cheek lyrics reflect the trouble between the sexes as well as women's pleasure in being both the objects *and* the *subjects* of desire.

Bharati's courtroom tirade at the end of the film results in more than a symbolic victory. The judge ruefully admits the court's (read Indian state's) failure towards women and sets Bharati free. The sequence's extreme lack of credibility undermines it and fails to vindicate the original indictment of the judicial system. Yet a lot has changed since the self-punishing Vandana in *Aradhana* a decade before quietly acquiesced to a twelve-year incarceration for defending herself against rape. If melodrama condenses profound public/private conflicts, at once exposing and reaffirming power relations (Gledhill 1987; Landy 1991), it is also a vivid emotional register in Hindi films. In *Aradhana* the centrality of affect shored up by the profilmic masculine fantasy acknowledges patriarchal oppression and proffers reverence in the form of a grand award from the state (fusing mother/nation/state)—an awkward and phantasmic compensation. On the other hand, in the post-1980s woman's film nothing short of "sweet revenge" compensates for women's suffering.

The 1980s rape-revenge film, fuelled by women's rage, dramatizes a public discourse that repudiates victimization and patriarchy and that is distinct from the pre-1980s obsessive "inscription" and "erasure" of sexual violence, *Teesri Manzil*-style. The topos of rape, a weapon against the weak, is used by filmmakers as a rhetorical trope to conjure images of power, coercion, and humiliation in conflicts between the culturally powerless and powerful.[28] Yet domination/subordination, as Priyamvada Gopal points out in the context of *Bandit Queen,* is not an eternal category but an unstable one, and the vengeful action fulfills this prophecy. Nor is "meaning," and here I reiterate her invocation of Susie Tharu: "so much total expression as a tension, a difference from that which went before" (Tharu 1989, 866).

I contend that the historical context is crucial to understanding the arrival of the avenging women's film, its success and role in the circulation of discourses between representation and reality.[29] In the films I have discussed—from the 1960s, 1970s, and 1980s—I see the discourse on womanhood in an orbit from reverence to rape, and then revenge. It is no accident that the sharp reaction to Mathura's rape in 1978 spearheaded the women's movement. Gopalan's anguished point is that, within the Hindi film narrative, it takes a woman's rape to permit revenge. Ironically, and rather more ominously, the rape-revenge genre's history reflects an unhappy reality. It took Mathura's (and Rameeza Bee's and Maya Tyagi's) rape for the nation to focus attention on women's rage organized as a movement.

Notes

1 Revised and reprinted with permission from *Screen* 40, 1 (Spring): 1999.

2 Three essays address this question: Shohini Ghosh, "Deviant Pleasures and Disorderly Women" (1996); Priyamvada Gopal, "Of Victims and Vigilantes: The *Bandit Queen* Controversy" (1997); and Lalitha Gopalan, "Avenging Women in India Cinema" (1997).

3 *Aradhana* descends from a long line of successful women's films, *Achchut Kanya/Untouchable Girl* (1936), *Aurat/Woman* (1940) and its remake *Mother India* (1957), *Sujata* (1959), *Bandini* (1963), and *Mamta/Maternal Love* (1966), to mention a few. I choose to discuss *Aradhana* because elements of repetition and difference make interesting comparisons to other films from its ouevre.

4 Here the legal discourse assumes the law is "soft" on women, contrary to the history of the Indian women's movement discussed later.

5 Successful outdoor shooting in *Junglee/Uncouth* (1960), *Kashmir ki Kali/Flower of Kashmir* (1963), *Sangam/Confluence* (1964), and *Evening in Paris* (1967) established this convention.

6 Viviani points out that the maternal melodrama, *Madame X*–style, repeatedly traces the mother's separation from the child. The mother watches the child "from afar; she cannot risk jeopardizing his fortunes by contamination with her own bad repute" (Viviani 1991, 171).

7 For a detailed examination of the mother–son–state relationship see chapter 3 of my *The Cinematic ImagiNation: Indian Popular Films as Social History* (Rutgers University Press, 2003).

8 Julia Lesage points to an irony in feminist film and television literature that, until recently, overwhelmingly focuses on the "castration threat" rather than on the "rape threat" (personal communication with the author).

9 In her "Life after Rape: Narrative, Rape and Feminism," Rajeswari Sunder Rajan (1993, 82) refers to the rape scene in Hindi films as "almost mandatory." Gopalan (1997, 51), however, reads it as an excuse for violent sex—though ultimately necessitating the woman's revenge. I am suggesting we examine the variations in staging rape.

10 Other films of its ilk are *C.I.D.* (1956), about a police officer tackling the mafia; *Jewel Thief* (1967), about international crime; and *Intikaam/The Test* (1968), about an escaped convict.

11 Rules governing rape trials are based on Sir Mathew Hale's opinion written to the King's Bench in 1671: since rape is a charge so easily made and so difficult for a man to defend against, it must be examined with greater caution than any other crime. See Susan Brownmiller's (1976, 369–70) seminal *Against Our Will: Men, Women and Rape*. She also cites John Henry Wigmore's *Evidence*, a primary treatise on evidentiary rules, which makes a similar argument.

12 *Shringaar rasa* is the mood of love, romance, and sensual pleasure—one of the nine *rasas* in classical Indian drama theory.

13 Writing against the editor's condemnation of the film *Panihari* (1947), Pandit Indra (1947, 47–48) says, "First of all I should warn the puritan editor that he is doing the greatest injustice to the industry by exciting the Government against our pictures....Does he want to turn our 'Romantic industry' into [a] heartless business institution? If romance[,] which he alleges [is]...vulgarity[,] is squeezed away[,] what will remain? Preaching sermons? Then why go to the pictures at all? We can attend temples, mosques and churches for sermons."

14 This shift might lend credibility to the feminist charge that the rape scene substitutes for the vamp. My own preferred reading, however, is that the vamp figure is at odds with a populist feminist discourse, which has increasingly become Hindi film's cachet.

15 Gopalan's suggestion (1997, 57–59) that women's agency can be depicted without gratuitous rape scenes, as in the exemplary Telegu film *Police Lock Up* (1992), is useful, but it does not explain the success of the rape-revenge narratives.

16 The film has remarkable parallels with, and might even be a creative adaptation of, Lamont Johnson's *Lipstick* (1976), a Hollywood film with a rape-revenge theme.

17 Barbara Ehrenreich's phrase to describe women's enthusiastic support for Lorena Bobbitt in her "Feminism Confronts Bobbittry," in *The Snarling Citizen* (1995).

18 *Bharati* derives from the word *Bharat,* the Hindi name for India.

19 Star currency is crucial in viewer expectations. Ramesh Gupta, played by Raj Babbar, not conventionally a villain, added to the quotidian nature of acquaintance rape.

20 Texts more open to reader interpretation.

21 "Conduct" was critical to the Supreme Court's verdict in Mathura's rape trial. According to the judges, Mathura's "boyfriends" and sexual liaisons prior to her rape pointed to her "loose" conduct. It was therefore difficult, the argument went, to establish whether she had consented to sex with the constables or not. In 1989 the courts ruled against Rameeza Bee on the same grounds.

22 *Anjaam/Consequence* (1994) is held exemplary in this respect, though several other films, *Pratighaat/Retribution* (1987), *Zakhmi Aurat/Wounded Woman* (1988), *Haq/Rights* (1991), and *Damini/Lightning* (1994), fit this female avenging category.

23 Inevitably, a woman's body registers violation or injury of one kind or another. In *Pratighaat* and *Damini* neither protagonist is raped. The protagonist in *Pratighaat* is disrobed in public, and in *Damini* a working-class woman is raped by members of the upper-class protagonist's family. In *Haq* the protagonist has a miscarriage, and the public and private conflicts coalesce when she takes on her politician husband, who is responsible for the miscarriage.

24 Rosie Thomas (1989) refers to Radha levelling a gun to kill her own son in *Mother India's* denouement as "the most powerfully horrifying image" (23). In *Mamta,* a Madame X–style variant of *Aradhana,* the protagonist/mother kills her extortionist husband and is defended in court by her long-lost daughter. The mother dies moments after learning that her daughter at least recognizes her maternal sacrifice.

25 This recapitulation is based on my participation as an activist in the women's movement through the 1980s. Rajyadhyaksha (1995, 416) echoes this sentiment in his write-up on the film: "The three rape sequences staged with voyeuristic relish, no doubt contributed to its commercial success."

26 Gopal's (1997, 96–97) sensitive iteration of the confusion unleashed by competing claims between Phoolan Devi's pain, the invasion of her privacy, and the commodification of her narrative in *Bandit Queen* point to the profound contradiction wherein rape is experienced as a private trauma despite the women's movement's effort to view it as a public issue, a manifestation of quotidian power structures and relations.

27 Williams quotes Jonathan Dollimore, "The Cultural Politics of Perversion: Augustine, Shakespeare, Freud, Freud, Foucault" (1990).

28 As Clover (1992, 153) argues, in "popular cinema's redefinition…rape [is] less an act of sex than an 'act of power.'"

29 Hindi cinema is wont to represent feminist discourses as well as to participate in the backlash against such discourses.

In the Name of the Nation: Images of Palestinian and Israeli Women Fighters

DORIT NAAMAN[1]

[15]

Introduction

Since the beginning of 2002 the Israeli–Palestinian conflict has seen a new flavour of resistance, whereby Palestinian women have joined the ranks of suicide bombers. Previously, upon revealing that I am from Israel, the North American response was often pity and compassion for having come from a war zone. My conversant would usually express sympathy and worry for the sake of my family in Jerusalem and ask questions about the situation. But since women started killing themselves, I have encountered a new set of baffled questions or requests for me to explain the phenomenon. The idea that women are sent to kill themselves, or choose to do so, appalls North Americans. On numerous occasions I have been told that the interviews with mothers who claim they encourage their daughters to kill themselves in this way, and wish they could do the same, are distressing. The photos of the women were featured in the media with stories emphasizing their beauty, intelligence, and mis-used future, and (at least) in North America a bewildered response ensued. It also seems that the gender shift in suicide bombers has resulted in a shift in attitudes towards me, from a victim to an expert. I—a woman, a feminist, and a Palestinian sympathizer—found myself asked to explain a phenomenon that I find anti-feminist. Moreover, since I am an Israeli, Palestinian suicide attacks—particularly those taking place inside Israel—are naturally emotion-ally charged for me. Nevertheless, the phenomenon of female suicide bombers and the responses to it challenged me to question the representation of women fighters in general and to try to complicate the North American discourse about Palestinian female suicide bombers in particular.

In April of 2002 I was shopping for gifts for my yearly visit to Israel, and a vendor said: "How can they send women to kill themselves and others? Are they animals? And this one, she had a future, she was engaged, she was study-ing, she was beautiful....What kind of a society is this?" He was referring to Ayat Akhras who, on 29 March 2002 blew herself up at a supermarket in Jerusalem, killing herself and two others and wounding dozens. Since 27 Jan-uary 2002, the day that Wafa Idris strapped ten kilograms of explosives to her-self and blew herself up in downtown Jerusalem, an excited discourse has emerged (both in the Arab world and in the West) on those "angels of deaths," or "Joans of Arc," depending on one's political position.[2] Even *Adbusters,* the leftist anti-capitalist magazine, published a full-page photo of Akhras, with a centred caption reading "Something to die for..." The designed pun on her beauty and her cause is not incidental. Whether *Adbusters* intended it or not, this language falls into traditional Orientalist lingo, and even under the most charitable reading, Akhras is, at the very least, romanticized and fetishized. To be fair, the photo is contrasted with obscured images of North American kids who supposedly commit suicide and have "nothing to live for," so the context for the photo-essay is neither the Palestinian fight for independence nor women suicide bombers. Still, this out-of-context use only draws more attention to its stereotypical implications (*Adbusters,* July/August 2002).

But the attention is not exclusive to the Arab world, and an array of ques-tions emerge: Why are the actions of Idris, Abu Aisheh, and Akhras more hor-rific than those of their male colleagues? Why did Sadam Hussein dedicate a memorial site for them and not for the dozens of male suicide bombers? The answer most clearly has to do with the very fact of their gender: violent women are conceived in the cultural imaginary to be deficient in the feminine qual-ities of nurturance and mercy. But the situation is more complex with women who fight for national liberation as they betray yet another stereotype, that of the mother-nation: the supportive, nursing, accepting meta-mother; the one who teaches mother tongue and the love of the country; the one who brings forth life (not death and destruction) and nurtures it. Moreover, the mother-nation is also the one who is supposed to raise her son to fight for liberation, to be a hero, but who does not go to war herself. Yet, as I show bellow, national liberation movements found interesting ways to incorporate women fighters as part of their myth of nationalist heroism. While these gender stereotypes are reflected in the reservations generated by women fighters, I see a serious cultural discrepancy at work: Israeli women were fighters in the 1948 war, and they are resuming those tasks in recent years after a long fight with the army over gender. While the Palestinian woman fighter is seen in the West as a demon, a product of a sick and distorted society, the Israeli woman fighter is considered a sign of progress, equality, and modernity.[3] A similar comparison can be made between the representation of women who serve in the Canadian or American armed forces, who are considered feminist, individualist, and competitive, and the representation of women who serve in the Iranian or Iraqi armies. The latter are always shown in large, seemingly conformist groups, holding guns, their faces stern, which presumably conveys the idea that they have been brainwashed and indoctrinated.

In this chapter I explore the cultural images of Palestinian and Israeli women fighters and attempt to address an array of issues regarding the intersection of gender with nationalism in general and with the historical context of the Israeli–Palestinian conflict in particular, from the days of the British mandate, to the 1948 war, to the present. I discuss the suicide bombers as part of a variety of tactics employed by occupied peoples in their struggle to become sovereign. These tactics range from fighting in armed forces, to supporting soldiers, to community organizations, and peace activism. I suggest that the representation of women during the struggle for liberation functions on a continuum from victims (of the occupier) to national heroines to monsters.[4] The application of these labels (both inside and outside their respective societies) is not solely a consequence of acts committed but, rather, of the interaction between gender, race, nationality, and a particular historical and media moment. In other words, a nationalist movement may incorporate women fighters and hail them, while outsiders may condemn them. At the same time, due to historical circumstances, similar acts may be hailed by outsiders with regard to one society (Israeli) and condemned with regard to another (Palestinian).

Cinematic Context

I begin with a brief analysis of violence that is enacted against women within the context of national liberation movements. I have in mind an image from Deepa Mehta's 1999 film *Earth*. Mehta tells a story of a Hindu nanny to a Persian family living in 1947 Lahore on the eve of the partition of India and Pakistan. The nanny, Shanta, is courted by three men: two are Muslim and one is

Sikh. At a time of growing ethnic and religious segregation, Shanta seems to be able to bring the men together, symbolizing a united, tolerant, and multicultural India. As the atmosphere in town gets tense, the militant Muslim, Imam Din, proposes marriage to Shanta as a means to secure her safety. But Shanta turns him down as she is in love with Hassan, the apolitical Muslim. The film ends with Hassan's death and Shanta being dragged by her hair (presumably to her death) by Imam Din. What is striking to me in this film, as in Moufita Tlatli's *Silences of the Palace* (set in Tunisia), is the equation made between the woman protagonist and the nation struggling for independence.[5] In both films the woman is like the nation—occupied—and in both the nation's independence does not guarantee the woman's liberation. In other words, both Mehta and Tlatli conclude that while the struggle to end colonialism (in Pakistan/India and Tunisia respectively) has succeeded, the struggle to liberate woman is still ongoing. The woman protagonist is not able to save herself; instead, she can aid the male fighters in achieving independence, only to be abandoned and oppressed by them afterwards.[6]

Male filmmakers also use the trope of the woman-nation as an evocative symbol of personal sacrifice for the good of the nation.[7] Michel Khleifi's *Wedding in Galilee* (1987) recounts the story of the wedding of a Palestinian mukhtar's (mayor's) son, which is performed under the controlling eye of Israeli army personnel, who manipulate the Mukhtar to invite them. The son, humiliated by these circumstances, suffers from impotence, and the bride— in a horrific scene—takes her own virginity, to save the honour of the family, patriarchy, and the nation.

In all these examples we see that the woman is presented as a victim of both patriarchy and nationalism, and if she makes a heroic gesture, it is always to benefit the nation (or patriarchy) rather than her status as a woman. In other words, she can become a national heroine only if she compromises or abandons her own (gendered) interests as a female subject, succumbing to the asexual role of the mother-nation.[8] Following this analysis, we can examine how these women negotiate the expectations nationalism has of them with regard to their gendered identity, and we can see what avenues are open or closed to them as national and gendered subjects. In particular, these films suggested that the women could choose either to be victims (of occupation and patriarchy) or to be nationalist heroines. But recent events made me realize that the heroine–victim dichotomy is too simplistic and that it does not account for the image of the Palestinian woman suicide bomber as a monster.

Nationalism and Feminism

Tlatli, Mehta, and Khleifi did not invent the fictitious and cinematic configuration whereby woman and nation are equated. In fact, feminism in Israel,
India, Tunisia, and Palestine (as well as elsewhere) had developed in tandem
with national liberation movements. Much like the American women's suffrage
movement—which emerged out of the comparison between the statuses of
women and African-American slaves—the diverse national liberation movements have taught women to fight for group rights, including women's rights.
In other words, American women activists realized that what they (or their husbands) were doing for others (i.e., African Americans) they were not doing for
themselves. Similarly, women active in national liberation movements saw
the parallels between occupation and patriarchal control, and they started to
fight for women's rights as well as national rights.

For Israeli women the fight started in the early days of the Kibbutz,[9] which
was supposed to be egalitarian and socialist. Yet, until the mid-1930s, women
did not partake in defence roles and were negligible in political or adminis-
trative posts. However, using socialist arguments, they slowly gained more
influential roles to the point that, during the Arab revolt of 1936–39, women
were an integral part of the Kibbutz defence system (Fogiel-Bijaoui 1992). At
the same time, women were fighting to participate in jobs generally considered masculine (such as agricultural roles), and eventually younger women
without children gained some access to those positions. But, according to
Sylvie Fogiel-Bijaoui (1992, 227), "women participated in the struggle for a
national homeland and eventual independence, but this in no way changed the
sexual distribution in the kibbutz. One of the reasons, we would argue, is that,
in spite of their feelings of frustration and anger, the war restrained women
from struggling for equality of rights, and caused them to fight for equality
of duties." It seems then that the inclusion of women in masculine positions,
including that of fighter, was possible only so long as it was perceived by the
patriarchal state institutions to be a national necessity rather than a feminist
act. However, the rhetoric and tactics of the national liberation movement
supplied women with tools for a (still ongoing) feminist struggle.

Similarly, Palestinian women were somewhat active politically throughout the British mandate as well as during the subsequent Jordanian and Israeli
rule, but their organizations (various forms of women's committees) were
formed primarily around distribution of charity, care for orphans and prisoners, and other traditionally feminine roles. However, since the beginning of
the first Intifada in 1987, feminist organizations have become active in fighting both the Israeli occupation and gender inequality. The Palestinian Women's

Action Committee was formed, and throughout the six years of the first Intifada over 1,000 women were arrested every year: 119 were killed, 460 were imprisoned for long terms, and 250 were deported.[10] *The Veiled Hope* (a 1994 documentary by Norma Marcus) and *The Women Next Door* (1992) both chart the evolution of a feminist identity alongside a national one. But *The Women Next Door* also shows a difference between West Bank and Gaza Strip women, whereby the former address gender inequality while the latter become more Islamist and traditionalist. In the West Bank a discussion emerges on domestic violence or the rights of women to work and study, while in Gaza women put on the veil.[11] The veil, which was sometimes hailed by nationalist movements as a symbol of cultural independence in the face of colonialism and global interventions, is a complicated symbol, used by different agencies for different reasons. Some feminists fight it as oppressive, while others adopt it as a means to avoid being objectified by the male gaze.

The veil's symbolic tension is also evident in independence struggles elsewhere. For example, in Algeria the French justified much of their colonialist activity by pointing to the inferior status of women,[12] and the Algerian nationalist response was to assign a political content to tradition. While women's participation in the Algerian National Liberation Front (FLN) armed struggle was marketed as a sign of the freedom women have under Islam, the veil was worn as a sign of patriotism. But after independence, the National Union of Algerian Women was negatively sanctioned, and women were "instructed to serve the woman's interest as wife and mother and not to abandon the ethical code deeply held by the people" (Nashat and Tucker 1999, 112). Once independence was achieved the veil lost its anti-colonial status and became a marker of traditional feminine performance.

In *The Women Next Door*, Amal Ouachadan-Labadi explains that the Palestinian Women's Action Committee in the Occupied Territories was established as an organization that fights at once for women's social rights and for national liberation. According to Labadi,

> If we want to go on with national liberation, putting aside our liberation as women, we would end up in the houses again. We will be locked up in our houses, and we do not want to repeat the experience of women in Algiers. We work for national liberation, where the women (as half of the population) will be equal to men in every aspect of life: work, education, marriage, divorce, inheritance, etc. (*The Women Next Door* 1992)

It seems clear that once national subjectivity is articulated, gendered subjectivity emerges as well, but it is not always the Western version of a gendered subjectivity. It is also evident that the nationalist project of statehood is rarely interested in freeing women from the confines of patriarchy, and therefore women's relationships to the newly established nation-state are complex. However, not all feminist organizations tie the two liberations together; some, as I discuss later, have questioned nationalist movements altogether, particularly as they relate to women.

The Woman Fighter

One of the mythic icons of the Jewish woman fighter prior the 1948 war is that of a Palmach[13] girl, hiding grenades in her bra. This mental image accompanied my upbringing, suggesting that women were brave and capable and that they contributed to Israeli independence as much as did men. Surprisingly, neither I nor my peers considered the evocative trope of (quite literally) explosive sexuality to be a possible aspect of the metaphor. The socialist model of equality underplayed female sexuality, and by the time I was a child—and Golda Meir a prime minister—power meant being "as good as a man."[14] Moreover, if women did use their sexuality to forward nationalist goals in the 1940s, this aspect of their contribution was eradicated from, or minimized within, official narratives: the myth concentrated on their bravery rather than on their tactics.

Naturally, the reality of the fight for Israel's independence was not exemplary of gender egalitarianism: only 10 percent of the Palmach members were women, and, during the 1948 war, only 20 percent of the Israeli army were women. Most women served as nurses, medics, communication specialists, and administrators (Bloom 1993). Very few served in combat roles, and those were controversial but necessary (due to the lack of trained male personnel). Combat roles for women were eliminated shortly after the war ended in 1949, when the army was able to train enough men. After 1949 women were drafted for a mandatory service period (now eighteen months) but were not positioned in combat units. However, in recent years, women have been trained for combat in ground troops; they have become tank and artillery instructors, and Israel has just seen the first woman pilot graduate from the air force's prestigious pilot course. The fight to get into the course was initiated by Alice Miller, and when the army denied her access to it, she took the case to the Supreme Court and eventually won. She also pleaded her case with a veteran air force commander, and then Israeli president, Ezer Weitzman. Weitzman responded by saying, "*Meidalleh* (little girl in Yiddish), why don't you go and knit socks for the soldiers instead?" This response publicly exposed the extent to which the patriarchal power structure in Israeli society is both hegemonic and oblivious to gender issues. After all, the presidency in Israel is not political but ceremonial, and Weitzman did not even consider that his response might offend at least 50 per cent of the population he represents. Women's organizations lobbied for Miller's inclusion in the pilot's course and sharply criticized Weitzman.

The Israeli army, however, was not the first army to draft and train women in the region. The Palmach women were often trained in the British army, which, since 1941, recruited women for its Auxiliary Territorial Service (ATS). Since the British did not want to send English women to the Middle East, they recruited 4,000 primarily Jewish, but also Palestinian and Armenian, women for their units, and even trained a few dozen to be officers (Bloom 1993, 129–30). These women volunteers were faced with sharp societal criticism and were regarded as deviant. Anne Bloom conducted interviews with those volunteers and found that, "if not labeled outright as prostitutes, they were called adventure-seekers, husband-hunters, or escapees from unhappy marriages. Many women reported that their families were ostracized" (130).

Similarly, after Wafa Idris committed suicide in Jerusalem, the articles in the Arab press tried to explain her behaviour by alluding to her divorce (due to her inability to bear children) and her unhappiness when her ex-husband remarried and had kids. And Anne Applebaum (*Slate*, 2 April 2002) expresses astonishment at Akhras's suicide bombing: "Not only was she not male, she was not overtly religious, not estranged form her family, not openly associated with any radical groups. She can hardly be described as a woman without a future. She was young, she was a good student, and she was engaged to be married."[15] In both the Palestinian and Israeli examples we see an attempt to associate the uncharacteristic behaviour of women fighters with personal, and particularly romantic, unhappiness. But when that explanation fails, the critics are unable to explain why a woman would choose such a path. In both societies this marginal behaviour is incorporated into a heroic national narrative that glosses over the problems these women experience in a male-dominated world. Israel prides itself on equality and uses the army, and the myth of women's participation in the 1948 war, as an example of its enlightened nature.

The Palestinians, in turn, hail the women fighters as national symbols, and, on 1 March 2002, the Fatah movement announced the establishment of a women's brigade in honour of the martyr Wafa Idris (*Al Quds*, 1 March 2002). In other words, while women are not considered or represented as equal to men on the battlefield (or off it), women fighters are put on a pedestal. It is important to note that Palestinian women also have numerous role models, the most famous being Leila Khaled (Black September airplane hijacking in Jordan) and Dalal el Moughrabi (1978 hijacking of a bus inside Israel): these women became a stronger symbol for Palestine than did any male fighter precisely because their behaviour was considered to be unique. And, as mentioned above, since the beginning of the first Intifada in 1987 many Palestinian women mobilized resistance movements, and many were arrested for active participation in the Intifada (Giacaman and Johnson 1989). Recently, an editorial in a Palestinian paper suggested that "he who marries a good girl will not be asked for a high bride price—a girl marries a warrior and asks for a rifle in place of a dowry" (*Al Quds*, 1 March 2002).

One of the differences between the Israeli and Palestinian women fighters is that outsiders consider the former to be courageous and the latter to be monstrous. The reasons for this are complex and are tied to historical as well as cultural norms that extend well beyond the scope of this chapter. Still, it is worth briefly articulating a few of these reasons. First, the 1948 war was fought when the world was recovering from the Second World War and was riddled with guilt over the Holocaust, so the images of Jewish women fighting for independence (in what was then coded as survival) were construed as courageous. Second, Israeli women were not seen as individuals but, rather, as part of a socialist system, the group, the kibbutz, the Palmach, and, later, the army. The collective nature of the struggle, and the inclusion of women as an integral part of it, softened gender-specific, film noir-ish patriarchal fears and, therefore, masked some of the issues at hand. In contrast, the Palestinian fighters are individuals, operating in cells with men but not trained or recruited in any organized fashion. Their national narratives of heroism are individualistic in nature and do not amount (yet) to the establishment of a group narrative.

Despite differences in reception in the West, I contend that, in both cases, through sacrificing their personal and private family lives (which are associated with femininity), the women become symbolic of, or synonymous with, the nation but then lose their prescribed gender identity as well as other aspects of their subjectivity.[16] To exemplify the loss of female subjectivity I refer to the film *The Battle of Algiers* (1965). This film covers the last few years in the FLN's fight for independence from the French, and, as mentioned above, women took an integral role in this battle. In one scene we see three women prepare to carry bombs from the (Muslim) Casbah to the French part of town. They bleach their hair blonde, shorten their dresses (or exchange them for 1960s Western-style miniskirts), put on makeup, and thus mask their Islamic, or North-African, appearance (see fig. 30). The film then shows each one of them

FIGURE 30 Scene from *The Battle of Algiers*, 1965 (Criterion).

FIGURE 31 Scene from *The Battle of Algiers*, 1965 (Criterion).

passing through the checkpoints, reassembling at a shop so that a man can install and set the bombs and then drop them off at ice cream parlours, coffee houses, and the race tracks—all places were the French spend a good deal of time.

This scene shows how women characters perform a particular (Western) sexuality and enact an identity that enables them to "pass" as French and easily move between the Casbah and the French city (see fig. 31). In assuming this mask, they exchange their "Arabness" for "Frenchness" and, ironically, gain an even stronger "Algerianness." But this willingness on the part of women to assume a visual identity in order to serve the nation suggests that their core identity is malleable. None of the male protagonists in the film could pass as French, so their identity is secured as Algerian or Arab—and, I would claim, as "men." However, women's visual (or ethnic) and behavioural (or gender) masquerade indicates that their femininity can be divorced from their national role; that is, as long as is necessary they are fighters but as soon as independence is achieved it is assumed that they will resume their "feminine" roles and become subservient wives and mothers. In any case, none of the female characters in the film is evolved and complex, none has subjectivity or much agency to begin with. We know nothing about their lives beyond their own screen actions, and we know nothing about their motives, ideological differences, and so on. I contend that the women represent an excess of symbolism: they are the heroic, suffering, struggling nation. And, as such, they are fetishized—not as sexual objects but, rather, as asexual national ones.

In films about Israel's early days women fighters take on a similar role to that mentioned above, thus losing not only a gendered subjectivity but also any subjectivity whatsoever. In *Exodus* (1960) Karen, the young Holocaust survivor, makes it to Israel only to fight and die for its establishment. She is stripped of a personality and a future of her own, and stands as a symbolic representation of European Jewry, which needs to die in order to facilitate the birth of the new Jew (represented in the film by Ari Ben-Canaan). In her fascinating book *Identity Politics on the Israeli Screen*, Yosefa Loshitzky suggests a unique reading of Karen's death and burial in the same grave with the "Uncle Tom" Arab, Taha. Loshitzky (2001, 9) points out that a subversive reading would indicate that the "Zionist state was established on the graves of the Palestinians and the Holocaust survivors." Either way, she shows that the symbolic nature of the character of Karen (and of Taha, for that matter) eliminates her subjectivity while enabling her to function as a dramatic prop. Similarly, Ella Shohat (1987, 58–76) shows that *Hill 24 Doesn't Answer* (1955), which supposedly tells the story of four 1948 fighters—three men and a woman—in actuality only tells the story of the men. The characters are a pro-Israeli Irishman, an American Jew, a Sabra (Israeli-born man), and an Oriental Jewish woman (see fig. 32). While the men each get to recount the story of how they got to that hilltop in a series of flashbacks, the woman is denied a story of her own; she thus lacks the individuality and unique identity given to the others. Shohat claims that this omission is a result of the woman being an Oriental Jew, but I would suggest that the combination of her gender and ethnicity serves as a double justification for not assigning her a story and, thus, subjectivity (see fig. 33).

To conclude this section I would like to suggest that women fighters are conceived as deficient with regard to performing a certain form of expected femininity (albeit they are not necessarily deficient with regard to sexuality);

FIGURE 32 Dead woman holding flag in hand, from *Hill 24 Doesn't Answer*, 1955 (with permission of Ergo Media Inc.).

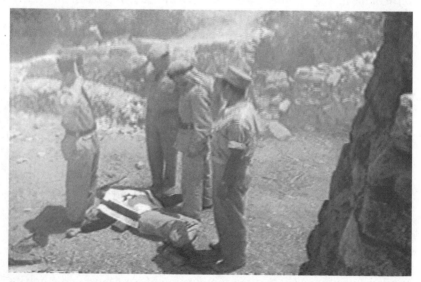

FIGURE 33 Dead woman covered with flag, from *Hill 24 Doesn't Answer*, 1955 (with permission of Ergo Media Inc.).

instead, they perform an aggressive and physical (or masculine) role, which the national project incorporates as one of its symbols of national struggle. However, by taking that symbolic role, women fighters are stripped of ethnic or gendered subjectivity and are, in fact, objectified as icons.[17] This objectification resolves patriarchal anxieties about violent women, or even about state violence in the hands of women, and at the same time produces a positive narrative of national struggle. To illustrate this point one can look at Santosh Sivan's *The Terrorist* (2000), which tells the story of Malli, a Tamil fighter chosen for a suicide bombing mission (designed after the 1991 mission to kill Rajiv Gandhi). Malli is a very young woman, a skilled and fierce fighter, committed to the cause, and determined to execute it. But when she finds out she is pregnant—as a result of a one-night affair with a Tamil fighter whom she later watched being killed by soldiers—Malli starts to have doubts, and eventually she revokes her mission. It is interesting to note that Malli thinks of the fetus as a boy, and her reason for continuing to live involves raising him to avenge his father's death. The film, then, falls into a patriarchal pattern, whereby Malli is accepted as a fighter (in avenging the death of her brother and fighting for independence) so long as she is neither sexual nor reproductive. Interestingly, it is patriarchy (in the form of an old man) that informs her she is pregnant (basing his assumption on an intuition and on her vomiting once), and immediately thereafter she "knows" that, indeed, she is pregnant. From that moment, too, the images start to emphasize her femininity, thus preparing the grounds for her to desert the mission, something the film clearly morally condones. In other words, as soon as her sexual subjectivity is enacted she is no longer a suitable candidate for the suicide mission" the icon of the nation now needs to take on the role of the mother-nation and raise her son to heroism.

Feminism and Peace Activism

Women fighters, as I show above, are accommodated by the nationalist project of liberation, but both their femininity and their subjectivity are compromised to accommodate patriarchal anxieties. Some women fighters see themselves as feminist activists, working towards a more egalitarian and open society. But some feminist organizations see nationalism, and particularly the armed forces, as standing in contradiction to the foundation of any feminist agenda. In what follows I address some feminist positions with regard to the place of women in the armed forces and in peace activism.

Wafa Idris was described by her family as a tomboy (Beaumont 2002) and by the Arab press (in some cases) as a feminist (Nir 2002) and a national heroine. However, the feminist label is tricky and context-dependent. While the Palestinian Authority now encourages women to participate in armed struggle alongside men, the question of whether these acts are feminist depends on different interpretations of feminism. The Jordanian daily *Al Dustour* stated in an editorial:

> Wafa Idris, like the rest of the young women of her generation, never dreamed of owning a BMW or of having a cellular phone. Wafa did not carry make-up in her suitcase, but enough explosives to fill the enemy with horror. Wasn't it the west that kept demanding that eastern woman become equal to man? Well, this is how we understand equality—this is how the martyr Wafa understood equality. (A. Chancellor, *Guardian*, 23 February 2002)

This cynical response alludes to a colonial (and neocolonial) configuration of a binary opposition between East and West, to Orientalist critiques of gender inequality in the Middle East, and to the demands of early waves of Western feminism to universalize the woman's question above and beyond race, ethnicity, and nationality. The article, then, uses the term "feminism" to mock a set of Western discourses about the Middle East and gender rather than to invoke a Middle Eastern form of feminism.

Some editorials have suggested that the phenomenon of the female suicide bombers should be read as an indication that Palestinian men cannot protect Palestinian women, and so women have to protect themselves. This explanation is also common with regard to the Tamil female fighters (Black Tigers) who opted to join the armed forces because, otherwise, they would face gang rapes and murder. Self-defence for a woman in a violent patriarchal society, then, is tied to the nationalist armed struggle, and while refusing the victim role is a positive move, it is not necessarily a feminist one. Moreover, neither Islam nor Judaism prevent women from fighting, and, in fact, self-defence is considered a virtue in both religions.[18] Ismai'l Abu Samad, a Hamas leader in Gaza, said: "Jihad against the enemy is an obligation that applies not only to men but also to women. Islam has never differentiated between men and women on the battlefield" (*Middle East Online*, 2002).

While Sheikh Ahmed Yassin (the spiritual leader of the Hamas movement until his assassination in March 2004) had some reservations, he, too, agreed that Islam does not prohibit women from fighting; in fact, in the case of an occupation it is the duty of a man, a woman, a slave, and a master to fight such occupation (*Afaq Arabiyah*, 30 January 2002). It is clear then that the "Joan of Arc" imagery, associated particularly with the suicide bombers inside Arab society, is not necessarily read as either subversive or feminist. According to Kamila Shamise (*Guardian*, 27 April 2002):

> Female suicide bombers are not a recent phenomena, they're just new to the Israeli–Palestinian conflict. The Tamil Tigers have recruited more women than men for suicide attacks, and not just because women are less likely to get searched

or to arouse suspicion. Men are considered more suited to training recruits, so it's just more efficient to have women kill themselves. No surprise to find men keeping themselves at the centre of things, relegating women to positions of service rather than strategy.

Shamise claims that, like Charlie's Angels, who do the work for "him" by risking themselves, the three suicide bombers (at the time of publication of her article) only enable Arafat to ensure that the centre of power remains out of reach of women's participation. The bafflement with which the Western world has met the phenomenon is due to overly simplistic explanations of why men engage in suicide bombing——that is, their fundamental religious belief, along with the promise that seventy virgins will await them in heaven. Alas, Shamise shows that the virgins, or *houris*, are genderless and that they await anyone who gets to heaven regardless of how they got there. She concludes by saying: "why would any woman be in a hurry to get handed over to a host of genderless virgins?" (*Guardian*, 27 April 2002).

In Israel, too, the inclusion of women as fighters is not automatically perceived as a feminist act. True, the decision of Israel's first prime minister, David Ben-Gurion, to remove women from combat—because he wanted to use them in the rear (Bloom 1993, 133) for less prestigious and less dangerous jobs— was clearly chauvinistic. But the opposite does not follow; that is, that inclusion of women in fighting forces is necessarily a feminist act. In fact, most of the feminist organizations in Israel are pro-peace and are decisively non-violent in their forms of protest.

Since the beginning of the first Intifada at least a dozen Israeli women's organizations have been working with Palestinian women to promote peace, dialogue, and non-violence. In this current Intifada a new movement has emerged: mothers and wives of soldiers go to stand at the roadblocks where their husbands and sons serve. They place signs reminding the soldiers to act humanely, inviting them to quit the army and go home. Another feminist organization, Machsom Watch, places daily teams of women at the roadblocks, where they observe the behaviour of the soldiers who control the movement of Palestinians. During Ta'ayush[19] activities it is generally agreed that, should the army stop the group on the road, the women members will negotiate with the soldiers. The idea is to break the pattern, to force soldiers to engage in a discourse with women who do not serve in combat roles, who do not share the same army experience and, therefore, who will not accommodate normative masculine army behaviour.

Some Palestinian and Israeli feminists question whether nationalism and feminism are compatible. In the introduction to their book *Women and the*

Politics of Military Confrontation Nahla Abdo and Ronit Lentin develop a fascinating dialogue with regard to the relationship between feminism and nationalism. Both see themselves as national subjects, and Abdo even comments on how, at one point in her life, circumstances forced her to be more a Palestinian than a gendered subject. And yet both see nationalism as problematic for women. Abdo writes:

> But as a feminist, I cannot but argue that nationalism is conceived by and for men (Anderson's "horizontal brotherhood"), without taking into account either the experience of women, or their active participation in national liberation struggles....My critique of nationalism also stems from my understanding of Zionist nationalism as a masculine construction, in which the "new Hebrew" was male, and in which diaspora Judaism was feminized, in contrast with Israeli nationalism.

Like many of the women whose narratives are presented in the book, Abdo's gendered identity is tied to a national one, but, as a result of feminist criticism, she started to steer away from nationalism. For these women dialogue across nationality, collaborative efforts, and peace activism are all natural consequences of their feminism. The Jerusalem Link, an umbrella organization made up of diverse Palestinian and Israeli feminist groups, and Women in Black (when they share events with Palestinians) are good examples of this approach to feminism.[20] In the recent documentary *This Is Not Living*,[21] which focuses on Palestinian women's lives under Israeli occupation, all the women interviewed ask for peace, for compromise, and for the end to violence. These women want to live a quiet and dignified life, and they do not condone violence because they are victims of it. Moreover, these women see the parallels between their oppression as Palestinians and their oppression as women.

With the benefit of a feminist analysis, these organizations also see a correlation between domestic violence in Israel and the conflict with the Palestinians. In a famous case from the first Intifada a soldier shot and killed a seventeen-year-old Palestinian woman who was sitting on her balcony reading a book. The soldier was tried but released, and two years later he shot and killed his ex-girlfriend (whom he had abused for years). The connection, or pattern, between these two events was somewhat contested then, but it became very clear after the first Gulf War. During that war most Israeli men sat at home with their families, experiencing the same anxiety that is shared at the "rear." Men reported feeling impotent and irritable, and, at the end of the war, Israel had seen a significant rise in domestic violence, with half a dozen murdered wives and the shelters for battered women filled beyond capacity (Sharoni 1994, 121–37).

In her work on gender and resistance in the Palestinian–Israeli conflict Simona Sharoni (1994, 123) traces the complex webs that connect and differentiate Palestinian and Israeli women: "Palestinian women have had to confront violence on two intimately related fronts: as members of the Palestinian community; and as women. Their homes and bodies have become the battlefields for these confrontations." But the Palestinian woman is not alone as Israeli women are also treated as occupied territories: their bodies are recruited for the national project of reproduction and their legal rights are restricted on numerous grounds (Sharoni 1994, 125). Sharoni emphasizes these connections between Israeli and Palestinian women because she believes that gender analysis could lead to alliances that would result in further understanding and compromise.

Conclusion

The women of Women in Black—an organization of Israeli women that has been demonstrating weekly against the occupation since 1988—often encounter verbal abuse. Men shout epithets at them, such as "whores of Arafat" or "Arab lovers," thus combining militarism with sexism (Sharoni 1994, 125). And here we have come a full circle: the Palestinian suicide bombers are Arafat's angels and the Israeli peace activists are Arafat's whores. Victims of patriarchal and nationalist history, and heroines by their own acts, these women, whether or not they foreground gender issues, choose to enact their subjectivity. But this subjectivity, especially when it chafes against the expectations of proper femininity, is sometimes coded as monstrous. The monstrosity, I believe, is entirely the creation of a fearful patriarchal imaginary, which cannot sustain the idea of capable, assertive, and violent femininity, and thus sets out to punish it.[22] Compounded with anti-Islamist, and anti-Arabic sentiments, the image of the female suicide bomber is projected back to us by a xenophobic and chauvinistic hegemonic mirror—the mirror of Western media. Not surprisingly then—and as a product of that hegemonic system—Colin Powell coined the term "homicide bombers." But in the Arab world these women are martyrs, freedom fighters, victims, and heroines who sacrifice everything for the sake of the nation. Both Israel and the world media marketed Israeli women fighters as innovative, egalitarian, and progressive, while they marketed Palestinian women fighters as individualistic, irrational, and barbaric. Wafa Idris volunteered in an ambulance for months during the Intifada, prompting Peter Beaumont to entitle his article "From an Angel of Mercy, to an Angel of Death" (*Guardian*, 31 January 2002). But Kitty, the Christian American nurse of *Exo-*

FIGURE 34   Scene from *Exodus*, 1960 (with permission of MGM).

dus, was willing to kill too, and this blonde angelic manifestation of woman-liness was never referred to as "an angel of death." The monster, I therefore con-clude, is in the eye (and mind) of the beholder.

Notes

1 I would like to thank the following friends and colleagues for reading this chapter and providing me with valuable criticism and suggestions: Benita Roth, Salma Abu-Ayyash, Elia Zureik, Nasrin Rahimieh, Susan Lord, and Annette Burfoot. This chap-ter is dedicated to my mother, Galit, Tal, Yael, Chana, Salma, Nahla, and the many other Palestinian and Israeli women in my life who keep an open dialogue, and who make an effort to believe in a life and a future for both of our peoples, despite the ever worsening situation in the Middle East.

2 It is unclear at this point whether the Palestinian female suicide bombers amount to a lasting sociological phenomenon. By March 2006 eight women had carried out successful suicide attacks. This chapter deals primarily with the first three, who killed themselves in the first few months of 2002.

3 This comparison requires some qualifications. At this historical moment (2006) Israel is a sovereign state with a strong army, while the Palestinians are stateless and with-out an army. This power structure has to be taken into account as one cannot discuss fighters without addressing the existence, or not, of an organized army. Still, the com-parison with which I am concerned focuses primarily on images of pre-state Israeli female fighters—a situation not dissimilar to the Palestinian predicament in that the Israelis were forbidden an organized and official army.

4 I should note here that, in comparison to the male suicide bombers, the women are humanized by being assigned an image, a name, and a life story. Still, within the context of gender expectations, they are demonized.

5 For a fuller discussion of *Silences of the Palace* see Naaman (2000).

6 In Tunisia, some laws have been instituted after independence prohibiting polygamy (for instance) and improving, at least to some extent, the rights of women.

7 For a fuller discussion of the "woman-nation" dyad see, for instance, Kaplan, Alarcón, and Moallem (1999); and Mclintock, Mufti, and Shohat (1997).

8 For a fuller discussion of the mother-nation dyad and the historical process of desexing the mother-nation, see Anzaldúa (1987); and Chatterjee (1993).

9 The Kibbutz is the ideological high point of Zionism. These collectives were established all over the country, the aim being to cultivate the land and to live communally according to the principles of socialism.

10 Data from *The Veiled Hope* (dir. Norma Marcus, 1994).

11 See also *A State of Danger*, a 1989 documentary by Jenny Morgan and Haim Bresheeth.

12 The United States recently used similar rhetoric to justify its bombing of Afghanistan. While women suffered severely under Taliban rule for over five years and the world did nothing to intervene on their behalf, the manhunt focused on Osama bin Laden was cynically marketed as an attempt to free Afghan women from an oppressive rule.

13 The Palmach was the armed wing of the Hagana, Israel's largest underground movement, which fought the British prior to 1948.

14 In a recent interview with *Ha'aretz*'s Adar Primor (19 April 2002), Jean-Marie Le Pen commented that Meir, like Margaret Thatcher, was "a true man" (19 April 2002).

15 It is important to mention here that it is particularly because the middle classes of Palestinian society are so hopeless that they rebel against occupation. Poor or rich, Palestinians in the West Bank and Gaza are restricted in almost every aspect of their life, robbed of nearly every freedom they deserve as human beings.

16 It is necessary to point out that male suicide bombers lose their subjectivity at the altar of the nation as they become Shaheeds (holy martyrs). However, this loss of subjectivity is not in any way a judgment pertaining to a lack in their gendered identity or sexuality.

17 While both cinematic and cultural figures who serve a primarily iconic function are always subject-less, in this case the iconicity is harnessed to produce specific narratives of national struggle.

18 For the Jewish code see Bloom (1993, 133). For Islam's attitudes see http://www.imra.org.il/story.php3?id=10155.

19 Ta'ayush is an Arab–Jewish partnership, a non-profit organization that emerged at the beginning of this Intifada and that attempts to provide humanitarian relief and to promote justice. To learn more about Ta'ayush see taayush.tripod.com.

20 More information on "The Jerusalem Link" and on "Women in Black" can be found on the website for the Coalition of Women for Peace at www.coalitionofwomen4peace.org.

21 *This Is Not Living* (dir. Alia Arasoughly, 2002).

22 There is a parallel here with post–Second World War film noir, in which women are assertive, sexual, and deviant. In these films they are usually punished by death or serious physical injury.

FIGURE 35 Prisoners tap dancing at Christmas concert, Kingston Prison for Women, 1952 (with permission from Canada's Penitentiary Museum Collection, Kingston, Ontario).

[sources]

Exhibitions

Holzer, Jenny. LUSTMORD. 1993. Haus der Kunst, Munich.

————. LUSTMORD. 1994. Barbara Gladstone Gallery, New York.

————. LUSTMORD. 1994. Bergen Museum of Art.

————. LUSTMORD. 1995. Monika Sprüth Galerie, Cologne.

————. LUSTMORD. 1996a. Kunstmuseum des Kanton Thurgau.

————. LUSTMORD. 1996b. Städtische Galerie Rähnitzgasse, Dresden.

Hutner, Simeon. No Humans Involved. 1993. USA: University of Southern California.

Lane, Abigail. Blueprint. 1992. Karsten Schubert, London.

————. Bottom Wallpaper. 1992. Group show, Kunsthalle, Lucerne.

————. Conspiracy Board Game. 1992. Karsten Schubert, London.

————. Making History. 1992. Karsten Schubert, London.

————. The Incident Room. 1993. Ha-Ha, Spacex Gallery, Exeter.

————. Bloody Wallpaper. 1997. Biennale-de-lyon, France.

————. Skin of the Teeth. 1995. Institute of Contemporary Arts, London, UK.

————. Still Lives. 1998. Museum of Contemporary Art, Chicago.

————. Whether the Roast Burns, the Train Leaves, or the Heavens Fall. 1998. Museum of Contemporary Art, Chicago.

————. Tomorrow's World, Yesterday's Fever (Mental Guests Incorporated). 2001. Milton Keynes Gallery, London, UK.

La Specola. Wax anatomical models. University of Florence, Italy.

Film and Television

ABC News. 1998. "A Closer Look: Women and the Death Penalty." Hosted by Peter Jennings. 13 January. USA.
The Accused. 1988. Jonathan Kaplan. USA.
Achchut Kanya/Untouchable Girl. 1936. Franz Osten. India.
Adua e le compagne. 1960. Antonio Pietrangeli. Italy.
Adynata. 1983. Leslie Thornton. USA.
Alien. 1979. Ridley Scott. USA.
Alien Resurrection. 1997. Jean-Pierre Jeunet. USA.
Alien 3. 1992. David Fincher. USA.
Aliens. 1986. James Cameron. USA.
Amar Prem/Eternal Love. 1973. Shakti Samanta. India.
Angst. 1983. Gerald Kargl. Austria.
Anjaam/Consequence. 1994. Rahul Rawail. India.
Antonia's Line. 1994. Marlene Gorris. Netherlands.
Aradhana/Prayer. 1969. Shakti Samanta. India.
Asylum. 1972. Roy Ward Baker. UK.
Attack of the 50-Foot Woman. 1958. Nathan Juran. USA.
Audition. 1999. Takashi Miike. Japan.
Aurat/Woman. 1940. Mehboob Khan. India.
L'avventura. 1959. Michelangelo Antonioni. Italy.
Bad Boys. 1995. Michael Bay. USA.
Baise-Moi. 1999. Virginie Despentes and Coralie Trinh Thi. France.
Bandini. 1963. Bimal Roy. India.
Basic Instinct. 1992. Paul Verhoeven. USA.
Battle of Algiers. 1965. Gillo Pontecorvo. Italy-Algeria.
The Bird with the Crystal Plumage. 1970. Dario Argento. Italy.
The Birds. 1963. Alfred Hitchcock. USA.
Black Widow. 1987. Bob Rafelson. USA.
Blowup. 1966. Michelangelo Antonioni. Italy-UK.
Blue Steel. 1990. Kathryn Bigelow. USA.
Body Beautiful. 1990. Ngosi Onwurah. UK.
The Body Snatcher. 1945. Robert Wise. USA.
The Book of Knives. 1996. Kim Derko. Canada.
Born in Flames. 1983. Lizzie Borden. USA.
The Bride with White Hair. 1993. Ronny Yu. China.
The Bride with White Hair 2. 1993. David Yu. China.
Broken Mirrors. 1984. Marlene Gorris. Netherlands.
Buddha's Palm/Yuloa Sunjeung (aka *Rulai Shenzhang*). 1964. Ling Wun. China.
The Burning Bed. 1984. Robert Greenwald. USA.
C.I.D. 1956. Raj Khosla. India.
The Cabinet of Dr. Caligari. 1919. Robert Weine. Germany.
Call Me. 1988. Sollace Mitchell. USA.

Candyman. 1992. Bernard Rose. USA.

Cape Fear. 1991. Martin Scorsese. USA.

La carne. 1991. Marco Ferreri. Italy.

Charlie's Angels. 2000. McG. USA.

Cherry Falls. 2000. Geoffrey Wright. USA.

Ciao maschio. 1977. Marco Ferreri. Italy-France.

City of Dreams. 2001. Gianfranco Norelli. USA: Palio Pictures, in association with the Canadian Broadcasting Corporation and the British Broadcasting Corporation.

Cliffhanger. 1993. Renny Harlin. USA.

CNN *Larry King Live.* 1998. Episode "Karla Faye Tucker: Live from Death-Row," 14 January. USA. Live transcript #98011400V22.

Come quando perché. 1969. Antonio Pietrangeli. Italy.

Cordélia. 1976. Jean Beaudin. Canada: National Film Board of Canada.

Crimes of the Heart. 1986. Bruce Beresford. USA.

Crouching Tiger, Hidden Dragon. 2000. Ang Lee. China.

The Crush. 1993. Alan Shapiro. USA.

Dahmer. 2002. David Jacobson. USA.

Damini/Lightning. 1994. Rajkumar Santoshi. India.

The Damned House of Hajn (a. k. a. *Invisible*). 1988. Jiri Svoboda. Czechoslovakia.

Daughter of Horror. 1955. John Parker. USA.

Deadful Melody. 1994. Ng Min-kan. China.

Deep Red. 1975. Dario Argento. Italy.

Deewar. 1975. Yash Chopra. India.

Defending Our Lives. 1993. Margaret Lazarus and Renner Wunderlich. USA: Cambridge Documentary Films.

Dementia. 1955. John Parker. USA: re-released as *Daughter of Horror,* 1957.

Dhund/Fog. 1973. B.R. Chopra. India.

Disclosure. 1994. Barry Levinson. USA.

Dolores Claiborne. 1993. Taylor Hackford. USA.

La donna scimmia. 1963. Marco Ferreri. Italy-France.

Double Indemnity. 1944. Billy Wilder. USA.

Double Team. 1997. Tsui Hark. USA.

Dracula 2000. 2000. Patrick Lussier. USA.

Dressed to Kill. 1980. Brian De Palma. USA.

Earth. 1999. Deepa Mehta. Canada.

L'eclisse [*The Eclipse*]. 1962. Michelangelo Antonioni. Italy.

Edtv. 1999. Ron Howard. USA.

Evening in Paris. 1967. Shakti Samanta. India.

"The Execution Tapes." 2001. *Sound Portraits,* Ray Suarez, National Public Radio. USA.

The Executioners. 1993. Johnny To and Ching Siu-tung. China.

Executive Decision. 1995. Stuart Baird. USA.

Exodus. 1960. Otto Preminger. USA.

Experiment Perilous. 1944. Jacques Tourneur. USA.

Extremities. 1986. Robert M. Young. USA.

Fair Game. 1995. Andrew Sipes. USA.

Fatal Attraction. 1987. Adrian Lyne. USA.

La Femme Nikita. 1990. Luc Besson. France.

Fire Dragon. 1994. Yuen Wo-ping. China.

Freeze Me. 2000. Takashi Ishii. Japan.

Friday the 13th. 1980. Sean S. Cunningham. USA.

Fried Green Tomatoes. 1991. Jon Avnet. USA.

Il futuro è donna. 1984. Marco Ferreri. Italy-France.

Gaslight. 1944. George Cukor. USA.

Gumrah/Deception. 1967. B.R. Chopra. India.

Halloween. 1978. John Carpenter. USA.

Halloween H2o. 1998. Steve Miner. USA.

The Hand That Rocks the Cradle. 1992. Curtis Hanson. USA.

Hannibal. 2001. Ridley Scott. UK-USA.

Haq/Rights. 1991. Harish Bhosle. India.

L'Harem. 1967. Marco Ferreri. Italy-France.

The Haunting. 1963. Robert Wise. UK.

The Haunting of Julia (a.k.a. *Full Circle*). 1978. Richard Loncraine. Canada-UK.

Heavenly Creatures. 1994. Peter Jackson. UK-Germany-New Zealand.

The Heroic Trio. 1993. Johnny To and Ching Siu-tung. China.

Hill 24 Doesn't Answer. 1955. Thorold Dickinson. Israel.

Hush. 1998. Jonathan Darby. USA.

Hush...Hush, Sweet Charlotte. 1964. Robert Aldrich. USA.

I Know What You Did Last Summer. 1997. Jim Gillespie. USA.

I Love You. 1986. Marco Ferreri. Italy-France.

I Spit on Your Grave (a.k.a. *Day of the Woman*). 1978. Meir Zarche. USA.

Insaaf ka Taraazu/Scales of Justice. 1980. B.R. Chopra. India.

Intikaam/The Test. 1968. R.K. Nayyar. India.

Io la cononsceva bene. 1965. Antonio Pietrangeli. Italy.

Iron Monkey: The Young Wong Fei Hung. 1993. Yuen Wo-ping. China.

Jeanne Dielman, 23 quai du commerce, 1080 Bruxelles. 1975. Chantal Akerman. Belgium.

Jewel Thief. 1967. Vijay Anand. India.

Juarez, The City of Dead Women. 1998. J.M. Hostate and J.B. Gallot. France: Tony Comiti Productions.

Julie. 1975. K.S. Sethumadhavan. India.

Juliet of the Spirits. 1965. Federico Fellini. Italy.

Junglee/Uncouth. 1960. Subodh Mukherjee. India.

Kashmir ki Kali/Flower of Kashmir. 1963. Shakti Samanta. India.

Kati Patang/Falling Kite. 1972. Shakti Samanta. India.

The Killer. 1989. John Woo. China.

The Ladies Club. 1986. Janet Greek. USA.

Lara Croft: Tomb Raider. 2001. Simon West. USA.

The Last Seduction. 1994. John Dahl. USA.

"Legacy of Pain." *The Fifth Estate.* 1999. Neil Docherty and Francine Pelletier. CBC. 1 December.

Lethal Weapon. 1987. Richard Donner. USA.

Lethal Weapon 2. 1989. Richard Donner. USA.

Life with Billy. 1994. Paul Donovan. Canada.

Lipstick. 1976. Lamont Johnson. USA.

The Long Kiss Goodnight. 1996. Renny Harlin. USA.

Loyalties. 1986. Anne Wheeler. Canada.

M. 1931. Fritz Lang. Germany.

Mamta/Maternal Love. 1966. Asit Sen. India.

Man Bites Dog. 1992. Rémy Belvaux, André Bonzel, and Benoît Poelvoorde. Belgium.

Maquila: A Tale of Two Mexicos. 2000. Sonia Angulo and Saul Landau. USA: Cinema Guild.

The Matrix. 1999. Andy Wachowski and Larry Wachowski. USA.

The Matrix Reloaded. 2003. Andy Wachowski and Larry Wachowski. USA.

Metropolis. 1926. Fritz Lang. Germany.

Meshes of the Afternoon. 1943. Maya Deren and Alexander Hammid. USA.

Misery. 1990. Rob Reiner. USA.

Mother India. 1957. Mehboob Khan. India.

Mother's Day. 1980. Charles Kaufman. USA.

Mourir à tue-tête. 1979. Anne Claire Poirier. Canada/Quebec.

Ms. 45. 1981. Abel Ferrara. USA.

Murder and Murder. 1996. Yvonne Rainer. USA.

Naked Vengeance. 1985. Cirio H. Santiago. USA.

Nata di marzo. 1957. Antonio Pietrangeli. Italy.

Natural Born Killers. 1994. Oliver Stone. USA.

"Newsworld Reports." 1999. *Newsworld.* CBC. 6 December.

Night Cries: A Rural Tragedy. 1990. Tracey Moffatt. Australia.

The Night Porter. 1974. Liliana Cavani. Italy.

The Notorious Mrs. Dick. 2001. Anne Pick. Canada: Real to Reel Productions Inc. in association with CTV.

The Numerology of Fear. 1999. Janine Marchessault. Canada.

Nurse Betty. 2000. Neil LaBute. USA.

Offensive to Some. 1996. Play by Berni Stapleton. Canada.

Office Killer. 1997. Cindy Sherman. USA.

The Old Dark House. 1932. James Whale. USA.

Opera. 1987. Dario Argento. Italy.

La parmigiana. 1963. Antonio Pietrangeli. Italy.

Pati Patni aur Who/Husband, Wife and the Other. 1978. B.R. Chopra. India.

Performing the Border. 1999. Ursula Bieman. Mexico/USA.

Peeping Tom. 1960. Michael Powell. UK.

The Piano. 1993. Jane Campion. Australia.

Play Misty for Me. 1971. Clint Eastwood. USA.

Pleasantville. 1998. Gary Ross. USA.

Poison Ivy. 1992. Katt Shea. USA.

Police Lock Up. 1992. K.V. Raju. India.

The Postman Always Rings Twice. 1946. Tay Garnett. USA.

Pratighaat/Retribution. 1987. N. Chandra. India.

Prom Night. 1980. Paul Lynch. Canada.

The Provoked Wife. 1991. Victoria Mapplebeck and Peter Day. UK: Faction Films.

Psycho. 1960. Alfred Hitchcock. USA.

A Question of Silence. 1982. Marlene Gorris. Netherlands.

Rebecca. 1940. Alfred Hitchcock. USA.

The Red Desert. 1964. Michelangelo Antonioni. Italy.

Repulsion. 1965. Roman Polanski. UK.

Sangam/Confluence. 1964. Raj Kapoor. India.

Savage Streets. 1984. Danny Steinmann. USA.

Scream. 1996. Wes Craven. USA.

Secret beyond the Door. 1948. Fritz Lang. USA.

Semiotics of the Kitchen. 1974. Martha Rosler. USA.

Senorita Extraviada: Missing Young Woman. 2001. Lourdes Portillo. USA: Xochitl Films.

Seven. 1995. David Fincher. USA.

Seven Women, Seven Sins. 1987. Bette Gordon, Maxi Cohen, Helke Sander, Ulrike Ottinger, Chantal Akerman, Valie Export, Laurence Gavron. Belgium/France/USA/Austria/West Germany.

Shame. 1987. Steve Jodrell. Australia.

The Silence of the Lambs. 1991. Jonathan Demme. USA.

Silences of the Palace. 1994. Moufida Tlatli. Tunisia-France.

Single White Female. 1992. Barbet Schroeder. USA.

Sisters. 1973. Brian De Palma. USA.

The Sky Is Falling. 2002. Chris Castillo. USA.

Sleepaway Camp. 1983. Robert Hiltzik. USA. 1983.

The Smiling Madame Beudet. 1923. Germaine Dulac. France.

So Evil, My Sister (a.k.a. *Psycho Sisters*). 1972. Reginald Le Borg. USA.

Il sole negli occhi. 1953. Antonio Pietrangeli. Italy.

A State of Danger. 1989. Jenny Morgan and Haim Bresheeth. UK.

The Stendhal Syndrome. 1996. Dario Argento. Italy.

Stories from the Riverside. 1994. Susanne Mason. USA: Filmakers.

Strait-Jacket. 1964. William Castle. USA.

Strange Days. 1995. Kathryn Bigelow. USA.

Sujata. 1959. Bimal Roy. India.

Sur Name Viet, Given Name Nam. 1989. Trinh T. Minh-Ha. USA.
Suspicion. 1941. Alfred Hitchcock. USA.
Suspiria. 1977. Dario Argento. Italy.
Swimfan. 2002. John Polson. USA.
The Swordsman. 1990. King Hu. China.
Tai Chi Master. 1993. Yuen Wo-ping. China.
A Tale of Love. 1995. Trinh T. Minh-Ha. USA.
Teesri Manzil/Third Floor. 1965. Vijay Anand. India.
Tell Me Something. 1999. Yoon-Hyun Chang. South Korea.
The Terminator. 1984. James Cameron. USA.
Terminator 2: Judgment Day. 1991. James Cameron. USA.
Terror Train. 1980. Roger Spottiswoode. USA-Canada.
The Terrorist. 2000. Santosh Sivan. India.
Thelma and Louise. 1991. Ridley Scott. USA.
Thief of Hearts. 1984. Douglas Day Stewart. USA.
This Is Not Living. 2002. Alia Arasoughly. Palestine.
Thriller. 1979. Sally Potter. England.
To Die For. 1995. Gus Van Sant. USA.
Torso. 2002. Alex Chapple. Canada.
The Truman Show. 1998. Peter Weir. USA.
Twister. 1996. Jan de Bont. USA.
Two Lies. 1990. Pam Tom. USA.
L'ultima donna. 1975. Marco Ferreri. Italy-France.
Underexposed: The Temple of the Fetus. 1993. Kathy High. USA.
Valentine. 2001. Jamie Blanks. USA.
The Veiled Hope. 1994. Norma Marcos. France.
Videodrome. 1983. David Cronenberg. Canada.
Violated. 1984. Richard Cannistraro. USA.
La visita. 1963. Antonio Pietrangeli. Italy.
Wag the Dog. 1997. Barry Levinson. USA.
The Watcher. 2000. Joe Charbanic. USA.
Wedding in Galilee. 1987. Michel Khleifi. Palestine-Belgium.
What Ever Happened to Baby Jane? 1962. Robert Aldrich. USA.
When Women Kill. 1994. Barbara Doran. Canada: Morag Productions.
White-Boned Sword/Bakgwud Yumyeung Geem. 1962. Ling Wun. China.
Why Women Kill. 1992. UK: BBC Worlwide.
Wing Chun. 1994. Yuen Wo-ping. China.
The Women Next Door. 1992. Michal Aviad. Israel.
Women Who Kill. 1994. USA: Films for the Humanities and Science.
Zabriskie Point. 1970. Michelangelo Antonioni. Italy-USA.
Zakhmi Aurat/Wounded Woman. 1988. Avtar Bhogal. India.

References

Abdo, Nahla, and Ronit Lentin, eds. 2002. *Women and the Politics of Military Confrontation: Palestinian and Israeli Gendered Narratives of Dislocation.* New York: Berghahn.

Agger, Inger. 1993. *The Blue Room: Trauma and Testimony among Refugee Women— A Psychosocial Experience.* London: Zed.

Allen, H. 1987. "Rendering Them Harmless: The Professional Portrayal of Women Charged with Serious Violent Crimes." In *Gender, Crime and Justice,* ed. P. Carlen and A. Worrall, 81–94. Milton Keynes: Open University Press.

Almodovar, Norma J. 1993. *Cop to Call Girl: Why I Left the LAPD to Make an Honest Living as a Beverly Hills Prostitute.* New York: Simon and Schuster.

Amnesty International. 2004. *Stolen Sisters: Discrimination and Violence against Indigenous Women in Canada: A Summary of Amnesty International's Concerns.* http://web.amnesty.org/library/Index/ENGAMR200012004. Accessed: 27 March 2006.

Anderson, Walter Truett, ed. 1995. *The Truth about the Truth: De-confusing and Re-Constructing the Postmodern World.* New York: Tarcher/Putnam.

Anzaldúa, Gloria. 1987. *Borderlands/La Frontera: The New Mestiza.* San Francisco: Aunt Lute.

Artz, Sybille. 1998. *Sex, Power, and the Violent School Girl.* Toronto: Trifolium Books.

Bal, Mieke. 1995. "Reading the Gaze: The Construction of Gender in 'Rembrandt.'" In *Vision and Textuality,* ed. Stephen Melville and Bill Readings, 147–73. London: Macmillan.

———. 1996a. *Double Exposure: The Subject of Cultural Analysis.* London: Routledge.

———. 1996b. "The Gaze in the Closet." In *Vision in Context: Historical and Contemporary Perspectives on Sight,* ed. Teresa Brennan and Martin Jay, 139–54. New York: Routledge.

———. 2001. *Looking In: The Art of Viewing.* Amsterdam: Gordon and Breach.

Balasubrahmanyan, Vimal. 1990. *In Search of Justice: Women, Law, Landmark Judgements, and Media.* Bombay: Shubhada Saraswat Prakashan.

Baldauf, Scott. 1998. "Death Row Has Its Own Gender Gap." *Christian Science Monitor* 90, 40, 23 January.

Balmain, Colette. 2002. "Female Subjectivity and the Politics of 'Becoming Other': Dario Argento's *La sindrome di Stendhal* (*The Stendhal Syndrome,* 1996)." *Kinoeye* 2, 12 (24 June). http://www.kinoeye.org/02/12/balmain12.html. Accessed 27 March 2006).

Bannerji, Himani. 2002. "A Question of Silence: Reflections on Violence against Women in Communities of Colour." In *Violence against Women: New Canadian Perspectives,* ed. Katherine M.J. McKenna and June Larkin, 353–70. Toronto: Inanna.

Barthes, Roland. 1974. *S/Z.* New York: Noonday.

———. 1981. *Camera Lucida*. New York: Hill and Wang.

———. 1988. *Image/Music/Text*. Trans. Stephen Heath. New York: Noonday Books.

Bataille, Georges. 1962. *Death and Sensuality: A Study of Eroticism and Taboo*. New York: Walker.

Baudrillard, Jean. 1983. *Simulations*. New York: Semiotext.

———. 1988. *The Ecstasy of Communication*. New York: Semiotext.

———. 1998. *Jean Baudrillard: Selected Writings*. Ed. Mark Poster. Stanford, CA: Stanford University Press.

———. 1999. "The Precession of Simulacra." In *The Blackwell Companion in Contemporary Social Theory*, ed. Anthony Elliot, 327–37. London: Blackwell.

Beatty, Sally. 2002. "Couch Tater Tots." *Wall Street Journal*, 1 April.

Bell, V. 1999. "Mimesis as Cultural Survival: Judith Butler and Anti-Semitism." In *Performativity and Belonging*, ed. V. Bell, 133–62. London: Sage.

Benedict, Helen. 1992. *Virgin or Vamp: How the Press Covers Sex Crimes*. New York: Oxford University Press.

Benjamin, J. 1984. "Master and Slave: The Fantasy of Erotic Domination." In *Desire: The Politics of Sexuality*, ed. A. Snitow, C. Stansell, and S. Thompson, 292–311. London: Virago.

Bernardo v Queen (unreported). Ontario Crown Court 1 May 1995.

Bernier, Joanne, and André Cellard. 1996. "Le syndrome de la femme fatale: 'Maricide' et représentation féminine au Québec, 1898–1940." *Criminologie* 24, 2: 29–48.

Birch, Helen. 1993. "If Looks Could Kill: Myra Hindley and the Iconography of Evil." In *Moving Targets: Women, Murder and Representation*, ed. Helen Birch, 32–61. London: Virago.

Birnbaum, Lucia Chiavola. 1986. *Liberazione Della Donna: Feminism in Italy*. Middletown, CT: Wesleyan University Press.

Blazwick, Iwona, and Richard Shone, eds. 1995. *Abigail Lane*. London: ICA.

Bloom, Anne R. 1993. "Women in the Defense Forces." In *Calling the Equity Bluff: Women in Israel*, ed. Barbara Swirski and Marilyn P. Safir, 128–39. New York: Teacher's College Press.

Bociurkiw, Marusia. 1990. "Je Me Souviens: A Response to the Montreal Killings." *Fuse* 13, 4: 6–10.

Bonaparte, M. 1995. "Some Biophysical Aspects of Sado-Masochism." In *Essential Papers on Masochism*, ed. M.A.F. Hanly, 432–52. New York: New York University Press.

Boozer, Jack. 2002. *Career Movies: American Business and the Success Mystique*. Austin: University of Texas Press.

Bordo, Susan R. 1987. *The Flight to Objectivity: Essays on Cartesianism and Culture*. Albany, NY: SUNY Press.

Braidotti, Rosi. 1991. *Patterns of Dissonance: A Study of Women in Contemporary Philosophy*. Trans. Elizabeth Guild. New York: Routledge.

———. 1994. *Nomadic Subjects*. New York: Columbia University Press.

Brasher, Brenda. 1999. "Women at the End of the World: Christian Fundamentalist Millenarianism as an Engendering Machine." *Journal of Millennial Studies* 2, 1 (Summer). http://www.mille.org/publications/summer99/brasher.pdf. Accessed 27 March 2006.

Brennan, Teresa, and Martin Jay, eds. 1996. *Vision in Context: Historical and Contemporary Perspectives on Sight.* London: Routledge.

Bronfen, Elisabeth. 1992. *Over Her Dead Body: Death, Femininity and the Aesthetic.* Manchester/New York: Manchester University Press/Routledge.

Bronson, D. (1989) "A Time for Grief and Pain," *Globe and Mail,* 8 December: A7.

Brown, Wendy. 2001. *Politics out of History.* Princeton: Princeton University Press.

Brownmiller, Susan. 1976. *Against Our Will: Men, Women, and Rape.* New York: Bantam.

Brunetta, Gian Piero. 1998. *Storia del cinema italiano: Dal neorealismo al miracolo economico 1945–1959.* 3rd ed. Rome: Editori Riuniti.

Buckley, Réka C.V. 2000. "National Body: Gina Lollobrigida and the Cult of the Star in the 1950s." *Historical Journal of Film, Radio, and Television* 20, 4: 527–47.

Bundtzen, Lynda K. 1987. "Monstrous Mothers: Medusa, Grendel, and Now Alien." *Film Quarterly* 15, 3: 11–17.

Burnside, S., and S. Cairns. 1995. *Deadly Innocence.* New York: Warner.

Butler, Judith. 1990a. *Gender Trouble: Feminism and the Subversion of Identity.* New York: Routledge.

———. 1990b. "Performative Acts and Gender Constitution: An Essay in Phenomenology and Feminist Theory." In *Performing Feminisms: Feminist Critical Theory and Theatre,* ed. S.E. Case, 270–82. Baltimore, MD: Johns Hopkins University Press.

———. 1997. *The Psychic Life of Power.* Stanford, CA: Stanford University Press.

Butler, Margot Leigh. 2000. "Epistemology, Politics, and Subjectivity in Artists' Collective Projects." PhD diss., Goldsmiths College, University of London, UK.

———. 2001a. "Making Waves." *Women's Studies International Forum* 24, 3/4: 387–99.

———. 2001b. "Swarms in Bee Space." *West Coast Line* 35, 2 (Fall). http://www.sfu.ca/west-coast-line/covers/butler.pdf. Accessed 21 March 2006.

———. 2004a. "The Hero of *Heroines.*" *Mosaic: A Journal for the Interdisciplinary Study of Literature* 37, 4: 275–97.

———. 2004b. "Missing Sarah." *The rain Review of Books,* September/October: 4.

Cadieux, Pauline. 1979. *La lampe dans la fenêtre.* Montreal: Libre Expression.

Caldwell, John. 1995. *Televisuality: Style, Crisis, and Authority in American Television.* New Brunswick, NJ: Rutgers University Press.

Califia, Pat. 1994. *Public Sex: The Culture of Radical Sex.* San Francisco: Cleis Press.

———. 1993. *Sensuous Magic.* New York: Masquerade.

Cameron, D., and E. Fraser. 1987. *The Lust to Kill.* New York: New York University Press.

Campbell, M. Freeman. 1974. *Bloody Matrimony: Evelyn Dick and the Torso Murder Case.* Toronto: Penguin.

Canino, Frank. 2000. *The Angelina Project*. Toronto: Guernica.

Capecchi, Saveria, and Cristina Demaria. 1997. "Gender Representation in the News." *Server Donne*. http://www.women.it/cyberarchive/files/capecchi_demaria.htm. Accessed 27 March 2006.

Caputi, J. 1988. *The Age of Sex Crime*. London: Women's Press.

Carlen, Pat. 1983. *Women's Imprisonment: A Study in Social Control*. London: Routledge and Kegan Paul.

Carlino, Andrea. 1999. *Books of the Body: Anatomical Ritual and Renaissance Learning*. Trans. John Tedeschi and Anne C. Tedeschi. Chicago: University of Chicago Press.

Carter, A. 1979. *The Sadeian Woman*. London: Virago.

Cartwright, Lisa. 1998. "A Cultural Anatomy of the Visible Human Project." In *The Visible Woman: Imaging Technologies, Gender, and Science*, ed. Paula Treichler, Lisa Cartwright, and Constance Penley, 21–43. New York: New York University Press.

Caruth, C. (ed.) 1995. *Trauma: Explorations in Memory*. Baltimore: Johns Hopkins University Press.

Cernea, Adrian. 1999. *Poly 1989: Témoin de l'horreur*. Montréal: Éditions Lescop.

Chatterjee, Partha. 1993. *The Nation and Its Fragments: Colonial and Postcolonial Histories*. Princeton, NJ: Princeton University Press.

Chun, Wendy Hui Kyong. 1999. "Unbearable Witness: Toward a Politics of Listening." *Differences: A Journal of Feminist Cultural Studies* 11, 1: 112–49.

Clarkes, Lincoln. 2002. *Heroines*. Vancouver: Anvil.

Clover, Carol J. 1992. *Men, Women, and Chain Saws: Gender in the Modern Horror Film*. Princeton, NJ: Princeton University Press.

———. 1993. "High and Low: The Transformation of the Rape-Revenge Movie." In *Women and Film: A Sight and Sound Reader*, ed. Pam Cook and Philip Dodd. Philadelphia: Temple University Press.

Copeland, Roger. 1990. "The Presence of Mediation." *Drama Review* 34, 4 (Winter): 28–44.

Court TV. 1998. "Court TV Legal Documents: Karla Faye Tucker Death Penalty Appeal." http://courttv-web2.courttv.com/archive/legaldocs/newsmakers/tucker/tucker1.html. Accessed 27 March 2006.

Creed, Barbara. 1990. "*Alien* and the Monstrous Feminine." In *Alien Zone: Cultural Theory and Contemporary Science Fiction Cinema*, ed. Annette Kuhn, 128–41. London: Verso.

———. 1993. *The Monstrous-Feminine: Film, Feminism, Psychoanalysis*. London: Routledge.

Crosbie, Lynn. 1997. *Paul's Case: The Kingston Letters*. Toronto: Insomniac Press.

Davey, Frank. 1994. *Karla's Web: A Cultural Investigation of the Mahaffy–French Murders*. Toronto: Viking-Penguin.

Davies, Michael. 2000. "'What's the Story Mother?': Abjection and Anti-Feminism in *Alien* and *Aliens*." *Gothic Studies* 2, 2: 245–56.

Davis, Keith, Irene Hanson Frieze, and Roland Maiuro, eds. 2002. *Stalking: Perspectives on Victims and Perpetrators*. New York: Springer.

de Beauvoir, Simone. 1949. *The Second Sex*. Harmondsworth: Penguin.

De Certeau, Michel. 1988. *The Writing of History*. Trans. Tom Conley. New York: Columbia University Press.

De Lauretis, Teresa. 1987. "The Violence of Rhetoric: Considerations on Representation and Gender." In *Technologies of Gender: Essays on Theory, Film and Fiction*, 31–50. Bloomington: Indiana University Press.

de Sade, D.A.F. 1966. *Justine: Philosophy in the Bedroom: Eugénie de Franval, and Other Writings*. Trans. R. Seaver and A. Wainhouse. New York: Grove Press.

De Vries, Maggie. 2003. *Missing Sarah: A Vancouver Woman Remembers Her Vanished Sister*. Toronto: Penguin.

Della Casa, Stefano. 2000. *Dario Argento, il brivido della critica: scritti sul cinema*. Turin: Testo and Immagine.

Derrida, Jacques. 1976. *Of Grammatology*. Translated by Gayatri Spivak. Baltimore: Johns Hopkins University Press.

———. 1996. "Structure, Sign, and Play in the Discourse of the Human Sciences." In *Knowledge and Postmodernism in Historical Perspective*, ed. Joyce Appleby, Elizabeth Covington, David Hoyt, Michael Latham, and Allison Sneider, 437–48. New York: Routledge.

Doane, Mary Ann. 1988. "Woman's Stake: Filming the Female Body." In *Feminism and Film Theory*, ed. Constance Penley, 216–28. New York: Routledge.

———. 1990. "Technohilia: technology, Representation, and the Feminine." In *Body Politics*, ed. Mary Jacobus, Evelyn Fox Keller, Sally Shuttleworth, 163–76. New York and London: Routledge.

Docherty, N. (producer) and F. Pelletier (co-producer). 1999. "Legacy of Pain" (video-recording), *Fifth Estate*, Canadian Broadcasting Corporation. Aired 1 December.

Dorland, Michael, and Priscilla Walton. 1996. "Untangling Karla's Web: Post-National Arguments and Cross-Border Crimes." *American Review of Canadian Studies* 26, 1: 31–48.

Dubinsky, Karen, and Franca Iacovetta. 1991. "Murder, Womanly Virtue, and Motherhood: The Case of Angelina Napolitano, 1911–1922." *Canadian Historical Review* 72, 4: 505–31.

du Gay, Paul. 1997. "Organizing Identity: Making Up People at Work." In *Production of Culture/Cultures of Production*, ed. Paul du Gay, 285–322. London: Sage.

Duggan, Lisa, Nan D. Hunter, and Carole S. Vance. 1989. "False Promises: Feminist Antipornography Legislation." In *Caught Looking: Feminism, Pornography and Censorship*, ed. Kate Ellis et al., 72–85. Seattle: Real Comet.

Dworkin, A. 1981. *Pornography*. London: Women's Press.

———. 1983. *Right Wing Women*. London: Women's Press.

Dworkin, Andrea, and Catherine A. MacKinnon. 1993. "Questions and Answers." In *Making Violence Sexy: Feminist Views on Pornography*, ed. Diane E.H. Russell, 78–96. New York and London: Teachers College Press.

Early, Frances, and Kathleen Kennedy, eds. 2003. *Athena's Daughters: Television's New Women Warriors*. Syracuse: Syracuse University Press.

Ehrenreich, Barbara. 1995. *The Snarling Citizen*. New York: Harper Collins.

Elsaesser, Thomas. 1987. "Tales of Sound and Fury: Observations on the Family Melodrama." In *Home Is Where the Heart Is: Studies in Melodrama and the Woman's Film*, ed. Christine Gledhill, 68–91. London: BFI.

Ermarth, Elizabeth Deeds. 1992. *Sequel to History: Postmodernism and the Crisis of Representational Time*. Princeton: Princeton University Press.

Erickson, Glenn. 2002. "Review of *Dementia*." DVD Savant. http://www.dvdtalk.com/dvdsavant/s149dementia.html. Accessed 27 March 2006.

Fahmy, Pauline, ed. 1994. *Events of Polytechnique: Analyses and Proposals for Action*. Trans. Gisèle Landry. Ottawa: Canadian Research Institute for the Advancement of Women.

Faith, Karlene. 1993. *Unruly Women: The Politics of Confinement and Resistance*. Vancouver: Press Gang.

Feaver, William. 1995. "Marvelous Sightings: Abigail Lane." *ARTnews Special Issue*.

Felman, Shoshana, and Dori Laub. 1992. *Testimony: Crises of Witnessing in Literature, Psychoanalysis and History*. New York and London: Routledge.

Fennelly, Carol. 1998. "To Die For." *Sojourners* 27, 4 (July/August): 14–15. http://www.sojo.net/archives/magazine/index.cfm/action/sojourners/issue/soj9807/article/980741d.html. Accessed 27 March 2006.

Findlen, Paula. 1996. *Possessing Nature: Museums, Collecting and Scientific Culture in Early Modern Italy*. Berkeley: University of California Press.

Firmstone, Julie. 2002. *Discerning Eyes: Viewers on Violence*. Luton, UK: University of Luton Press.

Fitzroy, L. 1997. "Mother / Daughter Rape: A Challenge for Feminism." In *Women's Encounters with Violence: Australian Experiences*, ed. S. Cook and J. Bessant, 40–54. Thousand Oaks, CA: Sage.

Flood, Richard, ed.1996. *Brilliant! New Art from London*. Minneapolis: Walker Art Center.

Fogiel-Bijaoui, Sylvie. 1992. "From Revolution to Motherhood: The Status of Women on the Kibbutz, 1910–1948." In *Pioneers and Homemakers: Jewish Women in Pre-State Israel*, ed. Deborah S. Bernstein, 211–33. Albany, NY: SUNY Press.

Fontana Dictionary of Modern Thought. 1977. London: Fontana.

Foucault, Michel. 1987. "The Ethic of Care for the Self as a Practice of Freedom: An Interview with Michel Foucault on January 20, 1984." Interviewed by Raul Fornet-Betancourt, Helmut Becker, and Alfredo Gomez-Muller. *Philosophy and Social Criticism* 12, 2/3 (Summer): 112–31.

———. 1994. *The Order of Things*. New York: Vintage.

———. 2001. *Fearless Speech*, ed. Joseph Pearson. Los Angeles: Semiotext.

French, Karl. 1997. *Screen Violence*. London: Bloomsbury.

French, S. 1996. "Partners in Crime." In *No Angels: Women Who Commit Violence*, ed. A. Myers and S. Wight. London: Pandora.

Freud, S. 1957 [1915]. "Instincts and Their Vicissitudes." In *The Standard Edition of the Complete Psychological Works of Sigmund Freud*, Vol. 14, ed. and trans. J. Strachey, 117–40. London: Hogarth.

———. 1977. *Three Essays on Sexuality*. Ed. A. Richards, Trans. J. Strachey. Harmondsworth: Penguin.

———. 1978 [1919]. "A Child Is Being Beaten." In *Sexuality and the Psychology of Love*, ed. P. Rieff, 107–32. New York: Collier.

Friedan, Betty. 1963. *The Feminine Mystique*. New York: Norton.

Frigon, Sylvie. 1995. "When Women Kill Violent Husbands in Canada, 1871–1946: Drama, Disqualification of Women's Voices, Resistance, and Male Tyranny." Paper presented at the British Criminology Conference, University of Loughborough, UK, 18–21 July.

———. 1996. "L'homicide conjugal féminin, de Marie-Josèphe Corriveau (1763) à Angélique Lyn Lavallée (1990): meurtre ou légitime défense?" *Criminologie* 24, 2: 11–28.

———. 1999. "Tuer pour survivre: récits de femmes belges, françaises et canadiennes." *Recherches féministes* 12, 2: 139–58.

———. 2000. "Corps, féminités et dangerosité: de la production de 'corps dociles' en criminologie." In *Du corps des femmes: contrôles, surveillances et résistances*, ed. Sylvie Frigon and Michèle Kérisit, 127–64. Ottawa: University of Ottawa Press.

———. 2001. "Paroles incarcérées: Corps et perspectives des femmes." In *Mémoires de femmes, paroles de femmmes*, ed. Lucie Hotte and Linda Cardinal, 49–82. Montreal: Les éditions du Remue-ménage.

———. 2002. *Maricide*. Montreal: Les éditions du Remue-ménage.

Frosh, Stephen. 1987. *The Politics of Psychoanalysis*. New Haven: Yale University Press.

Gadoury, Lorraine, and Antoine Lechasseur. 1994. *Persons Sentenced to Death in Canada, 1867–1976*. Ottawa: National Archives of Canada.

Gallant, Chris, ed. 2000. *Art of Darkness: The Cinema of Dario Argento*. Guildford, UK: FAB Press.

Gallop, J. 1997. *Feminist Accused of Sexual Harassment*. Durham, NC: Duke University Press.

Gatrell, Vic. 1994. *The Hanging Tree: Executions and the English People, 1770–1868*. New York: Oxford University Press.

Gavigan, Shelley. 1989. "Petit Treason in Eighteenth Century England: Women's Inequality before the Law." *Canadian Journal of Women and the Law* 3, 2: 335–74.

Ghosh, Shohini. 1996. "Deviant Pleasures and Disorderly Women." In *Feminist Terrains and Legal Domains: Interdisciplinary Essays on Women and Law in India*, ed. Ratna Kapur, 150–83. New Delhi: Kali for Women.

Giacaman, Rita, and Penny Johnson. 1989. "Palestinian Women: Building Barricades and Breaking Barriers." In *Intifada: The Palestinian Uprising against Israeli Occupation*, ed. Zachery Lockman and Joel Benin, 155–69. Boston: South End Press.

Ginsborg, Paul. 1990. *A History of Contemporary Italy: Society and Politics, 1943–1988*. New York: Penguin.

Gledhill, Christine, ed. 1987. *Home Is Where the Heart Is: Studies in Melodrama and the Woman's Film*. London: BFI.

Gopal, Priyamvada. 1997. "Of Victims and Vigilantes: The *Bandit Queen* Controversy." *Thamyris, Gender in the Making: Indian Contexts* 4, 1: 73–102.

Gopalan, Lalitha. 1997. "Avenging Women in Indian Cinema." *Screen* 38, 1: 42–59.

Griffin, S. 1981. *Pornography and Silence: Culture's Revenge against Nature*. London: Women's Press.

Gross, D. 2000. *Lost Time: On Remembering and Forgetting in Late Modern Culture*. Amherst: University of Massachusetts Press.

Guillaumin, Colette. 1991. "Madness and the Social Norm." Trans. Mary Jo Lakehead. *Feminist Issues* 11, 2: 10–15.

Hall, Edward T. 1966. *The Hidden Dimension: Man's Use of Space in Public and Private*. London: Bodley Head.

Hamilton Spectator. 1999. 'Vigil Honours Victims of Massacre', 3 December: NO5. (no author).

Hanssen, Beatrice. 2000. *Critique of Violence: Between Postculturalism and Critical Theory*. New York: Routledge.

Haraway, Donna. 1991a. "The Actors Are Cyborg, Nature Is Coyote, and the Geography Is Elsewhere." Postscript to "Cyborgs at Large." In *Technoculture*, ed. Constance Penley and Andrew Ross, 21–26. Minneapolis: University of Minnesota Press.

———. 1991b. *Simians, Cyborgs, and Women: The Reinvention of Nature*. London: Free Association Books.

———. 1997. *Modest_Witness@Second_Millenium.FemaleMan©_Meets_OncoMouse™*. London: Routledge.

Hart, L. 1998. *Between the Body and the Flesh: Performing Sadomasochism*. New York: Columbia University Press.

Hellman, Judith Adler. 1987. *Journeys among Women: Feminism in Five Italian Cities*. Cambridge, UK: Polity.

Higgins, Lynn, and Brenda A. Silver. 1991. "Introduction." In *Rape and Representation*, ed. Lynn Higgins and Brenda A. Silver, 263–77. New York: Columbia University Press.

Holly, Michael Ann. 1995. "Past Looking." In *Vision and Textuality*, ed. Stephen Melville and Bill Readings, 67–89. London: Macmillan.

hooks, bell. 1989. *Talking Back: Thinking Feminist, Thinking Black*. Boston: South End.

———. 1990. *Yearning: Race, Gender, and Cultural Politics*. Toronto: Between the Lines.

———. 1992. *Black Looks: Race and Representation*. Toronto: Between the Lines.

Hunt, Leon. 2000. "A (Sadistic) Night at the *Opera*." In *The Horror Reader*, ed. Ken Gelder, 324–35. London: Routledge.

Ingham, Helen. 1995 "The Portrayal of Women on Television." *Media and Communications Studies Site*. Aberystwyth, UK: University of Wales, Aberystwyth. http://www.aber.ac.uk/media/Students/hzi9401.html. Accessed 27 March 2006.

Inness, Sherrie A. 1999. *Tough Girls: Women Warriors and Wonder Women in Popular Culture.* Philadelphia: University of Pennsylvania Press.

Irigaray, L. 1985. *This Sex Which Is Not One.* Trans. C. Porter. New York: Cornell University Press.

Jayamanne, Laleen. 2001. *Toward Cinema and Its Double: Cross-Cultural Mimesis.* Bloomington and Indianapolis: Indiana University Press.

Johnson, Richard. 1999. "Exemplary Differences: Mourning (and Not Mourning) a Princess." In *Mourning Diana: Nation, Culture and the Performance of Grief,* ed. Adrian Kear and Deborah Lynn Steinberg, 15–39. London and New York: Routledge.

Jones, Alan. 1983. "Argento." *Cinefantastique* 18 (March): 20.

Jordanova, Ludmilla. 1989. *Sexual Visions: Images of Gender in Science and Medicine between the Eighteenth and Nineteenth Centuries.* Madison: University of Wisconsin Press.

Kannabiran, Kalpana. 1996. "Rape and the Construction of Communal Identity." In *Embodied Violence: Communalising Women's Identity in South Asia,* ed. Kumari Jayawardena and Malathi de Alwis, 32–41. New Delhi: Kali for Women.

Kapadia, Karin, ed. 2002. *The Violence of Development: The Politics of Identity, Gender and Social Inequalities in India.* London/New York: Zed.

Kaplan, Caren, Norma Alarcón, and Minoo Moallem, eds. 1999. *Between Woman and Nation: Nationalism, Transnational Feminism and the State.* Durham, NC: Duke University Press.

Kappeler, S. 1986. *The Pornography of Representation.* Cambridge: Polity.

Kelley, Caffyn. 1995. "Creating Memory, Contesting History." *Matriart* 5, 3: 6–11.

Kellner, Douglas. 1995. *Media Culture.* New York: Routledge.

King, John, Ana M. Lopez, and Manuel Alvarado, eds. 1993. *Mediating Two Worlds: Cinematic Encounters in the Americas.* London: BFI.

Kinoeye. 2002a. "Assault on the Senses: The Horror Legacy of Dario Argento." Special Issue, Part 1. *Kinoeye* 2, 11 (10 June). http://www.kinoeye.org/index_02_11.html. Accessed 27 March 2006.

———. 2002b. "Assault on the Senses: The Horror Legacy of Dario Argento." Special Issue, Part 2. *Kinoeye* 2, 12 (24 June). http://www.kinoeye.org/index_02_12 .html. Accessed 27 March 2006.

Kirsta, A. 1994. *Deadlier Than the Male: Violence and Aggression in Women.* London: Harper Collins.

Knee, Adam. 1996. "Gender, Genre, Argento." In *The Dread of Difference: Gender and the Horror Film,* ed. Barry Keith Grant, 213–30. Austin, TX: University of Texas Press.

Knox, S. 1998. *Murder: A Tale of Modern American Life.* Durham, NC: Duke University Press.

Kohli, Rita. 1991. "Violence against Women: Race, Class and Gender Issues." *Canadian Woman Studies* 11, 4: 13–14.

Kristeva, Julia. 1981. "Women's Time." Trans. Alice Jardine and Harry Blake. *Signs* 7, 1: 5–12.

———. 1982. *Powers of Horror: An Essay on Abjection.* Trans. Leon Roudiez. New York: Columbia University Press.

Kumar, Radha. 1994. "The Agitation against Rape." In *A History of Doing*, 172–81. New York: Verso.

Lacan, Jacques. 1977. "The Mirror Stage as Formative of the Function of the I as Revealed in the Psychoanalytic Experience." In *Écrits: A Selection.* Trans. Alan Sheridan, 1–7. London: Tavistock.

Lakeman, Lee. 1992. "Women, Violence and the Montréal Massacre." In *Twist and Shout: A Decade of Feminist Writing in* This Magazine. Ed. Susan Crean, 20. Toronto: Second Story.

Landy, Marcia. 1991. "Introduction." In *Imitations of Life: A Reader in Film and Television Melodrama*, ed. Marcia Landy, 13–34. Detroit: Wayne State University Press.

Laozi. 2001. *Dao De Jing: The Book of the Way.* Translated by Moss Roberts. Berkeley and Los Angeles: University of California Press.

Laplanche, J. 1995. "Aggression and Sadomasochism." In *Essential Papers on Masochism*, ed. M.A.F. Hanly, 104–24. New York: New York University Press.

De Lauretis, Teresa. 1984. *Alice Doesn't: Feminism, Semiotics, Cinema.* Bloomington: Indiana University Press.

———. 1987. *Technologies of Gender: Essays on Theory, Film, and Fiction.* Bloomington: Indiana University Press.

Lebel, Andrée. 1981. *La Corriveau.* Montmagny: Libre Expression.

Lévesque, Andrée. 1989. *La Norme et les déviantes: Des femmes au Québec pendant l'entre-deux-guerres.* Montreal: Les éditions du remue-ménage.

Lewallen, A. 1988. "*Lace*: Pornography for Women?" In *The Female Gaze*, ed. L. Gamman and M. Marshment, 86–101. London: Women's Press.

Lippi, Donatella, and Massimo Baldini. 2000. *La Medicina: Gli Uomini e le Teorie.* Bologna: Cooperativa Libraria Universitaria Editrice Bologna.

Lord, Susan. 2006. "Canadian Gothic: Multiculturalism, Indigeneity, and Gender in Prairie Cinema." In *Canadian Cultural Poesis*, ed. Sheila Petty, Annie Gerin, and Garry Sherbert, 399–419. Waterloo: Wilfrid Laurier University Press.

Loshitzky, Yosefa. 2001. *Identity Politics on the Israeli Screen.* Austin: University of Texas Press.

Lowry, Beverly. 1992. *Crossed Over: A Murder, A Memoir.* New York: Alfred A. Knopf.

MacCormack, John. 2002. "A Serial Killer's Dream." *San Antonio Express-News*, 4 March, n.p.

McKenna, Katherine M.J., and June Larkin, eds. 2002. *Violence against Women: New Canadian Perspectives.* Toronto: Inanna.

MacKenzie, Scott. 2002. "*Baise-moi*: Feminist Cinemas and the Censorship Controversy." *Screen* 43, 3: 315–24.

MacKinnon, Catherine A. 1987. *Feminism Unmodified: Discourses on Life and Law.* Cambridge, MA: Harvard University Press.

———. 1993. *Only Words.* Cambridge, MA: Harvard University Press.

Mclintock, Anne, Aamir Mufti, and Ella Shohat. 1997. *Dangerous Liaisons: Gender, Nation and Postcolonial Perspectives*. Minneapolis: University of Minnesota Press.

Malette, Louise, and Marie Chalouh. 1991. *The Montreal Massacre*. Charlottetown, PEI: Gynergy.

Mansfield, N. 2000. *Subjectivity: Theories of the Self from Freud to Haraway*. Sydney: Allen and Unwin.

Marchessault, Janine, and Kim Sawchuk, eds. 2000. *Wild Science: Reading Feminism, Medicine and the Media*. New York: Routledge.

Margulies, Ivone. 1996. *Nothing Happens: Chantal Akerman's Hyperrealist Everyday*. Durham: Duke University Press.

Marks, Laura U. 1999. "Fetishes and Fossils: Notes on Documentary and Materiality." In *Feminism and Documentary*, ed. Diane Waldman and Janet Walker, 224–43. Minneapolis: University of Minnesota Press.

Martin, Adrian. 1994. *Phantasms*. Melbourne: Penguin.

———. 2001. "Lady, Beware: Paths through the Female Gothic." *Senses of Cinema* 12 (February/March). http://www.sensesofcinema.com/contents/01/12/gothic.html. Accessed 27 March 2002.

Marwick, Arthur. 1998. *The Sixties: Cultural Revolution in Britain, France, Italy, and the United States, c. 1958-c. 1974*. Oxford: Oxford University Press.

Massé, M. 1992. *In the Name of Love: Women, Masochism and the Gothic*. New York: Cornell University Press.

Maynard, Joyce. 1992. *To Die For*. New York: Dutton.

Mellencamp, Patricia. 1995. *A Fine Romance: Five Ages of Film Feminism*. Philadelphia: Temple University Press.

Melville, Stephen, and Bill Readings, eds. 1995. *Vision and Textuality*. London: Macmillan.

Middle East News Online. 2002. 28 January. www.middleastwire.com:8080. Accessed 27 March 2006.

Millum, Trevor. 1975. *Images of Woman: Advertising in Women's Magazines*. London: Chatto and Windus.

Modleski, Tania. 1986. "The Terror of Pleasure: The Contemporary Horror Film and Postmodern Theory." In *Studies in Entertainment*, ed. Tania Modleski, 155–66. Bloomington: Indiana University Press.

———. 1991. *Feminism without Women: Culture and Criticism in a "Postfeminist" Age*. New York: Routledge.

Morrissey, Belinda. 2003. *When Women Kill: Questions of Agency and Subjectivity*. London and New York: Routledge.

Moussa, Helene. 2002. "Violence against Refugee Women: Gender Oppression, Canadian Policy, and the International Struggle for Human Rights." In *Violence against Women: New Canadian Perspectives*, ed. Katherine M.J. McKenna and June Larkin, 371–402. Toronto: Inanna.

Mulvey, Laura. 1975. "Visual Pleasure and Narrative Cinema." *Screen* 16, 3 (Autumn): 6–18.

————. 1989. *Visual and Other Pleasures*. Bloomington: Indiana University Press.

————. 1996. "Pandora's Box: Topographies of Curiosity." In *Fetishism and Curiosity*, 53–65. Bloomington: Indiana University Press.

Naaman, Dorit. 2000. "Woman/Nation: A Postcolonial Look at Female Subjectivity." *Quarterly Review of Film and Video* 17, 4 (Fall): 333–40.

Naficy, Hamid, and Teshome H. Gabriel, eds. 1993. *Otherness and the Media: The Ethnography of the Imagined and the Imaged*. Chur, Switzerland: Harwood.

Nashat, Guity, and Judith E. Tucker. 1999. *Women in the Middle East and North Africa*. Bloomington: Indiana University Press.

Nathan, Debbie. 1999. "Work, Sex, and Danger in Ciudad Juarez." *North American Congress on Latin America Report on the Americas* 33, 3 (November/December): 24–30.

Nelson-McDermott, Catherine. 1991. "Murderous Fallout: Post-Lepine Rhetoric." *Atlantis* 17, 1: 124–28.

Newman, Kim. 2000. "Four Flies on Grey Velvet." In *Art of Darkness: The Cinema of Dario Argento*, ed. Chris Gallant, 105–108. Guildford, UK: FAB Press.

Newman, L. 1995. *The Femme Mystique*. Boston, MA: Alyson.

Nichols, Bill. 1991. *Representing Reality: Issues and Concepts in Documentary*. Bloomington: Indiana University Press.

Oldenberg, Veena Talwar. 2002. *Dowry Murder: The Imperial Origins of a Cultural Crime*. Oxford and New York: Oxford University Press.

O'Shea, Kathleen. 1999. *Women and the Death Penalty in the United States, 1900–1998*. Westport, CT: Praeger.

————. 2000. *Women on the Row: Revelations from Both Sides of the Bars*. Ithaca, NY: Firebrand.

O'Shea, Kathleen, and Beverly Fletcher. 1997. *Female Offenders: An Annotated Bibliography*. Westport, CT: Greenwood.

Passerini, Luisa. 1991. "The Women's Movement in Italy and the Events of 1968." In *Women and Italy: Essays on Gender, Culture and History*, ed. Zygmunt G. Baranski and Shirley W. Vinall, 167–82. London: Macmillan.

Pearson, P. 1998. *When She Was Bad: How and Why Women Get Away with Murder*. Toronto: Random House.

Petro, Patrice. 1996. "Historical *Ennui*, Feminist Boredom." In *The Persistence of History: Cinema, Television and the Modern Event*, ed. Vivian Sobchack. New York: Routledge.

Pettys, Dick. 1984. Narration of execution of Alpha Otis O'Daniel by the State of Georgia. Associated Press. 12 December.

Pincus, Robert L. 1995. "The Invisible Town Square." In *But Is It Art? The Spirit of Art as Activism*, ed. Nina Felshin, 31–49. Seattle: Bay.

Plato. 1973. *Phaedrus*. Trans. Walter Hamilton. London: Penguin.

Poirier, Patricia. 1990. "Canadians Haunted by Montréal's Ghosts." *Globe and Mail*. 6 December, pp. A1, A5.

Polan, Dana. 1993. *In a Lonely Place*. London: BFI.

Prince, Stephen. 2004. "Violence and Psychophysiology in Horror Cinema." In *Horror Film and Psychoanalysis: Freud's Worst Nightmares*, ed. Steven Jay Schneider, 241–56. Cambridge: Cambridge University Press.

Rajadhyaksha, Ashish, and Paul Willemen. 1995. *The Encylopaedia of Indian Cinema*. New Delhi: Oxford University Press.

Randall, Margaret. 2003. *When I Look into the Mirror and See You: Women, Terror, and Resistance*. New Brunswick, NJ: Rutgers University Press.

Rapping, Elayne. 2000. "The Politics of Representation: Genre, Gender Violence and Justice." *Genders* 32. www.genders.org. Accessed 27 March 2006.

Rathjen, Heidi, and Charles Montpetit. 1999a. *6 décembre: de la tragédie à l'espoir— les coulisses du combat pour le contrôle des armes*. Montréal: Libre expression.

———. 1999b. *December 6: From the Montréal Massacre to Gun Control—The Inside Story*. Toronto: McClelland and Stewart.

Read, Jacinda. 2000. *The New Avengers: Feminism, Femininity and the Rape-Revenge Cycle*. Manchester: Manchester University Press.

Réage, P. 1972. *The Story of O*. London: Corgi.

Reik, T. 1962. *Masochism in Sex and Society*. Trans. M.H. Beigel and G.M. Kurth. New York: Grove Press.

Reynaud, Bérénice. 2002. "*Baise Moi:* A Personal-Yet-Angry Feminist Reaction." *Senses of Cinema* 22. www.sensesofcinema.com/contents/02/22/contents.html #baise. Accessed 27 March 2006.

Rorty, Richard. 1992. "Moral Identity and Private Autonomy." In *Michel Foucault, Philosopher: Essay Translated from the French and German*, ed. Timothy J. Armstrong, 328–35. New York: Routledge.

Rosenberg, Sharon. 2000. "Standing in a Circle of Stone: Rupturing the Binds of Emblematic Memory." In *Between Hope and Despair: Pedagogy and the Remembrance of Historical Trauma*, ed. Roger I. Simon, Sharon Rosenberg, and Claudia Eppert, 75–89. Lanham, MA: Rowman and Littlefield.

Rosenberg, Sharon, and Roger I. Simon. 2000. "Beyond the Logic of Emblemization: Remembering and Learning from the Montréal Massacre." *Educational Theory* 50, 2: 133–55.

Rowland, Wade. 2001. *Galileo's Mistake: The Archeology of a Myth*. Toronto: Thomas Allen.

Rubin, G. 1984. "Thinking Sex." In *Pleasure and Danger: Exploring Female Sexuality*, ed. C.S. Vance, 267–319. London: Routledge.

Rugoff, Ralph, ed. 1997. *Scene of the Crime*. Cambridge, MA: MIT Press.

Russ, Joanna. 1973. "Somebody Is Trying to Kill Me and I Think It's My Husband: The Modern Gothic." *Journal of Popular Culture* 6, 4 (Spring): 666–91.

Russo, Mary. 1994. *The Female Grotesque: Risk, Excess and Modernity*. New York: Routledge.

Sacher-Masoch, L. 1989 [1925]. *Venus in Furs*. In *Masochism: An Interpretation of Coldness and Cruelty*, ed. G. Deleuze, 143–271. New York: Zone.

Salzinger, Leslie. 1997. "From High Heels to Swathed Bodies: Gendered Meanings under Production in Mexico's Export-Processing Industry." *Feminist Studies* 23, 3 (Fall): 549–74.

San Roque, M. 1999. "Popular Trials/Criminal Fictions/Celebrity Feminism and the Bernardo/Homolka case." *Australian Feminist Law Journal* 13: 38–65.

Saunders, Gill. 1997. "How Wallpaper Left Home and Made an Exhibition of Itself." In *Apocalyptic Wallpaper: Robert Gober, Abigail Lane, Virgil Marti, and Andy Warhol,* ed. Donna De Salvo, 31–47. Columbus: Wexner Center for the Arts.

Saussure, Ferdinand de. 1983. *Course in General Linguistics.* London: Duckworth.

Schiebinger, Londa. 1987. "Skeletons in the Closet: The First Illustrations of the Female Skeleton in Eighteenth Century Anatomy." In *The Making of the Modern Body: Sexuality and Society in the Nineteenth Century,* ed. C. Gallagher and T. Laquer, 42–82. Berkeley: University of California Press.

Schneider, Steven Jay. 2000. "Kevin Williamson and the Rise of the Neo-Stalker." *Post Script: Essays in Film and the Humanities* 19, 2: 81–97.

———. 2002a. "Barbara, Julia, Myra, Carol, and Nell: Diagnosing Female Madness in British Horror Cinema." In *British Horror Cinema,* ed. Steve Chibnall and Julian Petley, 117–30. London and New York: Routledge.

———. 2002b. "Introduction, Part I: Dimensions of the Real." *Post Script: Essays in Film and the Humanities* 21, 3: 3–7.

Sharoni, Simona. 1994. "Homefront as Battlefield: Gender, Military Occupation, and Violence against Women." In *Women and the Israeli Occupation,* ed. Tamar Mayer, 127–37. London: Routledge.

Shaviro, Stephen. 1993. *The Cinematic Body.* Minneapolis: University of Minnesota Press.

Shipman, Marlin. 2002. *The Penalty Is Death: US Newspaper Coverage of Women's Executions.* Columbia, MO: University of Missouri Press.

Shohat, Ella. 1987. *Israeli Cinema: East/West and the Politics of Representation.* Austin: University of Texas Press.

Sielke, Sabine. 1996. "'I HAVE THE BLOOD JELLY': Sexual Violence, the Media and Jenny Holzer's 'Lustmord.'" In *Blurred Boundaries: Critical Essays on American Literature, Language, and Culture,* ed. Klaus H. Schmidt and David Sawyer, 221–47. New York: Peter Lang.

Silverman, K. 1993. "Masochism and Male Subjectivity." In *Male Trouble,* ed. C. Penley and S. Willis, 33–64. Minneapolis: University of Minnesota Press.

Simon, Roger I., Sharon Rosenberg, and Claudia Eppert, eds. 2000. *Between Hope and Despair: Pedagogy and the Remembrance of Historical Trauma.* Lanham, MA: Rowman and Littlefield.

Simonds, Cylena. 1994. "Public Audit: An Interview with Elizabeth Sisco, Louis Hock, and David Avalos." *Afterimage* 22, 1 (Summer): n.p.

Sisco, Elizabeth. 1993. "Forum I: Women Who Kill." In *Critical Condition: Women on the Edge of Violence,* ed. Amy Scholder, 41–73. San Francisco: City Lights.

Sobchack, Vivian. 1994. "Revenge of *The Leech Woman:* On the Dread of Aging in Low Budget Horror Films." In *Uncontrollable Bodies: Testimonies of Identity and Culture*, ed. Rodney Sappington and Tyler Stallings, 79–91. Seattle: Bay.

Spivak, Gayatri Chakravorty. 1988. 'Can the subaltern speak?' In *Marxism and the Interpretation of Culture*, ed. Cary Nelson and Lawrence Grossberg. Urbana: University of Illinois Press.

Sunder Rajan, Rajeswari. 1993. "Life after Rape: Narrative, Rape, and Feminism." In *Real and Imagined Women: Gender, Culture, and Postcolonialism*, 64–82. New York and London: Routledge.

Taiwo, Olufemi. 2002. "Racism and Philosophy." Public lecture at Queen's University, Kingston, ON, 8 February.

Tasker, Yvonne. 1993. *Spectacular Bodies: Gender, Genre, and the Action Cinema*. London and New York: Routledge.

———. 1998. *Working Girls: Gender and Sexuality in Popular Cinema*. London: Routledge.

Tatar, Maria. 1997. *Lustmord: Sexual Murder in Weimar Germany*. Princeton, NJ: Princeton University Press.

Taubin, Amy. 1993. "The 'Alien' Trilogy: From Feminism to AIDS." *Women and Film: A Sight and Sound Reader*, ed. Pam Cook and Philip Dodd. London: BFI.

Tharu, Susie. 1989. "Tracing Savitri's Pedigree." In *Recasting Women: Essays in Colonial History*, ed. Kumkum Sangari and Sudesh Vaid, 254–68. New Delhi: Kali for Women.

Thomas, Rosie. 1989. "Sanctity and Scandal: The Mythologization of Mother India." *Quarterly Review of Film and Video* 11: 11–30.

Thrower, Stephen. 2000. "*Suspiria.*" In *Art of Darkness: The Cinema of Dario Argento*, ed. Chris Gallant, 127–44. Guildford, UK: FAB Press.

Valdivia, Angharad N. 2000. *A Latina in the Land of Hollywood and Other Essays on Media Culture*. Tucson: University of Arizona Press.

Villiers de l'Isle-Adam, Auguste. 1982 (1886). *Tomorrow's Eve*, translation by Robert Martin Adams. Urbana: University of Illinois Press.

Virdi, Jyotika. 2003. *The Cinematic ImagiNation: Indian Popular Films as Social History*. New Jersey: Rutgers University Press.

Viviani, Christian. 1991. "Who Is without Sin: The Maternal Melodrama in American Film 1930–1939." In *Imitations of Life: A Reader in Film and Television Melodrama*, ed. Marcia Landy, 168–82. Detroit: Wayne State University Press.

Walker, L.E. 1984. *The Battered Woman*. New York: Springer.

Weaver, James B. 1991. "Are 'Slasher' Horror Films Sexually Violent? A Content Analysis." *Journal of Broadcasting and Electronic Media* 35: 385–93.

Wernick, Andrew. 1991. *Promotional Culture*. London: Sage.

West, Rebecca. 1998. "Lost in the Insterstices: A Postwar, Pre-Boom Enciclopedia delle donne." *Annali d'Italianistica* 16: 169–94.

Wilcox, Rhonda V., and David Lavery, eds. 2002. *Fighting the Forces: What's at Stake in Buffy the Vampire Slayer?* New York: Rowman and Littlefield.

Wilden, Anthony. 1968. "Lacan and the Discourse of the Other." In *Speech and Language in Psychoanalysis*, 157–311. Baltimore: Johns Hopkins University Press.

Williams, Linda. 1991. "Film Bodies: Gender, Genre, and Excess." *Film Quarterly* 44, 4 (Summer): 2–13.

———. 1995. "Film Bodies: Gender, Genre, and Excess." In *Film Genre Reader 2*, ed. Barry Grant, 140–58. Austin: University of Texas Press.

Williams, Stephen. 2003. *Karla: A Pact with the Devil*. Toronto: Cantos.

Wolff, Mike. 2002. "The Price of Modern Mexico." *Daily Lobo* (via University Wire) March 25.

Wood, Robin. 1986. *Hollywood from Vietnam to Reagan*. New York: Columbia University Press.

Woodward, Kathleen. 1991. *Aging and Its Discontents: Freud and Other Fictions*. Bloomington and Indianapolis: Indiana University Press.

Wright, Melissa W. 1999a. "The Dialectics of Still Life: Murder, Women, and Maquiladoras." *Public Culture* 11, 3: 453–74.

———. 1999b. "The Politics of Relocation: Gender, Nationality, and Value in a Mexican Maquiladora." *Environment and Planning A* 31, 9 (September): 1601–17.

Yeo, Marian. 1991. "Murdered by Misogyny: Lin Gibson's Response to the Montreal Massacre." *Canadian Woman Studies* 12, 1 (Fall): 8–11.

Young, G., and L. Fort. 1994. "Household Responses to Economic Change: Migration and Maquiladora Work in Ciudad Juarez, Mexico." *Social Science Quarterly*, 75, 656–70.

Young, Robert, ed. 1981. *Untying the Text*. Boston: Routledge.

Zarecka, Irwin. 1994. *Frames of Remembrance: The Dynamics of Collective Memory*. New Jersey: Transaction.

Žižek, Slavoj. 1991. *Looking Awry: An Introduction to Jacques Lacan through Popular Culture*. Cambridge, MA: MIT Press.

[biographical notes]

Jack Boozer is a professor in the Department of Communication at Georgia State University, where he teaches film studies, screenwriting, and adaptation. He has published widely on American film, including *Career Movies: American Business and the Success Mystique*. His work on individual films includes articles on *The Crying Game*, *Thelma and Louise*, and the history of femmes fatales. He is currently completing an edited book, *The Process of Adaptation*. His forthcoming articles include one on the year 1987 in Hollywood film for a series by Rutgers University Press.

Annette Burfoot is an associate professor in the Department of Sociology, Queen's University, Kingston. She has published in the sociology of science and technology (as editor of *The Encyclopedia of Reproductive Technologies*) and on the representation of gender in science fiction and science-as-fact. She currently studies the formation of modern medical imaging as a historical cultural science study from the point of view of feminist materialism.

Frank Burke is a professor of Film at Queen's University, Kingston. He has published *Federico Fellini: Variety Lights to La Dolce Vita* and *Fellini's Films: From Postwar to Postmodern* and has co-edited *Federico Fellini: Contemporary Perspectives*. He provided the commentary (along with Peter Brunette) for the

2006 Criterion DVD release of Fellini's *Amarcord*. He has published numerous essays on Italian and North American cinema and is currently writing a book for Edinburgh University Press on the Italian sword-and-sandal film of the 1950s and 1960s.

Margot Leigh Butler is a theorist, installation artist, and cultural activist. She has a Ph.D. in Media and Communications from Goldsmiths College, University of London, UK, with specializations in politics, philosophy, art, and science and technology studies. Her work has been published in *Women's Studies International Forum, West Coast Line, The Virtual Embodied,* and elsewhere. She lectures in Europe and Canada and is part of the Kootenay School of Writing collective. She lives in Vancouver, where she is curating a reading series called "'Tag, we're it!' or 'Implicatedness.'"

Lisa Coulthard is an assistant professor of Film Studies at the University of British Columbia, Vancouver. She has published on Quentin Tarantino, John Woo, Abigail Lane, Kiki Smith, and Stan Douglas. She is currently working on a manuscript on love in contemporary European cinema.

Sylvie Frigon holds a Ph.D. from the Institute of Criminology at the University of Cambridge, UK. She is Professor and outgoing Chair of the Department of Criminology at the University of Ottawa. She has co-edited (with Michèle Kérisit) *Du corps des femmes: contrôles, surveillances et résistances.* She edited a special issue of the journal *Criminologie:* "L'enfermement des femmes au Canada: une décennie de réformes" and authored the book *L'homicide conjugal au féminin: d'hier à aujourd'hui.* She has also published a novel, *Écorchées,* on women in prison. She is currently working with Chris Bruckert and Nathalie Duhamel on the social and professional (re)integration of women in conflict with the law and on the issue of mental health of women during and after imprisonment. Dr. Frigon founded the research and action alliance La Corriveau, which is concerned with socially marginalized and criminalized women. She is finishing a manuscript on the body and imprisonment for the Autrement collection in Paris and is writing a book on dance, the body, and imprisonment with Claire Jenny, choreographer and director of the Parisian dance company Point Virgule.

Susan Lord teaches film and media cultures at Queen's University in Kingston. Her main research areas are women's film culture, Cuban visual culture, new media, and translocal artist collectives. She is co-editor with Janine Marchessault of *Fluid Screens, Expanded Cinema* and co-editor of *Digital Poetics and Politics,* a special issue of the journal *Public.* She has published widely on women's film cultures. She is completing a manuscript about Sara Gómez and Cuban documentary in the 1960s.

Zoey Élouard Michele wrote her chapter in this volume, "Missing: On the Politics of Re/Presentation," while enrolled as a doctoral student in the Department of Sociology at Queen's University in Kingston, Ontario. In 2005, she left academic life to pursue a career in the skilled trades. She lives in Halifax, Nova Scotia, with her husband, René.

Belinda Morrissey teaches media and communication studies at the University of Canberra, Australia. She is the author of *When Women Kill: Questions of Agency and Subjectivity*, and has published articles in several journals, including *Social Semiotics, Continuum,* and *Australian Women's Law Journal.* She is the author of a chapter in the forthcoming *Inflections of Everyday Life.*

Dorit Naaman is a film theorist and documentarist from Jerusalem and teaches at Queen's University, Canada. Her research focuses on Middle Eastern cinemas (primarily from post-colonialist and feminist perspectives), and she is currently working on a book on the visual representation of Palestinian and Israeli women fighters. Her documentary work is about identity politics and the politics of representation, and she developed a format of short videos, DiaDocuMEntaRY.

Kathleen A. O'Shea, a nun for thirty years, is a social worker who does research on female offenders, with an emphasis on women on death row. She is a teacher, writer, activist, and lecturer with a great passion for what she does. She published *Female Offenders: An Annotated Bibliography, Women and the Death Penalty in the United States: 1900–1998,* and *Women on the Row: Revelations from Both Sides of the Bars.* She has recently finished a collection of stories of nuns who have befriended death row inmates. She lives and works at Innisfree Village, a lifetime facility for mentally handicapped adults in rural Virginia, and is currently working on *Hymns of the Revolution*, a novel based on her memoirs of Chile, 1965–1973.

Sharon Rosenberg is an associate professor at the University of Alberta, Edmonton, where she teaches in the theory/culture focus of the Department of Sociology. She works primarily in the areas of contemporary feminist and queer theorizing, trauma and memory studies, and pedagogy and culture. She is the editor of the special issue "Memorializing Queers/Queering Remembrances," for *torquere: Journal of the Canadian Lesbian and Gay Studies Association*; is co-author of *Troubling Women's Studies: Pasts, Presents and Possibilities,* with A. Braithwaite, S. Heald, and S. Luhmann, and is co-editor of *Between*

Hope and Despair: Pedagogy and the Remembrance of Historical Trauma, with R. Simon and C. Eppert. Rosenberg's current research considers the possibilities for non-indifference as a mode of living with and in regard for the legacies of those who have died violently.

Steven Jay Schneider is a Ph.D. candidate in Cinema Studies at New York University's Tisch School of the Arts. His books include *Horror International, Fear without Frontiers: Horror Cinema across the Globe, New Hollywood Violence, Horror Film and Psychoanalysis: Freud's Worst Nightmares, Dark Thoughts: Philosophic Reflections on Cinematic Horror, Underground USA: Filmmaking beyond the Hollywood Canon, Traditions in World Cinema*, and *1001 Movies You Must See Before You Die*.

Jyotika Virdi, assistant professor at the University of Windsor, Ontario, teaches film/media studies. Her research interests include postcolonial cultural politics, and she has published essays in *Film Quarterly, Jump Cut, Screen*, and *Visual Anthropology*. Her book, *The Cinematic ImagiNation: Social History through Indian Popular Films*, is forthcoming from Rutgers University Press.

Suzie Sau-Fong Young is an associate professor of cultural theory and film studies at York University, Toronto. She has an interest in practices of "place" (digital diaspora, national cinemas), inscriptions of "body" (cinematernity, Nature-TV), and theories of the "grotesque" (the pleasures of horror/David Cronenberg, the horrors of pleasure/Steven Spielberg).

[index]

Books in the Cultural Studies Series

Published by Wilfrid Laurier University Press

Slippery Pastimes: Reading the Popular in Canadian Culture edited by Joan Nicks and Jeannette Sloniowski
2002 / viii + 347 pp. / ISBN 0-88920-388-1

The Politics of Enchantment: Romanticism, Media and Cultural Studies by J. David Black
2002 / x + 200 pp. / ISBN 0-88920-400-4

Dancing Fear and Desire: Race, Sexuality, and Imperial Politics in Middle Eastern Dance by Stavros Stavrou Karayanni
2004 / xv + 244 pp. / ISBN 0-88920-454-3

Auto/Biography in Canada: Critical Directions edited by Julie Rak
2005 / viii + 280 pp. / ISBN 0-88920-478-0

Canadian Cultural Poesis: Essays on Canadian Culture edited by Garry Sherbert, Annie Gérin, and Sheila Petty
2006 / xvi + 530 pp. / ISBN 0-88920-486-1

Killing Women: The Visual Culture of Gender and Violence edited by Annette Burfoot and Susan Lord
2006 / xxii + 332 pp. / ISBN-13: 978-0-88920-497-3 / ISBN-10: 0-88920-497-7

Taking Pleasure in Success While Being Prepared for Difficulty

Sean's therapy was one element of a multifaceted approach to intervention. Though gradual, the impact of this intervention was powerful, and not just for him. Sean's outbursts started occurring less often and were less intense too. He and his mother began enjoying each other more. Both Carla and Sam found themselves appreciating their son's intensity rather than just dreading its consequences. Furthermore, as Sean's teachers provided steady skill-building help in school, they began to see big differences as well. Sean still had some trying days, but all the adults who cared for him could see that he was beginning to learn how to manage himself through hard times.

Sean and the adults around him needed help on and off over the next number of years, however. This is often the case. When kids struggle to manage intense emotions, we often see stretches of wonderful growth coupled with periods of backsliding. Sometimes family life has gotten more stressful; sometimes a teacher-student match isn't ideal. Perhaps the child has just lost a grandparent or pet. Maybe he's encountering a child in the neighborhood who is bullying him away from adults' eyes. Whatever the reasons, when kids start looking messier, we do best when we go back to the basics. We lean in and lean out. We offer the kind of skill-building help they haven't needed for a while. We set the bar for good behavior. Most of all, we remind ourselves to enjoy them and believe in their ability to do well. With our strategies on hand and our trust in long-term growth intact, these kids often right themselves and move forward once again.